BETWEEN
ME AND LIFE

BETWEEN
ME AND LIFE

*A Biography
of Romaine Brooks*

Meryle Secrest

Macdonald and Jane's · London

Published in Great Britain in 1976 by
Macdonald and Jane's
(Macdonald & Co. (Publishers) Ltd)
Paulton House
8 Shepherdess Walk
London N1

Copyright © 1974 by Meryle Secrest

ISBN 0 356 08382 9

Printed and bound in Great Britain by
REDWOOD BURN LIMITED
Trowbridge and Esher

TO ADELYN BREESKIN

My dead mother gets between me and life.
                    Romaine Brooks in 1958, at the age of eighty-five

ACKNOWLEDGMENTS

A biography has to be a collaboration between the person gathering information about a life and those with access to it. To use, therefore, the hackneyed phrase that "I couldn't have done it without . . ." is to restate a tired but bald truth. So many people were willing to listen and help, to write letters for or to me, send copies of articles, lend books, photographs, and letters and, most important, take the time to talk to me, on faith, since they could not know what role their information would have to play in a slowly emerging design.

I am particularly grateful to Dr. Joshua Taylor and the staff of the National Collection of Fine Arts in Washington, D.C., for making their files available and smoothing my path in a hundred large and small ways; Mrs. Gil Tatge, who generously acted as my intermediary, and Dr. Emilio Mariano, who provided access to the files at Il Vittoriale along with the copies of Romaine Brooks' letters to D'Annunzio; Madame Berthe Cleyrergue, who has the gift of almost total recall; Mme. Bettina Bergery, whose reminiscences of an epoch were mesmeric; and to Adelyn Breeskin, curator of contemporary painting and sculpture at the NCFA, without whose encouragement and help this biography could not have been written.

And special gratitude to Mrs. Laura Dreyfus Barney and François Chapon, curator of the Literary Library Jacques Doucet of the University of Paris, who is literary executor for the work of Natalie Clifford Barney, for permission to quote from Miss Barney's letters to Romaine Brooks.

I have particular reason to thank Francis Steegmuller and Shirley Hazzard, whose advice, encouragement and painstaking help have been given with a liberality that I can never repay.

I am equally indebted to Léon-Marie Emmanuel, heir to the estate of Romaine Brooks, for his generous permission to quote from Ella Waterman Goddard's letters to her daughter, to reproduce photographs owned by Mrs. Brooks, and to quote from Romaine Brooks' letters to Natalie Barney, Carl Van Vechten, Gabriele d'Annunzio, and others, and permission to quote from Romaine Brooks' unpublished writings, including her memoirs, *No Pleasant Memories*. I am particularly grateful to M. Emmanuel and his children, Philippe Emmanuel, Mme. Monique Grossin, and Mme. Elyane Cier, for their generosity and many kindnesses.

I would also like to thank Philip W. Amram, Barbara Bagenal, Harriet Bernstein, Mary Blume, Kay Boyle, Ambassador David Bruce, Laetitia Cerio and the Centro Caprense, Caroline Despard, Lovat Dickson, David Farmer, Ken Feil, Janet Flanner, Baron Luigi Franchetti, Donald Gallup, literary trustee to Carl Van Vechten, for permission to quote from the letters of Romaine Brooks in the archives of the Beinecke Rare Book and Manuscript Library at Yale; John Gallagher, Robert Gilkey, Myron Gilmore and I. Tatti, Elio Grandi, Graham Greene, Émile Gruet, archivist, and the Galeries Durand-Ruel, Jean Hugo, William Huntington, Matthew Huxley, Heather Jeeves, Philippe Jullian, Claudia Kidwell, Eyre de Lanux, for permission to quote from an unpublished essay on Natalie Barney; Herbert Lottman, Harry Lowe, Florine Lyons, Donald McClelland, Jan Muhlert, Paul Morand, Barbara Mullens, Anaïs Nin, Iris Origo, the Italian Ambassador Egidio Ortona, Len Randolph, Harold Raymond, Ben Ruhe, Dr. David Scott, Lisa Sergio, Roy Slade, Solita Solano, Norah Smallwood, Priscilla Smith, librarian, and the Freer Gallery of Art; Roger L. Stevens, William B. Walker, Mrs. Bruce Yorke, Mahonri Sharp Young, the Marchese Uberto Strozzi for permission to quote from his letters to Romaine Brooks, and Anthony Fothergill, executor for the estate of John Rowland Fothergill, for permission to quote from a letter and the extract from his father's unpublished memoirs, *Lest an Old Man Forget*.

In particular, I would like to thank the following for consenting to be interviewed: Sir Harold Acton, Helene Baltrusaitis, Yvon Bizardel, Laura Dreyfus Barney, Bryher, Adeline Cacan, Jean Cassou, Anna Cerutti, Mr. and Mrs. Anthony Fothergill, John M. Fothergill, Mrs. Hamish Hamilton, Aileen Hennessy, Alice DeLamar, Édouard MacAvoy, Betty Parsons, Professor Norman Holmes Pearson, Gino (Vittorio) Scodellari, Alan Searle, the Marchese Uberto Strozzi, Dr. Charlotte Wolff, and Dr. Richard P. Wunder. Sir Compton Mackenzie, who took a particularly warm interest in my work, died before this book could be published. So did Natalie Clifford Barney and Mme. Janine Lahovary.

The staff of Doubleday-France in Paris, under Beverly Gordey and Véronique Poderzay, provided a willing ear, practical help, and endless cups of tea.

Finally I would like to thank my editor, Diane Cleaver, whose patience, delicacy of understanding, and ability to see the possibilities of things, are rare qualities.

Meryle Secrest
Chevy Chase, Maryland

CONTENTS

Introduction   xvii

PART I

1 Forgotten   3
2 Caught   13
3 Saving the Saint   25
4 Departure   35
5 Disapproval   45
6 Dreams Attacked by Day   57
7 Climbing One's Wings   73
8 Sorrow of Rebirth   85

INTERLUDE: HELL, a short short story by Romaine Brooks   101

9 It Feeds on Our Illusions   103
10 Our Ride Through Life   121
11 Mother and Child   147

PART II

12 Asking the Way   171
13 We Weep and We Weep Alone   191
14 The Dead Friend   219
15 On Wings of Love   259
16 Life   281
17 The Inevitable Line   305
18 Time Separates   359
Epilogue: Unity of Good and Evil   385

Appendix   391

Bibliography   417

Index   423

All chapters titled after, and accompanied by, drawings by Romaine
Brooks.

ILLUSTRATIONS

following page 158

Family group, circa 1875: Ella Waterman Goddard, Major Henry Goddard, Beatrice Romaine as a baby, and her brother, Henry St. Mar, at seven or eight years of age.

Ella Goddard, 1875.
Romaine and Maya, circa 1886.
Romaine as a young girl.
St. Mar, aged sixteen.
"Roland" Fothergill, 1898.
Romaine, circa 1908.
Romaine as a lady of fashion, Paris, 1908.
John Brooks.
Renata Borgatti and Romaine with friends on Capri, circa 1917.
Romaine on Capri, circa 1899.
Romaine at Villa Cercola, Capri, circa 1923.
Bernard Berenson, Florence, 1948.
Romaine Brooks.
Romaine Brooks.
Romaine Brooks.
Ida Rubinstein, Paris, 1917.

following page 286

The Masked Archer, painting by Romaine Brooks, 1910–11.
Portrait of Fothergill by Romaine Brooks.

xiii

Natalie and Romaine in Geneva, probably not long after they met, circa 1915.

Romaine and Gabriele d'Annunzio, circa 1915.

Renée Vivien, Paris, circa 1900.

Lady Anglesey, 1902: inscribed to Romaine.

Self-portrait, 1900, age twenty-six.

Drawing of Romaine by Édouard MacAvoy.

Romaine, circa 1925.

Romaine, circa 1925.

Natalie Barney, nude study.

Natalie Barney in Florence during World War II at the Villa Sant'Agnese.

Natalie in riding costume.

Natalie and Laura Barney.

Natalie in front of the Temple of Friendship during the '20s.

Villa Cercola, Capri, circa 1920.

Château Grimaldi at turn of the century.

Romaine and Natalie, circa 1935, in Paris.

Romaine and Natalie at Beauvallon, France, 1936.

COLOR ILLUSTRATIONS

following page 190

Azalées Blanches, 1910. (National Collection of Fine Arts, Washington, D.C., U.S.A.)

Le Trajet, circa 1911. (Charles Philips)

Gabriele d'Annunzio, Le Poète en Exil, 1912. (Musée National d'Art Moderne, Paris, France)

La France Croisée, 1914. (National Collection of Fine Arts, Washington, D.C., U.S.A.)

Jean Cocteau À L'Époque de la Grande Roue, 1914. (Musée National d'Art Moderne, Paris, France)

following page 222

Ida Rubinstein, 1917. (Charles Philips)

Renata Borgatti au Piano, circa 1920. (National Collection of Fine Arts, Washington, D.C., U.S.A.)

Miss Natalie Barney, L'Amazone, 1920. (Musée du Petit Palais, Paris, France)

Una, Lady Troubridge, 1924. (National Collection of Fine Arts, Washington, D.C., U.S.A.)

Marchese Uberto Strozzi, 1961. (National Collection of Fine Arts, Washington, D.C., U.S.A.)

INTRODUCTION

Cycles of taste in art, like those in clothes, have their casualties along the way. The early part of the twentieth century is seen today as the great flowering of post-Impressionism, Fauvism, and Cubism in France; and art that does not fall into these categories is dismissed as if it never existed. Yet there were artists, then as now, who fashioned their work outside the areas of experimentation, and resisted categories; who were faithful to their own vision.

One of them was Romaine Brooks, an American by birth, European in education and point of view, who made a distinguished reputation in London and Paris between the wars as a portraitist of exceptional talents. Her spare and powerful works were widely acclaimed in Europe although, like those of Mary Cassatt, they did not travel well and were little noted in her native land. Her drawings are even more singular and in her experiments with abstraction she is considered by some to have predated Picasso.

In depicting the life of an artist, one can consider the work as its own phenomenon, separate from the life, or find its origins in the psychic composition of the artist. The work of Romaine Brooks cannot be separated from her life. It had its roots in experiences that marked and marred her and provided the obsessive themes for her portraits and drawings. She was handicapped by her childhood but not destroyed by it. She fought for the right to be herself as an artist and a woman in a socially repressive age. She was a member of a major intellectual circle; a friend of Robert de Montesquiou, Ida

Rubinstein, Somerset Maugham, Gabriele d'Annunzio, and Natalie Barney. She was a force to be reckoned with, and despite her times, an extraordinary woman.

She outlived those times. Tastes changed and, when her work was given a retrospective exhibition in New York and Washington in 1971, it was the first showing in over thirty years; she died forgotten. This biography is an attempt to restore the balance.

PART ONE

Forgotten

I

She had lost her sense of reality by turning to the stars. Eventually I lost mine by turning from her to my inner self, which is, perhaps, the same thing.

No Pleasant Memories

The last day in the life of Romaine Brooks was as unremarkable as all the days of her final years. Anna, her Italian-born housekeeper, got up at 5:30 A.M., just as she always did, and made breakfast in her attic room for herself and Gino. At 6:30 she went to a small dairy, Le Bon Lait, where she bought the usual liter of milk. She toasted bread from the day before and cooked two eggs, *oeufs à la coque,* and made *café au lait* as usual. Then she gave Romaine Brooks her breakfast. By then it was 7:30.

Romaine Brooks' appetite had remained excellent until the last couple of years, when her physical decline had been rapid. Breakfast was almost the only meal she would eat. Sometimes she took two hours over it and Anna would hear the patient tap, tap, tap of her spoon as she broke up lumps of sugar—she had a sweet tooth. Yet, she was insistent that three meals be served to her, whether or not she ate them, and she was used to being obeyed.

She did very little, those last two years. She could no longer walk but insisted on being carried to the bathroom, with Anna supporting her on one side and Gino on the other. She would spend hours in a daze, somewhere between sleeping and waking, and on the last morning, she scarcely stayed awake long enough to eat. Anna finally fed Madame with a spoon.

Madame would not, in any event, have spoken to Anna. Romaine Brooks reserved her conversations for Gino who, over the last twenty years, had become her chief confidante, "almost like a son," he has said. He ran the household, cashed the checks, negotiated with lawyers, bought and sold and, in the last few months, was instrumental in helping to get her will changed for the last time. She was always rewriting her will and had done so only fifteen days before. Her mind was still going back over the last, nagging problem of the will, as a tongue will worry at an aching tooth. The documents had been typed; she signed them, and went back to sleep.

She died at 2:30 that afternoon. Anna was sitting in the small room that adjoined the bedroom when she heard Madame making noises in her throat. She rushed to the phone and called Romaine's nephew, Maître Léon-Marie Emmanuel, a retired lawyer of Nice. He came at once in a taxi with his daughter, Madame Pierre Grossin, but when they got to the sixth floor, Tante Romaine was dead.

Anna and Gino dressed her in one of the black suits she always wore, with a white blouse, and her Légion d'Honneur ribbon fastened in a buttonhole. They combed her hair and laid her in freshly pressed blue sheets. She looked very good, Anna said. She seemed asleep because, "She hadn't suffered."

It was a small funeral, attended by members of the family and a few friends. There were no flowers, since Romaine detested them: green plants were sent. The family was undecided about where Romaine should be buried, since they were quite sure she would not want to be entombed with her mother. It was decided to place her body beside that of her brother, St. Mar, in the family plot and to use the epitaph she wrote herself, "Here remains Romaine, who Romaine remains."

The room in which she died is a transparent, apt, and perplexing metaphor for the unfulfilled life of the artist Romaine Brooks. Appropriate, because it states its theme in the black and white terms

6

in which she saw life; baffling, because there seemed no apparent reason why a woman, given a forceful and original talent, along with considerable material advantages, should have considered her life hardly worth living.

One can see this room from the Quai des États-Unis, the extension of the Promenade des Anglais which follows the faultless curve of the Baie des Anges at Nice. Romaine Brooks' main apartment occupies a corner of the top floor at 11 rue des Ponchettes, a pleasant street of apartment buildings running parallel to the quay and a block behind it.

The apartment, its french doors giving onto a balcony edged with the sunburst pleats of an Art Deco railing, commands a panoramic view of this long, gentle curve of the Mediterranean, intensely blue beneath a cloudless sky; palm trees break the intervals between famous old hotels, there is the painterly prettiness of the harbor, and the Corniche Inférieure winding around the cliffs toward Villefranche-sur-Mer.

Her bedroom, which included one of the two sets of french windows, was barricaded against the light. Outside the room, a small and commanding perch remote from the confusion beneath, there was a triumphant expanse of blue, opening into limitless vistas of depths and height, like the spaces cut into a Magritte canvas in which a room's objects have become exaggeratedly large and the window alone speaks of the blue beyond, in small, compelling terms.

Inside, however, the room was black. Shreds of the once-white filmy curtains, which used to drift in the breeze from half-open windows, had disappeared behind heavy black draperies tacked up to blot out everything: light, noises, intrusions of other thought. Every room on the sixth floor was similarly muffled. There were black cushions on the black-quilted double bed, the walls were of unreflecting, leaden gray, the room's single painting was curtained over with gray, and the only source of light, a lamp beside the bed, had a black shade. The light meeting her eyes dwindled to a pinpoint, and her world to these black and gray objects inside the walls of her bedroom. Romaine Brooks turned her face resolutely from

7

the light and waited for death. It arrived on December 7, 1970, when she was ninety-six.

I was fated never to meet her, although I had first encountered the paintings of Romaine Brooks about six months before her death.

Walking through a gallery devoted to the work of nineteenth-century American artists in the National Collection of Fine Arts in Washington, D.C., my attention was directed to a painting by an artist I had never heard of. It was Romaine Brooks' self-portrait, painted in 1923 when she was forty-nine years old. She was wearing a black top hat which shaded, but did not completely conceal, her eyes; a black jacket and gloves. Behind her was a ruined landscape.

What gave this portrait a compelling quality, which made it stand out in an assembly of more famous works, was its assurance. Everything had been ruthlessly pared down to a single dramatic statement: the palette of blacks and grays, the rigidity of the somberly dressed body, and the shells of buildings, looking like blackened logs in a dead fire. It was the aftermath of a holocaust: the only survivor was charred and burned, her face a mask of scars. It was a soul locked in its own despair, in private mourning for itself. Nevertheless, an enormous power came from the work. I looked at the right arm with its clenched fist and elbow held tightly against the body and was seized by the thought that this being had not died, after all, but still fought back with all its strength.

Romaine Brooks was, in the opinion of the National Collection of Fine Arts, which arranged a major retrospective exhibition of her work the following spring (March 1971), a neglected talent. She had made her name in Europe before and after World War I yet, like Mary Cassatt, had been ignored by her native land. I walked away, but the enigma of that painting was a riddle I felt as driven to unravel as she had evidently felt compelled to paint it. What kind of woman was capable of such unflinching self-appraisal? What kind of life had she lived? What caused her such despair?

I learned that she was still alive at the age of ninety-six and living in Nice. She had been famous in her day as a portraitist, documenting a certain intellectual, aristocratic, and homosexual world which had vanished after two world wars. Jean Cocteau, Ida Rubinstein, Gabriele d'Annunzio, the Marchesa Casati, and Paul Morand sat for their portraits. Romaine Brooks was in as much demand as a decorator in the then-daring color scheme of black and white. She had chosen, with unerring accuracy, to live in poetic places at moments of high drama: Capri at the turn of the century with Norman Douglas and Somerset Maugham, London and Paris a decade later, Venice with D'Annunzio during World War I. She met, in the literary salons, Pound, Joyce, Gide, Valéry, Colette, and Robert de Montesquiou. But she had lived too long and was forgotten. I was told that she had become eccentric, a virtual recluse. I could attempt an article about her, if she would agree to be interviewed.

I made enquiries among magazine editors I knew. I was prepared to fly to Nice, but no one seemed interested in the work of an artist not exhibited in the United States for over thirty years. I had almost renounced the idea, tantalizing as it was, when I had the good fortune to talk with Adelyn Breeskin, curator of contemporary art at the National Collection, who was preparing the Romaine Brooks exhibition.

I had known Mrs. Breeskin for several years, since she came to Washington from her position as director of the Baltimore Museum of Art to be the first director of the Washington Gallery of Modern Art. During her tenure, she introduced the work of a number of important but little-known artists, and I had complete confidence in her artistic judgments.

Mrs. Breeskin related that she had visited Romaine Brooks in Nice two or three summers before to discuss the transfer of her works to the National Collection. Mrs. Breeskin had taken a room at a hotel on the Quai des États-Unis and was promptly invited to lunch; Gino Scodellari, Mrs. Brooks' Italian valet and chauffeur, was dispatched to lead the way and open doors.

Romaine Brooks had put on a skirt for the occasion; she explained that her usual attire was pants and a jacket. There was a five-course luncheon, and Mrs. Breeskin concluded in her measured way, Romaine Brooks insisted on being her hostess in every respect: when Mrs. Breeskin went to pay her hotel bill, she was told that it had been taken care of.

A few shreds of their conversation remained in Mrs. Breeskin's

9

memory. Far from being withdrawn and morose, the artist was vivid and emphatic. She told a number of anecdotes, she joked, and gave the impression of a woman in full command of life, still vigorous in spirit if advanced in age. She was concerned about her eyesight, the transfer of her portraits, and the fact that she could not find her drawings. She believed, she said, that someone in her household "was making a secret collection" of them; with the finger of suspicion pointing toward Gino. Most of all, she was concerned about her memoirs; not a word, she insisted, must be changed.

The memoirs are in two sections, the first containing chapters about her childhood and young womanhood; the second, the period she spent in Florence during World War II. They had never been published and the Smithsonian Press was considering their publication, in connection with the opening of the exhibition. (The plan was dropped.) Mrs. Breeskin had found them a valuable source for the biographical essay she wrote in the exhibition catalogue. The memoirs would, she suggested, explain many of the overtones of the portrait which had baffled me. "No tears," she said cryptically, "but my, was she strong."

As I began to read *No Pleasant Memories* I found eloquent and irrefutable reasons for the somberness of the self-portrait. Here was an account of the mid-Victorian childhood of a mistreated and emotionally damaged child, with the mother as chief tormentor, of a demented brother, and an atmosphere of supernatural evil. It was a story of childish terror, of adolescent suffering, of the inner anguish that accompanies the death of hope, and the correspondingly valiant struggle not to be overwhelmed by life.

The more I read the more fascinated I became, though the story seemed hard to believe. It was a gothic nightmare, written out in stark good-versus-evil terms, as if for some naïve, turn-of-the-century audience; with Romaine Brooks as the helpless victim of a malevolent fate, virtually, a Joan of Arc in "golden armour," to use her own phrase. Could any life have been quite so melodramatic, the lines of battle quite so clearly drawn? I wondered whether Romaine's version of her early life could be checked against other evidence.

The memoirs had been read by a number of Romaine Brooks' friends who seemed to have similar reservations. Sir Harold Acton, the poet, novelist, and historian, who came to know her in Florence after World War II, was convinced that her memoirs contained a good deal of self-dramatization. Professor Norman Holmes Pearson of Yale University, who tried to have Romaine's memoirs published in the United States, thought they had been written from motives of revenge. Carl Van Vechten, the late novelist and photographer whose portrait she painted, refused to believe them.

"Did I dream it or did you really say yesterday in reference to my narrative of my early life, 'I don't believe it?'" Romaine Brooks wrote to him reproachfully in 1936. "If you said this to impress upon me how badly written it is, that of course, coming from you, is a point of view to be considered; but if you meant that you did not believe it to be a veracious story of my life, then *c'est toute une autre question* and you must . . . face a barrage of proofs . . ."

The doubts appeared to be based not only on the facts of the formidable story itself, but to arise also in instinctive reaction to the dominant tone of the memoirs, which is one of embittered outrage of a woman bent on bringing to justice those who would have destroyed her if they could. Yet Romaine Brooks demonstrates a curious reluctance to name her enemies. It would be useless to disguise her mother's identity and she does not try. But she omits her sister altogether, calls her brother (St. Mar) by the thin pseudonym of St. Amar, gives fictitious names to minor players in her private drama long dead, falsifies names of schools, towns, streets, and disguises dates. I was to find that this fear that readers would reach conclusions she was in fact at pains to make obvious, was typical of her ambivalence.

Such reservations tempered my enthusiasm but did not conquer it altogether. The memoirs had opened up too many avenues. The puzzles I found, and the paradoxical attitudes of the woman behind the words, only intrigued me further. Taken on their own terms, the memoirs made fascinating reading. Here was a natural storyteller —hampered by the stylistic conventions of her period, with its circumlocutions and stiff phrases that camouflaged meaning, like "sufficient chastisement"; yet capable of lighting up her narrative with eloquent descriptive passages and similes of sudden clarity and force. Living with her mother, Romaine said, in a terse and illuminating phrase, was "like living on an avalanche."

E. F. Benson remarked in his memoirs, *Final Edition,* that life has an uncanny way of spelling out a certain path. Things are perhaps the decrees of fate or, "the fantastic hazards of a fortuitous world"; circumstances began to conspire toward my biography of Romaine Brooks. Opportunities presented themselves unsought and events fell magically into place. I had no sooner felt the lack of a missing fragment than it was served up to me. Working on an outline of the proposed book, I entitled a chapter "Marriage to John Brooks" and was writing, "More research needed, reasons unknown," when the mailman arrived. Among the letters was one from the British novelist Bryher, who lives in Switzerland, but happened to be visiting her old friend, Professor Pearson, in New Haven, Connecticut, and had learned of my project. "People seem to be astonished at her marriage to John Brooks," she wrote in a letter which sent superstitious shivers down my spine, "but I believe I have the key to that puzzle."

Such eerie coincidences set me in a direction that was to have long-reaching implications. By the time the exhibition, *Thief of Souls,* opened in Washington in March 1971 (it moved to the Whitney Museum in New York two months later), my course was determined. But by then, Romaine Brooks was dead.

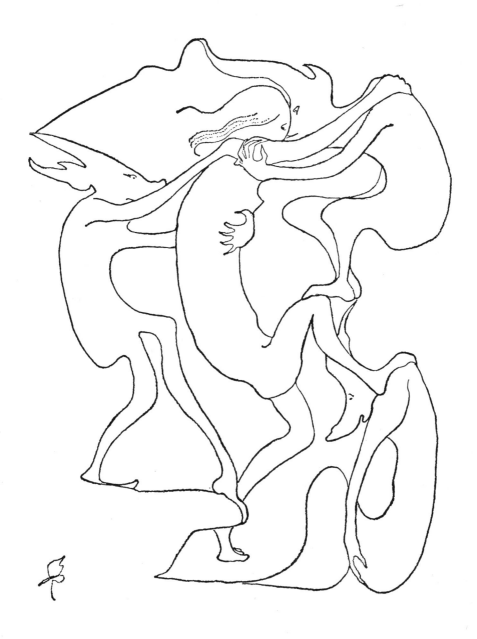

Caught*

2

To be caught in the vicious circle of another's life is to revolve perilously in another's perils.

Three photographs of Romaine's mother have survived. Two were taken in 1875, less than a year after Romaine was born, and the third is undated. The first is a family group of Ella Mary Waterman Goddard with her husband, Major Henry Goddard, the baby, Beatrice Romaine, and their son, Henry St. Mar, then seven or eight years old. Mary Aimée (Maya), who was then five, is not in the picture. There was one more child, Katharine, who died at the age of a year.

The family group is conventional and Victorian: with the mother seated in a tufted armchair, in satins, ribbons, and a frilly black hat, holding the baby Romaine and looking calmly at the photographer. St. Mar is a small figure perched on steps, in a velvet jacket heavily braided with white, a plumed cap set on his long blond hair; he looks apprehensive, a bit cowed, and clasps one arm across the other. The father, a balding and bulky figure, stands in the background. He seems to lean protectively forward and there is something deferential about his otherwise expressionless gaze.

The second photograph shows the thirty-five-year-old mother in close-up. One sees even, strong features, a heavy chin and a calm smile which seems full of optimism. In the third portrait, she is

* Also called, "Emprisonnée."

15

hatless, and her light brown curls are piled prettily on top of her head; there are frills and laces and a cameo on a ribbon around her neck. She looks serene but more confident, almost commanding.

Very little is known about Ella Waterman Goddard at the time of Romaine's birth and even less about her state of mind. She was born in 1840, one of two daughters (the second was Clara W. Dwight and there was a son, George) of Isaac S. Waterman, Jr., (1803–83) the kind of enterprising American one reads about constantly in the nineteenth century. Everything about him is legendary: his mysterious childhood in Barbados, his arrival in the United States where he apparently made several fortunes with mines in Salt Lake City and anthracite coal mines at Kingston, Pennsylvania; and the story that he was also a Quaker minister, supposedly connected with the founding of Rehoboth Beach, Delaware. Research at the Library of Congress, in Philadelphia and Rehoboth Beach, failed to verify any of this information. However there is no doubt that he was a multi-millionaire. In the 1870s he bought twenty acres in Chestnut Hill, Philadelphia, paying $55,000 for the property, an immense sum in those days. He built a handsome mansion there, now destroyed, where Romaine often stayed. She describes it as a child's paradise, full of flowers, butterflies, fireflies, humming birds, and katydids in the summertime. It stood among great trees and sweeping lawns and, since there was a small farm that supplied the needs of the house, there were horses and cows on the property.

When Isaac Waterman died, on March 10, 1883, he left a fortune and a lengthy will, leaving his children handsome yearly incomes from a trust fund. The will stipulated that only the grandchildren were to have access to the original capital.

Ella Waterman would have had the genteel upbringing considered proper for an heiress from a pious family. She grew up in a house on West 81st Street in New York City, took music and singing lessons, painted, read Shakespeare, liked to write poetry and meditate upon the nature of things.

Harry Goddard, the man Ella married, is an equally mysterious figure. It was a match, however, that would have pleased both sets of parents, since he was the son of a famous preacher whose sermons were so memorable that, years afterward, Romaine was pointed out on board a boat when the captain discovered that she was the grand-child of Pastor Goddard. In addition, Major Goddard was a Philadelphia descendant of the famous Providence furniture maker, and family tradition has it that he was distantly related to Napoleon via a cousin, Elizabeth (Betsy) Patterson of Baltimore (who married Jerome Bonaparte, the youngest brother of Napoleon). Romaine was constantly torn, in later years, between her dislike for her father and her desire to establish the Napoleonic connection. "I admire," she wrote, "the great achievers." So at times she told people that she was illegitimate; at others, that she was related to Napoleon Bonaparte.

Ella's marriage to Major Goddard ended in divorce, although it is impossible to know exactly when they separated. Romaine was born in a hotel in Rome on May 1, 1874, where her mother happened to be traveling at the time. In later life, when Romaine was putting forward her illegitimacy theory, she said that her father had left the household before she was born. But there is the matter of the 1875 family photograph and Major Goddard looming large as life over his infant daughter.

One only knows that Major Goddard faded out of the daguerreotype around the time of Romaine's birth and that he was an alcoholic, who probably died of cirrhosis of the liver.

These, then, were the circumstances surrounding Romaine's birth. She was the last child in a disintegrating marriage. She would certainly have been, by her very existence, an irritating daily reminder to her mother of the final months of a failed relationship. Ella Waterman Goddard moved permanently to Europe, taking along her children and their nurses as she pursued the life of a rich gypsy.

No Pleasant Memories, Romaine's unpublished memoirs, begins with the comment that "to be caught in the vicious circle of another's life is to revolve perilously in another's perils." That "other" was her mother, who, at the time of Romaine's birth, "was beautiful, autocratic, highly cultivated," and rejected her daughter.

Romaine's earliest memory centers dimly in a nursery peopled by a succession of nurses. There was Helen, who stayed for years, and an Irish nurse called Mary O'Neill, who had an inquisitive turn of mind. There were so many others that Romaine forgot their names. They were anonymous figures whose outlines blurred and faded when contrasted with the awful presence of the Powerful Being who lived outside. From time to time, Romaine would be taken out of the security of these four walls, "pushed within the very gates of the enemy," and then left in her mother's presence. Her earliest memory of this event is one of immense fear.

One day, she remembers that she was "dressed up in red like a monkey" and taken out walking with her mother. It was evidently some kind of social occasion, and Romaine, the baby, was on display. The long walk was too much for her small legs. She sat down in rebellion on the ground and started to cry. For this, she was dragged home, spanked, and put to bed.

Exactly what caused such terror in the child Romaine is never made clear by the adult. But it seems that one of the important factors was her mother's complete unpredictability. Romaine never knew what kind of reception she would get from her, and a child is bound to be apprehensive under such circumstances. She might be the object on which her mother would vent all her rage, "the whipping boy," for no reason that the infant Romaine could see. Or she might find herself grudgingly accepted, which was equally bewildering. What Romaine always knew was that she could never please her mother. She felt that she was not loved, and barely tolerated, yet even this precarious state could change without warning.

"The atmosphere she created was that of a court ruled over by a crazy queen; and before my brother showed definite and incurable signs of madness, she treated me either as one of royal blood—since I was descended from her—or else as a page in waiting, rather than a little girl. There was even a time when she dressed me up in replicas of the clothes my brother had worn as a very small boy. But she never failed to remind me that I was not good-looking like St. Mar, and indeed, my pale face and dark hair could in no way compare with his angelic blondness."

Ella Waterman Goddard appeared to be the kind of woman who presented a mask of placid self-assurance toward the outer world. To her, the family circle was the place where one could strip away the veneer, let down one's guard. Daily routine was nonexistent; "indeed, she had no consideration for Time and would have banished it altogether." She never seemed to go to bed and wanted her meals served at any hour of the day or night, whenever she felt like eating, or not at all. Ella had discovered that it was very relaxing to have the soles of her feet tickled. What would have driven most people insane apparently sent her to sleep, and she was imperious about having this need satisfied. Romaine was frequently made to tickle her mother's feet for hours, even though she found it intolerably tiring. Even if the "gaoler" fell asleep, she seldom slept soundly and Romaine did not dare to stop. Sometimes she would fall asleep herself and be surprised to find herself in the same place when she woke up.

There were moments when it was all too much for the little girl. She would go and hide under the table, looking out at the world from behind the tablecloth. "I felt safe in my tent by myself."

This image of a woman leading a socially correct, outwardly upright life, which masked a profound interior disorientation, raised immediate questions about the emotional climate in which Ella had been raised. Behind the moralistic Christian background there were other, sinister strains, indications of unacknowledged and profound emotional problems in the Waterman family. Sister Clara was an alcoholic and Ella chose to marry another. St. Mar became insane at puberty, and Romaine had a cousin, Mamie, on her mother's side of the family, who also went insane at puberty. Like St. Mar, Mamie was beautiful and blond, with long braids, and like him she was the oldest child. Romaine remembers that once, when she was sitting on Mamie's knee, Mamie opened her blouse and pushed Romaine's mouth to her breast, apparently under the delusion that Romaine was her baby. Mamie was kept shut up in rooms at the top of the house and it was known that she could be dangerous.

Once, when Romaine was staying at her grandfather's house in Chestnut Hill, she was awakened during the night by terrible screams. She was told that Mamie had thrown herself out of an upper window and met her death on the pavement beneath.

In telling this story in *No Pleasant Memories*, Romaine makes her first reference to her mother's obsessive interest in the supernatural. At the end of the nineteenth century, spiritualism was very much in vogue and Ella was fascinated by every aspect of it. Romaine's early memories involve seeing her mother sitting at a table with a medium, "with hands outstretched, waiting anxiously for the table to turn or for flowers to fall from the ceiling."

Ella thought she saw ghosts. She had forebodings. She knew that Mamie would die, she told the terrified Romaine, because, "One late afternoon, she was walking towards her room . . . when, in the corner behind a chair, she saw the crouching figure of the mad girl. As [Ella] approached to speak to her, my cousin rose and, floating in the air, disappeared out of the bedroom window."

Then there was a mysterious "Mr. R.," described as a friend of her mother's, who always spoke to Ella in verse and took her on trips. They went to Niagara Falls together, but Ella returned unexpectedly a few days later, alone. Romaine was told she was ill: "I remember her muffled and silent form in bed." One night, "at spirit hour," Ella told Romaine that "Mr. R." had been so upset at being forced to leave her (apparently, Ella had broken off the affair) that he had thrown himself over the falls. Ella had somehow known that this would happen. "'But listen,' she whispered, 'do you hear that sound?' I listened, and in the silence of the night I could hear the faint ticking of a watch. 'That is his watch, he left it on my table before his death.'"

On the subject of the spirits and their powers, Ella seems to have been as inconsistent as she was in other matters. At times she told Romaine about her psychic presentiments, filling her mind with morbid imaginings; at others, she imagined that Romaine was spying upon her and would descend on her in a rage.

This happened one afternoon when Romaine, about six years old, had dozed off to sleep in her mother's alcove bedroom, a small room curtained off from the sitting room, whose one door into a corridor was blocked by a huge wardrobe.

Ella was conducting a séance in the sitting room when she had a sudden conviction that she was being spied upon. She pulled Romaine upright roughly, demanding to know what she had heard. She had a whip in her hand.

"I was speechless with terror. As the whip was about to descend on my small body, St. Mar walked into the room and slowly advancing, placed himself between me and the whip, facing my mother. Though he said nothing her fury at once abated and she let me go."

Romaine saw clearly the unreasonableness of her mother's suspicions, which went so far as to order her to move the wardrobe to see if she could have escaped from the room by this route (needless to say, she could not). She was more than unreasonable, Romaine decided, she seemed to be possessed.

"I remember standing before a mirror supporting her arm in order to ease its weight as she stuck a long pin into her hat perched high on a structure of curls. The arm was heavy, but presently I found diversion looking at my mother's image in the mirror. It was evident that the hand was automatically directing the pin, for the raised eyes were fixed far above and beyond the hat, reflecting in their transparency some vision of colorless light. The hand at last fell down, but the eyes remained still focussed above, unconscious of the moment, unwilling to return."

Ella wrote diabolical poetry:

> Twixt you and me and other worlds
> Oh, demon of destruction,
> We seek to find our double selves
> Lost in Death's constellation.

She took "flights into space," and Romaine decided that her mother "had lost her sense of reality by turning to the stars." All this had a curious effect upon the growing child. It was Romaine's private explanation for her mother's unreasonable dislike of her: Her mother was going insane. Yet, another part of her implicitly believed that her mother could see visions and conjure up spirits. The image of Mamie's "apparition" and the fright she must have had when her mother demanded to know what she had heard in the séance, made a permanent impression on her.

Perhaps the most serious development was what this belief of Romaine's did to her conviction of her own impotence. Seen through the eyes of a child, a parent is already a Powerful Being. When he is in league with the unseen, that parent becomes omnipotent and the child's sense of helplessness in an onslaught of hatred from such a being must be profound. Yet Romaine tried.

She was becoming a silent, precociously observant child, outwardly conformist, learning how to conceal her emotions. She seldom smiled and she never cried. She would watch for her mother's moods in the grave manner of children who learn this method of self-preservation at an early age.

Romaine had the large, lustrous, slightly protuberant eyes of her family, as a photograph taken of her in Philadelphia at about this time shows. She is wearing a pleated plaid dress with a bow at the neck, a straw boater, and boots. She stands with one hand on the photographer's fake fence, beside imitation ivy that climbs artistically up the side of a false tree trunk, and gazes to the right of the photograph.

It is the uncomprehending stare of childhood, but intensified, as if her eyes had been permanently startled by the sights they had witnessed. The child's bewilderment is coupled with an air of helpless appeal, of being the victim of circumstances, "a small prisoner who knew that no help could come from without." This was the way Romaine looked at her mother and Ella's feelings of guilt turned into anger. She said that her daughter had "snake's eyes"; she had "devil's eyes."

Those first years were a succession of rooms for Romaine; in hotel after hotel, sometimes in Europe, occasionally in Chestnut Hill, Philadelphia, which lodged in her mind as the only home she had. There were always trunks, clothes, servants, and the angry voice of her mother, something to be avoided at all costs. Romaine would wander off down the hotel corridors and, at about that time, she started to draw. She would find a quiet corner and the objects she loved at Chestnut Hill. This was the spontaneous appearance of a talent and she was innocently proud of the results. She was arranging her drawings along the floor against the wall of her bedroom one day when her mother passed by. Ella bent down, picked up the drawings and took them away. Romaine never saw them again and from then on, she was told, she was not to draw.

"My reaction to this was very curious. Though terrified, I began to draw indiscriminately on all sorts of objects—on my mother's white boxes, on the window sills, and even with a pin on the polished wood of the piano. All these efforts I proudly signed."

Later, whenever Romaine sketched, it was in secret. Pencils and paper would be hidden away quickly when she heard the jingling of keys on the chatelaine her mother always wore, heralding Ella's approach. As an old lady, Romaine told a friend that this sound still haunted her.

This is perhaps the most serious of the accusations against her mother which Romaine makes in her memoirs. Ella was not only autocratic, demanding, vengeful, rejecting, ready to use a whip on her at the least provocation, but she tried to forbid her daughter the one thing in life that gave her pleasure; to prevent her from becoming an artist.

Romaine decided that Ella could not forgive either of her daughters for being healthy and talented (Maya was a natural musician) while her one son, St. Mar, was sickly and sorely troubled. Romaine would have to be punished for St. Mar's many deficiencies. Ella did not love Romaine. But she was capable of love: She loved St. Mar.

Saving the Saint

3

Some higher dispensation makes madmen of those who lose their way and fail to return with their riches.

Like his mother, St. Mar has, in *No Pleasant Memories,* a grotesque quality. He is the other figure looming like a gargoyle out of the narrative in Romaine's nightmarish vision of her childhood; and her feelings toward him are a complex blend of disgust, loathing, a grudging pity, fear, and implacable jealousy.

After her first child, Katharine, died at the age of a year, Ella Waterman Goddard looked forward eagerly, but with obvious apprehension, to the birth of her second in 1867. The confinement was a difficult one. There is a family story to the effect that, on the day of his birth, Ella sent her husband in search of a doctor but, he went to a bar instead and got drunk. St. Mar might have received a brain injury during birth, but what happened will never be known. However, the fact that he arrived after the death of one child and in such a precarious state of emotional and physical health is sufficient explanation for Ella's anxious preoccupation.

The details of his various physical and psychic ailments are equally unclear. He could have been tubercular (or consumptive, as Romaine put it). He could have had heart disease, as his mother thought. No one seemed to know exactly, and even the cause of his death, at thirty-four, is in some doubt; it might have been pneumonia or an infectious kidney disease. Ella was given conflicting opinions by a succession of doctors engaged to travel with the family (the doctors appeared to serve two purposes, Romaine said, to take care of her brother and act as mediums for her mother). Ella lavished on the pale and fragile St. Mar all the tenderness she refused Romaine.

Apparent attacks of pain would seize the little boy, usually at the most inconvenient moments. No one actually knew if he was really sick, since what St. Mar gave was a histrionic display of a person in his death throes. In a restaurant, or waiting for a train on a station platform, St. Mar would suddenly clutch at his chest and insist on being given a chair. Then, usually in a crowd of people, he would kneel on the ground with his chest against the seat of the chair, groaning loudly. At that point the doctor would step up with a small glass vial, snap off the end and roll the liquid (apparently, some kind of sedative) on a pad of cotton wool which the boy would sniff at, until the pain seemed to diminish and he was ready to take up his life again.

The fact that, as Romaine remarks irritably, St. Mar always picked the most inconvenient and conspicuous places to have his attacks, sounds like self-dramatization, or like the temper tantrums staged in a department store by a small child overwhelmed by the newness of the experience, the break in daily routine, and the obligation to be on his best behavior.

As a child St. Mar was physically fragile but otherwise normal in appearance. A second photograph of St. Mar in 1883 at the age of sixteen, shows a sinister transformation. His hair has been combed, parted in the middle, and plastered down on each side. He wears a high-buttoned collar, a white shirt, a plain tie, and the intense, fixed expression of the mentally deranged. Between the ages of seven and sixteen, insanity gradually developed. Romaine says that it appeared after an attack of scarlet fever when St. Mar was sent to recuperate with an overzealous and religious grandmother, probably the wife of Pastor Goddard. Mrs. Goddard would have considered it bad enough that the child was given the foreign name of "Mar," but to add "Saint" to it was an unconscious blasphemy for which an awful punishment would be meted out if its owner did not make profound amends. She filled his "sensitive and anemic" mind, Romaine said, with her own stern and puritanical view of life; in which a human sense of proportion seems to have played very little part.

Ella also blamed St. Mar's grandmother for his insanity. She said (in a letter written in 1885), "I attribute my son's sickness to the unnecessary religious pressure inflicted upon him by his grandmother. He was of a too nervous temperament to be bothered with such subjects."

Whether or not the stay with his grandmother was the precipitating factor, the general circumstances of St. Mar's life must have been as great a strain on him as they were on Romaine. The fact that his mother made him the preferred child and indulged his every whim, has to be weighed against the effect, on a fragile psyche, of living in a state of constant pandemonium; of meals at any hour of the night or day, of ceaseless travel from one hotel room to another, of séances and flowers falling from the ceiling. Living such a life, it would be easy to spin the contact with reality to a fine thread which the slightest jarring might snap.

Romaine's characteristic explanation, which has its own poetry, is that St. Mar was "incomplete"; born too soon. The concept of the Incomplete Being became one of her major themes. He was the divine fool, one of those whose madness had an innocence that protected them from life; as such, they saw things more clearly than others around them and perceived much more than they were ever given credit for. Reaching that slender gulf that separates genius from idiocy, they can vacillate between both in a way that is denied those who are condemned to stay sane. Or so St. Mar's tormented, but stubbornly sane sister, believed.

Romaine remembers seeing St. Mar pacing up and down the room, his hands clasped firmly behind his back, wearing a black velvet jacket which threw into sharp relief an untidy cascade of blond hair. His tight mouth was awry and unhappy; his blue eyes strangely sharp and questioning. He was always muttering to himself. On the one hand, he appeared to be begging some unseen presence to pardon him and let him be born anew. On the other, he would ask the same omnipotent being whether he had to die and go to hell; this was his "call to destruction," Romaine said.

St. Mar's monologues, spelling out his internal conflicts in such

29

innocent and pathetic terms, are like echoes of his mother's love-hatred for her own "demon of destruction." Romaine, too, saw life as a desperate battle in which good and evil fought for possession of souls. In the case of St. Mar, evil was winning.

Romaine must have been about five at the time and St. Mar would have been twelve. Her memories of the same period include evenings at Chestnut Hill, with wind and snow sweeping around the old country house. The two children are living there alone, attended by servants, and are having dinner at a long table. St. Mar is muttering an improvised, interminable grace. The servants have disappeared and the food is cold on the table. Romaine sits with bowed head, waiting for her brother to finish. She attributes her patience to "a childish sympathy or even admiration for my brother."

St. Mar's obsessions were focusing upon religion. In childhood, Romaine said, his preoccupations remained ascetic and pure, but as he grew older, the overtones became sexual, menacing, and obscene. Romaine did not elaborate, but certainly this first contact with adult male sexuality must have been frightening. St. Mar was convinced that God and His saints were persecuting him "like demons," and he saw similar demons all around him.

In a family in which it was a dishonor to be ill, Ella blindly refused to believe that there was anything mentally wrong with St. Mar. She insisted that St. Mar accompany them everywhere, even though Romaine was convinced that such constant traveling exacerbated St. Mar's symptoms. He must live exactly as everyone else did, his doting mother insisted. St. Mar refused to co-operate. Servants, nurses, and barbers were afraid to come near him, because of the weaponlike thrusts of his pointed elbows.

So St. Mar was left to his own devices and he began to look "like a fanatic long lost in the desert." Long, tangled hair, which was never combed or cut, covered his thin shoulders, and an untidy matted beard formed a curtain over his undeveloped chest. A small, waif-like face could be seen through the mass of hair, and fierce eyes were raised in defiance against imaginary enemies.

He looked like an object of revulsion to Romaine, but was the blazing sun around which Ella's pale moon revolved. She would go to infinite lengths to please him although, according to Romaine, her efforts were invariably unrewarded. She would tiptoe into his room while he was asleep and place some exquisite object on the table by his bed to surprise him on waking. St. Mar seemed less pleased than horrified.

Once Ella gave him a clock which told not only the time but the days of the week, the moons, the weather; it was "a small palace of crystal and gilded columns." Shortly after St. Mar awoke, strange noises were heard in his room. Ella and Romaine rushed in. They found St. Mar in the act of smashing the clock into a thousand fragments. He explained gravely that no Christian could possibly endure such a clock since it had the effrontery to begin the week on a Saturday.

As the favorite child, whatever St. Mar said or did was taken with complete seriousness. Since he liked to play the piano he must, of course, be a genius. St. Mar concurred in this opinion and occasionally gave recitals. Romaine's description of them is a model of indignant exasperation.

"My brother, crouched on the stool in his great overcoat, would close his eyes as if in pain. Then spreading his limp hands flat on the keys, he would move the fingers as though groping for sound.

"But suddenly he would awake as if in anger. Then the din of fifty madhouses could not have competed with the deafening sounds which he . . . drew from the piano," while his mother, her finger on her lips to enforce silence, stood beside her son in an ecstasy of delight. ". . . At last, like a deflated accordion, he would collapse to his former limp self and remain quietly on the stool until we had left the room."

The anger Romaine was forced to conceal at being required to play a role in this charade turned in upon itself. She wrote (much later), "Even now any loud, discordant sounds can bring palpitations and send waves of blood to my head."

Romaine was in the grip of violent feelings, struggling with the mingled jealousy and rage a child feels when it is openly, one might almost say callously, rejected in favor of another; who is made to feel that whatever she is or does will be inadequate by comparison. She was even dressed up in St. Mar's old clothes, a symbolic act whose unconscious message is, "You would be better if you were a boy."

31

It was St. Mar's right to be lavished with praise, adoration, and gifts, and Romaine's fate to be ignored, belittled, and rejected. Yet her every fiber rebelled against the injustice of being rebuffed in favor of a mental and physical cripple. She wanted a loving mother. She wanted to be the object of adoration, just as St. Mar was. Her yearning had the frenzy of a long, fundamental deprivation. Romaine longed like a lover for her mother, who yearned in her soul for her son.

Romaine saw how little St. Mar gave his mother in return. He seemed to ignore her. When Ella would tenderly draw his bedraggled head to her shoulder, her murmurs of, "My poor darling boy!" "My beautiful St. Mar!" were merely endured—or perhaps St. Mar didn't even hear them. He never gave love in return. In fact, he seemed to take a naughty child's delight in tormenting his mother. He would come up to her quietly with a cane and start prodding her toes. She would move away, pretending not to notice. St. Mar would follow, insistently prodding at his mother's feet and enjoying the game. Ella would not allow herself to be angry with St. Mar and found an outlet for her annoyance by shouting at Romaine.

Ella could do very little with this obstinate and hostile son. But she found that St. Mar would allow Romaine to do things for him that he would permit from no one else.

When Ella wanted to take St. Mar out driving, it was Romaine who gave him a presentable appearance. St. Mar would allow her to ·take a pair of scissors and hack away at the jungle of his hair and beard.

Only Romaine could persuade St. Mar to remove, occasionally, the stained and bedraggled coat he insisted upon wearing indoors and out. It was she who pulled him back when he would stare, fascinated, over the edge of a cliff, and who prevented him from drinking the exotic concoctions he brewed for himself out of leaves and flowers.

St. Mar had to be watched constantly. "One of his favorite pastimes, when he could escape my vigilance, was to throw bottles from a balcony on the heads of passers-by. An incident of this kind in a terminus hotel in Paris caused the arrival of the police. My brother

32

was caught red-handed, his pockets bulging with bottles. Only the evident state of his mind averted proceedings against him."

One never knew how St. Mar would react. Mrs. Goddard had bought an imposing château at Mentone, a matter of yards from France on the Italian side of the border. Driving out with his mother, St. Mar became the quintessence of cordial good will. The moment their carriage slowed down slightly, St. Mar's hat would come off, to be waved at the surprised customs officials who were lounging on benches almost at the gates of the château.

This charming eccentric could, in fact, be extremely dangerous.

Romaine was having dinner one day and St. Mar was facing her across the table, when he suddenly decided that he could see "an aggressor" standing behind her chair.

"Suddenly a large dinner knife came whirling across the table, missing me by inches. So intent was he on self-defense, that he neither noticed my presence nor saw me changing my place quickly."

Dealing with St. Mar took enormous patience. Romaine acquired that at an early age while waiting for him to finish mumbling interminably over grace and playing the endless games of cards that began in the evening and went on until the early hours of the morning. She could never allow herself the pleasure of winning a game, knowing what St. Mar's mad reaction would be.

One night they were alone together in a villa on the Riviera when Romaine was awakened by the smell of burning. She rushed into St. Mar's room and found him naked and leaning over the bed with a candle in his hand, trying to burn his nightshirt. He explained in his disquietingly soft voice, that the Invisible had worn it, and so he must destroy it.

Romaine agreed that the nightshirt should be destroyed, but she persuaded him to do this by throwing the smouldering garment into the bathtub. He agreed, and allowed himself to be dressed in a clean nightshirt and led back to bed.

To expect a younger child to become her brother's keeper is placing an unreasonable demand upon her. At times, Romaine found the responsibility "almost too heavy to bear." She felt that she was completely wedged between her brother and her mother, "a small prisoner who knew that no help could come from without." Her whole childhood was passed in humoring and appeasing their frightening moods, and for this she paid a heavy inner price. She herself was surprised that she survived.

To expect, moreover, that a child take tender and solicitous care of an Adored One whom she herself envied was so outrageous that even Romaine was aware of the paradox. She had every reason to vent her fantasies of revenge upon her brother, but appears not to have done so. In the terrible triangle of unrequited love that imprisoned them all, she did not blame St. Mar. He was the divine fool, as innocent a victim in his way as she in hers. When she was with him, she did not have to be with her mother, and that was an improvement in itself. His madness even seemed mild, compared with that of her mother. Finally, she discovered that he had grown fond of her.

"In his crazy fashion, his was the only protection I could hope to find . . . On occasions when my mother's mad mood would seek in me a victim, he would even intervene on my behalf. These interventions were so unexpected that from mere astonishment my mother instantly calmed down.

"My brother would walk slowly forward and stand in silence between us, his limp, stooping figure facing my mother. It was eloquent and sufficient to turn the scale in my favor.

"When I went away, I was told that he sought my mother, an unusual thing for him to do, and with shut eyes stood silent and motionless before her. It was his way of protesting against my departure."

To say that Romaine loved St. Mar in return would be to overstate the case. But she felt a maternal pity for him, and to that extent did become her brother's keeper. She identified with him, since he was as much an outcast as she was. His interventions gave the child Romaine a small space, however inadequate; a tiny corner into which she could retreat and tell herself, with anguish, all those things that she could tell nobody else.

Departure*

4

Physically I reacted favorably enough, but I am now convinced that mentally the effects of slum life were never effaced. In some dark corner of my inner consciousness these experiences had sown what would soon take the form of a secret craving for the negative exultation of those who are solitary and adrift.

Ella Waterman Goddard was lying regally on a couch in the room of a New York hotel. It was evening and Romaine, about seven years old, was standing beside her, in the company of a Mrs. Hickey, a plump and good-natured Irish washerwoman. It appeared that the two women had reached an agreement: Mrs. Hickey was going to be paid and in return, Romaine was to live with her. Romaine took her hand and followed Mrs. Hickey out of the room, to take up life in the tenements of New York.

It felt to Romaine like a rescue. Shortly before Mrs. Hickey appeared on the scene, St. Mar had been away undergoing "a cure" of some kind. It seemed to Romaine that her mother's attitude toward her had become increasingly embittered and hostile, as if Ella were blaming her daughter for being healthy when St. Mar could not be cured.

One day Ella dragged Romaine into a room, pulled off her velvet jacket and chopped at her hair in all directions with a pair of scissors. That Ella might have wanted a short-haired little girl, a boy-sub-

* Also called, "Dejection."

stitute, to make up for the one who was missing, did not occur to Romaine. She experienced the incident as a humiliation, a deliberate attempt on the part of her mother to make her as ugly as possible. "It is hard to make allowances for the many miseries I had to endure," she wrote in her memoirs.

Mrs. Hickey lived on the top floor of a Third Avenue tenement. Romaine remembered a long ride in a tram car and then a climb up an endless dark staircase.

William Glackens, in his ink, pencil, and watercolor sketches, paints a vivid portrait of the New York City of the turn of the century, which this development in her life opened up for Romaine. A hundred fat Mrs. Hickeys, their hair parted in the middle and slicked down into a bun, their aprons tucked under spreading bosoms, jostle their way down a crowded sidewalk holding the hands of five-year-olds, or carrying loaded baskets. Stalls full of apples and oranges bulge into the streets where children are playing games of stickball and frightening horses drawing carts. There is a jumble of clocks, of laundry flapping, of balconies rising like steps over the street, of bystanders like Glackens' man in a bowler hat who leans idly against a sign advertising "The Best Lager Beer, 5 Cents."

There is an implied contrast, in Romaine's memoirs, between the dark, immobile form of her mother cloistered in a muffled room (blinds drawn against the city, a clock ticking) and the abrupt shock of this change of surroundings. Romaine went from an atmosphere of wealth and eccentricity—where she was the despised child—to smells, noise, poverty, and a living scraped off the streets; a dangerous, marginal existence, but one that provided acceptance and warmth.

Perhaps Mrs. Hickey only existed in the limbo of childhood where fact and fantasy are inseparable, as the vision of a loving mother that Romaine wanted and therefore invented out of a casual visit to a poor woman's home. Or perhaps Mrs. Hickey really existed and did indeed take Romaine up a long flight of stairs and offer her a slice of bread and butter and a large cup of black coffee.

"I was put to bed on a sofa and for the first time in many months I slept the whole night through. On awakening next morning I noticed how light the curtainless window made the room, and how strange the fire-escape balcony looked outside."

Romaine's instinctive painter's eye recorded the ugly details of the room, including the clumsily framed cardboard pictures that Mrs. Hickey's son brought home from the shop where he was a salesman and had stuck up on the walls; and her rich-child's expectations were given a jolt by the discovery that most of her meals would be like the first one: strong black coffee and bread.

As an adult, Romaine reserved her tenderest self for servants who kept a peasant's simplicity about them. She tended to select women whose guilelessness and innocence of the world were far outweighed by their largeness of spirit. Mrs. Hickey must have been the model for these later choices because she at once encouraged Romaine to draw. She found pencils and paper and a small drawer in which the child could keep her precious possessions.

Then Mrs. Hickey introduced Romaine to another "artist," who lived across the fire escape balcony and drew all day long at an easel.

"He seemed to be the only thing in the room not covered with heaps of fuzzy woollen mats. He told me that his mother made the mats while he copied photographs. I admired his copies and he in turn looked wisely at my drawings. We became very good friends."

For Romaine, the life of a slum child became an endless adventure. She would creep down the long, dark, evil-smelling staircase apprehensively, trying to avoid the strange people who darted out from different doors on the stairs; and walk up and down the streets "in a daze"; though whether from euphoria or fear, or both, she does not make clear. She would often get lost and then a policeman would have to bring her home. She remembered running about on roller skates in a treeless square near their apartment, and her first contact with any group of children.

Her attitude toward this introduction mingled an instinctive longing to be part of the group with deep suspicion. She had already noticed the unconscious cruelty of young children; how roughly they played with each other and how they would pick on newcomers. Their favorite game was to put the unsuspecting one in the center of their line. Then, joining hands, they would all race down Third Avenue. At the signal, they would let go of the new child, who would be flung forward on his face. Romaine had no intention of letting that happen to her. But one day, they pleaded with her so earnestly and promised so faithfully not to do it, that she took the risk. She found her new friends as good as their word.

The reminiscences of this period are remarkable for the matter-of-fact quality of their telling, as if a child's automatic acceptance of such a radical change of surroundings had been retained by the adult. Things *were*, because they had happened; that was all; the child adapted and did not question, without a backward glance. Romaine makes it clear, however, that she was making a deliberate choice. When the opportunity to return to her mother presented itself, she turned it down.

It came about one afternoon when Romaine returned to the apartment and saw the figure of Mrs. Hickey drooping over two baskets full of clean linen. The washerwoman had gone to her mother's hotel as usual to return her laundry. But when she got there, she was told that Mrs. Goddard had left without leaving an address. Mrs. Hickey was rubbing her reddened, varicose-veined legs up and down. "No money for the washing—her weeping, kindly eyes turned to me—and a child on her hands, unpaid for."

Romaine stood beside her, shocked and silent. She knew perfectly well what to do, since she had memorized her grandfather's address in Philadelphia. All she had to do was to give it to Mrs. Hickey. But that would mean going back to her mother.

"Deliberately I remained silent, as children often do, and I effaced all memory of my life at Chestnut Hill. In perfect innocence I took my part in the general upheaval that was to follow."

The sudden loss of income caused an astonishing series of changes in the household, which dropped another significant notch on the poverty ladder. Mrs. Hickey moved to even cheaper rooms. There was one bedroom for her son, Mike, while she and a "frowsy" relative, who helped do the washing, and Romaine slept together in a kind of closet. "I can still smell the odor of that shut-in pen—a mixture of unwashed bodies and beer." The whole tenement was infested with bedbugs, and since Romaine was developing a fastidious distaste for all forms of insect life, she often sat up all night to escape them.

The rooms opened out onto a courtyard where there was a solitary tree, straggling and sooty. Nature had already given it up for dead, but Romaine loved it; to her, it was a precious and beautiful reminder of Chestnut Hill, and she anticipated the delightful pleasure of sitting alone under its branches. But this hope vanished when she discovered that the tree was the rallying point for all the children of the neighborhood, who flocked to it like sparrows.

There was no more money for bread and black coffee. Romaine lived on sweet buns, bought with the few pennies Mrs. Hickey left her before she went off to work every day. Romaine was almost always hungry and would rock herself energetically in a rocking chair, singing in a loud voice to drown the hunger pains. She ran about in the streets all day, playing with the neighborhood children, with whom she got on badly. She did not understand what went wrong, but it was always the same she said in the memoirs. At first, she was accepted enthusiastically by the group, which had, after all, raced her down Third Avenue without ever letting go. But the same children quickly turned hostile and chose her as their victim.

It was more than dislike, she decided; the children seemed to hate her. They made fun of her because she bragged about the fine clothes and velvet jackets she used to wear. They called her a liar and "saucer eyes" for the way she would stare. Even the children's mothers rose up against her, and when Romaine was sent to fetch water at the public tap with her heavy pitcher, the mothers would gather around, giving vent to their feelings "in rich and colored language." Romaine did not understand why this always seemed to happen. Her perhaps incomplete explanation was: "Evidently my nature is monastic and has been accentuated by an unusual childhood. Any effort on my part to be otherwise is only make believe . . . To the herd this deception, when disclosed, is a crime . . ."

Despite the hostility of the "herd," despite the hunger, the bedbugs, the trips to the corner saloon to buy beer for Mrs. Hickey, the time when she helped sell papers in the street, "crying out the news in a small piping voice," the time when she found Mike in bed with the frowsy relative, Romaine never once thought of going home. Her loyalty to Mrs. Hickey was complete, since Mrs. Hickey had saved her from her mother. She let her draw, she introduced her to other artists and would not abandon her, even though there was no more money for Romaine's support. When the father of a playmate, a prosperous butcher, wanted to adopt her, Romaine annoyed him by declaring that she would never leave Mrs. Hickey.

The fact that her mother had attempted to abandon her, impressed itself so deeply on Romaine that she told the story over and over again. Whether it happened just as she describes one cannot know, although a form of proof exists that something of the sort happened. Dr. Richard P. Wunder, a former curator at the National Collection of Fine Arts who interviewed Romaine in her old age, reported that a slight New York accent was still detectable in her speech.

Whatever the mitigating circumstances might have been, what Romaine experienced was abandonment. In leaving her mother without a backward glance, she was giving up the struggle to love her. What remained was not acquiescence, but outrage. The incident is her proof to the world of her mother's incorrigible wickedness. The fact that she was ready to endure great privation rather than return, demonstrates how badly she was treated as a child.

Romaine appears to have realized that the event was deeply significant. Her explanation was that it had sown "what would soon take the form of a secret craving for the negative exultation of those who are solitary and adrift." The incident reinforced the conviction that she was unlovable, although she did not know why. It was her fate to be the victim of circumstance, misunderstood and persecuted by everyone, like a medieval saint.

Romaine tried valiantly to come to terms with desolation. She could take a stoic pride, "a negative exultation," in her ability to endure without being broken. She could turn defeat into triumph by embracing the life of one cast off from human contact and adrift on a perilous sea. Since it was useless to want love and approval, she would stifle that need in herself; would put an emotional distance betweeen herself and others, so that they would lose their power to hurt her. She could take Peer Gynt's maxim, "To thyself be enough." It was an ominous development.

Even Mrs. Hickey was something of a disappointment. After Ella Goddard disappeared, the washerwoman managed to make contact with Romaine's grandfather in Philadelphia and Romaine concluded, years later, that the family might have acted to avoid the possibility of a lawsuit against the abandonment of juveniles. One day, when Romaine was out buying buns, she was told to run home quickly. She returned and found a gray-haired man sitting in Mike's bedroom. She knew him: he was Mr. Barr, her grandfather's secretary. They looked at each other in silence. Mr. Barr took a number of bills from a bulging wallet and asked Mrs. Hickey if that was enough. "She thanked him volubly, her features taking on that unhappy expression of intense pleasure I have so often noticed on the faces of the poor," Romaine wrote in disapproval, apparently feeling that Mrs. Hickey's greed had got the better of her affections. Then, not knowing where she was going, Romaine walked out to a waiting carriage with Mr. Barr, her dirty hand in his.

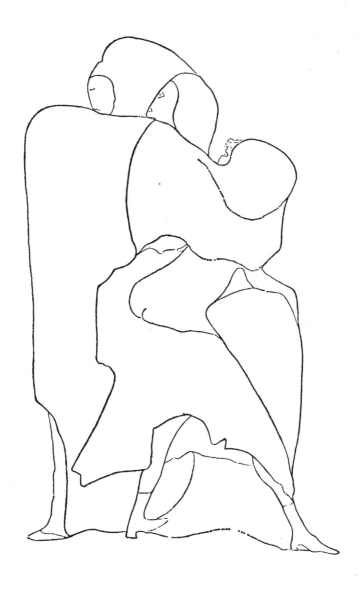

Disapproval*

5

This desertion, however, in no way affected pleasant memories of St. Mary's. My life there ever remained to me the one bright spot in the course of my troubled childhood.

Romaine was scrubbed clean by a lady friend of Mr. Barr and dressed in an outfit she remembers meticulously: "The frock was of lace over a silk slip; the hat was a wonder of cream Italian straw, black velvet ribbons and an ostrich feather."

After the reclamation, Romaine said that she missed Mrs. Hickey, so one Sunday she was taken there for a visit, dressed in her ostentatious finery. Her desire to make the visit might have stemmed from a desire to get even; at any rate, the visit was a triumph. Children of the tenement suddenly became her admirers and one of them, acting as a bodyguard, took her to Sunday school, where it happened to be the day for signing an anti-drinking pledge. (Romaine solemnly added her name.)

Romaine was not sent to join her mother but to her grandparents at Chestnut Hill, where she spent a summer recuperating. She was just eight and old enough, it had been decided, for St. Mary's Hall, an Episcopal boarding school in Burlington, New Jersey.

It had spacious grounds and green lawns sloping down gently to a fast-flowing river, and followed what Romaine called "the genteel

* Also called, "L'Oeil."

American tradition." Girls were supposed to be young ladies. Rough games and loud voices were discouraged with the comment that they were out of place. Instead, these children of wealthy and socially correct families were dressed up in stately white muslin dresses and took walks up and down the river banks, like Seurat's static figures juxtaposed against the dappled light and shade of a Sunday afternoon beside a stream.

The school's religious tone was orthodox. There was chapel twice a day, with hymns sung and the Bible read by the director, who was also a clergyman. Attendance was obligatory, only to be excused if one were ill enough to go to the infirmary. Sunday afternoons were spent in the partitioned alcoves where each girl slept. Presumably the time passed in meditation and prayer, although Romaine reports a good deal of cakes and candies being passed around, along with the Bible, with certain significant passages marked, and handed over the partition with smothered giggles. Romained found this mystifying.

Her education had been sporadic up to this point, but now she developed a sudden interest in reading, "lost between the real and the unreal." One book in particular seized her imagination. It was *At the Back of the North Wind,* a story about a little boy who played with the elements and was carried off one night by the north wind. It is not hard to see why such an escapist fantasy would have enchanted her and her dreamlike absorption did not go unnoticed. When she could not do her arithmetic ("My mind refused to divide, add or subtract") this book was pronounced the culprit and its reading relegated to Sundays.

Her natural artistic talent was similarly restricted. All the queer devils, ghosts, and spirits that she was always drawing were viewed with alarm. Instead, she was set to copying plaster models of cubes, blocks, and pyramids; and, later, Bibles, spectacles, and candlesticks. Romaine continued to give expression to her flights of imagination rebelliously, just as she had when her mother had prevented her from drawing. "I used to chalk on the blackboard, when I was alone, such ephemeral fancies as would relieve the tedium of the moment."

At about this point Major Goddard made his first and only appearance in Romaine's life. She had only dim memories of him as a small child, but she had, naturally, heard a lot about him from her mother, who always described her former husband in most uncomplimentary terms. One cannot know what Ella told Romaine. Perhaps she said that Major Goddard deserted her in her hour of need; or perhaps that he was a drunkard. Whatever it was, Romaine accepted her mother's evaluation of her father in the automatic manner of childhood, reflecting the same contempt for a man she had never seen.

Then one day he appeared at the school, "a somewhat bald gentleman with a long, drooping moustache." Romaine would not go down to the reception room to meet him and relented only when he sent up a box of caramels. That first conversation was labored and cursory. Perhaps sensing what his daughter felt, Major Goddard addressed most of his remarks to her principal. But he did talk about Romaine's gift for drawing before he left and said how much he admired Gustave Doré.

Although Major Goddard appears to have made a number of visits, they are not recorded in Romaine's memoirs. He seems to have been a well-intentioned but ineffectual man who had been dominated by his wife and must have been at a loss to deal with his strange, stubborn, hostile daughter. That he showed a certain courage in visiting her at all, Romaine was able to acknowledge later. All he had to live on was the small allowance his wife gave him, and he knew she would disapprove of his contacts with their daughter. When she found out about the visits, Ella reacted with predictable illogic, blaming them on Romaine.

Romaine's attitude toward her father did not change. "Belonging to one parent was a disagreeable experience; I had no desire to belong to another," she wrote. Perhaps this peevishness hid a resentment that her father had abandoned her to a cruel childhood fate. This would account for her readiness to accept her mother's evaluation of him. Now he was appearing in her life, requiring to be accepted if not loved, with no regard for his daughter's possible feelings.

Romaine only gives the barest clues about her refusal of a possible avenue of escape in this opportunity to make her first contact with her father and his side of the family. But there is an indication that she must have sized up her father, at some point, and found him wanting. The more he and unknown aunts and cousins came forward with sudden presents, invitations, and letters, she said, the more she shrank back into herself. Their faces and their kind intentions would not provide the support she needed; they were no match for her realities. And so her father faded out of her childhood, leaving no trace.

Hers were dangerous realities indeed; fantastic and elusive; full of dissolving shapes, hints, portents, murmurs of other worlds, of tragedies suppressed, of terrors choked back into the throat, of malevolent spirits peering over balconies and insinuating their suffocating presences along the silent corridors.

There was, to begin with, the physical setting of the school which, so benign at first glance, with its rolling lawns and rushing water, had hidden dangers for the unsuspecting, since the neighboring countryside contained "long stretches of stagnant marsh lands from whence arose miasmas and mosquitoes." Shortly after she arrived at the school, these miasmas began to make themselves felt. Whenever Romaine could escape the attention she was getting for being the youngest child in the school (as an exception, she was admitted a year early), she would find some corner to hide in. There she would shiver and shake not, as one might suppose, in an understandable release of tension from being the center of such attention but, she declared, from "chills and fever." She claimed that none of the adults noticed she was ill.

Her new environment held other terrors. It was said that the school was haunted. Years before, two little girls, close friends, had come from overseas to be pupils at St. Mary's but, shortly after they got there one of them died of a fever. The other child died of grief shortly afterwards. These little girls had been seen "roaming through the empty schoolrooms, clad in nightgowns, their black hair streaming behind them," and during the evening service at chapel they would pull aside the curtains and peer inside.

This story made a great impression on Romaine. She was already filling her drawings with ghosts and devils, peopling her imagination with the malevolent spirits who must be responsible for her fears. It was a short step to imagine that she could feel the presence of these ghosts. Perhaps she only dreamed that one night when she was walking alone toward the chapel, she "saw distinctly" the backs of the two little girls, their white nightgowns and black hair, opening the curtains and peering into the place.

These fears were too terrible to be revealed. They were, after all, indescribable; not to be separated from those moments when Romaine would file into her chapel seat, which happened to be in a front pew facing the other half of the school, feeling every eye fixed upon her and the weight of a hundred critical judgments and then, from behind the closed curtains, would steal the conviction that she was being watched. Romaine would go rigid, the blood would rush to her face, and she would feel like fainting. She underwent this ordeal twice a day.

Romaine correctly decided that such visitations by ghosts resulted from her mother's early influence, and eventually, she noted, she gained enough control over them so that she could will them to leave. She was aware that her acute self-consciousness in front of a crowd was somehow involved; a nervousness she never quite lost.

One of her earliest drawings, executed in her teens, is a fluid, writhing shape, forked and darted. In the center is a veined eye, its heavy outlines suggesting inflammation, suspicion. Compacted as stone in an inflexible face, the condemning eye has a rolling sidelong glare; the image was to become indelible.

Romaine could not know how much this was the result of her own condition. Those who become, through early malformation, self-disparaging and condemning, will imagine hostility emanating from others. He who has "no eyes" (a metaphor for a profound lack of inner confidence) and therefore no faith in what he sees, is obliged to look in the mirrors of others for his own reflection.

That she was bound on the wheel of the tormented and self-tormenting was poetically realized in her works. At the conscious level, Romaine saw her life in terms of Greek tragedy. She believed that the causes of her persecution were malevolent influences from outer spheres. It seems, she wrote, "that the demon ever hovering over massed humanity is more active for evil than for good."

Her friendships were a mirror of that secret world where destruction and self-destruction were intertwined. There was a little German girl, tiny for her age, with blond plaits sticking out at right angles from a small pink face. She was sitting on a high stool playing "Heimweh" at the piano with such ludicrous exaggeration that Romaine, who had been brought to the concert to meet her, fled as soon as the music ended. But a kind of reluctant friendship developed. Romaine was willing to sit and watch her play and noticed that the little girl always seemed to be chewing something; she thought it was gum.

"But I soon learned the awful truth which I never mentioned to a soul, so impossible it was to speak about. The little pianist, like a cow, chewed her cud! It would make me very ill indeed when, by the movement of her thin little throat, I saw the meal coming up and asking to be chewed over again."

The same mixture of fascination and revulsion is contained in a description of another school friend whose apparently normal exterior concealed a dreadful secret. Jane was also small and blonde, with a thin face bent low on her chest like St. Mar's, and pathetic gray eyes. It was a wordless friendship in which both were aware of a common bond. They appeared together in *tableaux vivants* given by the school, as the two little princes in the tower.

Then one year, Jane did not come back to school after the holidays. Romaine discovered that the little prince in the tableau was marked in real life for a dreadful fate: She was becoming a hunchback like her sister.

When Jane reappeared and invited Romaine to spend a day on the river on her father's boat, Romaine refused to go. Writing about the incident, she felt remorseful. Had she forgotten Jane so soon, or was she unwilling to recognize Jane's fate? she asked herself.

The four years Romaine spent at St. Mary's Hall were important in two respects. She was away from her mother's influence for a considerable, perhaps crucial, period of time. She was in an atmosphere that could be described as one of benign neglect. After the first uncomfortable months of scrutiny, Romaine became one more in a blur of anonymous faces. She was very happy at this apparent loss of identity. She had yearned to be left alone and it was finally happening. No one was giving her particular attention, but no one was making her the object of personal antagonism either. Contrasted with her mother's autocratic demands, the rules of the school seemed mild.

Following as it did the months of freedom with Mrs. Hickey, the period spent at St. Mary's Hall made a slight but significant change in her inner landscape which, to judge from another early drawing, was that of a lake filled with monsters. Romaine was beginning to believe in a beneficent God; very cautiously, since there was still her mother and the spirit world to be considered, but hopefully. She began to see Him as a potential ally for the future.

Like the rest of her generation, she was entering puberty in almost complete sexual innocence. There had been that one incident at Mrs. Hickey's, when she had burst in upon Mike and the frowsy relative together in a way that seemed to frighten her, even though she didn't know why. There had been certain things about St. Mar's behavior which were disturbing, but . . . she had forgotten them. When the girls at St. Mary's giggled over certain passages in the Bible, Romaine was perfectly blank, even faintly self-righteous. For her, the arrival of sexuality meant a spontaneous flowering of interest in her own sex that she would have considered pure and therefore true, since it was not tainted by the slightest sensuality.

At first Romaine found herself in an agony of admiration for some living or dead hero or heroine, analogous to the ecstasy of the contemporary preadolescent for the beautiful creature in intimate, maddening, and safe distance on a movie screen. Then her fantasies began to take the more substantial shapes of girls in the school, but they were always older and therefore safely separated from her by the natural barrier of age.

From the start, Romaine's crushes on older girls contained more than the usual edge of determination. Though adoring from a remote distance, she adored stubbornly, hopelessly, completely. When one of the girls who had been the object of her passion left the school, Romaine's reaction was much more than the usual trancelike staring through windows, the echoing memories of lonely footsteps down a path, the scribbled elegiac couplets, and the random small acts of retaliation against the world. She became physically ill.

Fortunately, Romaine was able to recognize that her reaction was

53

out of proportion to the event. She confided in a friend who visited her in the sick bay. The friend remarked, with what Romaine recognized as wisdom, that this was surprising since she, the friend, had never seen Romaine together with the object of her passion. Romaine confessed that she had never even spoken to her, and they both laughed. Fortunately, Romaine was developing an excellent sense of humor.

Since the converse of having a crush on a girl is to be yourself the object of another's admiration, Romaine had her share of admirers. She did not, as a more secure or narcissistic girl might have done, take the slightest interest. These were "little girls," she said, shrugging off their pathetic presents and letters with the comment that, "perhaps I already felt the irony of things that permitted such sentiments to come and go unrequited."

A young girl's normal stage of homosexuality is relatively brief, lasting until that point is reached at which she discovers boys. In fact, schoolgirls appear to arrive at this moment with inner clocks more or less uncannily synchronized, and those who were, at the age of twelve, writing despairing declarations of love to other girls are, by the ages of fourteen or fifteen, slipping the same messages of love, this time to boys, under the lids of their desks.

But there are a few girls for whom this inner metamorphosis never takes place and, by degrees, they become emotionally involved with older girls and teachers.

When this first happened to Romaine, she was barely aware of it. It was her fourth year at St. Mary's Hall, and their home room teacher was an elderly lady who also taught handwriting. Romaine knew that she was the teacher's "favorite," but, because that teacher was a model of discretion, only guessed later the extent of the woman's affection for her.

"The highest degree of perfection in this copy-book calligraphy lay in the ability to dash off scrolls, flowers, and birds with one dash of the pen; the whole making a beautiful and effective ending to one's signature. . . ." It was a bit like drawing and Romaine mastered it easily. No name or face of the teacher survives, but only the intense visual pleasure Romaine derived from such convoluted patterns of flowers and birds, heads bent over paper, no sound but the scratching of pens, the obedient whirr of thirty pieces of paper turning for a new exercise; a caressing, approving, swiftly passing presence. Then, the prize: a gold pen.

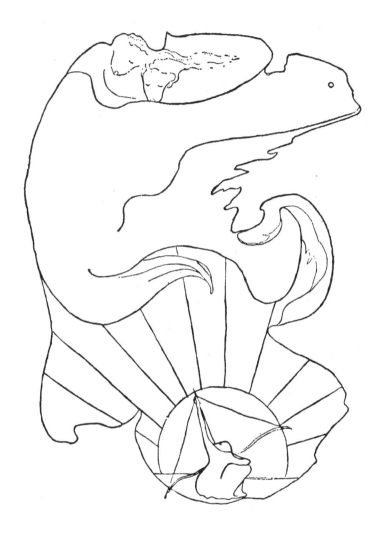

Dreams Attacked by Day*

6

As I grew older I was fortunate enough to be sent away from time to time; but . . . I never forgot that my fate was with these mad ones, and on my return I would find them again and be dragged precisely as before into their crazy round of existence.

Romaine Brooks retained some fragments of her early life. Packed in the recesses of trunks, they were taken out at intervals, examined, and returned to their obscure hiding places. One of them is a sepia photograph, slightly stained and creased, showing the mark of two drawing pins on its top edge, but in the otherwise good condition which would suggest nostalgic care. It is a portrait of herself and her sister, Maya, taken by Debenham and Gould of Bournemouth, when she must have been twelve and Maya, fourteen. Romaine stands against a table, wearing a loosely pleated sailor dress with a constrictingly high collar, and her sister sits in a chair beside her, her flat, wide and rather strongly featured face turned in wistful appeal toward the photographer.

Romaine is the real beauty. These half-formed features, still softly rounded, are more delicately designed. One is aware of a high, oval forehead hidden by a fringe, a small, straight nose, a soft, almost pretty mouth with a generous upper lip, and large eyes whose expression is not so much naïve as open, unsuspicious, accepting.

It was a look they would seldom have again; the fruit of four years

* Also called, "Les Rêves Attaqués Par Le Jour."

spent at St. Mary's Hall in surroundings where she was beginning to develop the belief that she was acceptable; would be accepted just for herself.

One sees in this formal testimony the germinal outlines of the kind of woman she could have been; was destined not to become. The cause is implied in the testimony itself. There is the correct opulence of the decor, with its scattering of brocade, columns, ferns, fur, and velvet; the pose of sisters grouped with arbitrary charm, their hands clasped, their heads tilted to the right appealing angle. All that this testimony implied, fell like an implacable framework around Romaine in the uncompromising nature of her mother's response when they met again after four years.

"As I greeted my mother in London," she writes in *No Pleasant Memories*, "and recognized the same mad, luminous eyes and unsmiling mouth, I felt the apprehension of a small animal caught in a net and for no good reason of its own.

"I was dressed in a sailor suit with a diminutive bustle that I hated and a high, starched collar that choked me.

"After a slight inspection my mother addressed me as one would a grown-up person: 'A bustle, a standing collar, and an American accent are inappropriate here.'"

At that moment, St. Mar came into the room. When Romaine left, St. Mar had been thin and delicate. She remembered the characteristic way he had of peering at life, as though he were groping through the confusion of his mind. Here was another shock, for the boy who should have been, at nineteen, in the first bloom of manhood, was an old man. Romaine could see the frail and prematurely bowed shoulders under the velvet jacket, the jut of the small face almost hidden behind its incoherent tangle of beard and hair, and a look on his face which, in her shock and horror, seemed to be that of the pale and pathetic Jane, the friend of St. Mary's Hall who was condemned to a terrible fate; identifying, for Romaine, the reasons for her empathy and revulsion . . .

Romaine and St. Mar had always understood each other on some essential level as children. Whatever directness of look passed between them, caused him to put up his hands to hide his face. Romaine knew she must do something quickly. She crossed the carpet, took one of his thin hands and shook it, sparing him the nakedness of his confrontation with himself and giving him the only reassurance she could have provided at that moment. "I was relieved to find that he not only recognized me but . . . seemed pleased at my return," she wrote.

The old life fell around her like a shroud, blurring the soft outlines of her face the way the London rain bemisted the windowpane; blotting out those dreams of other worlds, while inside the room, St. Mar's nervous fingers beat a monotonous tattoo against the glass of the window, and he accompanied it "with a curious, low, sing-song voice which was horrible to hear."

Nothing would ever change. It was a new city, a new suite of rooms, that was all. What Romaine felt was the same demonic energy, almost a presence outside of them all, that whipped them around the ring while her mother, the most driven of all and the one at the center, brandished the whip; demanding a more rigorous obedience . . . St. Mar was capering around the ring, followed by the doctor he hated, the valet who was afraid of him, her mother's terrified maid, Maya, and an English governess, who had been hired to teach the girls, but soon gave her notice.

As before, Ella stayed up all night and slept in snatches during the day. So did St. Mar. Whenever he found life overwhelming, he would retire to his bed and sip a mild solution of paregoric to ease imagined or real pains. At night Romaine was required to sit up with him playing long games of cards, or stay with her mother listening to her spirit-haunted soliloquies.

For the next two years, Romaine did very little except follow them around Europe. Their endless wanderings were symbolized for her in the exasperating problem of their twenty-two trunks, "identical black canvas mammoths," which accompanied them everywhere.

To begin with, the family was never able to travel anywhere and have all twenty-two trunks arrive. Some would get lost along the way. Some would be left in the luggage van and still others, their tickets mangled, would bury their way into the depths of the lost luggage office.

What was more, since the trunks were identical, nothing could ever be found. Ella would demand some item of clothing and a maid would appear, rattling a large bunch of keys, and sink to her knees in front of a trunk, her face eloquent with despair. She would try one key after another. Some would fit and some would not, but none of them would open a single lock.

Other people would offer to try, and the trunks would be opened, but the particular garment was not to be found.

"During the confusion my mother, reclining on her divan, would converse softly with congenial spirits; but should the garment not be forthcoming the ring-master within her was instantly resuscitated, cracking the whip. We would then show greater nimbleness, and 'Find the Garment' became more than an ordinary game." Romaine was the one who solved the mystery of the trunks and was given the responsibility for keeping track of the piles of linens, dresses, hats, coats, and shoes.

St. Mar detested scenes of any kind. Whenever they took place he would disappear into another room, drumming on the windowpane and trying to whistle. But he hated traveling even more. His dislike of it took the form of unpredictable and sometimes violent scenes in contrast to his usual apathy. The family would arrive, and St. Mar would refuse to leave the train. The doctor would try to pull him out. He would hit the doctor. The whistle would blow, the baffled face of the station master would appear at the window, several people would plead and tug. St. Mar would collapse as unexpectedly as he had resisted and allow himself to be hauled out.

St. Mar was always unpredictable. He might ramble around the room, confiding to people in whispers that terrible things had happened to him in childhood, things he had by a miracle escaped; that dreadful men had tried to murder him. Ella would mutter loyally, "That man should have gone to prison."

Nevertheless, he was capable of taking a rational, if macabre, interest in the world around him. There was a cholera epidemic one summer and St. Mar read the papers carefully for the daily list of reported cases. Each town was allotted its own exercise book and its cases were carefully recorded, with much smudging and rubbing out.

"Book after book was filled with lugubrious lists," Romaine recorded, "the interest of which lay in finding out the town that held the record for cholera deaths. I remember his telling me that Hamburg was the winner."

Romaine slid back into the old ways the way a drowning man's fingers relax their grip on a piece of driftwood and he surrenders himself to the depths. The emotional triangle was immutable. Ella loved St. Mar, who loved (as much as his muddled mind was capable of it) Romaine. And Romaine, for her part, was still attempting to gain her mother's love, although her attitude toward Ella was congealing into passive defiance. Romaine had learned at an early age to calculate Ella's moods and conceal her own feelings against attack: "I surveyed, rather than lived, my life," she wrote. This training would have given her watchful and guarded expression a certain deliberateness that Ella must have found irritating.

But it was more than a case of simply manipulating her mother out of trouble's way. "My mother I first feared, then watched, then judged," Romaine wrote revealingly. This, then, was the implacable look to which Ella was responding when she would hiss, "I will break your spirits."

Romaine added, "That she broke neither my spirits nor my back is a miracle worth recording." There is more than a hint of reckless pride in the remark.

The four years at St. Mary's Hall, which had done so much to alter her view of her life and herself, could not survive the whirlwind of fear and hatred in which Romaine was once more engulfed. How ridiculous it had been to think that the benevolent God of St. Mary's could possibly protect her from Ella's own God, Lucifer. Romaine knew that he existed because she had seen his swarthy, winged form diving to unknown depths on the covers of magazines her mother received. She knew he was the God of the Underworld, the demon of destruction to whom her mother wrote poems in a kind of perverse ecstasy, with whom she took flights into space; with whom Ella had made a sinister bargain. When confronted with Lucifer it seemed to Romaine, who already had vivid visions of herself as a second Joan of Arc, that "my golden armour melted away like a covering of snow."

63

No benign God, she was convinced, could protect her against Ella and her winged demon.

After two years of this inner stress Romaine, at fourteen, was close to a nervous breakdown. The family happened to be staying at a town in northern Italy when Ella, who had never forgiven St. Mary's Hall for baptising Romaine an Episcopalian ("I think the child entirely too young to understand the nature of such a performance," she wrote reprovingly), seems to have seized on the idea of sending Romaine to a convent. It was a way of getting even with St. Mary's Hall and correcting the supposed imbalance in her daughter's mind. A small trunk of new clothes was packed, Romaine was deposited at the school and left to adapt herself to a life of medieval Catholicism.

Somewhere in the back of her mind, Romaine had an image of Catholicism, compounded of the teachings of St. Francis, the beauty of old church music, and the sunny cloisters she had seen, whose calm seemed to radiate divine inspiration. The reality of the convent (unnamed) in which she found herself, was a bitter disappointment.

It was a dark building of gray stone bordered by recreation courts without a sign of grass or trees and walls as high as prisons. There were unheated classrooms, corridors whipped by the wind, and paved floors that were punishingly cold in winter. Instead of light, warmth, and hope, Romaine saw the convent as a place where hope was extinguished. It seemed to be a tabernacle erected to the transience of life.

In the year Romaine spent there, people died without warning. A frail nun who taught her catechism had a toothache and a swollen cheek one day and was dead the next. Another nun, who damaged her finger slightly while playing the organ, promptly expired. That slight accidents should have such drastic results was unnerving, but what was even more unsettling was the casual way in which death was accepted. It was a too-familiar presence. "They try to measure God," she wrote, "but only end in measuring their own coffins."

The mother superior might have been the personification of death. Romaine, who had been prepared to make an elaborate curtsey upon first meeting her, was amazed at the old woman's astonishing ugliness. This monstrous yellow face, with its great flabby mouth falling over a stiff black and white bow, was like an ogress in the fairy stories she had read at St. Mary's Hall. She was a witch from the deep forest who trapped and devoured little girls.

The fact that the mother superior was particularly interested in Romaine (such an unusual case, an American mother concerned over her child's misguided religious indoctrination who hoped her daughter would take the veil), only made it worse. The appearance of the mother superior deepened Romaine's conviction that she was fated to live in a nightmare with monsters.

She was taken down to a dormitory, filled with rows of beds, where she was to sleep, and shown the clothes she was to wear.

"The combined chemise-nightgown of thick linen, with long sleeves and high neck was . . . to be worn night and day in order to prevent any display of anatomy when getting in and out of bed. It was discreetly changed every Sunday and this . . . was to be no easy matter, for the clean one had to go on before the other was off. There were also long black stockings in the trunk, and among them I saw what seemed to me a particularly ugly green pair. My nerves were evidently in a bad state for after declaring that these stockings were impossible to wear I, who never cried, began crying."

Romaine had been wearing relatively short skirts just below the calf. These clothes were removed and replaced by a gown of black-and-white checks which effectively covered ankles, neck, and wrists in the pursuit (she was told) of modesty and the salvation of her soul. Then the long hair which covered her shoulders was twisted back into a bun and her bangs plastered back to show her high forehead. Feeling as uncomfortable as she must have looked, she was taken to a refectory where two hundred identically dressed girls were being served soup from a huge black cauldron and listening to a nun reading from a high pulpit.

Romaine disliked the monotonous convent diet. Breakfast began with a small cup of black chocolate and stale rolls without butter, followed by lunches of beetroot salad, chunks of tunny (a Mediterranean fish) and cheese, which Romaine unwillingly learned to eat with a knife.

The dehumanizing effect of the clothes was bad enough; but Romaine was even more unsettled by the dormitory's rows of beds.

She asked for a screen and it was provided until the nun in charge, tired of carrying the heavy object in and out, suggested to the other girls that Romaine needed it to hide some physical deformity. Romaine, her pride galvanized, waved the object away.

But the screen came back on Saturdays after Romaine discovered the limitations of the weekly bath. She had an American respect for hygiene and such modern inventions as tooth brushes. Romaine found that the only parts of their anatomy the Italian girls ever washed were their hands and face (once a day) and their feet (on Saturdays.)

"Being used to other ways I would try to bathe in my small foot-tub behind the screen. Hearing the unusual splashing of water the anxious sister on the other side . . . would call out, 'Soltanto i piedi! Soltanto i piedi!' (Only the feet! Only the feet!)." It was suggested to Romaine that such washing was unhealthy and that she would surely brush her teeth away.

Romaine became the center of attention for the other girls, who had never met an American before. They surrounded her in a chattering circle, touching and prodding her to see if she were real. She spoke very little Italian and her foreign accent was the subject of much mimicry, but (in contrast to St. Mary's Hall, where she had found such scrutiny uncomfortable) Romaine seems to have enjoyed this acknowledgment of her difference, her uniqueness.

She took on the role of the class jester, regaling her classmates with caricatures, drawn on the blackboard in rapid strokes before the start of classes. Ella the mad ringmaster and the poor, befuddled St. Mar with his bottles and cholera books, were particularly appreciated. Romaine had just put the finishing touches on a tonsured priest with uplifted hands, when a sister appeared and snatched the chalk out of her hand.

Since the convent believed that every talent should be put to use, Romaine was appointed draftsman. She reproduced life-size heads of Christ crowned with thorns from miniatures, scenery for the convent plays (an outsize cardboard angel seated on a tomb) and, on the feast days, made cardboard placards of cooks bearing the meager menus on monumental stomachs.

Romaine was led to understand that as soon as she took the veil she would be trained as a drawing teacher. It was meant as a compliment. In fact, the convent was properly diligent in its task of guiding the foreign Protestant to a recognition of the error of her ways. A rotund priest talked about confession and extreme unction, subjects which seemed frivolously irrelevant to Romaine, compared with the diabolical designs of her mother. The convent, she considered, had nothing new to tell her about death. Her memoirs make a passing reference to what seems to have been her first and only suicide attempt, when she drank a homemade brew of sulphur matches soaked in water.

Finally, the mother superior dangled a locket on a chain in front of her nose and told Romaine that it would be hers on the glorious day when she was converted. What was more, all the girls in every convent of the order would have a holiday.

Romaine remained unmoved. When on walks in a "crocodile" of convent girls in their black-and-white checked dresses and black capes, she would look up at a passing window and choose it as a future hide-out. She longed to escape, but until that magic moment came, she was determined to resist in the only way she knew: passively. It was the only path possible for a martyr, and Romaine was convinced that she was becoming one. She was persecuted on all sides, but she would prevail because of her saintlike and heroic endurance.

Although outwardly obedient and compliant, willing to tell her beads, learn the Lord's Prayer by heart in Latin and Italian, and answer questions on the catechism, Romaine would refuse to kiss the ivory body of Christ on the altar once a year; would refuse to understand when the subtleties of divine faith and the state of grace were explained with such clarity and patience.

She was either stupid or stubborn. The convent was losing its patience, although Romaine did not know this. She had concluded that the only way out for her was to get ill. She was praying to the God of St. Mary's Hall for a Protestant miracle.

Romaine's description of the Christmas she spent at the convent is Dickensian. It is the classic vision of the child barred from human happiness: "I see myself alone, shivering with cold in the schoolroom, seated at my desk . . ." She can hear her classmates opening up their Christmas hampers and exclaiming over the contents somewhere in the distance. There is nothing for her, but she is not aware of any emotion, only a sharp pain in her side which forces her to lean over the desk. Her classmates notice the lack of a hamper and pass by, silently . . .

The days that follow are a blur because her Protestant God has answered her prayer, or her own obsessive longing to escape is having the desired effect; and she gets ill. She is swept up in a confusion of seemingly disparate events. The convent has become like an up-turned ant hill. People rush distractedly in and out of corridors. A sister adjusts her veil and hurries toward the chapel. "Run quickly," she calls out. "Put on your veil. The mother superior is very ill. You must pray for her."

Romaine joins the others in the chapel and prays there for two days, with short breaks only for meals. Then, it seems to Romaine, who is now running a high fever, that she finds herself standing beside the body of the mother superior. The ogress-tormentor of the fairy tales has been vanquished. A pale gray bonnet surrounds the flaccid yellow flesh, ugly even in death. Somebody is urging Romaine to kiss that shrunken cheek. She draws back in revulsion.

Now she is walking through deserted cloisters. Where have they all gone? Romaine realizes that she is ill and is looking for help. She climbs to an upper floor, equally silent, finds a heavy curtain and pulls it back. She finds herself on a balcony, looking down over the chapel which is heavily draped in black velvet and filled with the stale scent of incense and death.

In her confusion she thinks that not only life, which has already been denied her, but even death has receded, leaving her in an intolerable vacuum. She is driven backward by the suffocating weight of the black velvet, obliterating all sensation, into airless corridors along which she gropes for an exit; some kind of culmination. She finds her classroom and falls on her desk.

It is a long descent; an accelerating fall hurtling past stifling curtains, clifflike walls, poisonous whispers, cadaverous cheeks, the airless constriction of her life; heavily sinking down through the terror of nothingness and into the promise of oblivion.

Pleurisy and pneumonia keep Romaine in bed for weeks. The

nuns ply her with their superstitious remedies. They pray around her bed. They give her bitter quinine to drink and holy water that tastes like the bilge water of a ship. They thrust the sharp frames of saints' portraits under her pillow.

Romaine tosses restlessly, longing for tea, yearning for the oranges growing in her mother's garden, dreaming of wind rushing in from the sea and rebelling fitfully against the room's fetid sickroom atmosphere. She gathers up her last resources of strength to crawl to the door and open it.

Ella comes to visit in a rustle of petticoats and fluttering ribbons. She pronounces the air too stale and sits in the far corner near the door. They sip on Italian champagne prescribed for Romaine's recovery. Ella chatters about her tiring trip from the Château Grimaldi at Mentone, which she has recently bought, and about St. Mar, whose voice is calling her, she says. She bends over the bed, depositing a gold coin (a Louis d'Or) beside it, along with a photograph of herself, and leaves. Romaine is childishly delighted with the visit and the photograph. She spends several weeks in bed reading the books the convent thinks are suitable (*Addio al Protestantismo* is the unmistakable title of one, and the other is Queen Victoria's diary) and draws contentedly for hours at a time.

Romaine is numbly prepared to go back to her regimented, impersonal life. But her refusal to admit the error of her ways has convinced the convent that the American child is most certainly damned and must be expelled. It was a victory, but in case Romaine might be tempted to see it as such, it was draped with funeral banners. Romaine was seated in a dark room in the center of a circle of nuns who rose, one by one, to point accusing fingers at her and categorize her shortcomings (she drew cartoons of priests, she refused to kiss the dead mother superior . . .) and then let her go. Romaine went back once more to her mother.

The house in which she found herself, the Château Grimaldi, still exists on a hillside overlooking the Riviera town of Mentone. Its eighteen front windows and large terraces command now, as they did then, a spectacular view of the Mediterranean.

The château stands in extensive grounds beside a ruined, thirteenth-century tower which was an outpost of the Crusades for Charles d'Anjou. Everything should have conspired to produce a dream of romantic perfection, yet the castle, built of granitic gray stone, suggests not art but the self-satisfaction of the *nouveau riche*. Succeeding owners have removed some of the claptrap ornamentation, revealing the naked outlines of a bunker, the monumental finality of a tomb. Ella was pleased to call it her little cottage.

The château's thirty rooms and four floors required an imposing staff of servants, even for those days. Ella Goddard's fortune was equal to the task and there was a cheap supply of household help from Mentone. There were seven or eight servants in the house, including a butler and two valets, three coachmen on staggered hours so that a carriage and pair could be available around the clock, and a small boy with a pony trap. There was another staff to take care of the grounds, terraced with the lush semitropical plants and trees of the Riviera.

Surviving photographs testify that in her interior decor, as in her choice of house, Ella exercised the same cloying bad taste. Her esthetic sense imagined that its object was to stun the viewer. She achieved this by cramming every room with decoration: frescoed walls, garlands of flowers twisted around pink columns against gold backgrounds; suits of armor and swords in the hall; oriental draperies, etiolated tapestries, shelves of leather-bound books embossed with gold; porcelain knickknacks prized by her generation; and marble statues after Canova. She upholstered her furniture in brocades and velvets, draping swags of satin around the balconied windows. Half the house was arranged for her and half for St. Mar. Romaine saw with relief that she would have the top floor to herself.

Coming from the Spartan gloom of the convent to this riotous display was, for Romaine, like emerging from a cavern into a carnival. Her response to her mother's taste was the instinctive wince of someone who takes ugliness as a personal affront. That she was revolted is revealed in her description of St. Mar in an old overcoat, scuttling like a black beetle across the gaily flowered carpets and through rooms glimmering with the sheen of silks and satins. He found the decor as offensive as Romaine did, but for other reasons.

What looked to Ella like a pleasant shower of spirit flowers (carved from bracket to bracket on a heavy oaken buffet) appeared to St. Mar to be a nest of evil intentions. He would stand in front of the offensive object, muttering angrily.

Arriving at the château, Romaine had seen the sun glittering on the sea and sensed the languorous and inviting beauty of the garden. Yet even this gave her no comfort.

"The broad marble steps, steeped in the sun, leading up to the house; the exotic trees surrounding it; the myriad flowers bathing in their fragrance; all were powerless to change its inner darkness. The building was like a hot stone lying in a sunny garden which, when turned over, displays the damp, unpleasant insect life beneath.

"I fought hard to keep in contact with the sunny outer world, but my efforts were in vain . . ."

My efforts were in vain. At fifteen Romaine found herself at a frightening impasse. The damage had been done in childhood when, lacking the acceptance and love a child needs in order to develop a healthy sense of inner worth, she was made to feel that she was not acceptable *unless* she became someone else. So Romaine did what a child does. She turned against herself, using the measuring stick of the outside world and finding herself wanting. She was not loved; therefore, she must not be lovable. She reasoned unconsciously that she must be without intrinsic worth.

No one can go on living with this view of himself. So a solution offered itself to Romaine in the shining mirage of the person she could become. Since she was already a martyr, she could become a saint; heroic, beloved of the gods, pure and invincible. The arrows of outrageous fortune would not pierce the golden armor she would construct around herself.

Creating an "ideal" self is the attempt to resolve an anguish that would otherwise be unendurable. But perfection is not within the grasp of mankind. As soon as man begins to reach out for the Infinite he finds, like Faust, that the price is self-destruction; he cannot help but see and assess the yawning chasm between who he would be and what he is.

Romaine had an extraordinary poetic insight into her inner world, which demonstrated itself in her writings as in her art. Her descriptions of this period are the first reference to the double self she felt she was becoming: a figure of saintlike dimensions on the one hand, and a worthless human being on the other. Her basic creative drives were urging her in the direction of inner integration and self-expression at a moment when she saw, with a sadness born of despair, the extent of her inner division.

She must have dimly realized that both internal visions were less than the truth. She knew somewhere that her goal of sainthood was (as she entitled her drawing) only a dream which the chill light of reality would attack and expose. And her experience at St. Mary's Hall had allowed her to hope that she was not worthless; that she was a valuable being on whom a beneficent God could smile. It was a belief that did not survive the crushing weight of her mother's disapproval and the further dehumanizing effects of a year in a convent. So she lost the conviction of worth that would have saved her; and accepted her double self because she did not see any way out.

Romaine conformed to her mother's expectations outwardly. Since Ella insisted upon having her present, and rushed through the rooms like a whirlwind calling her name if she were not, it seemed easier to follow her mother's erratic movements blindly; to take obedient turns fanning her during the heat of a Mediterranean summer and to acquiesce without question to long drives in the carriage over the midnight hills. But inwardly, Romaine was mourning the loss of that other, true self. She was terrified that she was descending through a trap door into a private hell.

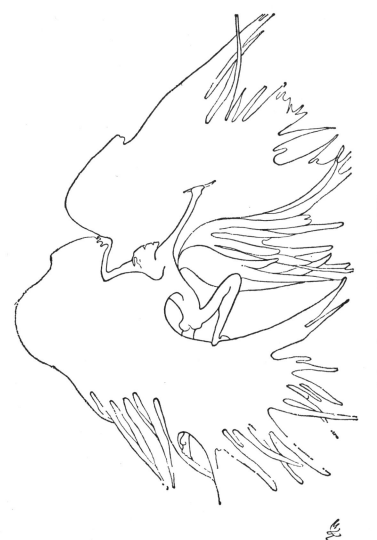

Climbing One's Wings

7

We leap into dangerous waters. Lucky is he who, with the return of a wave, is landed higher than he was before.

Romaine liked more desolate coastlines than those afforded by the Riviera. The western tip of Britain might have been more to her taste; or perhaps a deserted cove of rocks rusted with dead seaweed, where the slate-colored tide froths white around bleak promontories. No sound but the rumble of the surf far below one's feet and the tunnel-like howl of the wind, and the whirling cry of gulls overhead, their abandoned flight stirring depths of answering yearning as they fling themselves into the wind, plummeting like a stone; then pull out just as suddenly with their powerful wings, climbing steadily higher . . .

The glorious spread of wing worn by Icarus in Herbert James Draper's nineteenth-century painting, or the arched wing of a swan, as the neo-classicist Sir Lawrence Alma-Tadema might have painted it, became the symbol around which all Romaine's dreams of escape were clustered. Or the swan itself, plump white feathers flocking over its wings. To glide upward like a swan and conceal oneself behind the closed shutters of an attic window . . . Or to mount a winged white horse, its body in a rearing arabesque. To be plunged forward, the hooves scrambling for a hold, and then take to the air in one soaring white flight; this became her obsessive desire. Romaine filled her notebooks with drawings of wing spans that refined themselves into a wing poised for flight. It became the symbol with which she signed her work, as much her own as Whistler's butterfly. Her drawings were of angels, winged horses, and birds.

It would be six years before Romaine arrived at the then-legal age of independence, twenty-one, and could make her break for freedom. She seems to have spent those years in listless waiting, hoarding her energies for that moment. What happened until then hardly mattered. In 1891 she allowed herself to be sent away, at the age of seventeen, to Mademoiselle Tavan's Private Finishing School for Young Ladies in Geneva, Switzerland.

There are no photographs of Romaine at this time in her life, but one can guess, from clues in her memoirs and paintings of the period, how she might have looked. After the disappointing experience at the convent, Ella had given up hope of making Romaine into a nun and seems to have decided to groom her for a wealthy marriage. So Romaine arrived at her new school in the clothes that would equip her for her future role with her thick silky hair hidden under a boater, perhaps, or a diminutive bonnet tied under the chin with an enormous white bow; dressed in a costly striped taffeta frock lined with pure silk, which rustled busily under the flowing lines of a cape; wearing kid gloves, and carrying a parasol.

The boarding school had an international clientele: English, Russian, American, German, Greek, and Egyptian girls of wealthy families who had led sheltered lives as children and would have equally constricted lives as the decorative wives of the bourgeoisie. There was no thought of serious study. What mattered was knowing which fork to pick up and which inconsequential remark to drop; in short, how to move in the best circles. If a girl wanted to fill in her time learning another language, writing poetry about Swiss mountain peaks, painting the picturesque villages, or singing operatic scales, the family involved was inclined to be indulgent, as long as she remained a dilettante.

Most of the girls were, in fact, accepting a role in life that Romaine would have openly rebelled against if she had considered it at all; which she did not. The idea that she should make a wealthy marriage never crossed her mind. She knew she was going to escape, even if what lay beyond that moment was hidden in the coralline haze of uncertainty. But her conviction of difference made her uneasy since she believed that her sad destiny made it inevitable that "the herd" would attack her, sooner or later. Her first months were spent in trying to deflect their wrath in advance, smiling hopefully as she passed by with a great rustling of the new silk-lined dresses whose lavishness she viewed half in shy pride and half in derision.

If Romaine hoped to slip through two years at Mlle. Tavan's without being noticed, she was bound to be disappointed. There was, to start with, the fact that she never took notes in class but spent her time filling her exercise books with sketches. She could not remember a single date in history but knew the Lord's Prayer in Latin and Italian; she told hilarious stories about living in a convent, she recited eerie poems in class which she said her mother had written, about death and the sorrows of rebirth. Romaine was, although she did not realize it, hard to ignore.

First there was Hélène, a Greek girl with red hair, whom Romaine thought ugly. She discovered that Hélène could rattle off, in alphabetical order, the list of *"Personnages Célèbres"* in the Larousse Dictionary, and Romaine developed, for this formidable feat of memory, the admiration of one who can hardly remember a question, let alone its answer.

One day, Romaine defied a school regulation to visit Hélène alone in her room. Admiration was the explanation, Romaine wrote unconvincingly. She was relieved to have the visit discovered and to be told not to repeat it since, she said, being adored without adoring in return was "a wingless state," and even one's own "ineffectual flappings" when in the grip of a new love, were to be preferred. In such matters, Romaine retained the innocence of the ten-year-old schoolboy she felt she was. She had no idea what the outcome of such infatuations could be. It seems likely that she had allowed her curiosity to take her further than she really wanted to go, and that she seized on an excuse to cut it short. But Hélène was angry.

Then there was a young Russian girl who developed a great admiration for the sketches Romaine drew so casually in her exercise books and gave herself the job of collecting them. The girl had lost her nose in an accident so that she looked rather like a monkey. Romaine said that she must have made her revulsion too obvious, and the girl withdrew, hurt.

Then there was a pretty Romanian with a weak face, who fancied herself as a musician. Romaine, who was developing an excellent voice, would sit beside her in rapture as the girl played the piano. Romaine was, in fact, gaining something of a reputation as a flirt. "My dear old Don Juan," Karina, one of her classmates, wrote teasingly during the summer vacation, "Your letters are always so much like yourself, like your own graceful pretty little person that, reading them, I can scarcely realize that there is such a great distance between us, that I cannot take your hand and look into your eyes or kiss your pretty red lips . . ."

Bit by bit the very ostracism that caused her agony, Romaine said, was coming about, because she herself was in a vicious circle. Surrounded by rejection and hostility as a child, she was now easily hurt, suspicious of others' overtures of friendship, and ready to see a slight in the most harmless remark. Romaine would be testing the sincerity of such friendships by behaving in a hostile way herself and provoking the very outcome she feared.

Romaine did not see the part she played in this exchange. In her eyes, she was the "different" girl who only wanted to be left alone, but whom "the herd" was determined to persecute. It was unjust. She was indignant, then angry. If she hit back as hard as she could, it was only in self-defense.

Romaine sensed the signs of a gathering storm. Hélène and the Russian girl were inciting the others against her. Romaine was too proud to notice or make the slightest attempt to prevent what she knew was to come. One friend who would stand beside her was all that mattered. But the Romanian had been won over by the other side and had deserted her in her hour of need. Romaine felt betrayed. The opinion of "the herd" did not matter; it could think what it liked. But to lose the friendship of someone you admire and need, in whom you have confided; that was a bitter disappointment.

News of the battle reached Mlle. Tavan, whose well-meaning reaction was to attempt a reconciliation. A group of girls met around the schoolroom table and Romaine took her seat stiffly, sensing hostility all around her. Suddenly, she got up and went over to the

Romanian girl, placing her arm around her. Then she made a sarcastic speech in French about the value of a lifelong friendship.

There was nothing for anybody to say and Romaine stalked out. She spent a lot of time alone in her room after that, drawing "sad, drooping figures under . . . sad, drooping willow trees" and another drawing, of Death rocking the cradle of doomed babies.

While in Geneva Romaine had painted a couple of competent oils of a Swiss village, almost the only landscapes she ever attempted, and she had also shown a talent for music. Ella decided that Romaine, now nineteen, could finish her education in Paris, where she could study music and art in an "artistic" atmosphere and lose the atrocious Swiss accent she had developed.

Romaine was perfectly agreeable. In two years she would be free and would need to earn her own living. As an artist she would probably starve to death, but other people told her she had a good voice. So why not become a singer?

Ella found an advertisement in *Galignani,* the Paris *Herald Tribune* of the day, placed by a Monsieur and Madame Givend in Neuilly, who boarded girls of good families and prepared them for a singing career.

Romaine arrived in Paris in the Gay Nineties, that decade of so much speculation and legend which supposedly caught up its inhabitants in a life of endless pleasures. Romaine doesn't even bother to mention the fact. For her, Paris in September 1893 meant streets that all looked alike, all tinged by the pale Paris sky, which drains them of color and turns them into muted silhouettes of sepulchral grays, like an overexposed photograph. These are curious backwaters, still discoverable, where the paint flakes off the ornamental balconies, gray shutters stay bolted against the mid-day heat, there is a subterranean rumble from the Métro, and then the silence spreads like a stain over the street; a cat crosses on noiseless feet . . .

Romaine's first impressions of the Givend family were not encouraging. Monsieur Givend tended to have violent fits of coughing at meals and would attack a trail of ants through his dining room with the side of his dinner knife, wiping it off in his napkin with a flourish that made Romaine shudder. Then there was Toto, a rheumy old dog who was given the run of the house and allowed to poke his repulsive nose into everybody's plate.

The house was dark and stuffy, and Romaine's sunless room overlooked what the Givends airily described as their garden. It turned out to be a swamp with an open cesspool in the middle, where the family would dump its dirty water and slops.

These were trifling drawbacks compared to the dismay Romaine felt when she met Louise Givend, who acted as her father's accompanist. Louise's enormous gray eyes looked out from a sharp, painted face crowned with a mop of frizzy hair. She was almost as short as Toulouse Lautrec, and between the outlines of her shoulder blades, Romaine could see the unmistakable hump of the hunchback.

Romaine's reaction to Louise was the instinctive loathing she felt for the physically or mentally deformed. She tried hard to concentrate on French grammar and spent the dreary days of study learning to sing the page's song in *Les Huguenots*. But Louise was exerting an influence over her. Against her will, Romaine was drawn to return the look of those gray eyes, fastened upon her own.

Why didn't Romaine ever come and visit her in her room, Louise wanted to know. It was much gayer than Romaine's. "I had no diversions whatever and . . . the day arrived when, in spite of my repugnance, I found myself knocking at Louise's door."

What a pathetic, grotesque little creature Louise was, and to think that Ella hadn't even noticed her hump and told the Givends she was glad that Romaine would have someone to go out walking with! How shudderingly awful! How dreadful that she, Romaine, must be driven to seek out this monster's company! Obviously Louise was outside humanity, really, with a body like that, and so perhaps could exert some strange attraction . . . So Romaine reasoned, unaware that Louise was a metaphor for the monsters and dwarfs of her drawings; or that Louise's compelling lure provided symbolic proof of the growing power of Romaine's self-destructive forces and of the battle between her two selves.

"There remains vivid in my memory a picture of this misshapen little creature as she sat by the window almost lost in a huge armchair, plying her needle with long, clawlike fingers, to the brightest of pink underwear." The next time Romaine came, Louise was trimming the ferocious pink garments with a violent yellow lace. "For whom else should it be?" Louise replied to Romaine's inevitable question. "I wear them when with my lover."

Romaine was stunned into silence at the thought of this pathetic girl actually making love to anyone. The mental image raised all kinds of questions that Romaine had so far managed to avoid. Louise was delighted to provide the answers. She delved into the bottom of her closet and came up with pornographic books published in Belgium and photographs of the 101 positions of love, from Holland. Read these when you are alone and preferably in bed, Romaine was warned.

This then, was Romaine's abrupt initiation into sex: pornography and graphic photographs which left nothing to the imagination. The crude awakening had a mixed effect. On the one hand, Romaine was revolted: Louise's mind had been warped, no doubt, from the foul odors which seeped into the house from the garden; surely this was the only reason why she actually seemed to enjoy such things. Romaine hated the sly way these matters were discussed. As for the books themselves the crude, bestial act had nothing to do with the beauty of like minds meeting and mingling. Her own poetic attachments to girls could have no connection with the degradations inflicted by men on women. And yet . . . Romaine could not stop thinking about it.

"Lewd visions and dialogues, not wholly comprehended, would obsess me during the whole day, even when singing the page's song; which remains in my mind inextricably associated with this period of initiation."

For all their revolting secrets, the Givends of Neuilly had a certain reputation in Europe as trainers of young voices. When she went there, Romaine was the only pupil. But some time after her arrival she noticed that preparations were being made for a newcomer in the bedroom next to her own. Then the stranger arrived.

Romaine descended without enthusiasm, unwilling to meet anyone doomed, as she was, to live with the Givends. Suddenly, she heard the deep notes of a marvelous contralto, a voice so thrilling that "the interior of the stuffy little house fairly heaved with . . . its resonance."

The voice belonged to Clara Butt, a large peasant girl with enormous hands and feet and the "blocked-in features of the working class," who was destined to become a famous English singer. She was a year older than Romaine and studied briefly with the Givends before moving on to more famous teachers, Bouhy and Etelka Gerster in Paris (in 1895) and then to a triumphant career at Covent Garden and on the British concert stage.

Romaine did not consider Clara particularly intelligent, but what she did have was enormous kindness, sympathy, and good humor. Clara became more than just a diversion. She actually made life worth living again. Through Clara, Romaine felt her faith in her own creative abilities rejuvenated. Clara was the talisman Romaine needed in order to counteract the poisonous influence of Louise. When Louise tried to pass "certain books" to Romaine again, Romaine brushed her off as if she were a flyspeck on her sleeve.

Romaine probably loved Clara. She would spend hours sitting silently in her room, holding her hand, while the suspicious Madame Givend hovered outside, listening at the keyhole. The day Clara left the Givends was a bitter moment for Romaine.

"Almost covered by huge chrysanthemums—it was the season—she [Clara] drew me to her, whispered some words I did not hear, then, kissing me, left the house forever. I ran to her room. The floor was covered with chrysanthemum petals . . . Her fragrance was alive about me . . . I thrust into my blouse a forgotten black veil—a token of loss and mourning."

Romaine says in her memoirs that she ran away from her mother at the age of eighteen.

But letters from her mother, found in Romaine's effects after her death, date the rupture quite closely to between May 21 and June 4, 1895, when Romaine was living with the Givends, and barely a month after she had celebrated her twenty-first birthday, on May 1.

One wonders why Romaine was so anxious to give the impression that she broke away from home three years before she actually did. One reason might have been that by the time Romaine came to write *No Pleasant Memories*—in the 1930s—the concept of a child becoming independent at the age of eighteen would have been well established, and Romaine's struggles to escape from home at twenty-one might have seemed to her a little lame. But the overriding reason is that Romaine was vain about her age. When she finally acquired her first American passport in 1935, at the age of sixty-one, she quietly deducted six years from her life and told the immigration authorities that she was born in 1880. She maintained the pretense for years.

Nevertheless, for a wealthy girl to take up an independent life at any age would have been considered so daring as to be unthinkable in the 1890s. She had not been equipped to be self-supporting but to make some man a charming wife. Such a girl would have been exhibited in society, but otherwise closely supervised. As a matter of course, Romaine's mother paid elderly women to accompany her on walks in Paris. Life for her would have been much more confined than for a working-class girl who would necessarily have had greater freedom of action and would have been at least partly self-supporting.

In making the break from her mother, Romaine, who had vivid memories of poverty, had no idea whether her mother would ever support her again; her hopes for self-advancement might easily have rested on whatever influential contacts her mother could make. She was not lightly choosing a life of poverty over her family's material comforts. Her solitary childhood had had the good result, however, of forcing her back on her own resources. Even though she felt "pathetically inadequate," she knew that she had either to take charge of her life or forever caper around the ring to the commands of a mad ringmaster. All her strength and pride and all her courage were gathered to make that single-minded leap of desperation.

Romaine's mother arrived in Paris shortly after Clara had left the Givends. Ella might have been *en transit*; Romaine seldom bothered to ask. But she was perversely glad to see her mother, hoping that the "extreme discomfort" of her presence would somehow make her forget her grief at Clara's departure. It seemed that Ella was about to put St. Mar on the train for Mentone alone, the first time he had been separated from his mother as an adult.

When Romaine arrived at her mother's hotel, Ella was already in a carriage waiting for her. They made for the station while Ella muttered to herself, pulling her gloves on and off and staring ahead vacantly; she seemed increasingly lost in "other worlds." They found

St. Mar just as the train was about to leave, seated in the company of two extremely pretty women. One was a blonde, the other a brunette; both were decked out with feathers. Romaine also noticed a red-haired, bewhiskered young doctor standing stiffly in the background.

One of the pretty ladies took St. Mar's limp hand and shook it in their direction. Another moment, and the train was on its way to the Riviera. It was the last time Romaine saw St. Mar alive.

As they returned to the hotel, Ella grew increasingly uneasy. "It is all for his good! It is all for his good!" she kept repeating. That night, Ella could not sleep. She paced up and down in her room, calling St. Mar's name, stopping only to accuse Romaine of dropping off to sleep. As morning came, Romaine was sitting at a table, her head on her arms and her mother was packing. "I can hear his voice! He is calling me!" Ella said.

Romaine sat up wearily. She heard her mother's words as if from a great distance, overlaid by a momentous decision: She would leave Neuilly and her mother.

Ella ran back through the room, wearing a coat, a bonnet, and a veil. "I hear his voice. He is calling me! I must go! I must go!" she cried. She flung the door open and ran down the corridor, crying out, "St. Mar! St. Mar!"

"'I must go! I must go!' I drowsily repeated and I was conscious of speeding onward till the faint call of 'St. Mar!' and its echo, was lost forever far away in the past."

Sorrow of Rebirth*

8

When I try to look back on that particular period of my life, I am forced to conclude that one's past self can be almost a lost entity, a stranger one imagines can be brought back, understood and followed. But how can one pretend to understand such a composite of contrary impulses?

It was very still in the hotel bedroom after Ella left it. Let us imagine, since the memoirs are no guide, that the room overlooked a court-yard; that the french windows, draped with white, lace-edged muslin, were partly open and that the soft, milky light of early summer flooded in. It drifted over the unused double bed (still immaculately turned down for the night), the porcelain bowl with its delicately sprigged pitcher, the embroidered white hand towels on a rack, and a small, glass-topped table near the window, underneath which a pair of black boots had been flung. They lay as they had fallen, one precariously upright and the other sprawled on its side. Above them, Romaine's limp left arm was extended across the table's mirrored surface and her black head was half buried in its elbow.

A small sound disturbed Romaine. She sat up, her eyes half-blinded by a glitter of motes in sunlight and saw the figure of a middle-aged woman dressed in black. She was standing silently, examining Romaine's stockinged feet and matted hair with an expression of sour astonishment. It seemed that this was a widow hired before Ella left to take Romaine out for walks. Her husband,

* Also called, "Les parents entraînent leurs enfants."

she said with a sniff, had been a much-respected oboe player at the Opera. She seemed to take it as a personal affront that when she arrived Ella had departed and Romaine was asleep. She was determined, nevertheless, to see Romaine safely back to Neuilly. She had, Romaine noticed, a double row of false teeth, and her large sucker mouth puckered up and expanded rhythmically like that of a fish.

Romaine yawned and insisted that, since her mother's hotel had been paid for, she intended to sleep there for the rest of the day. The widow examined Romaine for a moment, her mouth contracted into a knot of disapproval. Then she pulled on her gloves and left.

As soon as the woman was safely out of the door Romaine sprang into action. She pinned up her hair, buttoned her boots, slipped on one of her mother's black cloaks, hailed a fiacre, and made her way back to Neuilly.

She was lucky enough to find the Givends out. She explained to the tousled maid who opened the door that she was going to stay with her mother for a few days. Then she stuffed her wardrobe of veils, ties, and sailor blouses into a suitcase and escaped into the waiting carriage.

She had saved up 1,000 francs. Her mother had sent 500 of them in a letter (May 21, 1895) as a "little extra" to buy a new dress and mantle. Romaine told the driver to take her to the avenue de Clichy in the eighteenth *arrondissement*, where she knew she would be able to find a room. She chose a small, sparsely furnished one on a top floor overlooking the avenue and almost immediately regretted it since the great Parisian boulevards, then as now, reverberated with the clang of traffic from early morning until late at night. The room was also unpleasantly close to a toilet which consisted, as did most Parisian sanitation of the period, of an unceremonious hole in the floor.

Still, it was the dream of the convent walks made real; the small high window above the street where she could look out in solitary safety at life. It was freedom, however cramped and unsatisfactory. Romaine, writing her memoirs thirty years later, could not imagine why she had stayed in such unsavory quarters for as long as she did. She decided that she must have found some perverse satisfaction in making herself as uncomfortable as possible.

She sees herself venturing down to the street as timidly as she had risked a walk on Third Avenue in New York at the age of six; imagining herself blending into the anonymous life of the city and unaware that a single girl with an American accent and a teen-age wardrobe would be bound to attract attention. She remembers breakfasting economically in her room, calculating carefully how long her money would last; picking up an armful of morning papers and poring over the classified advertisements with the dedication of one who hopes to discern, in their cryptic phrases, avenues of golden opportunities. What could the advertisement in *Le Journal* mean, "Remunerative work for those who have free evenings at home?" A native caution prevented Romaine from finding out. The numerous ads for artists' models seemed more promising. Abandoning her girlish sailor blouses, Romaine put on a grown-up, tight-waisted, long dress that she privately detested, pinned a sailor hat on her head and sallied forth to the Quartier Latin.

The artist was an Englishman who rather liked her and let it be known that she could sit for him on a regular basis. Although earning money was the thought uppermost in Romaine's mind, her artist's eye could not help evaluating what the Englishman painted: a languorous girl in a sailor hat, seated on the green banks of a river which existed only in his imagination.

He gave her tea and cakes, assured her that her mother was legally obligated to support her and warned her in a brotherly way against becoming a *cocotte*. Only girls who were really good at it, he said, would come out on top. Romaine found the whole conversation amusingly irrelevant. She was much more interested in talking about art. She was really an artist too, she said, and to prove it, drew a series of devils' and angels' heads on his sketch pad. Far from being impressed, the Englishman merely laughed in an infuriating male way.

Thirty years later Romaine looks upon her youthful self with bemusement as she orders a lemonade in the Pavillon Chinois, looking around her at the beautifully dressed and bejewelled women, her eyes dilated with nervous astonishment; going to the Palais de Glace and noting, with tremulous excitement, upon the crowds of *boulevardiers* and notorious beauties of the period who skated languidly past in striking sports costumes, or jostled each other as they strolled along the promenade; their eyes, alluringly bright, darting to right and left.

Most daring of all, she immediately joined a bicycle class. The subject had come up before Romaine's escape in one of her mother's letters. "To tell you the truth," Ella wrote, "I fear you would lose your head—and rush out of the Bicycle Garden—down the Champs Élysées." It was all right, Ella supposed, if Romaine intended to take this doubtful amusement in some segregated area like a private garden or the countryside, and probably good for her health. But for a woman to bicycle around in full public view was somehow disgusting to the really well-bred.

Romaine ignored such reservations and was soon industriously cycling up and down the Bicycle Garden, her legs pumping, her skirts bouncing, her pale skin flushed with gratified effort, not caring how unladylike she looked. She remembers some dangerous rides at night in the Bois de Boulogne with the others in the bicycle class, when the only light was the bobbing glow of the red Japanese lanterns dangling from their handlebars.

The moment of reckoning was linked in her mind with a fall off the bicycle. She was suddenly bumped back to earth with a lump on her nose and a repair bill which would, when paid, take a generous bite out of what remained of the 1,000 francs.

Romaine had not been in contact with Ella since she made her escape. She dreaded the confrontation, and, instead of writing herself, left it to her sister Maya to break the news. Maya, who was spending that summer in Paris, dutifully told Ella what Romaine wanted her mother to believe: that she had gone to London to become a governess. In due course Ella replied with pointed remarks to Maya about being "a sneak"; and with other words meant for Romaine's eyes.

The tone of the letter was such that Romaine never considered asking Ella for money. But the English artist's assertion that Ella was legally obligated to support her returned to her mind. There must be some way to get a monthly allowance, however much Romaine shrank from attempting it herself.

She thought of Dr. Alexander Hamilton Phillips, who had taken care of St. Mar for many years and was still with the family at the

Château Grimaldi. In those days it was customary for a wealthy family to put a physician on the payroll, and Dr. Phillips had been engaged as a young man before he had the necessary qualifications to practice medicine in the United States. As a result he became financially dependent on Ella's good will.

He was, Romaine remembered, tubercular, a slight figure with thin blond hair falling over his collar, protruding blue eyes, and a receding chin. In addition to his ability to handle St. Mar, Phillips had the added qualification of being able to evoke spirits. At his mere request in a séance, they would write words on a special slate placed face downwards on the table. His emotional ties to the family were equally complex. He apparently pinned his hopes on marrying Ella, but although it seems likely that they had an affair, Ella never considered marrying him. So Phillips turned his attentions to Maya, then twenty-five, who had been in love with him for years. (They eloped to New York later the same year Romaine left her mother and were married in the Little Church Around the Corner.)

Romaine found Phillips a sympathetic figure, and he seemed to be the one most likely to intercede with Ella on her behalf. She wrote to him secretly, and in due course Phillips paid a formal call.

The long climb up the stairs to Romaine's room on the avenue de Clichy made Phillips cough and left him exhausted. But as soon as he could talk he gave a formal speech to the effect that Romaine should return to her mother. Romaine made an equally solemn statement of refusal. That done, they got down to business. Phillips drafted two letters for Romaine to send: one to Romaine's cousin, who managed the Waterman estate in Philadelphia, and a second to Ella at the Château Grimaldi. Romaine remembers being delighted by his use of the word "consanguinity."

As her mother believed Romaine to be in London, there was the problem of how to mail the letters. Phillips suggested the "Isis" post office in London, which would mail letters from any foreign country to their destination, keeping their point of origin a secret. If Ella knew where Romaine actually was living, Phillips thought, she might engage private detectives to bring her back.

"He left after convincing me that my fate lay entirely in his hands. . . ."

An innocent phrase, devoid of apparent overtones. And yet, the melodrama of the memoirs might conceal the presence of still more incidents, equally improbable in their stark implications of fate conspiring to destroy the soul of a human being; intimations of things glossed over beneath a polite phrase wherever the principals in that drama might still be alive to raise objections; of monsters far below the silent waters which nose their sinister way to the surface, are glimpsed in dim silhouette, and then swallowed again in the murk of the interior lake. Here are some possibilities:

Scenario Number 1: "The Virgin Despoiled." In her old age, Romaine retold the same events one night, seated around the fire at Grandson, the Swiss estate of Janine Lahovary. It was the same man, Alexander Hamilton Phillips, the familiar figure from childhood to whom she had turned in her youthful desperation, when he seemed to be the one person who could help her.

But this time the apparently benign figure, coughing, already ill with the tuberculosis that would kill him, made a cynical proposal once he was alone with Romaine. He would help her, but she would have to sleep with him.

Romaine is desperate. There is no one else who can help; she is trapped. She consents. There is one night of love, perhaps only one, perhaps others since the memoirs hint of other visits . . . He leaves, she writes; he does not reply. She is pregnant.

The child, a little girl, is born in her room. She struggles through the ordeal alone. No one must know; Romaine gives the illegitimate baby to a convent, and five years later, upon inheriting half of her mother's estate jointly with Maya, Romaine returns to claim her daughter. She learns that the child died at the age of two and a half months.

According to the memoirs, Phillips was overcome with a violent fit of coughing in a subsequent visit, which brought on a hemorrhage, and he had to be helped down to a waiting cab. The memoirs state that Phillips died shortly after that visit (he actually died seven years later at the age of forty-four) and omit the fact that he married Maya and they had two daughters, Beatrice and Liliane. Romaine did not know until later that his words were instrumental in obtaining the monthly allowance on which she would depend for the next five years. "It is evident above all," she concludes with perhaps intentional irony, "to whom I owe my debt of gratitude."

Move to Scenario Number 2: "Revenge of the Rejected Suitor." Phillips wanted the mother, but she used him cynically and then spurned him for another. He takes his revenge on her by seducing first one daughter, then the other. He capitulates suddenly to Maya's insistent pleas that they elope, before Maya or anyone else knows the truth; knowing that, once he is a respectable brother-in-law, the family will be forced to suppress the scandal. Phillips makes his financial future secure by marrying the daughter still in her mother's favor and assuages his conscience by urging the mother to give an independent income to the girl he has wronged.

Scenario Number 3: "I Lost My Head." Maya might have suspected, while refusing to believe the evidence of her intuitions, that Phillips had had an affair with her mother. She adored him so much that she was willing to be his second choice. She has sympathized with Romaine, given her whatever small sums she could afford, written letters on her behalf, and even envied her freedom. Now she is presented with evidence of joint treachery. There is a stormy scene of reconciliation with Phillips. She spurns him indignantly. Phillips falls to his knees. He is perhaps in tears. He has discovered that she is the one he truly loves. It was a moment of madness brought on by his sexual frustration and longing for her. She smiles through her tears. They elope impulsively, glad to put the Atlantic Ocean between them and this disastrous news. No wonder that relations between the sisters are strained for years, and Maya refuses to have her existence even hinted at in Romaine's memoirs.

Scenario Number 4: "An Unscrupulous Sister," places the same event in yet another light. There never was an illegitimate child born in a room high up over the thunderous roar of the avenue de Clichy. Instead, there was only Romaine's calculating self-interest and her deliberately provocative behavior the day Phillips climbed the stairs to her sparely furnished room. In this hypothesis of what took place, Romaine is using every weapon at her command in the game of high stakes she was playing, knowing that Maya is not the second choice of Alexander Hamilton Phillips, but his third.

In the remaining Scenario, "Daydreams of Old Age," Romaine no

93

longer remembers what really took place almost sixty years before. Reality has become mingled inextricably in her mind with snatches of half-forgotten dreams, with the fantasies of what almost happened, and romantic self-dramatizations. She is weaving a feminist parable to demonstrate man's callous exploitation of womankind. Her story is offered as proof of the odds against which she, a penniless young woman, was struggling during that critical first year of freedom.

Ella capitulated in September of 1895.

The letter you sent to America was forwarded to me.

I wish you to understand that my executors have no authority to pay out my money to you or to anyone without my consent.

Considering the manner in which you ran away, you have nullified even a right to consanguinity.

I am much amused at your logic—to earn your own living independently of me and yet ask for my money to do so.

However as I know it is not so easy to set the Thames afire as you had supposed I enclose you Frs. 300—which you must promptly acknowledge to me—particularly if you wish me to assist you in the future.

It was far from being a generous settlement and Romaine was to complain about it all her life, but it was adequate. It was the relatively secure basis on which she could begin to plan her life.

Yet, months of apparent vacillation followed. Instead of studying art, which had been her dream for years and would seem the logical course, Romaine took voice lessons. Instead of remaining in Paris, she moved to a remote country village. It was inexplicable. Was she, perhaps, with child? A pregnant woman taking singing lessons was one thing, but a pregnant woman arriving in full view of an art class, was another. It would be logical, as her pregnancy advanced, for Romaine to retreat to a village outside Paris for several months, where she would not be known; and to spend the period of waiting there, taking solitary walks in the forest.

But perhaps Romaine was not pregnant at all. Her escape had been a complete success. She was not only free of her mother's influence, but she had money as well. She could do anything she wanted, and like many others whose fantasies have become fact, she did not know what she wanted to do. As if it were a fortune she did not deserve, she frittered her freedom away in a panic of indecision; darting first in one direction, then another. She was baffled, when she came to write her memoirs, because she could find no explanation for this.

Romaine addressed herself to buying new clothes, since her schoolgirl wardrobe was unsuitable for an aspiring singer. Her teacher directed her to dressmakers who, he assured her, wouldn't mind waiting for their money. They turned out to be two sisters whose unassuming manners hid calculating hearts. Their specialty was to find some pretty girl and dress her up to attract a rich lover. Then they expected to be paid back with interest. Romaine tried to ignore their muttered references to *un type* as they sketched and measured and basted and pinned, while snippets of lace, velvet, satin, and brocade fell to the floor. For the moment, Romaine was pleased enough with the results to sit for her photograph on the second floor of 39, avenue de Wagram. It was taken by Marcel Vernet who was, as was customary, also a painter and miniaturist.

Her head is almost buried in an immense chinchilla collar and her neck has disappeared underneath a massive white bow. There is a puffed velvet sleeve, a frivolous hairdo of bangs and curls, and her enormous eyes look out in a plaintive smile, hesitantly anxious to please.

Romaine was studying hard: earnest hours spent going over and over the title role of *Le Petit Duc*, then being performed by Mademoiselle Lavallière at the Théâtre des Variétés. Romaine was aware of the incongruity between her own American accent, her toneless delivery, and the impetuous sentiments sang, as the little duke wrenched himself away from his beloved: "Here is love, there is war/It's to war that I must go/I love you, do you hear me, I adore you . . ." So Romaine sang resolutely, feeling ridiculous.

It was the moment of the Victorian music hall; of men who sailed through the air with the greatest of ease; of little girls who once had a sweet little doll, dears; whose daddies wouldn't buy them a bow-wow; who were only birds in a gilded cage (married to old men,) but were secretly in love with the man who broke the bank at Monte Carlo. To avoid learning songs of this kind was impossible. So Romaine, swallowing her distaste, dressed in a Kate Greenaway costume with a poke bonnet stuck on top of a wig of yellow curls, made her debut on the stage of a cabaret in a side street near the Tour St. Jacques, singing, "Just a little bit of string/Such a tiny, tiny thing . . ." turning to the left and right with a roguish smile and holding up an imaginary piece of string to the audience.

Romaine was a great success and sang at this working-man's *café-chantant* for several weeks. She has a memory of long rides in a tram car to the other end of Paris, the smell of the greasepaint she plastered over her face and arms, and the pale manager who would invite her to join the listless group of performers at supper, served on a long table after the café closed.

Why, she asked herself, had she stayed in that unpleasant furnished room so long? Why had she tried to become a singer even though she had little talent and lacked any dramatic gift? Why did she force herself to go on singing an idiotic song in a dreary café? She must have a "curious twist of mind," no doubt caused by her "unusual" upbringing. Only this could account for the way in which, as a young woman, she persisted against difficulties for a victory that brought only negative results. So Romaine tried to explain her self-punishment and insistent guilt at a time when she might have been enjoying life for the first time.

It was early summer, 1896. Romaine suddenly gave up her job at the working-man's café and left her furnished room on the avenue de Clichy for a room in the house of a young couple who took in boarders at five francs a day. They lived in a small village, a half-hour's train ride outside Paris, and their villa was in an isolated spot near a forest, something Romaine noted with approval. She decided to take long daily walks there.

One sees the solitary house at the end of the village, perhaps surrounded by a grove of cypress trees whose insistent black-green, the one dense spot in a sunny landscape, Vincent Van Gogh found so intriguingly difficult to paint. That stubborn spot of black can serve as a symbol for Romaine's state of mind at the moment when she arrives to claim her new quarters. As she opens the gate, she notices a little boy, about four years old, in the garden. He looks up at her and growls like a dog, his bullet head lowered as if he were about to charge. Then he throws his pail at her.

Romaine is so surprised that she stands motionless for a moment. Then a young woman hurries out of the door, tugging at her skirt, wiping her hands on an apron. She slaps the child's face and he goes off, howling. In a shrill voice she offers to show Romaine the rooms.

As Romaine chooses her bedroom she notices soft lights in the woman's blond hair and a "clear, candid look" in her eyes.

They are joined by the young husband, who confides that Romaine is their first boarder. His wife was once a student at the Conservatoire de Paris, he said, looking at her with love and admiration. "What a nice couple!" Romaine thought. "But how is it possible that they should have such a horrid child? I decided that the little boy was deficient in some way and . . . dismissed him from my mind."

After Romaine had been living there for some weeks, she was coming back from a walk earlier than usual when she discovered another little boy in the garden. This one must have been about three years old.

He did not scowl or throw things. Instead, he looked at her with dim, expressionless eyes and pointed to a straggly row of flowers. "There aren't any flowers for me," he whispered.

Romaine was taken aback by such sweeping pessimism from such a tiny child. Could it be, she wondered, that there was another "deficient" child in the house? She took him to her room and gave him a candy. He walked off with it, apparently not comforted. Romaine never saw him again.

Then, one damp morning, the little blond woman appeared holding a pale blond baby in her arms. "He is ill," she announced. "He has had colic." At that point, she sat the baby down on the wet grass on his bare bottom.

Romaine was stunned. Could this be some strange new cure for colic? Was the woman, who had never said a word about the children, running a baby farm and trying to keep it a secret? Romaine got her answer one day during a meal when the conversation turned to the difficulty of getting back and forth from the house. "And to think I could afford a horse and trap," said the blond woman, "were it not for my three children!"

Here then, was the truth. The mother plainly hated her children and kept them shut up in a top room of the house. Two of them

97

would soon be dead, and the oldest, "whom ill treatment had converted into a brute," would grow up to murder his parents one day.

That is all Romaine wrote. She did not confront the parents. She never burst into that room on the top floor of the house where three miserable children were kept confined and abused. All she can do is take grim satisfaction in the retribution that finally came.

It is strange that Romaine's memoirs recall the incident in such detail, and that she should have been at such pains to ignore the obvious, to ransack her mind for logical explanations; to assume that the children must be mentally abnormal. She chose to be mesmerized by the clear, candid look in the mother's eyes and to ignore the grating edge to her voice, the casualness with which she slapped her little boy's face and plopped a sick baby's bare bottom down on the wet grass.

"There aren't any flowers for me . . ."

Unconsciously, Romaine must have known what was happening; but she could not allow herself to be aware because she could not deal with it. She was in a convalescent state, still nursing her own wounds, protecting herself from knowledge that would have exacerbated the pain. It was all too close to memories of being walked up and down like a red monkey, then slapped and sent home, of hair chopped off in a rage, of whips, and faces warped with hatred. The little child on the staircase, walking away with a candy clutched in his hand, might have been herself. She felt his sorrow acutely because it was her own. But she was as powerless to defend him against his parents, to come to his rescue, as she was to come to her own. This paralysis of the mind, the refusal to see what was happening and the inability to do battle against it, was a metaphor for her impasse. She had barely managed to escape from her mother; but she was still bound.

Interlude: The Jester at Home

Interlude: Hell,
a short short story by Romaine Brooks

I was watching a tiny little girl seated on the low stone ledge of a building. Her hands, which she held up in front of her, were being slapped very hard by her mother.

The slapping went on more and more violently and the little hands were very red. It must have hurt a great deal, but curiously enough the child was not crying. Her small face was pale and tense and she was gazing as though fascinated into the eyes of her angry parent; there evidently she saw something that forbade her crying.

I was wondering what the misdeed could have been to merit such punishment, when the young mother glanced in my direction. The expression of her eyes startled me for I saw in them the glitter of madness. Her anger had been promoted by her own demon.

And the little girl . . . She belonged to that terrifying other side of things; that child's hell on earth—the mad parent.

It Feeds on Our Illusions

9

Surely it was for me to tread the hard way of those who follow an ideal.
Is one ever poor who contains that ideal?

Romaine left Paris in late 1896, about a year and a half after her
break for freedom, with a third-class ticket in her pocket. She was going to Rome to study art at last. The station is vast and cavernous;
sounds swell out, reverberate against the glass dome and mingle with
gray smoke which leaks into the outer air and wreathes the edges of
platforms, making their slick gray surfaces seem vaporous and insubstantial.

The baby girl had been born. She had been secreted away in some
nameless convent, and her mother, free at last, was placing the greatest possible distance between them. Or, there was no child. Romaine
lingered in the modest villa outside Paris for several months, studying
music and walking in the forest, until the undefined, hardly understood moment when she awoke from her self-imposed nightmare.

"An operetta singer indeed! and dressed up like a monkey! And
the artist within me, the urge for sacrifice and hard work, those undeniable signs of the artist?" So she bundled together the new clothes,
the velvet coat edged with chinchilla, and all the dresses with their
wasp waists and bustles and provocative necklines, and sent them
back to the little dressmakers.

Rome appears to have been an arbitrary choice. Romaine might just as easily have studied in Paris, but Rome appealed to her; it struck a melancholic and responsive chord. Her imagination focused on a particular mental image, perhaps a composite of childhood visits and the delicately precise pencil studies by Ingres of the Appian Way, reaching toward the horizon as sharp as an arrow, or broken at intervals by long shadows of umbrella pines and piles of abandoned masonry that once were temples, palaces, statues. All this gave an air of romantic desolation.

Here, where so many thousands of pilgrims had passed, lacerating their feet on the road's jagged stones, where the memory of their presence was almost palpable, she too would walk. Such bruising thoughts were in harmony with her dissonant mood.

She remembers the trip as an endless jolting along in darkness, being squeezed into carriages whose hard wooden benches became intolerable after a few hours; then the confusion of the first days, when she lost her ticket and took someone else's suitcase; a disinterested offer of help proudly refused. Then she found a studio in Via Sistina and moved in.

It was not particularly comfortable, with a bed in a grubby, windowless alcove where she would curl up in distaste at night; but it did at least open out onto a garden. The studio was reached by a long, dark corridor which smelled, incongruously, of roses. The corridor was never lit and returning at night meant a perilous shuffle, one hand on the wall while the other guided the flickering light of a small wax taper.

The studio had one advantage. It was not far from a small restaurant, the Caffè Greco in Via Condotti, which was a haunt of students, artists, and writers at the turn of the century. The Caffè Greco allowed customers to pay their bills at the end of the week, giving a small discount, and served as an informal information center for foreigners. Romaine made enquiries there and discovered that she could study free of charge at La Scuola Nazionale. She submitted a sample of her work and was accepted. She also joined a sketch class that met every night at the Circolo Artistico.

She was working morning, afternoon, and evening. She filled her sketchbooks with the material at hand: drawings of the garden, studies of her face seen in the mirror, and drawings of her left hand "in all possible foreshortenings."

Every month Ella sent her 300 francs in bills and every month, Romaine dutifully acknowledged their receipt. A packet of the letters of receipt was found in Ella's effects after her death, kept, Romaine explained darkly, to prove that her mother had never left her without support. On this sum, Romaine wrote, she was able to make ends meet. But she had no financial resources and lived in fear that the money might not arrive. One month, the worst happened. The envelope had been tampered with and the money was stolen.

She wrote back to tell her mother, but expected no reply. She had a month to wait and some loose change, that was all.

Romaine did not ask anyone for help; in any event, she knew no one in Rome. It did not occur to her to try to earn money. She did a characteristic thing: She stuck it out. She was beginning to take what would become an almost demonic pride in not asking for help, whether the support were emotional or practical; and in proving to herself that she could be, like Peer Gynt; enough to herself. This, then, was to be her first test. She accepted her self-imposed martyrdom. "Not for one instant did I admit of . . . defeat. . . ."

She stopped going to the Caffè Greco. Instead, she went to the dairy for a glass of milk and a bun. This daily diet might have been disastrous, but the buns contained the seeds of pine cones (called *pignoli*) and were perhaps, Romaine decided, more nourishing as a result. She survived for a long time and, toward the end of the month, when even this meal was in short supply, stayed in bed and waited, "with a very empty stomach," for the arrival of the next allowance. Fortunately, it was not late.

When Romaine returned to the Greco, she was relieved to find that no one knew the reason for her absence but was somewhat surprised it had been noticed by a young English painter who sat opposite her at table. He was blond and very near-sighted and always ordered boiled eggs and potatoes instead of the usual pasta. They would discuss the pre-Raphaelites, and the young man would conclude that only the great Burne-Jones could have given Romaine's face the soulful expression it lacked.

On the day of her return, the English painter stared at her in open admiration and said that he had never seen the soul so manifest on her face before. Romaine refrained from telling him what starvation will do for the expression and ate her first good meal in a month.

They took long walks together, and on one of these, exploring the Coliseum, Romaine was horrified to find that her friend had disappeared. Then she heard his voice, faintly. "He actually fell into a lion's den." She helped him out, smoothed him down, and found his glasses. He was, she said, engaged to an English girl, but whether in admiration for her hollow cheeks or in gratitude for being rescued, the Englishman changed his mind and asked Romaine to marry him.

"It is doubtful whether at that time I was able to analyze my feelings about such a conventional affair as marriage . . ." Romaine appears to have used the proposal as an excuse to drop him.

One of the annoying consequences of living in Rome alone was, Romaine found, that one could not walk anywhere without an escort. One of her fellow students had suggested that what she needed was a man to protect her, and while rejecting the idea indignantly, Romaine found it a dreadful nuisance that she could not go on the simplest errand without running the gauntlet of the Italian male. Then, as now, he was adept at sidling up to an attractive woman on the street and taking a hefty pinch out of what ought to have been the fat part of the body but was, in Romaine's case, as thin as the rest.

Inside the Scuola Nazionale, things were not much better. Like the serious male art student of her day, Romaine was dependent upon an apprenticeship in classical drawing from the nude. But one of the reasons why there have been so few women artists is that they were traditionally barred from life classes until late in the nineteenth century. In a society that actually concealed piano legs beneath pantalettes in a paroxysm of Victorian piety, a woman who drew a naked male was considered beyond redemption.

As late as 1893, women were not admitted to life drawing classes at London's Royal Academy, and when they were the model had to be partly clothed. The decision to admit women to the Scuola Nazionale in Romaine's time must have been recent, and in 1896–97 Romaine was the only woman student.

This was the social climate in which Romaine, the female foreigner, took her seat every day at life classes. Since she could not possibly be a lady, she was therefore fair game.

One morning she found, lying on her high stool, a particularly disgusting postcard (Romaine delicately refrains from saying exactly what it was). She immediately knew whom to suspect. It was her neighbor, an older student with a beard and eyeglasses, who had been staring at her pointedly for some time. She swept the object to the floor and sat down.

The second morning, she found another suggestive postcard on her stool. That one went the way of the first. But on the third morning, when there was an open book on her stool with certain passages underlined and her neighbor seated in front of her was whispering urgently, "Signora! Signora!" it was too much.

"Seizing the book, I leant forward and smacked his face with it. His glasses fell off; he became crimson. I stood up, fully expecting to be hit back . . . Then, as there was no retaliation, I . . . [expressed] my indignation as best I could and . . . walked out of the room."

Romaine's forceful action caused a hurried reassessment of her probable morals at the school. When she returned, she was greeted by an atmosphere of respectful silence, and if she dropped a pencil, a dozen gallant young men suddenly appeared to retrieve it.

But the fact that she was a woman in a man's world was a constant irritation. She never knew when it would put her in an equivocal position.

Some time later, one of her mother's wealthy lady friends came to the studio saying that she would like to buy a drawing. She was the kind of woman Romaine observed drinking tea in the English Tea Room; a woman from the society Romaine detested and usually was at pains to avoid. In leaving her mother she felt that she had broken her ties with the tribe called "society," yet she forced herself to be cordial and disliked herself for it.

This particular lady was overweight and out of breath from navigating the long, dark corridor. She sat down and compared the barren room with the Château Grimaldi in a few well-chosen phrases.

Then she caught sight of some drawings from the life classes which Romaine had tacked to the wall.

"Is it possible that you draw *these?*" she said, her eyes dilated with horror.

These were the clinical studies of the naked male form which Romaine had done at the Scuola. The poor woman, who had come expecting to find some harmless water colors of picturesque models set against ruins, gathered herself up and hurried away. Romaine discovered later that the lady had returned to Ella and reported, in vivid detail, that her daughter had gone mad.

In later years, Romaine loved to retell the incident as an example of the days when she used to *épater les bourgeois.* But when it happened she was rather embarrassed, slightly uncomfortable, and distinctly relieved to meet John Rowland Fothergill.

John Rowland Fothergill had a shock of brown hair, straight brows drawn together across a well-defined forehead, a long upper lip, a firm chin, and the somber, somewhat self-consciously premeditating look of a young man who, at twenty-two, intends to make the world take him seriously. He was the quintessence of the good-looking Englishman. That he knew it shows in the length of his hair and the way his gray tweed suit is enlivened by a fulsome black bow, calculated to give the flaunting look of a Byron.

He had been educated at Bath College, then St. John's College, Oxford, Leipzig University, and the Slade School of Art, where he met Epstein and Augustus John. He was gifted in art and literature, was a protégé of Oscar Wilde, and knew Lord Alfred Douglas. His interest in archaeology had brought him into contact with E. P. Warren, a wealthy American esthete and collector, who was at that time forming what would become the famous collection of classical antiquities at the Boston Museum of Fine Arts. Fothergill worked with Warren for twelve years as one of several assistants paid to travel around Greece and Italy looking for possible acquisitions.

I first heard of Fothergill from the Anglo-Florentine historian and novelist Sir Harold Acton, when I visited him at Florence in 1971. Sir Harold knew Romaine Brooks well in her later life, and refers to their friendship in his second volume of autobiography, *More Memoirs of an Aesthete.*

Speaking of Romaine's work, Acton told me that one of the finest portraits Romaine ever painted was of Fothergill, who was one of the few men she liked. The portrait was "more virile than most," he said. He did not know where it was, or whether it still existed. Fothergill had died some years earlier, and Acton had lost touch with his widow and sons.

Sir Harold continued: "Romaine told me that Fothergill came one day when she was out and stole the portrait from her, because she did not want to give it to him." Those who knew Romaine were well aware that she never wanted to part with her portraits.

It seems likely that this was the first full-scale exploration of personality that Romaine attempted in her painting, and therefore an important event in her development as an artist. If the portrait could be found, much might be learned from it, and after this talk with Sir Harold Acton, I embarked on the search.

Finding the portrait turned out to be harder than I had expected, despite the fact that Fothergill had become something of a celebrity in his day. Some years after Romaine knew him, Fothergill wrote widely read books on his experiences as owner-manager of The Spreadeagle, Thame, near Oxford, and other inns: *An Innkeeper's Diary* (1931), *Confessions of an Innkeeper* (1938) and *My Three Inns* (1949). The Spreadeagle was a charming old pub, frequented by an intellectual clientele of undergraduates and dons from Oxford. It became a weekend place for artists, writers, and prominent politicians from London. Fothergill was determined not only to have properly cooked food but to have intelligent, beautiful, and well-bred people to eat it. He succeeded.

Fothergill became as much a personality as his guests as he presided over his establishment in a white coat and buckled shoes. Every room was exquisite, the food consummately well-cooked, and the service impeccable. His fastidiousness also meant constant crises behind the scenes: Fothergill never could find a staff quite good enough. His guests adored his lively, caustic wit until they had to suffer under it; Fothergill was capable of asking a young couple whose morals he suspected not to come back. His arbitrary attitude toward potential customers was such that he would turn them down simply because he disliked their notepaper or style of writing.

"If he was often uncharitable in his judgements," the *Times* of

London obituary remarked charitably when Fothergill died in August 1957, "he was capable of sporadic generosities and understanding courtesies that helped to offset these other qualities."

I began my search for the missing portrait with Fothergill's old publisher, Chatto and Windus, Ltd. of London. Norah Smallwood, a director, provided the address of Fothergill's widow at Rugby, and the information that a former senior partner of the publishing house, Harold Raymond, might have information.

Mr. Raymond was sorry that he had nothing more to add. He had lost touch with Fothergill after the last book was published in 1949. He added, "Fothergill had very much an artist's face. Augustus John did a sketch of him once."

My telegram to Fothergill's widow was undeliverable. I later learned that Mrs. Fothergill had died. Obituaries of Fothergill published in 1957 established the whereabouts, at that time, of Fothergill's two sons. One of these, John, was attached to a firm in Durban, South Africa; the other, Anthony, was an electronics engineer with a company at Rugby.

Anthony's old company no longer existed. There was one last possibility: that he worked for the company into which it had been incorporated, at Leicester. The personnel office there politely informed me that such details were never given by telephone. I could, if I wished, write to the personnel manager. I sent off a query without much hope.

In the meantime, Romaine's great-niece, Monique Grossin, had found a photograph of a handsome young man which, she said, was the only picture on display in Romaine's apartment in Nice when she died. Romaine's servants, Gino and Anna, were quite sure that it was a photograph of St. Mar, and Monique fancied that she saw a family resemblance about the eyes. Why, then, was the photograph signed "Roland" with such a clear and distinctive hand?

A day or so later, at Nice, I was going through a pile of old papers when I found what seemed to be the faded photograph of a portrait. It was signed "John R. Fothergill, Rome, 1899." The distinctive and elegant handwriting was the same, and the "Rs" matched exactly. Further proof: the painting might have been a mirror-image portrait of the same face. It suddenly dawned on me that Fothergill's middle name was Rowland and he had simply dispensed with the "w."

I now knew that Romaine Brooks and John Fothergill had known each other in Rome in 1899, and that "Roland" had retained sufficient hold on Romaine's imagination to be first in her thoughts some seventy years later.

On my return to London I found that Anthony Fothergill—who told me he was now known as "Tony"—had replied to my note. At first he could not recall ever seeing a portrait of his father by Romaine Brooks, and doubted its existence. But he wrote again later, saying, "As regards the portrait, we do have it, hanging in our sitting room! I was confused by my father's writing on the back of the frame which reads 'by Beatrice Brooks,' but then 'Goddard' is also mentioned and so after what you told me I was in no doubt that it was by Romaine (is Beatrice her second name?). Also mentioned:—'About 1905' and 'U.S.A. Phil. then Paris.'"

When Roland knew her, Romaine was still using her first name, and she was not yet married to Brooks.

Before I left for Leicester to see the portrait, Monique Grossin sent me an old letter she had found. It was from John Fothergill, on The Spreadeagle, Thame, stationery, dated July 17, 1925, to Romaine in London, where she was apparently having an exhibition. He was very glad that she had stuck to art against all the odds and he was sure, he said, that she had not been spoiled as a result of her success.

He still had her portrait of him, ". . . to my shame—unforgiven by you for all I know or could imagine and it is full of memories and I shall never forget how the first carbon sketch contained all that came later . . ."

Here, then, was a further piece in the puzzle. What could Fothergill mean by his reference to still having her portrait to his shame, unless the story that he had stolen it from her were actually true?

Fothergill's letter concluded wistfully, "If ever you could come here and let me see you again, it would be a great day."

The sitting room of the Fothergills' beautiful fifteenth-century cottage outside Leicester was the quintessence of English country charm: chintzes, the fine sheen of antiques, a grandfather clock;

pink hyacinths fragrant on the window ledge. The portrait I found hanging there was not what I expected, and I understood Fothergill's brief reference, in his letter of 1925, to the fact that Romaine had completely changed her style. This painting of a strong, almost compelling personality in three-quarter face bore little relation to what came later. It was a formal study in the late-nineteenth-century academic tradition. In fact, the only quality in common with her later work was its somber color scheme. The face was cameo-sharp against a black background, and the outlines of shoulder and bow at the neck were almost lost in the inky darkness.

Nevertheless, the portrait was painted with confidence and a sure dramatic sense. Romaine did not see Roland as a poetic, romantic figure, the way he saw himself. She caught, in the way the expression of the eyes contradicted the set of the mouth, a certain ambivalence, as if she sensed the inner bewilderment masked by the show of determination. There is the feeling of a perceptive imagination at work that I had not expected to find in this first major portrait by Romaine.

Mrs. Tony Fothergill showed me, at Leicester, a hand-written manuscript, loosely bound. It was Fothergill's unpublished autobiography, written when he was almost eighty, titled, *Lest an Old Man Forget*.

In 1898 Roland was twenty-two. Newly in Rome, he was dutifully visiting the monuments, wandering through the streets and occasionally acting as a guide. He had discovered the Caffè Greco and become friends with a pair of Italian boys and a beautiful American girl, two years older than himself.

He said that she had studied painting in Paris and had tried in vain to seduce Clara Butt. She was very poor and living in a studio with fleas on the floor which introduced themselves to you the minute you walked in, but she came from a family of millionaires. Her mother had taken a young man as her second husband, become jealous of her daughter and thrown her out with a tiny allowance. Roland found the lovely B. (Beatrice) absolutely fascinating. But his motto, he said, was "no time for love." So he got her to agree that their affair should last only three months, at the end of which he would be leaving for Greece.

"How happy we were and the rest of the story I cannot write . . .
I dare to hope she may think only of our visit to the Villa d'Este . . ."
They parted painfully and Roland went to Greece. When he returned
to Rome Beatrice had left.

The story might have ended there. But in 1905, when Roland
was back in England, he found a registered letter on his breakfast
table one morning. Inside it was £25 with a note from Beatrice
saying that it was what she owed him. Her address had been well
inked out, but with a little ingenuity Roland was able to make it out
from the sunken obverse, and they met again.

Beatrice's mother had died and she had inherited a fortune. She
was living in a sumptuous house on Tite Street, a combination studio
and apartment, and had married John Ellingham Brooks, a poet and
homosexual. The marriage had lasted only a few months and she
dismissed him saying, " 'See I don't want to be made a domestic
receptacle for you, go back to your boys in Italy'—and he went."

Beatrice began to paint Fothergill's portrait. Roland was living in
a small village outside London at Lewes House, working with E. P.
Warren and a group of young archaeologists. He described it as "a
monkish establishment with an ample table and a well-stocked wine
cellar." Sitting for a portrait was arduous; it meant traveling up and
down a score of times. It also meant enduring Beatrice's long and
boring tirades about women's suffrage. They quarreled half way
through, but the portrait promised to be such a good one that Roland
stuck it out. Then the broken romance, "no longer romantic," ended
forever.

But Roland continued to ask Beatrice for a photograph of the
painting without success. One day when Beatrice was out, he went to
the studio in Tite Street, told the housekeeper that he was taking
the portrait away to be photographed, and brought it home. Despite
Romaine's protests, he kept it.

When Roland left Beatrice for Greece, he took her photograph
with him and showed it to an older friend, a professor, who told
him that she had a cruel mouth. Perhaps she was cruel. As an old
man, he tried to remember through the fog of sixty years, and perhaps his theft of the portrait was an attempt to get even. "But I

remember her only as tender and loving like a child. She had a pale sensitive face with great black eyes and warm black curls."

In this and other matters, Romaine's memoirs are misleading through her determined use of pseudonyms. However, now that I had so much, finding Fothergill, the twenty-two-year-old "Roland" disguised as "Ronald," was a matter of turning to the right chapter.

She was aware at once, Romaine said, that she was attracted to him. What she felt was a double tendency: clear eyes, smiling mouth, and an air of shining youth, juxtaposed with the clever Oxford graduate's overlay of cynical sophistication, which had already drawn fine lines around his mouth and engraved a frown between his strongly marked brows.

They met at the Caffè Greco. She had stopped there one afternoon on the way back from the Scuola to buy a cake or sandwich which usually took the place of dinner. She was about to bite into a cake, when her eyes met the amused glances of Roland, whom she had already met briefly through her English artist friend.

He walked up to her, shook hands, and began to lecture her about eating such rubbish as cream puffs. She would never put another one into her mouth, he said, if she knew in what a "beastly awful" way they were made.

Romaine, who barely took any interest in food, took the lecture in perfect silence. She was fascinated, and when he offered to walk her back to her studio she did not refuse automatically, as she would have done with the Italian boys at the Scuola; and found herself making plans to see him again.

That evening at the café they were met by the English artist who had wanted to marry Romaine and whom she thought had left Rome forever. The three of them suddenly decided that night to go to Assisi to see the frescoes by Giotto.

They traveled third class on the train, each carrying a piece of soap and a tooth brush as luggage, and Romaine made a Burne-Jones-like drawing of herself asleep, with her head on Roland's lap. When they arrived, she made a number of studies of the churches and towers of Assisi.

The Giottos were a revelation. Romaine stared at them. Then she suddenly said that she was wasting her time and wanted to go back to Rome to start working, a remark which "my companions ascribed to an almost presumptuous faith in my own abilities."

Romaine does not state what is implied in Fothergill's reminiscences: that they lived together. But she says that they were constant companions; "there was not a single ruin, gallery or monument in Rome that we did not visit."

She thought him witty and clever. He already knew Oscar Wilde and reflected some of the brilliance of that personality. "His paradoxes came straight from the master but they were new to me, so I admired the pupil."

Her original impetus to go to Rome, made up as it was of a mood of melancholic asceticism, in which she saw herself as an outcast, a "black-cloaked traveler," put the city into a certain perspective for her. It allowed her to live an undisturbed life in a cloistered studio, and required total dedication to her art, and for that she was grateful. She felt her sturdy independence, but she had not yet experienced the beauty of Rome, and Roland brought it to her. He was a Greek pagan in that respect, she thought.

He laughed when she showed him the small edition of *Childe Harold's Pilgrimage* which never left her pocket, calling the book old-fashioned; and told her to read John Addington Symonds and especially Walter Pater, whose philosophy of the cult of beauty for its own sake had a marked influence on English esthetic thought at the turn of the century. Romaine did not fully understand Pater, but she read *Marius the Epicurean** and responded intuitively to "the wonder of a prose that could lift one to a Greek world of polished shadows."

Roland made her re-examine what she was seeing, and she "Marked him trace/Under the common thing the hidden grace/ . . . Till mean things put on beauty like a dress/And all the world was an enchanted place." (Quoted from Lord Alfred Douglas, *The Dead Poet*.)

Roland's main interest at that time was archaeology, and he con-

* Written in 1885, this is the best-known work of Walter Pater (1839–94), English critic and essayist. Pater was associated with the pre-Raphaelite movement and espoused the esthetic ideal at the same time as he rejected asceticism. "What she liked in Walter Pater I don't know," said Romaine's friend, Sir Harold Acton, "but she absorbed him into herself."

fided that he had once been very much in love with the marble head of a beautiful Greek boy he had found in some excavations. This made perfect sense to Romaine. She confided that while she was at school in the Italian convent she had conceived a kind of macabre passion for a dead nun, whose photograph she kept lying hidden on her chest against the coarse linen of her chemise.

When Roland left Rome Romaine was in despair. She felt her sudden loneliness acutely. She didn't want to see anyone, or even to paint; everything conspired to remind her of Roland. But, she was able to discipline herself, and so at last set to work harder than before.

She has very little to say in her memoirs about their subsequent meeting in London, seven years later. She does not tell us that she was the one to re-establish the contact, that she painted a portrait of him, or that he stole it from her.

She simply describes their first meeting, when she had tea with him at Lewes House. The brilliant boy who had been her closest companion had become dreary and faded. The young man who talked so brilliantly about the ideas of Wilde, Symonds, and Pater, who could discuss the origins of every ruin in Rome, whose curious mind was challenged by everything from Greek heads to cream puffs, and who had turned her world into an enchanted place, had become jaded, superficial. He spent the afternoon complaining that his friend E. P. Warren had become maniacal on the question of women, and wishing he had stayed with Romaine. His one remaining passion seemed to be horse racing.

So Romaine transferred her later disillusion, during the hours spent talking while she painted the portrait, to that first meeting. Roland, the boy with so much promise, disappointed her as a man. She took no further interest in his life except to remark that "he never became anything at all, sad to relate."

What seems to have happened is that both met at a crucial moment in their lives. When Romaine met Roland in 1898, and for some years afterward, she was toying with relationships with men that were more than friendships and something less than love affairs. She told herself that she was not interested in marriage. She repudiated, indignantly, the subservient role a wife would have been expected to play in those days. She was an outcast, therefore chosen. The expression *lapidée* (one who is stoned; i.e., a martyr) creeps into her work for the first time. It was the title of a magazine published in Paris that championed those who are attacked in life by Philistines. Since Christ had been of their number, Romaine felt it an honor to belong to such a group. She was marked and set apart; therefore conventional relationships were out of the question for her, she believed. She did not examine the deeper implications.

Nevertheless, Romaine was not quite ready to give up the idea of a relationship with a man. Nor was Roland, in 1898, quite ready to accept all the implications of a marriage. He was torn between homosexual attachments and heterosexual ones, just as Romaine was. After Romaine painted his portrait in 1905, he was married briefly to a woman who refused to consummate their marriage. At the end of a year, Roland had a nervous breakdown. In his second marriage, he was able to resolve his ambivalent feelings.

It is doubtful that Roland and Romaine ever had a physical affair. Theirs was the flirtation of walkers on the same tightrope. He thought of her as something less than a woman since (he told her once), "You are not like other girls. Your face is even more frank and open than any boy's"; and she could think of him as something less than a real man, therefore safe. When they met seven years later and Roland hinted that he wanted to abandon his monkish life for marriage, Romaine withdrew with finality. But she kept his photograph for seventy years.

Our Ride Through Life

IO

The other, the melancholy self, will sleep as long as I live here. These were my thoughts as I drove up the dusty road that runs between old walls and powdered oleander trees, or along the vineyards that looped with green the sea and Vesuvius paled in distant blue.

My mother was only a phenomenon I had been watching fearfully all my life. Death, the climax . . . nothing more.

To Norman Douglas it was Nepenthe "gleaming with golden rocks and emerald patches of culture." It was the authentic home of Dionysus for E. F. Benson, the most enchanting spot he had ever seen for Somerset Maugham, Arcadia for John Ellingham Brooks, and to Romaine, arriving there in the summer of 1899, it was still so unspoiled that she could hardly believe it existed.

Nobody knows any more what Capri was really like before the tourists and hotels and souvenir stands and holiday cruisers and foreign money made their inroads. The phrases of those who wrote about their stay there, years after the fact, are charged with the rosy hue of distance, intensified by nostalgic desire; so that it is impossible to tell any more whether it ever rained, if there were bedbugs on the ceiling, and whether anyone ever had an attack of diarrhea. All that remains is the shimmering vision of Capri rising through the mists, lit here and there by a fitful ray of sunlight, half shrouded in "pearly mystery," a perfect jewel embedded in a sea of fathomless blue.

Like John Brooks, they remember the buxom fisherwomen who picked them up like puppies off the boats and carried them through the surf to shore on their strong brown backs. They think of sinuous women who tossed trunks onto their heads as if they were bales of straw and made their statuesque way up the winding stony path to the village square (there was no funicular in those days), of unpretentious inns where, Somerset Maugham said, you could get board and lodging, wine included, with a view of Vesuvius thrown in for four shillings a day.

In that summer of distant memory, one can wander, as E. F. Benson did, up to Anacapri, climbing deserted steps built by the Greeks, and be a guest at an authentic marriage feast with mandolins, piles of macaroni, and jars of Capri wine under the vines. The red pomegranates are always in bloom there, and as dusk falls, they seem to glow in the darkness. The sky slips from palest blue into violet gray. Lizards flick in and out of the moldering walls, and as the stranger strolls through the narrow streets, almost suffocating under the heavy smell of the vines, he finds himself, like Benson, trembling with an irrational anticipation; as if Dionysus himself were waiting around the next bend in the road, with grapes in his hair and a goblet of wine in his hand.

Romaine was there for the summer. It was fashionable to leave Rome during hot weather to escape the fever prevalent in those days. The departure of Roland had left Romaine obscurely depressed. She had decided that she needed to study in Paris and thought she might be able to earn money in Capri by selling paintings.

She arrived in a state of vague unease, which increased after she had moved into a small pension which had the lowest summer rates. It was crowded with boisterous tourists, and during meals she was as self-conscious as she had been at St. Mary's Hall, feeling every eye upon her. At night trying to sleep, she would hear the strange cries of birds and find herself staring out into the transparent darkness of a southern sky. She would stand on the cliff beneath the Castello and be overcome by a violent urge to throw herself into the sea.

The sensation of being taken back to a pagan world, of being suspended in a time warp, took hold of her imagination. She would try to paint the peasants, who would pose for a few centesimi, and find herself unable to finish. The island was full of musical sounds, both stirring and unsettling: the rhythmic calls and responses in the vineyards, flutes on the hillsides, and the distant, strangely churning whine of bagpipes. Romaine would hear them and throw down her brush.

What stole over her was not despair, but the paralysis of convalescence. Her depression was being eroded, little by little, by the sounds and sights to which she could not help responding. In this ancient world one could live without ambition, breathing the soothing air like someone who has been suffocating; allowing the island's beauty to work its gradual healing. Bit by bit Romaine began to feel that she had left the other melancholy self, the black-cloaked traveler, behind.

After some searching, she found a studio in the poorest quarter of Capri. She kept a faded brown photograph of the spot. One sees old stone houses, an archway, wash hanging out on a line in the sun, and an old man sitting on a chair sucking a pipe. One walked through the rough archway, made by pulling stones out of the wall, into a courtyard shaded by fig trees, and then to a deserted chapel, one high bare room with a red-brick floor, which still had its Gothic window.

The studio contained a dilapidated divan mattress, a chair, and had a primitive kitchen-bathroom in the back. Since it was in such a modest quarter, the rent was only 20 lire a month. Romaine moved in at once. Where else, she reasoned, could she find orange groves and vineyards practically on her doorstep and have a view from her terrace of the Castello and the sea?

She would look back on the days spent in her abandoned chapel as the happiest of her life. She was a nun and this was her cloister, her convent's narrow cell within which she could exult in her perfect solitude. Years later, she almost bought a church, in order to decorate it with frescoes, then abandoned the attempt to recreate that first, simple happiness.

Romaine bought herself a tall and rickety desk that she found on sale and hung a curtain over the lower part of it to hide an iron washstand. She arranged her library of ten books on top of it and put a high stool in front. Then she climbed onto the stool, picked up a pen and sat there as if about to write. She would sit there for a long time in the bliss of her self-satisfaction, of being enough to herself again. But, had she known that she was about to change her solitary state, that half smile of triumph would have changed into a frown of apprehension.

While Romaine was sitting motionless at her desk with her pen poised, John Ellingham Brooks was probably spending a morning on the beach with E. F. Benson, like the one that author describes in *The Book of Months.*

They would go down as usual to the Bagno, a white pebbly beach that had small islands of sand one could lie on, carrying a straw case of cigarettes, a flask of wine stoppered with vine leaves, and books. They would swim out through the limpid waters to a brown rock covered with seaweed, then dive into the crystalline depths until they had exhausted themselves and would lie like corpses the sea had heaved up, while the surf swirled around their feet and the hot sand burned their backs.

Or perhaps Brooks was spending his usual morning hour ruminating over minute shades of meaning for his translation of the Hérédia sonnets. He saw it as the work of a lifetime, his Omar Khayyam, his slender but immortal claim to fame. In the pursuit of this goal he polished and repolished indefatigably, finding the morning well spent if he had refined a single thought; reading an occasional sentence aloud with deep satisfaction before remarking that (of course) there was a great deal more to be done.

He might have been seated in earnest study of a Beethoven piano sonata, industriously going over and over the same bars while continuing, said his exasperated friend "Dodo" Benson, to make the same elementary mistakes of fingering. When going down the scale with his right hand, he would pass his second finger over his first (an invention of his own) rather than using his thumb and passing his finger over that, like every other pianist in the world.

After lunch and a siesta, he might potter around the garden or play with his cats or walk his fox terriers. He might pick up something by Meredith, D'Annunzio, Leopardi, or Walter Pater; whiling away the hours pleasantly until it was time for an *apéritif* at Morgano's, the wine shop just off the piazza.

Brooks was an Englishman who had studied law at Cambridge. He went to Heidelberg to learn German, and there met the twenty-one-year-old Somerset Maugham, urging him to read Shelley's translation of the *Symposium*. He talked about Renan, Cardinal Newman, Matthew Arnold, and Swinburne and fired Maugham with enthusiasm for Italy and Greece. He was so persuasive about his choices, that the future author accepted such judgments with the fervor of a convert and only decided, years later, that some of those choices had been erratic.

"I was divided," Maugham remarked in *The Summing Up*, "between enthusiasm for the romantic epicureanism of the matter and the embarrassment occasioned by Brooks' delivery, for he recited poetry like a high-church curate intoning the litany in an ill-lit crypt."

At some point, Brooks went to Italy and took a boat over to Capri for a couple of nights. Then he sent back to Naples for his luggage. Like many other British homosexuals who had left England after the trial of Oscar Wilde, he was convinced that to remain would place him in real danger of public exposure. Capri was quite another matter, and Brooks simply stayed on.

By the time Romaine met him, Brooks must have been about forty, although he looked years younger. He was, by common agreement, uncommonly handsome and only his short stature marred his physical perfection. He had a broad brow, a strong nose, pale blue eyes, and a mouth whose thin upper lip suggested an asceticism that was contradicted by the pouting fullness of the lower. He had a mass of curly hair and the kind of hesitant, wistful look of a storybook poet.

Just how Romaine met her future husband is not known, but it was impossible that she should not, at some point, have been introduced to John Ellingham Brooks. Capri might be innocent, sensuous, and miraculously intact, but it was not exactly undiscovered. The downward path to international fame and touristic ruin had already been beaten out by a certain type of expatriate intellectual who, whether for reasons of health, money, or a fastidious craving for exclusiveness, had arrived at the conclusion that Capri was the most idyllic spot on earth. By the time Romaine found Capri, a group of brilliant and eccentric expatriates had already established themselves there, and they all knew each other.

Axel Munthe was probably the first to arrive. The Swedish doctor, psychiatrist, and writer came to Capri in 1875 at the age of eighteen, discovered an ancient chapel on the side of a hill haunted by ghosts and made it the goal of his lifetime to restore it with "garlands of vines and avenues of cypresses and columns supporting white loggias, peopled with marble statues of gods . . ." The manner in which his wish was poignantly granted many years later, became the unifying theme of his famous book, *The Story of San Michele*.

Somerset Maugham made the same kind of spontaneous commitment to the island twenty years later, in 1895, when he was twenty-one. For him it was not only the unspoiled, almost legendary beauty of the island, but the people he met there: the American colonel at Anacapri who had fought on the side of the South in the Civil War, and the regulars at Morgano's who spoke with such fascinating erudition about art and beauty, literature and Roman history.

Then there was Norman Douglas, Scottish diplomat, editor, and writer, who put Capri on the literary map with his devastatingly acute observations of its exotic social flora and fauna in his novel, *South Wind*, a best seller for years; the American artist Vedder; Charles Lang Freer, self-made American entrepreneur and connoisseur, patron of Whistler, who founded a museum in Washington, D.C., to house his exquisite collection of Japanese and Chinese art; and E. F. Benson, whose father had been the Archbishop of Canterbury and who wrote innumerable numbers of light, forgettable novels.

There were also, in this group of the wealthy, intelligent, and formidably gifted, others less well-known who provided the raw material for the fiction of Douglas and Sir Compton Mackenzie. There were the Misses Perry, who lived in a dazzlingly white house of Moorish architecture and served their guests goblets of potent Capri wine floating with strawberries and herbs. There was Thomas Spencer Jerome, unpaid American vice-consul and Roman historian of enormous erudition who proved to his own satisfaction that the

Emperor Tiberius was not a sadist who threw children off the cliffs and that the monstrous legend was an invention of Tacitus. There was the Baron Jacques d'Adelsward-Fersen, sometime poet and writer who liked to dress in an embroidered Chinese robe and smoke opium in his den with a select group of friends. There was the artist C. C. Coleman, who had a wife in an insane asylum and was in love with his peasant model Rosina; and unknown numbers of poets and writers, and artists with long hair, white umbrellas, and boxes of paints.

Romaine had no intention of meeting any of them. She couldn't help it. She had been discovered and immediately adopted by Mrs. Snow, a curious lady of indeterminate age who took a proprietary interest in Romaine's psychic and physical well being. She had plenty of money and a husband who lived in a gloomy house somewhere in London, and although her reason for being on Capri was never explained, she probably drifted there the way John Ellingham Brooks happened to arrive at the spot and immediately built his life around it. There was in that circle on Capri, at the turn of the century, the kind of unspoken truce of those who have similar reasons for escaping from the claustrophobic respectability of late-Victorian society. Nobody raised an eyebrow if the Baron d'Adelsward-Fersen chose to surround himself with beautiful boys, or if C. C. Coleman committed adultery with a peasant mistress, and nobody speculated about the private lives of the Misses Perry who had never ever had gentlemen friends; or an outwardly correct member of society like Mrs. Snow, whose husband seemed to have been left permanently behind.

It was Mrs. Snow, with her booming voice and invincible optimism, who helped Romaine find a studio, who invited her to the parties she gave in her suite of rooms filled with flowers and crucifixes (plenty of cold lobster, iced soda water, and brandy), and who introduced her around to wealthy people as a talented young portraitist. Through Mrs. Snow Romaine got her first commission. She was paid 50 lire in partial payment for a portrait of R. Barra, an American author, and she immediately spent the money on her wobbling desk.

C. C. Coleman was particularly fond of Romaine, and she became enough at ease with him to call him Uncle Charley. He was the group's elder statesman, a tall, ruddy-faced man whose cloud of white hair seemed to mass itself into a free-form sculpture and whose infectious enthusiasm for life expressed itself in interminable pink and blue paintings of the same view of Vesuvius.

He had an extraordinary decorative gift, as a torn photograph Romaine kept of his Capri studio demonstrates. A tapestry hangs on the wall above a divan decorated with an ornate geometric throw and silken cushions; surrounding pots, hookahs, and skulls are grouped together in inspired confusion. The feeling is Renaissance, or perhaps Pre-Raphaelite, and although Romaine usually detested such exuberant clutter, she liked his house and his garden even more.

It, like the studio, had an idiosyncratic strangeness that set it apart from the rest of the island. Fig trees grew more curiously twisted here than anywhere else, and there was an oleander tree growing in the small inner courtyard of the house, filling it with decorative branches of red flowers which pressed their way inside the doors and windows.

Uncle Charley was, like Mrs. Snow, an inveterate collector of people. One of his friends, the Englishman James Whipple, had been an explorer and kept a picture of his dead wife in her wedding gown in his living room with a wreath of flowers beside it. He decided that the way to bring some life to the island was to have roller-skating parties on his terrace, but the idea never caught on. Then there was Charles Freer, who had retired at forty-five after making a fortune with the New York, Kingston, and Syracuse Railroad and was traveling around the world collecting the art of Whistler, and then, because that artist had been so influenced by Japanese prints, Freer turned his attention to collecting them as well.

Freer's villa on Capri, the Villa Castello, had a magnificent view over the white town, backed by Axel Munthe's hill of San Michele on the one hand and the blue Mediterranean on the other. Added to this was the decorative outline of Vesuvius trailing a plume of smoke some twenty miles away. The house was filled with books, its floors were a marvel of varicolored mosaic fragments that had been ripped up from old villas, and its garden was a riot of oleanders, grape vines, fountains, and flower beds.

When Thomas Jerome, an authority on the Mithraic cult of sun worship which had been practiced on the island for centuries before

Christianity, decided that they should all re-enact one of the ceremonies, Freer was the one who provided the costumes. The ceremony was to be held in the Grotta di Matromania, a great natural cleft carved out of the cliffs 1,200 feet above the sea and facing east, which contained the ruins of an altar and what seems to have been a Mithras temple, where the appearance of the sun rising at dawn from the sea was celebrated in antiquity. Freer had just come back from a trip to the Orient and had brought a number of white kimonos which they all put on. Jerome, in spectacles and a beard, wore his fastened with a long striped belt and had wrapped a silk bandeau around his hair. Romaine clutched her kimono around her like a bathrobe and has a photograph of herself in the shadow of some bushes, with a garland of leaves wrapped awkwardly around her hair. Freer, Whipple, Coleman, and Brooks presumably wore the same.

They walked in procession to the grotto, chanting verses from the *Rubaiyat* of Omar Khayyam which Brooks had set to music. Arriving at the Grotta di Matromania, Romaine sang "Yon rising moon that looks for us again" and Jerome, "in propitiation doubtless for singing of the moon when we were worshipping the sun," droned on about Mithras until they all fell asleep. In order to wake everybody up, Whipple performed a magical trick in which he first brandished a "broken" leg into the air and then stood up to demonstrate that it had miraculously joined his body.

This incident, which is recorded in Romaine's memoirs and an old newspaper clipping Freer saved, is the first indication that she had already met John Brooks and that both were taking part in the kind of mock heroics that the expatriate circle liked to invent for themselves. He was, she said, the poet and musician of the island, sharing a villa with Somerset Maugham and E. F. Benson; the kind of person who knows everyone, is on good terms with everyone, and is seen at the best parties.

It is true that people were sometimes exasperated with Brooks. It was either because he seemed to live serenely on nothing at all: "'That fellow Brooks,' one could hear them saying," Pino Orioli wrote in *The Adventures of a Bookseller*, "'it's all very well. There he is and how does he get away with it? No money whatever, plays with his cats, strums the piano, reads all the latest books from England . . . and hasn't done a stroke of work in his life.'" Or, because they were asked to subsidize Brooks' idleness, as were his friends, who were perpetually expected to give him loans. "His whole life was a lie," Maugham remarked testily in *The Summing Up*, "but when he was dying . . . I am convinced he would have looked upon it as well spent."

They liked him nonetheless. He was the eye of the storm, the calm center of the hurricane. Around him raged the passions of the gifted and famous, those who burned to brand their names on life. They might be seeking cities they would never find, but Brooks, so apparently content (to their eyes), seemed to have found a secret that they could never share. For his part, Brooks seemed to be at his most serene in the tormented company of others, a paradox which would seem to hint at certain unexamined storm centers of his own.

Brooks had an instinct for excellence. He had his own limited but exacting code. It was necessary to know that a Larañagas was the best cigar, that Clos Vougeot was incomparably the best Burgundy, and that one could sense creative power, experience, and technique in the particular way in which a certain soup had been seasoned; just as it was necessary to know which were the most exquisite contemporary writers and which people unquestionably had the best minds. He had no creative gift, but he was a great appreciator; and his choice was unerring. He picked out Maugham, Douglas, E. F. Benson, and Compton Mackenzie as his friends, and he chose Romaine Brooks.

Romaine has nothing to say about her friendship with Brooks on Capri in her memoirs, an omission that is all the more curious given the space she devotes to Roland. Since it was impossible to disguise Brooks with a pseudonym, and since she was probably still angry with him when she wrote her memoirs in the '30s, she was apparently obliged to say nothing.

One can only speculate that theirs was the certain attraction of opposite temperaments. Brooks was immoderately vain about his good looks and not above taking advantage of them, whereas Romaine lacked the slightest interest in her physical appearance, was artlessly unaware of the power of her haunting gaze, and happiest when ignored. The attention of an occasional male threw her into a panic and then a rage until she had forced the admirer back to a comfortable distance.

Brooks, so cheerfully able to ask for money from his friends, never felt under the slightest moral obligation to the lenders; whereas it was a point of pride, amounting almost to an obsession, for Romaine never to ask for anything from anyone.

Romaine undoubtedly agreed with Maugham that she had never met such a lazy good-for-nothing in her life, and just as certainly was unable to suppress a grudging admiration for his serenity. Romaine was not only as single-minded and driven to express her talent as Maugham, but her proud reserve concealed a raging fire storm of feeling, rather like the tongue of fire licking around the inner edge of a volcano, likely to erupt at any moment. On the other hand, Brooks seems to have been remarkably free of passionate outbursts. He was what he seemed, a discreet homosexual who could also enjoy quite tender friendships with women as long as those did not demand too much of him, an attitude that exactly matched Romaine's need for friendly-but-distant male contact. Brooks was a loyal friend who would never jeopardize a relationship by examining its emotional bases too closely, as Romaine invariably did. In contrast to Romaine, his expectations of others were modest. So he had a great many friends, being able to tolerate almost anyone.

Brooks, who lived seemingly outside the boundaries of late-Victorian society, who dismissed the work ethic as if it had never existed, was, at base, as correct as a London banker. He believed in stability, the family, clubs, and the right ordering of things. Had life not dealt him one queer card, he would have conformed in every respect and thoroughly enjoyed it. But Romaine, who had escaped from the straitjacket of her mother's world of suffocating social obligations, remained in fundamental rebellion all her life.

Such differences of temperament always exert a magnetic pull one upon the other, based upon reluctant admiration for what each lacks. What Romaine undoubtedly admired most about Brooks was the quality that sustained his indolence: a conviction of absolute rightness. Friends might sometimes be at malicious pains to demonstrate Brooks' lack of the slightest talent for writing or playing the piano;

but he remained unmoved, living each day with the cheerful delusion that he was building up an immortal fame for himself. This self-confidence, which Romaine felt most lacking in herself, allowed Brooks to take it pleasantly for granted that he should be admired, emulated, talented, sought after by others—and taken care of.

They were delighted with each other. Romaine chose Brooks as her confidant. Like Maugham, she allowed him to form her literary tastes, sang the songs he picked out for her, and fussed over and rearranged his life.

Although Romaine never painted a portrait of Brooks, she was painting several others, thanks to the indefatigable Mrs. Snow. The first had been of R. Barra, an odious little man with fat legs crossed at a writing desk, seated in profile facing a geranium pot on a window, the better to show off his carefully trimmed beard and bull neck. Then there was Mrs. Snow herself, looking very much as she does in *South Wind:* "her handsome profile and towering gray hair inducing her to cultivate an antique pose, with a view to resembling 'La Pompadour.'" In a painting that survives only in a photograph, Romaine took careful note of the commanding profile, the slightly lowered eyebrow, and the towering mass of hair. The portrait is unidentified, but it exactly matches the profile of Mrs. Snow in another of Romaine's faded photographs.

Romaine's work on Capri is that of a groping young artist. It has a delicate pastel quality, as though she were applying paint in coats that are water-color thin. There is a feeling for interval and the sharp rectangular outlines of objects and the moment, as though she were trying to freeze movement with the immediacy of a camera. There is an attempt to give weight and roundness while retaining this spontaneity. There is, most of all, a sensitive awareness of character, showing why she chose portraiture over the picturesque streets, vineyards, and views of Vesuvius that one might have expected from a penniless painter dependent on the tourist trade. She is attempting to make her own statement and succeeds best in another portrait which only exists as a photograph, that of Don Alessandro Farraro, a Catholic priest on the island. It is a young man in profile, with full, fleshy cheeks. The portrait admirably suggests a nature that is both sensuous and calmly self-knowing.

Since these early works exist only as photographs, there is no record of the colors Romaine was using then. She says that she was painting the brilliant colors of the Capri landscape, its sharp sunlight and blue shadows, although she was not pleased with the results; the colors failed to harmonize with the artist's side of her nature. She sold a painting of a Capri child holding a bunch of berries to James Whipple. Another canvas, of a sunny pergola with green vines and purple grapes, was much in demand.

One of the people who wanted a copy was Charles Freer. He was dividing his time between Detroit, Paris, and Capri, and his laconic diaries of that period make frequent references to "Miss Goddard," interspersed with notes of lunches, *festas*, swimming parties, trips to the Blue Grotto, and dinner by moonlight with Axel Munthe.

Romaine was distinctly flattered by Freer's interest in her work. He was a man of evident and fastidious taste, with a formidable knowledge of contemporary art; one who would go to enormous lengths to inspire his friends with his own appreciation of genius. Agnes E. Meyer, the late wife of a Washington publisher who came to know Freer well, described a late afternoon visit to his house in Detroit when Freer suggested that they sit and contemplate two superb Japanese screens. He and his guests lay back on pillows sipping champagne and watching the exquisite Japanese mountain scene fading imperceptibly into the twilight.

That a renowned collector should want to buy one of her works was important to Romaine. But their friendship was perhaps more important for another reason. Freer was discussing art with Romaine at a moment when she was dissatisfied with her work. He must have spent a great deal of time talking about Whistler, who was making such daring experiments in the harmonics of color; whose subtle renderings of the English scene might consist of a virtuoso range of indeterminate grays, and who had offended conventional artistic sensibility by his radical descriptions of two portraits simply as "Arrangements in Grey and Black." Whistler as a prophet whom the truly enlightened admire and emulate, Whistler as a master of tone; this must have been the thrust of Freer's many conversations with Romaine. At any rate, before Freer, Romaine was painting faithfully bright pictures, but two or three years later she had moved to England, taken a studio on Tite Street where Whistler lived, and effected the radical change in her palette which was to bring her international recognition.

Freer must have told Romaine she had a gift that needed developing and that she was wasting her time on Capri. She needed to study the Old Masters in museums. She needed more training, and Paris was the place to go.

So Romaine returned to Paris for several months that fall, enrolled in the Académie Colarossi and began to study for three classes a day. It was very expensive. It left her very little money for meals and she was often hungry. Winter was coming on and she had no warm clothes to wear. While studying at the academy, she had become friends with a wealthy young Russian girl, also a student, who took her to visit her parents. Sensing her financial plight, the family made a frequent point of inviting Romaine for dinner.

One day they made her the present of a handsome winter coat: a black astrakhan. Romaine bundled it up and placed the fur coat on their doorstep; then she fled. She needed it desperately, but she couldn't accept their charity.

There was the incident with R. Barra, now in Paris, whose portrait Romaine had managed to finish. She took it to him, hoping for payment. He insisted that he had no intention of completing payment unless she were willing to sleep with him. He tried to kiss her. She resisted and was crushed against the wall . . . She managed to escape, but she had left the rolled-up portrait behind. Barra never paid for it . . .

Then there was the incident with Freer, the wealthy connoisseur who had taken an apparently paternal interest in Romaine's future. He, too, was in Paris. She was delighted to accept his invitation for dinner. But he took her to a variety show where some flamboyantly dressed women paraded about coquettishly in front of the men. Freer seemed to be watching her closely, as if he were trying to initiate her, into . . . what? Then he invited her to London to take a trip up the Thames with him . . . so she knew.

These incidents, the months of semi-starvation, the proud refusal of badly needed help, the struggle to get one's due from men who seemed to offer friendship but only wanted one thing, formed the background for a severe psychotic episode.

Romaine was driving herself pitilessly, as though a severe dissatisfaction with her work were spreading out to her life in general. Her memoirs of this period are full of accounts of overtures from men, indicating that she was also feeling abused by men. She wanted their disinterested friendship, but for complex reasons she did not want to be an object for their desire.

Being openly rejected in favor of a boy as a child, Romaine was now, more than most women of her time, resentful of men and envious of their apparent ability to exploit women with impunity. Her early feelings of indignation and jealousy of St. Mar had solidified into an intense envy-hatred for men in general; a wish to be as powerful, even invulnerable as they seemed to be; an implacable desire to get even. It was an emotional mechanism that has been described as "identification with the aggressor."

Whether what prompted her breakdown were a violent urge toward self-destruction, triggered by a sudden insight into her need to be perfect and the impossibility of ever measuring up to that goal; or whether it were the outcome of vindictive resentments against men which had no outlet, cannot be known. Perhaps there were many reasons, the way a group of random events in a life can conspire to dislodge a delicate emotional balance. She became physically ill.

Romaine's memoirs refer to this period as a bout of pneumonia, during which she was being nursed by her kind Russian friends, who supplied the doctor. She was threatened with "lung trouble," she said. The doctor prescribed some months of rest in Switzerland. But how was she to afford it? Then she remembered the village of Gruyère, where Mlle. Tavan used to take her girls on summer vacations. It already had a certain artistic cachet since Gustave Courbet had lived there when forced into political exile from France, and it was still cheap. So Romaine went to work there for several months in the early spring, painting mostly out of doors.

Even Romaine realized how close she was to insanity at this period. Years later, she told Janine Lahovary that she used to take daily walks in the forest, and everywhere she went she took a gun. One day, she glimpsed a man. Just saw a silhouette out of the corner of her eye; a threatening male figure. She took out the gun. She told Mme. Lahovary it was fortunate that the safety catch was on, or she would have shot him.

When she had recovered some time in the late fall of 1901, Romaine returned to Capri, to the chapel studio she had managed to retain, to her friends, looking for the calm contentment she had found there. She found Brooks contemplating suicide. The vast still lake of his languor had been broken, but the furies that pursued him were economic rather than emotional. He had been living on his capital for years and now it was exhausted. He had no idea what he would do so as to be able to do nothing.

Romaine hoped that his rich friends would help him out. She felt herself unable to help since her mother made it pointedly clear that, by leaving her, Romaine had forfeited all hope of inheriting from the family estate. Moreover, Romaine was convinced that, like Queen Victoria, her mother would live forever. That very year, the queen died. Then Romaine happened to read an announcement in the New York Herald:

"Mr. Henry St. Mar Goddard, the brilliant son of Mrs. Ella Waterman Goddard and Major Henry Goddard, has died at Nice of an illness that cut short a promising career . . ."

St. Mar died on December 24, 1901. Shortly afterward, Romaine received a letter from her mother, commanding her to return.

Romaine had not seen Ella for six years. She told herself that she had her own life. She had studied art in Paris. She had a studio on Capri. She had already painted and sold four portraits. She had friends to whom she could return. It did not help. She was filled with a claustrophobic panic, feeling the net tighten, smelling the sawdust in the circle, hearing the crack of the whip . . . What spoke was her conviction that she would never be able to escape again; as if she sensed, at some fundamental level, how much she was still bound to her mother.

She said a sad good-by to Brooks. She left her dog, Marco, in care of the kind Mr. Whipple and, feeling ungracious, allowed him to peck her cheek as a reward. She hid the two hundred lire she had just received for Mrs. Snow's portrait in a box as a promise to herself that she would return.

Then Romaine took the long train journey back to Nice in a mood of malignant self-criticism. "I have not gained complete independence through my work . . . Such friends as I have chosen are of no use . . . I have not grown up . . . I do not possess the slightest trace of . . . worldly wisdom." These were her thoughts as she watched the Italian landscape giving way, bit by bit, and saw the lush gardens of her childhood with their tangled masses of greenery, the succulent olive trees, and the small, pretty towns of the French Riviera slipping past her carriage window.

Ella was not staying at the Château Grimaldi but in one of the six apartments she had bought in the last few years. She would completely furnish one, then close it up, move on to another set of bare walls and begin again.

What Romaine was mentally prepared to meet was the demanding, autocratic Ella; the woman who would assess and coolly find wanting. She was totally unprepared for what she found when she drove up the avenue Victor Hugo and the cabdriver deposited her and her luggage on the doorstep. Before she could ask the concierge for the number of her mother's apartment, a figure appeared on the landing at the top of the stairs. It was Ella, transformed.

Ella, who wore such fastidiously fluttering fussy clothes, was wearing some kind of black dress that seemed to have been thrown on in a fit of absent-mindedness and slept in for days. Ella, who was always so incorrigibly vain about her appearance, had stuck a blond wig on her head without bothering to tuck away wisps of gray hair that escaped all around it. But the biggest transformation was in her expression. The habitual look of cool rebuff, across which other emotions would flicker like shadows on a wall, had become a mask of despair.

Romaine walked up the stairs toward her. Neither woman said a word. Ella simply turned and led the way through an open door into a shuttered room.

It was very still; very dark. After the brilliant sunlight outside, Romaine was temporarily blinded. She could barely see Ella's face but felt that her mother was looking at her intently. Bit by bit she began to make out the objects in the room dedicated, Ella said, to the memory of St. Mar.

A large glass case filled one side of the room. Inside it was the sheet on which St. Mar had died; on it was a plaster cast of his hand. Around the glass case were dozens of death masks, arranged in pairs and propped up to face each other. This, Ella muttered, symbolized St. Mar's dual nature, which death had united. It was also meant to help him on his journey to some astral sphere. A mention of the word "lunar" caught Romaine's imagination and she had a momentary image of her mother, St. Mar, and the spirit world lit up by an unearthly glow, pale, unnaturally bright . . . There were photographs of St. Mar on his deathbed around the room, framed in black. His long blond beard had been cut and Romaine hardly recognized him; his thin childish face had wasted away almost to nothing. Romaine found her mind wandering frivolously and was unable to stop it. His nose, she thought, was all that was left. It stuck out defiantly, daring Death to do its worst; insisting that it, at least, was still alive.

St. Mar could not really be dead; but he was dead. In the confusion of Romaine's thoughts, one predominated: that Ella seemed transfixed. She had constructed a tomb of St. Mar's memory, but she had not accepted the fact of his death and was trying to bind him to her by these repetitive acts. If she could not have his flesh, she was determined to retain his presence.

Ella handed Romaine some flowers. You are an artist, she told her. Arrange these flowers artistically around your brother's coffin.

Romaine stared at her. The funeral had already taken place and the object at which her mother was pointing was a bier, not a coffin. She obeyed out of habit, tracing a careful cross. When she looked up again, Ella had left the room.

Ella was waiting for permission from the Italian Government to have St. Mar buried on the grounds of the Château Grimaldi. She had planned an elaborate mausoleum in his memory in that shadowed garden, with its palm trees, its rocks and terraces carefully planted with exotic flowers. In the interim, St. Mar's coffin was being kept in a vault in the large cemetery of Caucade just outside Nice. One side was paneled with glass so that Ella could see St. Mar's face. Permission was never granted, and St. Mar is buried in the family plot at the Cimetière Anglais. It is a small cemetery, overgrown with weeds, standing beside an abandoned chapel, its air of forlorn neglect intensified by the constant roar of jets taking off and landing from the airport nearby.

In trying to communicate with her dead son, Ella had engaged the services of Cheiro, a curious character who, Romaine said, wanted to marry her mother. He liked to wear make-up, was rather stout, and invariably wore a tight frock coat and tails. Cheiro achieved a certain fame as a society palmist and occultist, claiming to have made many successful predictions, including the death of Rasputin. He liked to call himself Count Louis Hamon, and wrote several books about his "sensational personal experiences."

Romaine does not record whether Cheiro ever succeeded in invoking St. Mar's spirit. But her sister, Maya, said that after St. Mar died a place was always set for him at the dinner table, and sometimes all the silver would start to jingle. The servants were terrified of Ella and convinced that she had supernatural powers.

That first dinner was eaten in almost complete silence. Ella chewed mechanically, as if she did not know what she was eating, and if she spoke, it was only to talk about St. Mar. She would lean on the table and put a hand over her eyes as if overcome with fatigue. Romaine would feel herself relaxing slightly, but then she would stiffen as she caught sight, between the spaces of her mother's fingers, of one staring eye.

The homecoming had been even more of a strain than Romaine anticipated. That night, as she got ready for bed, she became convinced that Ella would somehow visit her in the night. So she rigged up an alarm system. She tied one end of a piece of string to a door-knob and the other to the bed. Then she balanced a log of wood on it so that if the door were opened, the noise of the log falling would be bound to wake her up. She went to sleep, planning her escape.

In the morning her fears seemed irrational, and Romaine decided to stay as long as she could. She found her mother getting dressed. The evening before, Ella had seemed only preoccupied and vague, but this morning she appeared to be completely disoriented. She kept muttering that it was the day of St. Mar's funeral and that she was going to the cemetery. Ella asked which wig one should wear to a funeral. To humor her, Romaine answered that she liked the one she was wearing, but before she could offer to adjust it, Ella had left the room.

As Ella went down the stairs she was muttering to herself. Her carriage was waiting. She would not get into it but insisted on walking behind it all the way to the cemetery, as though it were a hearse.

When Ella came back her mood of disoriented grief had changed to rage against the world. Why, Ella said, pacing up and down in the room, had the Riviera played her false? Why hadn't it given St. Mar back his health, as it was supposed to do? Life was bent on destroying her, she screamed, beating on the walls as if, Romaine thought, she were trying to push them back.

Ella fell on a couch exhausted, calling for a maid. A young girl appeared and, as if from long habit, knelt down and began to massage Ella's eyes and forehead. Romaine attempted a reassuring smile at the maid, who seemed frightened; but the smile faded as she saw her mother's eyes opening to stare at her uncannily.

This, Romaine thought, is the emotional atmosphere to which I have condemned myself. She took occasional walks along the Promenade des Anglais, then as now the main thoroughfare for thousands of tourists from all over the world. They, the sun, the sea, and the cloudless sky seemed to exist, but at such a remote distance that Romaine felt as if she were losing contact with reality.

Ella Goddard survived her son by ten months. She died on November 1, 1902. In those months, her physical and mental state deteriorated rapidly. Her determination to hold onto St. Mar by fair means or foul was on a collision course with her realization that she could not bring him back to life; the result of this despairing obsession was literal self-destruction.

Ella spent some of those months writing an involved children's story which was, in reality, a fairy tale for herself. It was about a baron whose lost son is miraculously restored to life by a magician on Christmas Eve—the day she lost St. Mar.

A Tale of Christmas Eve Masque was privately printed at what must have been great expense—the flyleaves are in padded lilac satin and the glossy white paper looks brand new after seventy years—and is an incidental indication of Ella's literary preferences: "Swaying to the rhythm of the dreamy dance, arching her silver-sandalled, delicate feet, waving her rounded arms encircled with brilliants, yet seemed she in all her movements to veil and re-veil her face with a fold of the scarf, or a strand of the golden hair that fell to her waist."

Romaine had thought for years that her mother was insane, although Ella had always managed to appear perfectly normal to the outside world. But now Romaine became convinced that her mother's distraught appearance, her delusions, her violent swings of mood, and her obsession with St. Mar, were so marked that a qualified observer would have to come to the same conclusion.

When she explained Ella's symptoms to a doctor in Nice he was sympathetic, but said that nothing could be done unless Ella were willing to commit herself to an insane asylum in front of witnesses. This seemed so unlikely as to be out of the question.

Romaine wanted to know why Ella seemed to need to drink such vast quantities of water. The doctor looked grave. He wanted to examine Ella, and since this was also out of the question, the doctor suggested that Romaine obtain a specimen of her mother's urine.

When this was tested, Romaine was astonished to learn that Ella had an advanced case of diabetes which had apparently gone untreated for years. The slightest aggravation, the doctor told her, might prove fatal. While Romaine was wondering how to get Ella to see him, her mother began to complain of pains in her elbow. It seemed that during one of her fits of depression and rage Ella had banged her elbow against a wall and it was beginning to be painful. As the pain got worse, Ella's entourage was ordered to take turns massaging her arm.

Although Romaine and Cheiro massaged most of the night, the arm got worse. So Romaine called in the doctor she had consulted, and Ella allowed him to look at her arm. When Romaine explained that they had been rubbing it for twenty-four hours, the doctor said that in such a severe case of diabetes it was the worst thing they could have done.

Madame, he must have told Ella, you are a sick woman. Ella would have waved such a verdict aside, of course. On the other hand, the pains in her arm were getting much worse. She was, in fact, in intense pain. She became delirious. She was seized by violent fits of vomiting. During one of them, her false teeth were thrown across the room. The doctor picked them up. Romaine watched her mother's eyes following his movements as he put them out of reach.

It took Ella a long time to die. Periods of agony were followed by moments when she was more or less coherent. Romaine stayed in the room watching her mother and observing that the injured spot on her mother's arm, once red and inflamed, now looked as white and hard as marble. When Ella fell into a merciful coma the doctor gave her an injection to revive her. It was necessary, he said in his efficient French way, to do everything possible to keep the dying conscious in case they might have a final word.

Ella did indeed have something to say: words of intense hatred for Romaine.

"It was not delirium. She knew that she was dying and I, alive, watching. I wondered if such hate could die with death. Might it not, as earth-born ombra, always hover over me?"

When the doctor left the room momentarily Ella, who seemed to have found new strength, insisted on getting out of bed. On one occasion she stood up, then staggered; Romaine caught her just before she fell. Ella wanted to be taken to St. Mar's mortuary chamber. She seized a black silk jacket from a chair and threw it around her shoulders.

Romaine managed to get her as far as the door of St. Mar's room. Then Ella stopped, started to tremble and insisted that she could not go through it. There was an invisible object in her way; to humor her, Romaine pretended to push the object aside. Ella clung closely to her daughter as she was led through the doorway, still terrified.

The room seemed, Romaine thought, more desolate than ever. Light was shining harshly on the photographs, the bier, the glass case, and the dozens of plaster casts of St. Mar's face, throwing bizarre shadows across his nose; that face which seemed such a pathetically inadequate object for so much devotion.

Romaine helped Ella to a couch and her mother lay there for some time, increasingly restless. She started calling for St. Mar. Then she began to rave so insanely that Romaine was terrified. To speak was out of the question; even to show herself was dangerous. Romaine stood behind Ella's couch, trying to calm her "by force of will." Ella

144

finally fell back exhausted and Romaine was able to leave her long enough to get help.

Ella's final moments were equally agonizing. She had been in a daze, but she suddenly sat up in bed and asked clearly for a glass of water. Romaine heard somebody muttering that Ella was not ready to die yet. But Romaine knew better; "I had seen her clawing at the sheet as if some force within her was impatient to be off." Besides, Romaine thought, the dog in the garden outside was howling; a dog always knows.

Ella drank the water and sank back down on the bed. She made a sweeping movement of her arm, dismissing everyone in the room except Romaine. She had something to tell her daughter, as if she were about to leave on a long journey but were turning back for something she had forgotten.

Ella could barely speak. Romaine saw her mouth open and move slowly, trying to form words. Then, Romaine understood; her mother was asking for forgiveness. It was a tense moment. Their eyes met. Ella seemed to become more anxious. As she was about to speak the door opened and Cheiro burst in, declaring that he was sure Ella had something to say to him alone.

But Ella had nothing more to tell anyone. She died with a shudder, whispering, "But it is so cold! So cold!"

Mother and Child

I I*

To me she is the root enemy of all things. (From Romaine Brooks' note-books.)

"Dear B." as her affectionate mama liked to address Romaine in her letters, must have forgotten that she was anxious to see her mother again after four years in the Episcopal girls' school in New Jersey. What Romaine's memoirs describe is a disjointed, confused period at the start of the summer vacations, when the other girls had left and a nurse, somewhere in the background, was packing her trunks. She remembers a new sailor suit with a chokingly high starched collar and the unpleasant smell of naphtha balls. She let it happen in a state of trance, she said, until the moment when her brother's doctor, sent across the Atlantic to fetch her to London, was waiting in the parlor . . .

But want it she must have done. "As Romaine is so anxious to come I shall make arrangements for her to do so in June or July," Ella wrote in 1885. "I intend my daughters to continue their studies together as they are the natural companions for each other . . ."

* This chapter reconstructs certain incidents in the relationship between Romaine Brooks and Ella Waterman Goddard, from the latter's point of view. The chapter is based on a group of letters from her mother, dating from 1885, when Romaine was eleven, which were found in her effects (see Appendix, p. 393); a deposition given by Ella's personal maid, Constance Finch, in support of a claim brought by Ella's second husband, George S. Crampton, against her estate in 1905, and upon information from Miss Natalie Barney.

Ella wanted to see Romaine. St. Mar was so much better now, that she could turn her attention to her daughters. He had almost completely recovered from his alarming psychic state after returning from that too-long stay with Grandmother Goddard, whose single-minded absorption with religion was truly morbid; the way she had filled St. Mar's mind with her obsessions was quite frightening, and he had suffered much as a result. Ella could not help but be disturbed to learn that now Beatrice Romaine was being drawn into the same tight net by the Episcopal school that had already confirmed the child without her mother's permission. Beatrice was entirely too young. She might even have other deficiencies after four years in an American environment.

Isaac S. Waterman must have been an unyielding man. Like other Americans of his generation, he assumed that worldly possessions rewarded the righteous; therefore, the rich were morally superior by virtue of their money. However, this did not let them off the spiritual hook. Because they were so much more worthy than the poor, they had a correspondingly greater obligation to cultivate their spiritual gardens. It was more than a question of good breeding; it was right feeling. They must be the exacting masters of their conduct. They must be vigilant in weeding out whatever noxious faults they found of vanity, of selfishness, of discontent, of foolish spendthriftness —whether of money or talents—or the temptation to wriggle out of onerous obligation by evasiveness and lying. Those feelings that were unacceptable must simply not be felt. He and his children must have an unerring sense of upright behavior.

Ella was her father's daughter in every respect but religion. She had drifted from his tyrannical Christianity in the directions of her tastes and sympathies, molded as they were by the modern directions being taken in poetry, art, and music. She had evolved from a mental image of the face of God as an ivory statue, his white hair in a violent halo, toward the metaphysics of Symbolism. She adored Baudelaire and passionately admired the Belgian artist Jean Delville, with his extraordinary vision of a red-haired and beautiful Satan stepping over a luminous tangle of sleeping bodies. She believed in the certainty of inner vision and of those secret regions of the soul where music knits threads of flowers in a garden, where a face glows fleetingly from the window of an empty room, and where a dream, glimpsed like a mirage in the rippling eddies of a fountain, has more truth than sunlight through a breakfast window.

It was her moral duty as a parent to inculcate in Maya and Beatrice Romaine the highest possible standards of behavior. After all, as blossoming (even gifted) girls, who would one day be wives and mothers themselves, they depended upon her to point out the right path. It was only her darling St. Mar, so frail, so pathetically dependent upon her vigilant care, who could not be expected, naturally, to measure up to standards of any kind. He must be watched over tenderly, like a delicate stalk in a hothouse.

When completely sane Ella did not believe in corporal punishment, even though she must be on guard against a regrettable impulsiveness when pushed too far. But she usually thought the better of it. In bringing up children properly, one simply took care not to spoil them. So much could be accomplished instantly by the right look of disapproval.

Having satisfied her immediate desire, upon seeing Romaine again, to root out whatever undesirable traits had developed during her long absence, Ella allowed herself to experience affectionate feelings for Beatrice Romaine. The child seemed much more content. She smiled more easily and her eyes had lost their air of habitual alarm, as if she saw spirits rising from behind her mother's chair; the look she had had since those early years when she was so silent, so stubbornly aloof, never seeking her mother out as Maya and St. Mar had done, but simply following her out of the room with her enormous eyes. That look stirred strange feelings in Ella's heart, flickerings of painful emotion to which she could not give a name, but which made her impatient, even angry. It was uncomfortable to be looked at so, to feel spying eyes upon one when one hoped for an exhausted moment of privacy, of rest . . . and without cause. It must be Romaine's unreasonableness that was at fault.

Everyone was saying that Maya and Beatrice Romaine made a charming pair, and so they did, both with the same heavy hair falling softly around their shoulders, the same poetically broad brows, the same finely molded hands, the hands of musicians, artists. They should have more photographs taken ensemble, perhaps on the cliff at Lyme Regis, looking out over the broken grasses toward the coast of France, or seated at the piano at Chestnut Hill, heads bent low, familiarly close . . . If anything, Maya was more difficult than Beatrice in some ways. "Dear B." was so extremely fond of St. Mar. He seemed particularly fond of her; had he not come up to his mother and put his head on her shoulder, in silent reproach, when Beatrice went away to school? Beatrice never lost her patience with him, the way Maya did; really, Ella believed that "Dear B." even protected St. Mar against Maya at times. The way Maya would pinch St. Mar sneakily at moments would make one think—if one did not know better—that Maya was wickedly jealous of her brother. Yes, Ella really felt that the moment had come to return Beatrice to the family circle. So a governess was engaged and the girls began to learn by rote a list of the Saxon kings.

The next thing to be said about Ella Waterman Goddard is that she was a profoundly disappointed woman who blamed the Major for the break-up of their marriage. He had seemed so gentlemanly, so full of deference, he had seemed to have a gentle, peaceful heart; and yet he had always withheld from her the one thing she most needed. She could not count how many times she had tried to make him respond, had threatened to hurl the Meissen out of the window, had torn up the useless money, had ripped his collar, had in her desperation threatened to destroy everything she valued, to destroy herself . . . His eyes would go blank and he would retreat behind a stubborn mask of polite concern. Ella wanted love, but he was incapable of finer feeling. What he had to give her was brutish, disgusting.

What the Major would not give, Ella, in her pride, would not ask for. This, then, was what her impregnable stare concealed; too-vulnerable needs that clamored like tiny mouths demanding the nourishment which others would never give. Others could only take from her, draining her of blood, and so she learned to stop asking. She became enough to herself, living her life according to certain precepts, taught since childhood, with the satisfaction of knowing that her behavior was always, where others were concerned, comme il faut; beyond reproach. And if Ella had reflected on that, she might have wondered why even though she spent her life living up to her expectations of herself, she gained so little satisfaction from it; why a profound inner restlessness drove her from city to city all over

Europe, that even denied her rest, except during moments of dangerous exhaustion. She might have wondered about the bitter bargain she had made when she allowed these acts of scrupulous obligation to take the place of the death of hope.

In this bleak inner world in which there was so little pleasure in living and no peace of mind, Ella could take comfort from St. Mar. His illness put him outside her framework of duty and, therefore, within reach. He was, as dear B. so charmingly put it, an incomplete being. Perhaps he was an angel, as she had thought in her mingled joy and confusion after his birth when, although the Major objected, she had insisted that he be given the name of Saint.

St. Mar was man before the fall. His fumbling innocence ensured his purity. He, at least, would never leave her. That he ignored his mother sometimes, that he could be irrational, even violent . . . all these things must be born patiently since they were the stigmata of his affliction; they must be born joyfully as the price to be paid for the gifts he had to give.

None of these things troubled his mother. It was only occasionally, when St. Mar would seem to shrink from her like a delicate anemone, would seem to curl up into himself in an agony of pain as if he could not bear her breath on him, that Ella would feel a moment's terror . . . But these moments never lasted, and afterward he would allow her to stroke his hair and touch his mouth with her fingers, murmuring words of endearment as his arms dangled limply by his sides.

Perhaps Dr. Phillips was right in thinking that St. Mar's health might be restored if he had an extended stay in a mild climate; certainly, he always seemed improved in Marseille and Antibes. Yes, she might very well take a villa on the Riviera. It had been so many years since they had a real home of their own. It would be pleasant to settle somewhere, to gather around her beautiful things, mild air, flowers, palms, the scent of gulls' wings; where she could always hear, as the muted background to her poetic fancies, the rhythmic pulse of the sea.

The Château Grimaldi became the focal point of Ella's life until her death in 1902, her first real home for years. When she was in it she felt lighter, freer, gayer. She would spend all day in the garden, the view was heavenly, St. Mar seemed to improve and would take lunch and tea al fresco with his mother. The fresh air should be a great tonic and medicine for him.

"This month is certainly the most delightful here in regard to climate—flowers etc.," she wrote one May. "—and yet it is the time the strangers homeward fly—But the Spring is pleasant everywhere —if not for its reality—for its promise—

"I am not quite sure when I shall be on the move. I am having the house put in order preparatory—so that I may be able to be on the wing when the Spirit moves—I do not think it well for St. Mar to remain through the approaching summer heat—I thought something of going on to Venice for the Exhibition—but am not really decided—

"There are lots of birds in the garden now—and lots of frogs croaking at nightfall—the Mosquito is just beginning to sound the tocsin—but Nets are prepared to catch the lively angler—as well as the poor fish—"

She might go to Dieppe, which was so much like the English climate, rain, rain; then a little sun followed by wind, wind; where one was obliged to light a little gas stove in the rooms, but which was much better than Paris for St. Mar since he could walk out more freely. And there was something very tonic about the climate, bracing and refreshing; one could run on the *plage* in careless attire, free as the air.

Ella loved Paris in the summer. Her room at the Athenée on the rue Scribe was very airy and the manager very attentive. The clothes were always freshly amusing, as she told "Dear B." or "Dear Romayne" in her letters. "Did you know," she wrote, "the fashions are 1835 for the time being, before *I* was born if you please! There are leg-o-mutton sleeves, fan-tailed skirts and tall combs and it's quite a Miss Fanny style, amusingly old-fashioned."

Ella liked to go to the theater and laugh. She went to the fashionable Cirque d'Été and was very entertained. There were wonderful performing dogs that looked almost human, graceful horses, and an equestrian dancer, a second Lois Fuller, who became airborne, flapped her wings under the changing rainbow tints of electric-colored lights and looked quite angelic.

While Beatrice was still studying at Mlle. Tavan's finishing school in Switzerland, Ella took her first trip up the Nile (in April 1893) and wrote to "Dear B." at length to tell her she had traveled as far as Luxor. It was a lotus-eating life, she wrote, good medicine for a tired spirit and harassed nerves. One simply drifted along, watching the scene shift as noiselessly as the sands themselves, the boat's gliding movement punctuated by the monotonous groans of the colorful crew, while the sun beat down on their heads or the occasional wind, blowing across the "sunny solitudes," sent invigoration through their veins.

The landscape she passed was a constant visual delight: palm-domed villages; the occasional oasis in the wide yellow slopes which looked like an old-world island in a tropical sea, where women in dark veils moved mysteriously through the groves; or a silent circle of dark-mantled men, with birds wheeling over their heads and pale water rippling at their feet.

But dusk was the most beautiful of all moments. The shadows bled color, fading into tender violet and velvety gray. Then suddenly the western sky would be shot through with deepest orange, intensified as the color met the water and pulsated there like something alive.

"I have not yet fancied myself 'Pharoah's Daughter,'" Ella wrote, "but who knows if the obstinate faith (of 5,000 years!) held by this Ancient people in the Resurrection of the Body—was not after all justified?—Perhaps many a Protean soul has returned in Modern Briton or Gaul to behold the dis-entombing of the treasured casket —or to peruse un-consciously the pictured record of former days on earth—"

To travel—well, there was always something to tell "Dear B.," in letters, that was amusing to recount, though it might not always seem so at the time. The trip she and St. Mar made from Marseille to Algiers in the winter of 1893 was something that she, for one, would never forget. With an express boat, the trip was supposed to take twenty-four hours; this one took thirty. "The boat danced like a cockle-shell—and the sea was like the end of the world!—We bolted right out into misery—and there was an instant sound of lamentation and woe and gnashing of teeth all round. Strange to say, St. Mar's spirits rose with other folks' stomachs. But in the night he had his own spell of trouble—indeed I was rolled off the berth 6 times—everybody was tumbling around."

Arriving at Algiers, the steamer could not put in at the dock because of the heavy seas. Instead, a small flotilla of boats manned by contemporary Algerian *pirates* was dispatched to bring the passengers to shore. Ella regretted to report that the first group fell into the water; the boat capsized with them, baggage and all. The *pirates* fished up the people and thoughtfully confiscated the baggage.

There was a slight delay while all this was happening. She herself "respectfully declined to proceed" until a few more people had met the same wet fate. She was interested to observe that, although the passengers got very wet the *pirates* seemed to stay very dry. She thought it might be as well to remain on board as a kind of *ballast*.

Finally, the moment came. She and St. Mar went down the gangway and made their leap in pitch dark, with the rain falling in torrents and the wind screaming in their ears, into the arms of a bold pirateer who picked them up bodily and dumped them down in a boat. Then they sat cheerfully in the pouring rain, forbidden to put up their umbrellas, while the *pirates* poked them with oars and made for the shore.

Ella had been taking an indulgent interest in Romaine's life at Mlle. Tavan's. "How does the singing come on?" she wrote in one of her letters. "What do you sing? Would I had wings like a bird!" She was most interested in Romaine's developing talent for art. She "nearly died laughing" at Romaine's sketch of one of the school's mountain rambling expeditions, and she thought the miniature Romaine had painted of her sister, Maya, a good attempt for an amateur. The upper part of the face was "quite like," although the mouth was a little crooked. But the general impression was good. Do one of yourself, Ella urged. Indeed, Romaine had applied herself so well to her studies at Mlle. Tavan's that Ella had more or less decided to send her to Paris.

"Will you try the effect of change?" she wrote in the summer of 1893. "I have it in my mind to let you study art—in an Art City—You seem to have a predilection for it.—(and it is to your credit to wish to occupy yourself with that amusement)—I will see you soon—" . . . "I want to see how you are and what you need to fix you up a bit—

and you can go to an art school probably for a while—and sing also—And then we can decide afterwards for the winter's location."

In fact, it was time for Romaine to have a little fun, and so Ella set about looking for a suitable pension for her in Paris. When Romaine moved in, she seemed well satisfied.

Ella wished, however, that Romaine would write oftener, "& tell me what you do & who you see & what interests you most—My life is more or less monotonous under the circumstances but you must have plenty to speak about—and as I have already said to you—I have too many letters—business or friendly—to attend to already—and am not always able—But your correspondance is sufficiently limited and you can very well take a little trouble to write—even if it is not a pleasure to you . . .'"

Ella was beginning to wonder if Romaine only wrote when she wanted money. There had been last year's problem with the dentist's bills. How could a child possibly run up such a figure, just to have a few teeth attended to? The price was far too high. Romaine was obviously letting herself be a "cat's paw" for people who were only after her money.

There was the problem of her allowance. "In regard to 'pocket-money' you seem to imagine it as necessary to your being as bread & beefsteak—it is a good education to learn to dispense with a lot of trash which makes a Napoleon burn a hole in the purse and leaves the useful out."

Romaine was always insisting that she never had enough clothes. "If you want more fine of course you can have it," Ella wrote. But why was Romaine complaining that her hands were cold? "I think I sent you a muff—before with your tippet—what did you do with it? If you've lost it—you should have bought a pair of flannel-lined gloves—until you could get another—

"This was not to be thrown away at a caprice—I had a tippet & muff that I brought to Europe after I was married 3 years—and had bought 2 years before as a girl for me by my mother—" As regards her other clothes, "You had better let Mme. Givend get you a warm solid winter dress—perhaps a sufficiently cheerful color that you can walk out in or wear for usual little vacations of a few intimate friends. With the remainder of the money (I sent 600 frs) you can get a muff and buy a few yards of white silk—to add to the length and drape the waist more if necessary of the silk I had made for you—"

Romaine seemed to have been getting very careless about money lately, dispensing with it as casually as she had apparently lost her muff. She seemed to think that there was a bottomless well of money, and when you wanted some, you simply dipped a bucket down for more. It was so parvenue to value everything by a fancy price. "But my dear Beatrice *you* are not Miss Vanderbilt—and it would be cruel to give *you* a false idea—Although I might not wish to advertize the actuality—But there is always plenty of *occupation* of *mind* for a *real* lady—indeed the daughters of the Princess of Wales make their own dresses for an occupation—as I have heard their mother did for economy, once upon a time . . ."

Perhaps more troubling than Romaine's dissatisfaction and careless spending was Ella's growing suspicion that Romaine was not telling her the truth. Ella saw it when she was last visiting Romaine at the Givends, and if St. Mar had not been so sick, she would have done something about it. The Givends were behind Romaine's sudden demands for this and that, complete control of the money, more coals in her room. "They were playing their little airs off on you—and you were inflating & giving one or two to me second-hand—like a dear, foolish little monkey, & soon were grinding me out like a coffee mill."

As for art lessons, Ella would attend to it at her convenience. "These accomplishments are extras which it will give me pleasure to afford you—as I can best do—but you must not get impatient or forget yourself or attempt to push me on or dictate such matters in a hurry. That I could not allow. You will always gain more with me by gentleness and consideration."

In another letter Ella wrote, "Why, when I am interesting myself —in spite of St. Mar's sickness—why do you throw cold water on me —by impatience—and even by a spirit of dictation—which is absurd —but I suppose you do not realize it. You seem inclined to turn your nose up at everything I began. Can you not see that there are times when, as you are doing nothing to help—the least is to try not to worry at me. Well—I won't scold—but it seems a pity that you are often so . . . resentful of advice or restraint from your mother whom

Family group, circa 1875: Ella Waterman Goddard, Major Henry Goddard, Beatrice Romaine as a baby, and her brother, Henry St. Mar, at seven or eight years of age. (From the collection of Maître Léon-Marie Emmanuel)

Ella Goddard, 1875. (Maître Léon-Marie Emmanuel)

Romaine and Maya, circa 1886. (Maître Léon-Marie Emmanuel)

Romaine as a young girl. (Maître Léo Marie Emmanuel)

St. Mar, aged sixteen. (Maître Léon-Marie Emmanuel)

"Roland" Fothergill, 1898. (Maître Léon-Marie Emmanuel)

omaine, circa 1908. (Maître Léon-Marie nmanuel)

Romaine as a lady of fashion, Paris, 1908. (Philippe Emmanuel)

John Brooks.

Renata Borgatti and Romaine with friends on Capri, circa 1917.
(Maître Léon-Marie Emmanuel)

Romaine on Capri, circa 1899. (Maître Léon-Marie Emmanuel)

Romaine at Villa Cercola, Capri, circa 1923. (Maître Léon-Marie Emmanuel)

Bernard Berenson, Florence 1948. (Maître Léon-Marie Emmanuel)

Romaine Brooks. (Maître Léon-Marie Emmanuel)

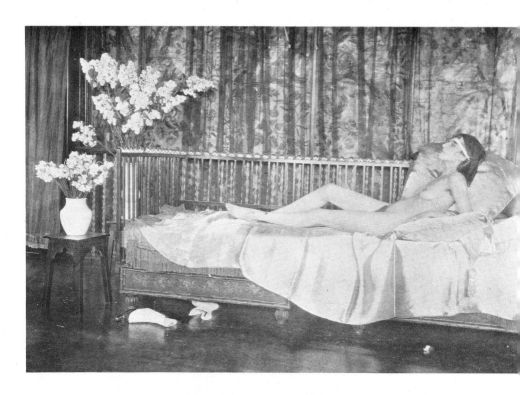

Ida Rubinstein, Paris, 1917. (Maître Léon-Marie Emmanuel)

you could accept it from—in an attentive & pleasant spirit without humiliation—"

Romaine had always been a difficult child, hard to please, easily influenced by the envious; a wild, stubborn spirit.

"You know that you have a little inclination to 'Perversity.' Haven't you? and you sometimes go a little two-sided—and sometimes a little wild-tempered, well,—all have some faults—but it annoys me when I feel chilled by some of those actions—just when I want to do something for you—and feel a pride in you—In many things you are quite sympathetic—we have many similar tastes—And it disappoints me when you are not always so—or not true to your *best* self—and I become more exacting—or more indifferent apparently than I really wish to be. But I want you to act 'straight' with me."

Well, Ella had left well enough alone only because she was seriously preoccupied elsewhere.

"St. Mar was very ill—I thought he would die—I was awake night & day for a long while—he suffered a good deal until he began to pick up strength again and I got him over the worst—until this Spring . . . he had a kind of relapse & for 48 hours was in almost constant suffering.

"I felt exceedingly discouraged again—for nothing seemed to entirely alleviate the pain until a remedy was apparently hit upon.

"It was said to be a heart difficulty. But much dependent upon general conditions of health—I am glad to say he has improved again & seems generally better—but I never can brag—because it seems to me that is the time that he gets ill—but if he continues to improve now I have good hopes for the Spring—He sleeps and eats pretty well & his nerves seem stronger—

"As for me—I have been very glad I came—they say my coming saved his life—

"I have had a very troublesome arm—stiff and painful & swollen and had to have a great deal of massage . . . I know I went about for over 2 weeks with the same pair of stockings—until I noticed the people staring at my feet—and discovered that one stocking had no foot —and the other only half a one left—while in serious trouble one

159

does not bother about those things—I did not often undress for a long time . . .'"

So this, then, was the reason why Romaine hadn't written. Ella stared at Maya's letter. Then she threw it down and stood up, walking to the window automatically. This was why she was always dunning her mother for money! Why she never had her white silk arranged. Why she seemed so evasive and deceitful. Ella cradled her arm, which suddenly felt much bigger and as heavy as stone, exquisitely painful . . . This was why Romaine seemed so evasive and deceitful. Why would she want to do something like this? Why? Why? How like Romaine to hide behind someone else, to make Maya break the distasteful news. Ella experienced the sudden nauseous taste in the mouth of someone who has been innocent, unsuspecting, while all around, friends are plotting his destruction. She was being slapped in the face. She was also being misjudged and abused. But she should have been more astute. If it had not been for St. Mar's illness, she would surely have sensed it in the atmosphere, in Maya's averted eyes, in Romaine's evasions, those words half sliding into silence . . . At this moment of impact, Ella wanted to hit back as hard as she could.

"I was certainly rather astonished at what you informed me," she wrote to Maya on June 4, 1895. "I was rather of the opinion that she had visited some acquaintances—and imagined it very fine to sail off in a highty-tighty way having achieved the wonderful age of 21 (which most young ladies are not at all delighted at)—hoping to cause great sensation in the ranks of learning of the Declaration of Independence.

"At those years we are supposed to have a little sense sometimes —although a good many postpone it indefinitely. But if the young woman really intends to go to London to see the Queen—or to frighten a little mouse under her chair—or to set the 'Thames afire' —why is all this circumlocution . . . if none can prevent her?

"Teaching brats is not very exhilarating—people usually do that when they find no other suitable 'lady-like way' of getting something to eat—or to help support some bothersome afflicted parent—teaching young men is often more remunerative—pro.tem—but there is a good deal of competition in both lines. I should not suppose a very high-styled family likely to take in to teach girls a comparatively unknown nomad—However I have afforded her a fine education & she has had advantages to become quite accomplished but I think she will weary of continued self-restraint—She seems to have Bohemian instincts . . . and she would enjoy the life . . . But whatever 'plan' she has in her head—the person who aids & abets her in the *dark* to move *slyly* under the circumstances—is necessarily a *sneak*—unless the person has been victimized by falsehood or misrepresentation.

"However I fancy she will—as usual throw aside any ladder when she feels fresh enough—having an absurd estimate of the immense privilege of her preference . . .

"But indeed nowadays '*nous avons changé tout cela.*' In the breeches-wearing, bycicle striding, bold & vulgar '*fin de siècle*' female needs no petticoat at all! She tears around the world—an unmarked battery on wheels—and her fair disciples are found everywhere following their own 'lesser lights' as fishers of men—mere excrescences of egotism & selfishness—'*Emportement*' is natural & excusable in the young—but I have always realized in the 'departed' a fund of duplicity—as well as a certain violence—of intrigue—repulsive in one so young.

"Often exacting & thankless when one's heart was warm—perverse & impatient of Rebuke in a manner exasperating to one interested—wishing to be a law unto herself—and a law unto her betters sometimes—Indeed, one was often obliged to suspect her of some mischievous outside '*caballizing*' even a little *treachery*.

"Yet she was also occasionally—if not very often, quite endearing—very entertaining—even sympathetic. It was a great pity she had not more stability."

Ella sealed the envelope with her usual red wax, stamped with the distinctive E. How could Romaine possibly survive as a governess in London? She was bound to come back.

But Romaine did not come back. Bit by bit, her image faded until it was as vague as the portrait of her that hung in a dim corner of a corridor in the Château Grimaldi, a face whose features habit had made anonymous. The servants said that Romaine had run away to a convent. Ella never heard the rumor, and if she had, she would not have bothered to correct it. One did not speak about Romaine in her presence, that was all. The monthly allowance was sent ("Please acknowledge receipt") and, at Christmas, there was an extra 100 francs with which to buy a present, along with a stiff little note. Ella did her duty by Romaine and heartily hoped that she would never have to see her again.

If only Maya had said a word. Maya, the other observer in the drama of their lives, who could have completed the story and shifted the perspective by pointing out the paradoxical facets that would have given it weight and substance. Maya watched and locked the painful evidence away in some inner fortress. She was adamant on that one point. Romaine must disguise the identity of St. Mar and act as if she, Maya, did not exist.

One catches tantalizing glimpses of the Maya who was, even to those who lived with her for the last thirty years of her life, an enigma. Nothing about her could ever be explained. There were only the facts of her elopement, knowing (as she must have) that Phillips had been her mother's lover; her early attempts to get financial support from her mother, and the birth of Ella Beatrice in 1899, followed shortly afterward by the birth of Liliane.

One only knows that the early years of Phillips and Maya were difficult, even desperate ones; that, at some point after the birth of Ella Beatrice, Maya and her mother were reconciled; that Maya, for inscrutable reasons, allowed the child Ella Beatrice to live with her mother; that Ella was indulgently fond of her first grandchild, giving her a ruby locket engraved with the words, "From Ella to Ella"; that she fed the year-old child on an exotic and erratic diet that included venison; and that it was only when the baby girl developed a grave intestinal complaint that she was returned to her mother. Maya was there when St. Mar died on Christmas Eve, 1901. She was there when Romaine, summoned back to Nice, arrived at their mother's apartment. She saw her husband die in 1902, and although Romaine didn't record it, she too was at their mother's deathbed when she died late in the same year. She would not discuss it.

Maya was, the children of her older daughter said, as much the lady as Tante Romaine was the Bohemian. With a staff of ten servants to look after her, she died in an enormous house with fifty-eight rooms, in which she had entertained the Queen of Portugal. She had nothing to do all day, yet she would become outraged if her chauffeur were a second late arriving; she seemed unable to tolerate the least slight to her *amour propre*. Yet, paradoxically, she was unable to scold her servants for such lapses; she shrank from it.

Her grandchildren, Philippe Emmanuel and Monique Grossin, remember the ritualized visits they made to Maya; being ushered in, seated on straight-backed chairs, and solemnly regarded. Their grandmother was waiting to be amused and entertained. As children, that was their role. In old age, Maya saw very few people, since she detested strangers and was stiffer than ever in unfamiliar company.

Maya was in all things a conformist, full of absurd prejudices, a relentless snob, and incapable of a spontaneously loving gesture. Yet her grandchildren regarded her with very little malice. Even as children, they knew she was locked inside a private prison. They respected her need for distance and, in the last weeks of her life, Maya began to tell Philippe, who was living with her, something about her childhood; as if she regretted her long silence and yearned for one final moment of contact. Like Ella, she shivered as she died, "It is cold, so cold," she said.

Even if both daughters had abandoned her, for Ella there was always St. Mar. Since the dreadful months of illness in 1895, St. Mar had much improved. He looked untidy; there was no doing anything with his beard, and it was a constant battle to get him to change his clothes; he had a child's tenacity for the familiar. But he seemed perfectly content. He could entertain himself for hours on end just by drumming on the windowpane. To hear him rambling through the house was a sound which Ella had incorporated into her life. There was the background rumble of the sea and the awareness of St. Mar's feet shuffling across thick carpets and half sliding down the marble corridors. Ella knew without looking when he would pause gravely in front of some object and he would make a scattering run at the room, as if he expected the furniture to retreat from him in disarray.

163

Her awareness of him was so automatic that a sudden silence would cause her to listen uneasily and go in search of him.

St. Mar's amusements were harmless. She enjoyed giving him pocket money, since he gained such pleasure out of the least thing. There had been the monkey he bought. What a pity it bit a child and had to be shot. Of course, he never won anything from the lotteries he was always entering, but the thought that he might, seemed to keep him perfectly content. Since he had his own coachman, he could come and go as he pleased with, of course, Dr. Henning always in attendance.

Ella had been at a dreadful loss when Phillips left. Apart from anything else, she had depended upon him to know St. Mar's ways, and for a time she thought there was no replacing him. But finding Henning had been a wonderful stroke of luck. He had been most diligent in regularizing St. Mar's life, making sure that he took his meals on time, accompanying him wherever he wanted to go in the most good-humored way. She could leave St. Mar with Henning in perfect confidence. He had a fund of common sense even though he was so young, and he had some delightful college chums, particularly George S. Crampton, a young doctor just out of medical school. He was a bright handsome fellow with rosy cheeks; a strong and healthy-looking fellow from the country, as Constance Finch, her confidential maid, chose to describe him. It is true he had no breeding—Henning said that he was the son of a bookseller from Rock Island—but he seemed willing to learn; yes, most willing.

Ella Waterman Goddard married Dr. George S. Crampton in November of 1898. Their honeymoon trip was aboard a boat to Genoa, traveling with St. Mar, Dr. Henning, and Ella's personal maid, Constance Finch; then to the Château Grimaldi. The marriage lasted barely a year before Crampton left. The reasons for the break were complex: a thirty-year difference in their ages, Crampton's fondness for gambling, Ella's extreme jealousy and possessiveness, and her preoccupation with St. Mar who, believing himself supplanted in her affections, threatened to kill Crampton. The precipitating factor was a dream Ella had from which she was awakened by Constance shaking her shoulder. She had been screaming,

"Murder!" loud enough to wake up the household. The murder she feared was that of St. Mar.

From that moment, Ella began to pay meticulous attention to St. Mar, and when Crampton left she hardly noticed.

Ella blamed herself for not having seen how thin St. Mar was getting. She blamed Henning, whose infuriating view seemed to be that life or death was a choice St. Mar alone could make. She called in other doctors. St. Mar continued to weaken. Ella watched him waste away in front of her eyes. During the months of her marriage to Crampton, St. Mar had chosen some fork in the road and now refused to come back. This illness was much worse than the one before. Then, there had been a violent struggle through which she had sustained him. She had pulled him out of the river, retching but alive. Now, there seemed to be no moment of crisis. He simply died, refusing to eat, refusing to drink, pushing her away, muttering angrily, and clenching his clawlike hands in feeble spasms. Then his eyes went blank. Ella thought she heard a dog howling at that moment, but it was her own voice.

After that, nothing much mattered. One put on something, anything, as long as it was black and one stuck something on one's head, though whether it were a wig or a bonnet one hardly noticed. One thrust one's feet into some shoes, clutched at a cape, and flew down over the stairs, and perhaps the cape fell off and lay there forgotten because one had not remembered to tie the ribbons. One ate nothing, or everything. Since one could not taste it did not matter. As for sleep, one had always survived without it.

To neglect her physical needs was more than an act of penance for Ella but an indication of her despair. Even though she had bound St. Mar to her by the all-embracing, devouring strength of her love, he had evaded her. He had triumphed over her by dying. Ella looked into the void of her life without St. Mar, and what she saw horrified her.

In those aimless corridors of the mind, nothing could be regulated or ordered. It was a secret and terrifying world where mirrors flamed with beautiful menace, where sound shattered echoing faces; it was the vision of Jean Delville; good had been vanquished and one saw the annihilating beauty of an ecstatic surrender. Ella groped, in her confusion, at what still seemed to be real: the cake of powder on Cheiro's face, his labored breathing in the séance, the plaster cast of St. Mar's face, the moment of release in late day as a maid's delicate touch smoothed, smoothed out the pain in her head; the comfort of fashioning one's own fairy tale, of restoring a lost child to a distraught parent . . .

Ella thought of Maya and then of Romaine. Romaine's flight was a bitter, unresolved issue in Ella's life. One by one, people had left her; first the Major, then the two girls, then Crampton, and now St. Mar, and she was weary of confrontations. She thought now of the peace of reconciliation. St. Mar had always loved Romaine, and perhaps her presence would lead him to make one last gesture; would reunite the mother with the son. They would sit quietly in his room, united in their loss, and St. Mar would steal through the door, perhaps as he had been; truly angelic, a little child in a white nightshirt, offering his cheek to be kissed.

Ella never knew, even remotely, what confused and complex feelings she had for Romaine. Had she allowed herself to perceive them for a moment, she would have recoiled in horror. There was a special circle in Dante's *Inferno,* reserved for parents who did not love their children. It could not be so; therefore it was not. If Ella remembered a moment of keen disappointment on discovering that she had given birth to another girl and not a boy as she had hoped, Romaine must never know it. She would be scrupulous in her care of Romaine. "To be kind and considerate—to be charitable in theory as in act to those who differ in opinion as well as in matter—are spiritual ethics for this world—and mighty hard ones to learn," she wrote once.

But Romaine must also play her part. She must make allowances for her mother, must understand that there were times when Ella was too burdened with worries about St. Mar to give her full attention and not insist, like a stubborn, spoiled child, upon having the center of the stage. The proof of proper parental influence is in "*right* direction of *right* feeling—not in utter selfishness & self seeking." What Romaine lacked, she must be taught. Romaine must see that her mother was giving as much as she could and be content with that, ready to repay. Why was it then, on those fleeting moments when Ella let down her guard and would grope for Romaine's hand, that Romaine suddenly became so hard and ungiving?

Well, all of us had faults. As Romaine grew older, Ella found herself looking forward to her infrequent returns from school. Romaine loved to recite her mother's poetry in a loud, clear voice and had an instinctive appreciation for it that was very fine. She shared Ella's response to music, and they sang very prettily together. She could be so sympathetic when she wanted to be. And amusing! Romaine had made Ella laugh so hard once that she almost choked.

Romaine returned, but not in spirit. She could not, out of duty, ignore the strength of her mother's need, which was immediately apparent when she caught sight of her at the top of the stairs. St. Mar's death had dealt Ella a fatal blow yet, while doing what was expected of her, Romaine remained unmoved by her mother's grief and felt nothing; she was numb. It was clear that nothing had changed. Romaine had always done what her mother expected, but these attempts to conform were means to an end: that of winning Ella's love. She had not won her love. Her rival, St. Mar, seemed to be desired even more passionately in death than he had been in life. Both Ella and Romaine were agonized by loss, and both in such pain that neither could see what the other needed, or have given it.

When Ella died, perhaps it was in the comforting belief of her passage into a Spirit World, taking the same path that St. Mar had taken, to follow him where ever he had gone. Perhaps she died in loneliness and terror, afraid to discover that the void of the last months was the only reality and that her hopes for love, for closeness, or a forgiving God, had been the real illusions. Perhaps the outlines of objects around her became distinct, the pair of false teeth placed out of reach, the silk cape thrown on the chair, as the efficient French doctor roused her for a final moment of consciousness and his voice was clear and cool, "Mrs. Crampton! Mrs. Crampton, can you hear me?" Perhaps Ella found Maya's face and then Romaine's and saw the handle of the door turn and click and Cheiro a shadowy shape behind it, whispering urgently; and perhaps Romaine pulled the sheets up around her neck as Ella tried to speak, her useless tongue blurring the words, asking for forgiveness; and perhaps Ella never saw Romaine stiffen or her hard, cold look as she refused.

PART TWO

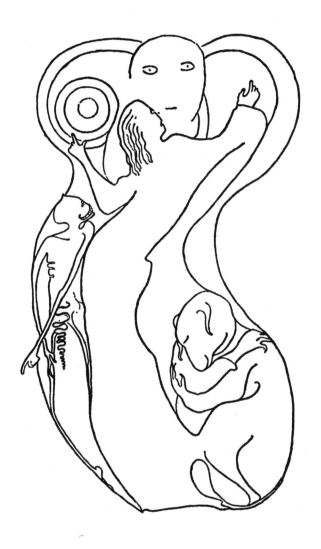

Asking the Way

12

The death of my mother and brother had not liberated me mentally and I felt that some part of me still remained with them.

Romaine must have wandered through the Château Grimaldi on one of those mornings following her mother's funeral in a kind of daze. It would have seemed vastly empty, that enormous house overlooking the glittering Mediterranean, its airless corridors opening onto one deserted room after another, where blinds were half-drawn against the morning glare, where a stray breeze ruffled a tapestry, and sunlight showed dust on polished silver. These silent terraces were scattered with leaves and pigeon droppings, and geraniums stood stiff-legged in forgotten stone pots.

She and Maya owned it all.

"From possessing almost nothing," she wrote in her memoirs, "I now had six flats in Nice alone, another in Monte Carlo, one in Dieppe, an unfurnished one in Paris and a château near Mentone . . ." There was no end to what they had inherited. Each of the thirty rooms was jammed with objects, and every closet, crammed full. Romaine found a trunk full of wigs, another full of false teeth, a third containing nothing but gloves. Wardrobes overflowed with clothes, furs, linen, and quantities of the old laces Ella loved. The shelves of the library were packed with leather-bound books embossed in gold. She pulled one out; it was on logic, inscribed to St. Mar from his mother.

Romaine went through the closets and found a small fortune in gold and silver coins which her mother had hidden against some nameless catastrophe. She pulled a pink satin sachet off an upper shelf and a plaster death mask of St. Mar fell on her head. A large box contained more masks, carefully packed in straw.

The knowledge that she was enormously wealthy left her dazed. Her memoirs attempt to grapple with her state of mind at that period; it seemed perfectly blank. She could not feel the slightest flicker of emotion upon her mother's death; not at the moment of her dying, not when her body had been laid out, surrounded by candles, and she surveyed her mother's features, contorted with pain; or at the moment when her mother's chief maid had kissed that sagging cheek and been shocked when Romaine refused to do the same.

There were so many dresses and furs, so many bonnets, shawls and cloaks, shoes and gloves, and matching sets of pink and blue lingerie. Romaine threw clothes on her mother's bed in piles and stood in front of a mirror, holding first one dress and then another against her, lacing herself into corsets, thrusting her feet into satin mules and leather boots; squeezing her hands into gloves of silken leather and pliant suede. She must have surveyed the results with a small smile of triumph before her mood changed. This costly ostentation was the antithesis of the statement she intended to make; it had nothing to do with her. She would give these clothes away. She would order a few plain, tailor-made coats and skirts from Redferns; something to befit her new status as heiress; subdued, elegantly simple.

She moved her things into her brother's suite of rooms but found their frescoed walls of pink-and-gilt columns an affront to the eye. Romaine had them covered over with a simple, restful gray paper. Similarly, his furniture was replaced with comfortable and unpretentious chairs from the library, and plain oak tables which she found in the servants' quarters.

Romaine had always longed for a life-size clay figure. It was the goal of the artist, something she had wanted for years; it was the symbol of the unattainable. It was bought and never used. Yet she could not bring herself to throw the figure away, even when its dusty body, years afterward, lay in an upper gallery of her studio.

Romaine had always wanted a volume of the complete works of Walter Pater, so she bought an elaborately bound edition of his works and then made the fatalistic discovery that she did not enjoy it half as much as the old, cheap edition she had carried with her as a student.

She was establishing herself in a new life and removing, bit by bit, like someone scrubbing old wallpaper off a wall, the remnants of her mother's presence. Yet the imprint stubbornly remained; Romaine was convinced that her mother haunted her.

The visitations began immediately, Romaine said, the night her mother died. Too tired to go back to her room downstairs, Romaine had gone to sleep on a bed in an empty room. In the early hours of morning, she found herself sitting upright and covered with sweat, her heart beating. She was about to scream with fright when she heard the muffled sound of a slow, intermittent thudding on the door.

Romaine was convinced that it was her mother. Not knowing what was to come, she waited patiently until dawn for her mother's mood to change, just as she had done in childhood. When she went into the bathroom from which the noises came the following morning, she found Ella's black silk underwear scattered on the floor; the clothes she had been wearing when she died.

The ghostly visit is a curious echo of a letter Ella wrote to Romaine in which a presentiment of her sister Clara's death took the form of an insistent doorbell ringing in a dream:

"I thought that my mother, my father, George, & the Major were altogether with me in the old W. 81 house—and I was in father's bed. I got up & went wandering through the house with them—when suddenly it became dark night & the front-door bell began to ring violently—and a voice said it is Mrs. D—your sister Clara—and I saw Clara come in—but quite pale—although she looked young.

"In my dreams it always seems long ago—It is strange how, as one grows older, no matter what the present may be, still the Spirit so

175

often reverts to the memories of youth. They seem more real than the present . . ."

Romaine moved into a hotel on the Promenade des Anglais at once. Madame Guy, who had been hired to take Romaine out walking in Paris five years before, had kept in touch with the family and had come for the funeral. Romaine was glad to see her; she seemed like a bulwark against unseen terrors. The lady moved into the room in which Romaine herself had slept and Romaine went to sleep in her hotel room with relief.

That night, the same thing happened: the realization that she was awake and terrified; then the muffled rappings on the door. Although paralyzed with fear, Romaine managed to stay sane, she said, through force of will. This would explain why, in time, the ghostly visits ceased; "yet I was always conscious that there was still a haunting presence which inspired fear, though it eluded even the abstractions of a dream."

To prove that these visits were real and not figments of her imagination, Romaine records that Madame Guy had a similar experience. When she asked that lady next morning if she had slept well, Madame Guy implied that she had had a ghostly visitation but, being a good Catholic, had been able to dispatch the apparition through prayer. Romaine offered further proof. Some time later the flat in which her mother died was completely destroyed by a mysterious fire and the concierge reported that ever since their departure the tenants on the floor below had been disturbed by heavy thuds coming from the empty apartment; as if a body were falling out of bed.

Then there was the night that Romaine, who moved into St. Mar's suite in the Château Grimaldi, thought she heard him crying her name. St. Mar's voice sounded so unhappy that Romaine was filled with the same anxious compassion she had felt for him as a child. She called his name repeatedly but had no response.

In the morning, Madame Guy asked Romaine why she had come all the way to her room in the night asking for help, but when she got up to open the door Romaine was not there.

That Romaine felt haunted by her mother and brother should not be taken literally, but rather as a poetic realization that she sensed herself still imprisoned. The death of Ella and St. Mar could not possibly give Romaine any relief since she realized, at some essential level, that she had incorporated her mother into herself. If she were still bound, the fact that she had become an heiress, that she was completely independent, would make no difference. Romaine was in a kind of mourning for herself, although she did not know it.

In those months following Ella's death, Romaine felt herself becoming submerged in the same phantom world from which she had narrowly escaped once before. Try as she would, shadowy curtains seemed to hang all around her, preventing movement in any direction. She was filled with lassitude, the victim of morbid fantasies.

The lush beauty of the Riviera gardens seemed, as before, to conceal poisons, revolting insects, dankness, decay; they symbolized an inner disintegration. She wrote a short story about these "Riviera Jungles" (see Appendix, p. 404), which links the diseased and rotting forces of nature with an archetypal old woman who was trying to lure her to her death, an erect figure who seemed to tower over her like a tree, with a blank face surrounded by wisps of black hair. In the story, Romaine expressed all of her childish terrors, her conviction that her mother was out to destroy her, in death as in life. At that moment, she was engaged in a violent inner struggle to escape alive.

Even Madame Guy was beginning to loom up like a monster out of childhood. That lady must have noticed the look of irrational terror in Romaine's eyes because she remarked that Romaine was becoming just like her mother. Romaine reacted with irritation, yet sensed the justice of the remark. She was making an enormous effort to pull back from the abyss; to escape just in time.

Then Madame Guy asked her when she was going to paint again. Romaine had completely forgotten that other life but suddenly, it was the only one she wanted. How could she have neglected for so long the only thing that really mattered? She immediately made plans to leave. It was, she said, a victory.

Romaine never returned to the Château Grimaldi. Her sister, Maya, recently widowed, lived there with her baby daughters and subsequently married Emilio, Comte de Valbranca, a flamboyant Italian who had ingratiated himself with the Portuguese court and been given a diplomatic sinecure in Monte Carlo. He appears to have been a despotic figure who married Maya for her money and made their marriage intolerable by petty acts of meanness and jealousy, refusing to give her any money, spying on her movements, and opening her letters.

Since Romaine wanted her financial share in the property, Maya and the Comte did not live at the château for long. It was sold to a Russian doctor who was experimenting with monkey glands to rejuvenate the aged and kept his monkeys in cages along the palm-shaded walks and terraces of the château. "The very air [which Ella] would have had vibrate with loving calls to St. Mar . . . is now filled with the chattering plaints of Voronoff's chimpanzees," Romaine wrote with transparent satisfaction.

Romaine made a nostalgic return visit to Capri in the spring of 1903, a year after she had left it.

Nothing had changed. Her chapel studio was still there. She packed up the few books she owned, the canvases she had painted, and put the 200 lire she had hidden away in case of need into an already bulging pocketbook. She took a last lingering look at the broken-down desk and high stool where she had spent so many blissful hours. As she turned the big rusty key in the old lock for the last time, Romaine felt a wave of unhappiness. "I knew somehow that the simple, almost monastic, life so congenial to me, was now over."

That she might have continued to live in such monastic simplicity, did not occur to Romaine. She took it for granted that her artless life as a poor student was over; as if her mother's death and her subsequent inheritance had placed her at an inexorable remove from the life she most wanted.

Money had its compensations. She could be everybody's fairy godmother, and so she gave presents to her friends. Mrs. Snow received an elaborate chatelaine jingling with ornaments, and Uncle Charley, an ugly Renaissance hanging, an expanse of silk and velvet embossed with a coat of arms, which she had originally bought from him and ended up sending back as a present because she couldn't get to like it.

John Ellingham Brooks came in for most of her solicitude. He was in worse financial shape than before and was slowly selling his possessions to buy food.

Romaine found him living in a dilapidated villa, blissfully unaware of a species of ticks which covered his dogs and crawled up the legs of the table while they ate lunch. Brooks also appeared as harmoniously able to ignore his debts, spending hours swaying on a piano stool and struggling with Debussy, Bach, and Brahms.

Romaine was concerned for his future. His debts had to be paid off, his friends placated, his house put in order, and an income supplied. Why she should have felt it her responsibility to take care of Brooks, Romaine could not imagine. Her memoirs only state, "Nevertheless, I married him."

Brooks had proposed marriage the year before and Romaine had then thought that the whole idea was absurd. Returning to Capri in the spring of 1903, her mood had changed. She decided that "a pleasant unity through isolation might be achieved."

If it were such a patently ridiculous idea, why did Romaine do it? Her friends, who were as hard-pressed to offer explanations as Romaine was herself, thought that she might have married Brooks out of gratitude for his kindness when she was poor and alone; or that she wanted the socially accepted role of a married woman; or that she wanted the freedom that the married state afforded. At the turn of the century, single women, even wealthy ones, were presented with endless petty restrictions upon their freedom of action, both social and legal.

Although a marriage of convenience sounds plausible, Romaine herself provides the evidence against it. A description of the marriage, omitted from the final version of her memoirs, makes it clear that she did not want to go through with a marriage ceremony. She considered it a "bourgeois convention," and was annoyed when Brooks insisted upon it. (A small leather diary for 1903 has one laconic entry for Saturday, June 13, which says only, "Married.") She had managed to live as a single woman for several years and knew how to survive; financial independence could only make life easier.

What Romaine wanted was companionship. She would have had strong reasons for not feeling lonely, but nevertheless the death of her mother and brother within the space of a year had left a great void in her life. Romaine wanted to feel united with someone and marrying Brooks, who knew how to keep a charming and friendly distance from a woman, who shared the same interests and had been the companion of so many delightful hours on Capri, looked like the ideal solution. They could continue to lead separate lives. For Brooks, marriage would mean financial security, and for her, it would make no demands of any kind, while giving her the comfort of knowing that she was no longer alone against the world.

But if Romaine thought she would gain without losing, she was to be disillusioned. Almost at once she discovered that their ideas of what this marriage was to be like were very different.

Romaine had wanted to take a walking tour of England for a long time. She would just take a knapsack and a sketchbook, and the harmonious contact with nature would be its own restorative, she thought. It seemed like the very thing for her and Brooks to do together. It would also provide the excuse to abandon the "many hateful prerogatives of my sex," beginning with the layers of clothes women were forced to wear: the stiff silk petticoats, the hats, gloves and parasols, the absurdly corseted waists, and the ridiculously exaggerated bustles. She could start wearing men's clothes. So Romaine ignored the warning signals coming from Brooks and spent cheerful hours in "Our Boys Shop" in London ordering a genuine sports outfit.

When Romaine appeared in her baggy trousers and big shoes, with her hair cut newly short, Brooks was horrified. She could not possibly appear with him looking like that, Brooks said; it would permanently damage his reputation. Romaine realized then that Brooks was unconventional in only one respect. The fact that she was independent-minded did not make the slightest difference. What Brooks really wanted was the dutiful wife of an English squire.

Romaine was at an impasse, although she did not try to resolve the dilemma as had the French artist Rosa Bonheur (1822–99), who adopted masculine attire at an early stage in her career while insisting that she was still a truly feminine woman with a closet full of dresses, and that she wore men's clothing for practical reasons. Romaine knew that she was in revolt; but she was too much a victim of her own insecurities to risk the loss of social approval.

Romaine apparently never took the walking tour with Brooks and did not wear pants for some years. She seems to have worked out a characteristic compromise, wearing the social uniform when it was unavoidable, but replacing it, by degrees, with increasingly severe coats and skirts, which she designed herself. In marrying Brooks, Romaine was making a deliberate break with conventional male-female relationships. She might even have expected Brooks to approve of her metamorphosis into a pseudo male. What she certainly strove for was a more honest understanding of each other's frailties and needs, delicately perceived and respected. What she found instead seemed duplicitous and disillusioning.

What began badly quickly developed into a major conflict. Romaine wanted to live as she pleased; Brooks wanted outward propriety. Romaine wanted freedom from onerous social obligations; Brooks wanted an elegant house in London and social position. Brooks was becoming the symbol of hateful restriction, just as her mother had eight years before. He was no longer the *lapidé*, misunderstood and ostracized by the narrow social mores of his day; someone whose rights she could champion against the world. He was society's advocate in disguise, trying to fit her into a straitjacket.

Brooks was impossible to live with. He was forever puffing on a pipe, filling the rooms with fumes that made her sick. He had dreadful manners; why, he even put his feet on the table. Romaine hints that Brooks had established a *ménage à trois*, in their house on Capri, since there was a boy friend sulking in the background, looking disconsolate, even ferocious (at the thought, presumably, that he had been supplanted in Brooks' affections by a wife).

Perhaps most irritating of all was Brooks' complacent assumption that he had an equal voice in disposing of "our" money. Then Brooks suggested solicitously that it was time for Romaine to make her will, just in case something should happen to her. "Now something was indeed happening to me, but of a very different order from that which was agitating [Brooks]," Romaine wrote.

Their marriage lasted about a year. In a letter C. C. Coleman wrote to Charles Freer in September 1904, he commented, "Mrs. Brooks has returned to London. Brooks is not with her and was not when she was here. *They are parted forever.*" (Italics his emphasis.) And so they were.

To escape from Brooks and move to London became synonymous

acts in Romaine's memoirs. She says as little about the reasons for this decision as she does about her marriage and its quick collapse. One can only speculate that London must have looked like fresh territory to explore, unsullied by grating memories; that Charles Freer's enthusiasms had fallen upon receptive ears, and that Romaine wanted to identify in some way with that clear break from nineteenth-century tradition which Whistler personified. The circumstantial evidence is strong: she moved to London a matter of months after Whistler died and took a studio in the same block as his famous White House, in Tite Street, Chelsea.

She planned her break with typical care. First, she rented another house, which had a tower, in Capri and often slept there at night despite Brooks' comment, "What on earth will the people in Capri say?"

Then one day she announced that she was making a trip to London, alone. Brooks' opposition was finally overcome when they agreed to meet there later.

Romaine's next step was to buy the studio in Tite Street. She moved in and, before Brooks was due to arrive, wrote him a letter saying, in effect, that she did not want him to join her. She was depressed, she said. She could only find release in solitude and hard work. But this Brooks refused to understand, as usual. His reply expressed intense disappointment. She had not given him a fair trial, he wrote.

The fact that Romaine could be extraordinarily rude and extremely loath to break unpleasant news to anyone were paradoxical aspects of her psyche that existed harmoniously. In this case, a direct confrontation with Brooks was to be avoided at all costs. So with typical deviousness, she tried to loosen the bonds of marital obligation so imperceptibly that he would not notice. Predictably, Brooks made great efforts to save their marriage. He followed her to London and, since she must have taken the precaution of not giving him her address, took to haunting the places where he might find her. Brooks' persistence paid off. One day, he caught sight of her passing by in a car and followed her to her house. He made his entrance after persuading the maid that he was her husband and therefore had a right to come in unannounced.

Romaine heard his voice just in time to lock herself inside her studio. "We were soon talking on either side of the door," she wrote. "His intention was to sit where he was until I came out, he said. I replied that my intention was to live in South America or some other out-of-the-way place and to deprive him of his income. This clinched the argument and he departed."

Later, Romaine told a slightly more emphatic version of the same confrontation. According to this story, Brooks got as far as the doorstep of her studio. She told him, "If you take one more step, I'll cut your allowance." Brooks stepped back.

Romaine bought Brooks off at the reported sum of £300 a year, a figure which perhaps intentionally echoes the 300 francs a month given to Romaine by her mother. It was not, even for those days, a generous settlement. "Enough for meat, but not enough for pickles," according to Maugham's long-time companion, Alan Searle. "She screwed him down to the last halfpenny."

For twenty years before Romaine moved there, Tite Street had been the fashionable artists' quarter for those who were prosperous enough to afford the rents. Whistler built his large studio there and planned to start a school. John Singer Sargent was painting portraits of the famous, Ellen Terry and Henry James, at No. 31. No. 52, More House, opposite Sargent's house, where Romaine may have lived, was built in 1882 by John Collier, an artist who painted "The Last Voyage of Henry Hudson." Oscar Wilde and his wife, Constance, took a house up the street in 1884.

If Romaine lived at No. 52, More House, it would have provided ample studio space for her. It is a large, heavy black-brick house, with an imposing bay window. The house Romaine owned had a chapel at the end of its small garden, and the back rooms were filled with sounds of doleful hymn singing. They also would have resounded with the noises of a slum since the house backed onto Paradise Walk which was, in those days, a notorious street where ladies did not walk alone and hordes of dirty children swarmed like flies. In front of the house one was likely to hear the crying of sick children being brought for treatment to the Victoria Hospital for Children on the corner, demolished in the 1960s.

By the turn of the century London was in "a strange period of transition: the hideous taste and prosperity of Victorian and Edwardian England still survived, but Mrs. Pankhurst rallied supporters from a balcony in Glebe Place and Suffragettes with banners marched down the King's Road. Ragged children still ran barefoot in the back streets of Chelsea, but people still believed in heroism and wept when Captain Scott, who lived in Oakley Street, died nobly in the Antarctic," Thea Holme wrote in *Chelsea*.

Romaine found it fascinating. Whistler, Oscar Wilde, and Beardsley were all dead, but there were equally interesting figures to meet: Conder, Lord Alfred Douglas, Sickert, and Max Beerbohm.

She did not much admire Sargent, and so she never bothered to meet him even though he lived in the house opposite hers. But she very much admired the work of Charles Conder, whose water colors on silk, Jeremy Maas wrote in *Victorian Painters*, are "drowsy evocations of *fin-de-siècle* lassitude." Romaine bought several of his paintings; to her, Conder's delicate designs seemed to encapsulate a dreamer's dim memory of color. They became friends and she discovered that this gentle man was slowly killing himself with absinthe. She remembers a long pale face, lanky hair, and a low voice murmuring disconnected mysteries, like some reincarnation of St. Mar. When she met him, Conder had just married a widow, Mrs. Stella Maris Belford, who was supposedly curing him of his addiction. This curious lady, however, seemed even sicker than her husband.

Whenever Romaine went to visit them she would be met at the door by Mrs. Conder who always had some part of her face freshly bandaged: an eye, her nose, or her forehead. It was very mysterious, since one would not suspect her husband of hurting a fly, much less giving his wife a black eye. But Romaine eventually discovered that the lady was an epileptic. During an attack she was likely to fall and bruise herself against the furniture.

The lady with the bandages so terrified Romaine that she discontinued her visits. She learned afterward that Conder had died in an insane asylum and that his wife had been burned to death in her sleep when her bed caught fire from a cigarette she had been smoking.

Romaine also became friendly with one of London society's most exotic members, Lord Alfred ("Bosie") Douglas. Douglas had somehow survived the savageries perpetrated on both their names after Oscar Wilde had been convicted of sodomy in 1895 and sentenced to

184

two years at hard labor. Wilde was bankrupted, his wife and two children fled to Switzerland under an assumed name, and "the whole of fashionable London turned from him in horror. Gently nurtured ladies, who had not the faintest inkling of what the crime was of which he was accused, found themselves unable to pronounce his name. The words 'Oscar Wilde' were like a shameful disease which would not be mentioned and must at all costs be stamped out. And stamped out his name was, from playbills and programs, at the theaters where *An Ideal Husband* and *The Importance of Being Earnest* were being performed. Actors went on acting, audiences went on applauding and laughing, while between them was a conspiracy to believe that the author, like Bunbury, did not exist," Thea Holme wrote.

Douglas, however, was still making the rounds of polite parties, even if the eyes around him were deflected or chilling. Romaine's impulse to defend him was automatic. But there was more than that between them since, John Glassco recalled in *Memoirs of Montparnasse* some twenty years later, Douglas was a small, handsome man with an overwhelming charm.

Romaine expected to find Douglas prematurely aged and disillusioned and was astonished by his buoyant, youthful optimism. They flirted mildly, much as Bosie was to do with Natalie Clifford Barney, to whom he was briefly engaged. Romaine thought Bosie saw in her "a dark edition of his own unquenchable youth, hiding a like rebellion against the world and its censure," and she must have found, in Bosie's enthusiasms, his lack of rancor, and his romantic response to beauty, a seductive reminder of that other, more intense, friendship with Fothergill. She walked a characteristically delicate edge, treating him as more than a friend and less than a lover. He sent her his book of poems, *The City of the Soul,* inscribed romantically with the quotation: *"Nous avons souvent dit d'impérissables choses."*

But, as with Fothergill, the interlude with Bosie was a male friendship whose consummation was to be feared. Perhaps they really had made undying declarations to each other. But such flowery and self-congratulatory compliments were becoming a trifle too insistent. Romaine had abandoned her work for Bosie, and when she allowed herself to be so deflected, even momentarily, a "deeper self" deserted her, Romaine decided. So she gave him up.

Romaine was at a critical juncture in her work. She had filled her house with the medieval English wainscoting and Jacobean furniture which she admired for the moment, hired servants, and equipped herself with a tall oaken easel and plenty of new paints and brushes. The treasured clay model had been set up in a corner of the room, and she surveyed her work. As usual, it seemed pathetically inadequate.

Despite her cheerful color scheme, her models looked sad and introspective. Perhaps the best canvases she had executed were certain heads painted without models, but in those days artists were not encouraged to take such flights of fancy seriously.

Romaine was so discouraged that it seemed useless to go on painting unless she could somehow start again from scratch, forgetting all the rules and painting only what she really felt.

"The result was still another melancholy self-expression: a young man with head bowed over a pink tie, and evidently in the last throes of dejection," she wrote in her memoirs. "But it so happened that this head was accepted for an exhibition and even such light success as that, brought encouragement."

A moment of deep discouragement can sometimes be the crucible in which a creative change of direction is forged. The first factor in such a change for Romaine was the undeniable influence Whistler had on her work. Romaine never intended to imitate him slavishly: "I wondered at the magic subtlety of his tones but thought his 'symphonies' lacked corresponding subtlety of expression." What she did do was to take his theories to heart. She must have studied his juxtapositions of closely related tones and the way he used neutral backgrounds to provide the properly dramatic setting for a small area of strong color. She must have known how much his pared-down, semi-abstract compositions had been inspired by Oriental art; that, against the vogue of the day, he lit his portraits in a subdued light so that they looked flat instead of round; that he thought in painterly terms rather than homiletic or literary ones.

Whistler's influence would not have been so pervasive, had it not accorded with Romaine's own inchoate yearnings for a satisfying self-expression. Everything that had happened on Capri, her distaste for the blazing Mediterranean colors which she was obediently reproducing, her perhaps instinctive decision to move to London, her affinity for the thick gray fog seeping through the windows of her house in Tite Street, and the crepuscular moods of the hymns she was forced to overhear on Sundays, had the inevitable result of focusing her artist's eye on one color. That color was gray.

The Cornish coast, where mists, rain, and wind bleached the colors out of the earth and sky, was a faithful mirror of the muted and wistful shadows of her dreams. In late 1904 Romaine went to St. Ives, known even then as a center for artists. She took a small studio where, when the sea was stormy and the wind high, waves would be dashed against the walls of her studio and over the roof.

Such a bleak outpost, which would have immobilized a more gregarious and less melancholic temperament, provided the ideal ambiance. D'Annunzio recognized, in a poem* (which he wrote in praise of a 1912 self-portrait in which Romaine has posed herself against sea and sky), that such a setting had come to symbolize, for her, her own unflinching ability to endure.

This, then, was the victory: one had survived because of one's ability to stare horror in the face without flinching. In that, if nothing else, one could take one's pride. It was a small step from sufferings unwillingly endured to the display of self-inflicted wounds; to the identification with landscapes that embody these conflicting emotions, and to the choice of colors that suffuse the soul with their imperceptible, yet implacable, stain.

Romaine was staying at a small hotel frequented by artists who came to St. Ives to paint pictures of quaint fishing villages. The group invited her to see their work; but since they were only reproducing the sentimentally picturesque, while she was struggling to express an inner reality, Romaine mentally dismissed it. Then they asked her to give a show of her own. She was most reluctant and must have yielded out of a perverse desire to punish. When the group of artists arrived at her studio, they were presented with eleven or twelve pieces of cardboard lined up on the mantelpiece, each one showing its successful or unsuccessful gray attempt.

Such a Dadaist display of non-art would get respectful attention

* See Appendix, p. 407.

nowadays. In 1904 it must have been considered a shocking affront to the serious artist, as much a nose-thumbing as, Ruskin declared, Whistler's "Nocturne in Black and Gold," was to the public. Romaine was, like Whistler, flinging a pot of paint at her colleagues, and they trooped out without a word.

She must have stayed at St. Ives for months, making hundreds of such experiments with a perfectionist's zeal until, she noted with satisfaction, she was able to pin down grays so elusive that she could barely see them.

Although Romaine retained her contempt for scenery, she did make one or two early experiments with black, white, and gray which used the subject matter at hand. Two small paintings in plain black frames on Windsor and Newton canvas were discovered with her effects in Nice. They are both slightly different views of the same fishing boats. They might be early studies for a larger work, "The Charwoman," now at the National Collection of Fine Arts, which shows an old lady in a boater and apron at a window, looking out over boats in a harbor.

The composition is the harmonious statement of mood for which Romaine had been groping in those months of study. The old lady in profile appears wistful, but does not so much dictate her mood of suffused nostalgia and regret upon the background as seem to reflect it; it dapples off her face like light bouncing off still water. Instead of simply reproducing an image, Romaine is imposing a point of view upon a work for the first time. She has taken major strides toward a coherent vision, one that she was to develop with great effect in the following two or three years.

Other works from that period are slightly less successful, though each has something of the same wistful charm. "Le Bonnet à Brides," also at the NCFA, is another well-composed character study, and a third, "Maggie" (at the NCFA), a portrait of a young girl in pigtails and a large red hat, is a sensitive study of a young English girl whom Romaine briefly considered adopting.

Still other studies of women's heads were found among Romaine's effects; earlier, less-successful versions of work she exhibited later. They are interesting only as proof that she was making repeated attempts to master an extremely limited range of tones. A self-portrait in black, white, and gray, may date from this period. She paints herself in three-quarter face, wearing a large black-and-white hat with an upturned brim, which seems to overwhelm the thin face underneath it. She looks to the left of the canvas, and the fearful, watchful expression in her eyes is identical to that of her photograph at the age of nine.

The choice of a color scheme, if this is not an overstatement for Romaine's palette, once hit upon, became hers for life. She wore black, white, and gray; she decorated in black, white, and gray, and she painted so faithfully within its limits that the color scheme served as an instant artistic signature. Nothing could have been better calculated to attract notice, and her timing was perfect. In France, exponents of official Salon art were reeling before the onslaughts of the Impressionists and post-Impressionists and prominent theorists like Maurice Denis who believed that a painting, before it was anything else, was "a flat surface with colors arranged in a certain order."

In London, Whistler had fought a similar and finally successful battle against the sentimental inanities of the story-telling paintings of the Royal Academy with their mermaids, dragons, and Spanish galleons; asserting the artist's right to call his works arrangements in black and gray.

Romaine, who only wanted freedom to pursue her own vision, wherever it might lead her, had her way prepared by artists like Whistler, for whom discipline, subtle understatement, and esthetic values stood for everything. It was a new wave, and she was on it. She moved to Paris.

Azalées Blanches, 1910. (National Collection of Fine Arts)

Le Trajet, circa 1911. (Charles Phillips; National Collection of Fine Arts)

Gabriele d'Annunzio, Le Poète en Exil, 1912. (Musée National d'Art Moderne, Paris, France)

La France Croisée, 1914. (National Collection of Fine Arts)

Jean Cocteau A L'Epoque de la Grande Roue, 1914. (Musée National d'Art Moderne, Paris, France)

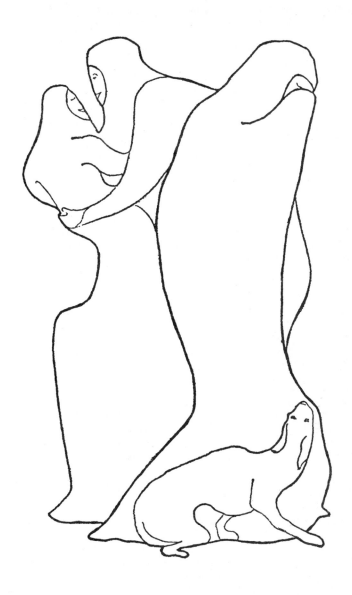

We Weep and We Weep Alone*

13

The exhibition was a success.

When D'Annunzio said that Romaine Brooks was "the most profound and wise orchestrator of grays in modern painting," he was not simply paying a politely lavish compliment to a friend, but giving voice to the general opinion. After fifteen years of solitary effort, Romaine Brooks had her first exhibition in Paris at the Galeries Durand-Ruel, 16, rue Laffitte, May 2–18, 1910.

The exhibition established her overnight as an artist of the first rank. A total unknown, she had arrived fully formed on the French scene, been measured against the most rigorous artistic standards of the day, and found worthy.

She exhibited thirteen paintings, all dating from 1905, following her visit to St. Ives, and all of them studies of women or young girls, although only two were actual portraits ("Portrait de la Princesse Lucien Murat," and "Madame Legrand au Champ des Courses," which was identified in the show as "Le Chapeau à Fleurs.")

Besides the three successful works painted at St. Ives ("The Charwoman," "Le Bonnet à Brides" and "Maggie"), she showed "Jeune Fille Anglaise, Yeux et Rubans Verts," a portrait of a young girl in a white dress with hands clutched anxiously in her lap; "La Jaquette Rouge," a despairing study of a nude girl waiting behind a screen in

* Also called, "Quand nous pleurons, Nous pleurons seuls."

193

a doctor's office; "La Veste en Soie Verte," a serene and harmonious portrait of a young woman balanced precisely above a skirt as big as a tent, her eyes downcast under a kind of plumed beret; and "Le Piano," in which a young girl in profile listens raptly to music which is being played out of sight, to the far left of the canvas. She also showed her first nude, "Azalées Blanches," of an unknown woman who reclines the width of the canvas, silhouetted against a kind of black wing, which throws an enormous pot of white azaleas into sharp relief; an image of sensuality refined, as exquisite and delicate as Ming porcelain.

"Esquisse," which was also on view, is unlike any of these works. It is the profile of a widow, a subject whose fascination for Romaine can be explained as the image of her bereaved and frantic mother, still icily unapproachable at the moment of her greatest grief; or as Romaine herself, fated to walk through life as a solitary, black-cloaked traveler, mourning some private loss that has left an unfillable void.

The portrait, which she also called "Woman in Mourning" and "La Veuve," since she liked to give several titles to her works, depending upon the exhibition in question, could have had a further significance for the artist when it was painted in 1910 since she felt newly bereaved by the loss of a recent love.

While these other studies of women and girls are impeccably finished, "Esquisse" is the rough and powerful result of a single sitting. The subject was a woman knitter, whom wealthy ladies would employ in those days like seamstresses to come to their homes and work on articles of clothing.

When the tricoteuse, recently widowed, arrived in her costume of stark mourning, Romaine was so inspired that she immediately began to paint the monumental outlines of the woman's body, her heavy black hat, worn forbiddingly low on the forehead and balanced by a regal fall of back draperies, and the brooding, grief-stricken and inflexible profile.

The portrait was to have been completed the next day. But the naïve Parisian, by now properly impressed with the idea that she was being painted, appeared decked up in her most elaborate finery. Romaine, amused and exasperated, refused to continue. Since she was a perfectionist, very few of her works were left in this raw state and

"Esquisse" testifies to the power with which she could seize the moment when her imagination was aroused.

Taken together, the thirteen canvases that Romaine Brooks showed at the Galeries Durand-Ruel six years after her stay at St. Ives are a statement of mature talent and a triumphant vindication of her determination to become an artist ("I was born an artist. *Née* an artist, not *née* Goddard"), achieved at the cost of a total break with her family, then years of poverty and concentrated effort.

The main theme that was to dominate her work (lightened occasionally by an acute sense of the absurd which could extend to caricature) was the essential loneliness of the human predicament. Her figures are locked into a forbidding silence, a frozen psychic space in which one senses, in an eerie way, the presence of violent emotions held rigidly in check. The lessons learned from Whistler have been applied to express a barren inner landscape, composed as meticulously as a Japanese *haiku* poem and stated in dramatically bold, oversize canvases with a color scheme pared down to the point of invisibility.

The power and austerity of the work was noted by Hilton Kramer of the New York *Times* when a retrospective exhibition was held at the Whitney Museum in New York in the spring of 1971. (It followed a larger exhibition at the National Collection of Fine Arts in Washington.)

"She is . . . a painter of remarkable powers. Her portraits are at once very strong and very cold," he wrote. "Her figure paintings—especially the female nudes—are impressively eerie, suggesting a kind of icy eroticism. Color—if one can really call it color—is generally limited to black, gray, and white. The structure of certain paintings is almost architectural in its rigor. There is nothing improvised or spontaneous in this style; there are few easy delights for the eye. But there is a force in this pictorial style that an earlier epoch than our own would have had no hesitation in calling masculine."

Kramer continued, "What we see in her pictorial style is the end of the Whistler inheritance, transmuted and crystallized into a personal vision." Certainly her work owed nothing to the most important art movement of the nineteenth-century, Impressionism, or to the post-Impressionists who were having an important exhibition in London that same year (Van Gogh, Gauguin, and Cézanne). Romaine Brooks painted as if they did not exist although, from our vantage point, it seems hardly possible that she had not been influenced by the Fauvists, who had held their first exhibition in the Salon d'Automne five years before, or by the experiments of Picasso, who had painted his revolutionary "Les Demoiselles d'Avignon" in 1907.

"It is sometimes hard to remember that the art world of Paris in the second decade of the twentieth century was not dominated by a single trend in painting," Dr. Joshua C. Taylor, director of the National Collection of Fine Arts, wrote in the catalogue to the 1971 exhibition.

"The simple scheme we call history arrives after the fact. Thrilling experiments in perception and form coexisted with a persistent preoccupation with spiritual values and the nature of human existence. An acutely self-conscious intellectual society pursued its goals of infinite choice and refinement with a critical awareness that separated it markedly from an earlier preciosity; a nice sense of irony quite transformed the 'decadent' sentiment of the late nineteenth century."

Romaine Brooks was already moving in Right Bank social circles, for whom whatever curious experiments might be being conducted in the Left Bank ateliers were simply not relevant. These were the titled, the famous, the elegantly scandalous, and the intellectually élite. This was the world she courted and chose to reflect, and her canvases, with their merciless rigor, self-conscious refinement, and fastidious irony, had an enormous appeal for it. Nothing that happened to Romaine Brooks afterward quite equalled the success of her first exhibition. But, before the show opened, she had a bad attack of nerves.

The Galeries Durand-Ruel were, at that moment, the most famous in Paris and specialized in the Impressionists. The same year that Romaine showed her work, they exhibited Manet, Monet, Pissarro, Redon, Cézanne, Renoir, and Mary Cassatt.

When Georges Durand-Ruel invited her to show there, Romaine was properly aware of the value of the offer. She prepared for the exhibition with her usual thoroughness. The Galeries Durand-Ruel walls were covered with red plush, which Romaine considered an unsuitable background for her work. So, just as Whistler had done thirty years before,† she redecorated it completely, covering the red with a simple beige material which would show off her subtle tonal dissonances to best effect.

Once finished, she surveyed the result and was stricken by an attack of doubt so violent that she would have canceled the opening if she could. How could she possibly expose her inner self to the world like this? Reveal the truth about herself, that she was, in fact, as despairing of life as the introspective faces on the walls? How could she take such an enormous risk?

She was deluged with praise from newspapers and magazines in Paris, and London the following year, when essentially the same show was exhibited at the Goupil Gallery in June 1911. The best critics bent their powers of analysis to isolate those elusive qualities that made the art of Romaine Brooks so distinctly arresting.

The critic Claude Roger-Marx, who wrote the introduction to the catalogue, thought that her art was addressed "to those intelligences and those chosen sensibilities who are fascinated by the exploration of character but who, rejecting obvious effects as offensive, prefer to categorical affirmations the delicate allusion of implication; they do not ask for light but for gentle shadow;

"Not color, nothing but nuance;

"Not contrasting effects, but a reigning harmony.
It is an art of strong significance and exquisite expression: one believes it made to order to illustrate the aphorism of Edmond de Goncourt: 'The rare is almost always the beautiful.'"

Romaine's friend, Robert de Montesquiou, called her a "Thief of Souls," considered her work almost perfect in its severe, bitter constraint and found the portrait of his close friend, Madame Cloton Legrand, a *chef d'oeuvre* (then bought it). Arsène Alexandre predicted that the strong, subtle canvases would be a revelation to the public. "These pensive portraits, these severe yet penetrating harmonies, reveal a genuine originality and emerge with much charm," he wrote in *Le Figaro*.

Albert Flament, writing in *Le Trottoir Roulant*, called her a painter

† In 1874 Whistler had the then-radical idea than an art gallery should provide the proper environment for his work; so he repainted its walls gray and added palms, flowers, blue pots, and bronzes. The result was much admired, but not imitated, and was still considered daring at the turn of the century.

whose talent was "curious, very rare, original, at once simple and vigorous and a rarely-achieved harmony . . . One of the most original feminine talents of our time . . ."

Louis Vauxcelles predicted in *Gil Blas* that "After Cecilia Beaux and Mary Cassatt, the name of Romaine Brooks is the only one among those from across the sea to remember."

Only Guillaume Apollinaire, writing in *L'Intransigeant,* had any reservations at all. Her paintings, he said, had a somber elegance; pale faces, black robes, silhouettes like memories; everything Romaine Brooks presented had this same severity. She painted with strength, he said, but with sadness, too much sadness.

Romaine Brooks' artistic unity of approach, a single-minded vision coupled with its ideal means of expression, had the weakness implicit in such strength. It is not surprising that the poet Apollinaire's sensibilities should have been affronted by the single note which an exhibition of her work was bound to strike. Her stylistic method necessarily limited her to the portrayal of a certain range of moods, but it would be more accurate to say that her limitation came from within. She saw her subjects filtered through a pervasive melancholy which never completely left her and which tinged everything she saw like a delicate wash of color, subtly deadening the emotional tone and giving a hard edge to the outlines of her figures, so that the final impression is less elegant than limiting, confining.

Few critics in 1910 addressed themselves to Romaine Brooks' skill as a portraitist, but from the vantage point of her total work one sees the same closed, enigmatic expression on the faces of many of her sitters as one sees in the portrait of a young debutante which she exhibited at the Goupil Gallery the following year. The girl, who is formally dressed and stands beside a porcelain turkey, her arms hanging like leaden weights, has the hopeless look of someone who feels herself to be pitilessly observed; her resigned anguish could be Romaine's own. (As Mahonri Sharp Young observed in *Apollo* magazine, Romaine seemed to be painting her own despair.) Since Romaine was wealthy enough to have the luxury of choosing her subjects, she might have responded unconsciously to such a quality in a particular face; perhaps she imposed it arbitrarily. At any rate, what one knows about these people: the Baroness Émile d'Erlanger,

Elisabeth de Gramont, Paul Morand, Natalie Barney, and Anna de Noailles, is very little. They are almost petrified statues, their eyes turned in upon themselves.

The exceptions are the faces Romaine wanted to caricature, like the smug and conceited Madame Errazuriz or the decorator Elsie de Wolfe, later Lady Mendl, whom Romaine painted in an absurd bonnet in juxtaposition with a white china goat; and the portrait of Una, Lady Troubridge, lover of Radclyffe Hall who wrote *The Well of Loneliness,* is a tour de force of ironic commentary.

There are three portraits in which the marriage of subject with mood works to the fullest enhancement of both. One is the portrait, painted in 1919, of the pianist Renata Borgatti, who was a close friend. She sits at the keyboard, profoundly lost in thought, her eyes closed; a powerful black figure leaning over the piano. Here the limited palette, the strong line, the somber mood, and the pared-down composition, strike the perfect chords. The second is "Madame Legrand au Champ des Courses," which probably did more than any other work to establish Romaine's reputation in Paris as a portraitist of subtlety and power, and which is now on permanent exhibit at the Musée du Petit Palais. Romaine met this society woman through the Princesse de Polignac and Robert de Montesquiou, both of whom adored her, while cordially detesting each other. The lady is returning from a day at the races. She sits on top of a gig, in black except for a rose thrust into her jacket, and somber despite an architectural marvel of a black hat which balances her form and the composition superbly. She is wealthy and fortunate, even loved. Yet her expression of wistful melancholy is more subtle than world weariness, more profound than disillusion; almost a coming-to-terms with life's limitations. It makes the work linger in the mind like a Debussy nocturne. The third is the 1923 self-portrait in which Romaine is wearing a black top hat. It is a completely honest and powerful self-evaluation.

Although Montesquiou considered her a thief of souls, implying an ability to steal into the hearts of her sitters and extract their most profound secrets, those moods Romaine Brooks portrayed most successfully were a reflection of her inner state. These were the psyches with which she was in harmony, and it was to these that she gave her delicacy of insights. For the rest, people she did not immediately understand, Romaine could be remarkably unobservant and intolerant.

"No she wasn't perceptive," said the Marchese Uberto Strozzi, who was a close friend of her old age and thought of her as a rock ("but a very charming and wonderful rock").

"She was too one-sided to be that. She didn't sympathize with people at all and would dismiss them for trivial reasons. She was very hard on people she thought silly and she decided Cocteau's drawings were silly, so she was finished with him."

When Romaine first met Cocteau in 1914 he was young, enthusiastic, relatively unknown, and just beginning to be noticed in the Parisian social-intellectual circles to which he aspired. She could see the Eiffel Tower from the glass-covered terrace of her mansion on the avenue du Trocadéro and had been contemplating it for some time. In a city of conformingly uniform lines, the tower was a rebel; bold, ugly, powerful, and stubbornly there. The fact that others were horrified that she should admire the Eiffel Tower, asking her why she didn't prefer something beautiful (like the palace of Versailles), seemed the persuasive argument for painting it. But Romaine needed someone to pose in front of it. Then she met Cocteau, probably at a party at Misia Sert's flat on the Quai Voltaire. Madame Sert had married for the third time. Her new husband was the Catalan painter Jose-Maria Sert, a close friend of Diaghilev, and the ballet impresario often brought Cocteau to their parties.

The conversation drifted to the Eiffel Tower, and it seemed that Cocteau had just written a poem about it. He seemed the perfect person to pose.

Romaine remembers that Cocteau was finicky about drafts and needed to be placated while he was posing with frequent cups of coffee and chunks of American chocolate layer cake.

Romaine was delighted with the portrait, which originally contained two other figures of women (she cut the canvas in half and exhibited the discarded section separately as "Jeunes Filles") and even more pleased when it was acquired by the Musée d'Art Moderne. She liked to quote Somerset Maugham to the effect that Cocteau would be remembered only because of her portrait of him.

She saw Cocteau as an outsider, with something of a schoolboy's air still about him; vulnerable and therefore someone to champion; and her portrait of him as a hollow-cheeked young introvert with a sharp chin and a scrawny neck, drooping in front of the steel-gray silhouette of the Eiffel Tower, is suffused with her own melancholic romanticism. Romaine did not see in his face the gleam of radical daring and the vital imaginative force that was to make him famous.

She misjudged him, Romaine says sorrowfully, and was saddened and horrified when she saw Cocteau's other side, that of the little boy who delighted in malicious gossip. He was not, after all, one of the world's walking wounded but one of its tormentors; he sided with those who threw the stones. He was spreading malicious rumors about her, and there was nothing she could do to defend herself, since she could hardly go around behind him saying it wasn't true. "So I had to let it pass." Montesquiou, who had never liked Cocteau, and had also suffered under the whiplash of Cocteau's devastating mimicry, and who had warned her against him, was right, after all. Cocteau was an *arriviste,* a social climber, and that said it all. So Romaine dismissed Cocteau from her life, demonstrating what her penetrating friend, the Marchese Strozzi, saw correctly: her tendency to sum up, oversimplify, and in condemning, misjudge.

Cocteau tried to mend the breach with Romaine several times. He sent her flattering letters, including an undated card which says simply, "I've written, 'There are people about whom one asks oneself, upon meeting them, how one could have lived without knowing them?' I write this to you."

Whenever he met her, he tried to reconcile with her. She used to meet him on board Lady So-and-So's yacht and he would take a chair next to her, but Romaine thought, "What's the use?"

Then Maugham, who did not know they had quarreled, invited them to the same lunch. Romaine came, determined to be difficult. She sat there in perfect silence through the whole meal; which didn't matter, because Cocteau was animated. "He was the life and death of every party," Alan Searle remarked, "because he couldn't stop talking."

Romaine's abortive friendship with Cocteau was an example in miniature of her encounters with Parisian society in general; that is to say, tangled, involving premature judgments on both sides, and doomed to fail. Romaine distrusted "the tribe called Society." This distrust had manifested itself at an early age in her immediate dislike for a new principal at her boarding school in New Jersey; a fat, silly woman who forced her unwelcome attentions upon Romaine only because (the child thought) she had snobbishly decided that Romaine's social status was worth the effort.

Such a distrust of society was not the result of a single casual encounter, but rather the complex response of the third generation to the brazen social-climbing of those who came before.

Grandfather Waterman was the original *arriviste*. His daughter Ella, while considering herself far above such mundane considerations as worldly status, was piously convinced that Socialism could not work because it would create discontent, instead of removing it. (It was in the nature of humankind to always want more, and people should learn, instead, to be thankful for what they had.) Ella was, of course, gratified to be the favorite of the governor's wife and also invited to dine with old French families of the finest breeding. Ella did not, like her father, believe that the American rich were more worthy by virtue of their money; what she believed was that the European aristocracy was more worthy, by virtue of its bloodlines.

Romaine looked at society with undeceived eyes, seeing its hypocrisy, its self-serving rationalizations, and its trivialities (she thought such people were garrulous bores). But while rebelling against society's strictures, she took her place in it, just the same.

That she was aware of embarking on a course that ran counter to her truest self, is the recurrent theme of her memoirs of this period. Why then, did she undertake the detested conventional life? Her answer was that when our ghosts no longer need to manifest themselves, it is because "they have found their way in, they are now one with us"; and, she continued, impose their will upon us. Romaine believed that her mother was controlling her actions in some supernatural way; not knowing that the child in her was still seeking her mother's approval, still accepting without question her mother's assumptions. Secretly, she still believed that Mother was Right.

The social climate in which Romaine found herself only served to increase the inner conflict. This was still Proust's world; of lives played out against the battleground of the right drawing room. To be accepted, one must conform to senseless rules, like employing a professional *poseur de cartes* (usually an impoverished member of a good family) to take around the thousand to fifteen hundred cards that, the rules decreed, must be left at other great houses each year.

One must learn self-defense, since beneath the civilized veneer it was a ferocious and cynical society, full of ruthless battles. The witty Comtesse Melchior de Polignac called it "the worldly circus," and in 1967 the American composer Ned Rorem, in his *The New York Diary*, still found that "French society consists of those who pronounce (Lord and Minoret), those who are pronounced upon (*les dames du monde*) and those who sum it up with 'the gift of the retort' (Cocteau, Noailles or the middle-class talents: Mauriac, Bourdet, etc.)."

Romaine persisted, because she was ambitious. She knew that a portrait painter, then as now, could only be as famous as the people who would pose for him. She had the example of John Singer Sargent, who lived across the road in Tite Street; and Sargent's Italian equivalent, Giovanni Boldini, who had achieved fame in Paris by judiciously committing to canvas the right faces of the *Belle Époque*. In order to have famous and influential sitters one must, like John Fothergill launching The Spreadeagle at Thame, meet the proper people and move in the proper circles. In short, one must court society.

Romaine was also vulnerable. Because of her childhood she was primed to see an insult in the most harmless remark, and was hypersensitive to criticism; yet more than usually needful of others' approval. There was another reason. As a little girl she had wondered whether the fat lady principal would go on cultivating her if she knew that Ella was eccentric and St. Mar was mad. As an adult she knew that she would be given *"une réputation"* and become the butt of sly looks and private innuendo if society discovered that she was deeply committed to loving her own sex. So she was forced to equivocate, play a certain role on the surface, acutely aware that she had a great many secrets she did not want unearthed. She detested her own hypocrisy and blamed "them" (the rest of the world) for forcing it upon her.

Romaine did not know what Natalie Barney had serenely discovered: that society would tolerate unconventional behavior as long as its outward forms were adhered to. Romaine had been taught, and believed, that daring and manners were mutually exclusive propositions. So she took a mansion on the fashionable avenue du Trocadéro (later, the avenue du Président Wilson) when she moved to Paris in 1905. She employed a butler and a chef, had first a carriage and then a chauffered car, went to the right parties, painted the right people, and was presented to an English monarch. She had photographs taken of herself as a lady of fashion, covered with feathers, white ermine and pearls, with a properly vapid expression. She conformed to society's outward forms: the cards sent and received, the invitations meticulously addressed, the formal and meaningless phrases at the ends of letters (*"Je vous prie d'agreer l'expression de mes sentiments les meilleurs"* was one of her particular abominations), while chafing under their constraints. She saw herself as a solitary, hardworking artist who only wants to be left alone, and who is made the butt of the world's jokes.

Those first years in Paris her life, she said, was exactly like a film she had seen of an underground animal whose burrow is uncovered on one side to allow inspection of him as he goes about his work. He continues, innocently unaware that he is being observed at length. So was she being spied upon and gossiped about and persecuted by the idle and malicious, an innocent victim of circumstance. Her eventual solution was to withdraw but, before that happened, Romaine suffered what seemed (to her) to be a succession of gratuitously bruising experiences with society. These encounters confirmed her view that "Hell is other people," as she wrote in her diaries years later.

"Like some curious animal in a cage I was at first stroked and admired, then jeered and jabbed at . . ."

Romaine first attracted notice shortly after she moved to Paris and began to decorate her mansion in a highly original manner that was inspired by the innovations of style she had seen at Tite Street, and which were years ahead of their time on both sides of the English

Channel. When he decorated Whistler's White House, the architect, Edward Godwin, took the then-radical step of painting the interior in one color: white. Oscar Wilde had done the same. "I have," he noted, "a dining room done in different shades of white, with white curtains embroidered in yellow silk; the effect is absolutely delightful and the room is beautiful."

Whistler and Godwin shared the view that daily life should be as governed by the esthetics of art as a painting. They found the Victorian overstuffed furniture, flowery wallpapers, heavy curtains, and tasteless pattern indiscriminately laid upon pattern violent assaults upon the eye. Whistler threw out the curtains to let in the pale London sunlight, painted his walls plain blue, gray, or black, and replaced thick carpets with simple Japanese mattings. Indeed his spare, elegant interiors owed a great deal to Oriental art.

Romaine, who had been momentarily taken by the medieval, found this simple, severe style in perfect harmony with her own mood and made imaginative use of it. She began to compose the interior of her house with the same general principles in mind, predictably choosing black, white, and gray. The effect, upon a society used to houses decorated in Louis XV or Louis XVI, with paneled walls, murals, brocades, and plenty of gold leaf, was a revelation. A fulsome newspaper account of her life, about 1911, gives almost as much space to a description of her house, as to her early struggles.

The salon was painted a delicate light gray with accents of black, and the only spots of color were the Old Master paintings on the walls. The house was a storehouse of beautiful old furniture found in antique shops (including Oriental pieces, after Whistler's pattern) and everything was designed by Romaine, to the last detail. The brocaded hangings were made to her specifications, and the soft velvet carpets on the stairs and in the hall (a plain light gray) were edged with a narrow black border she had designed herself.

Perhaps the most interesting feature of the house was the roof garden. The whole front, overlooking the city and the winding Seine, was of heavy plate glass, while at the back of the garden there was a mural decoration, which the artist had painted, representing a balcony. A crowd of people were about to step into the garden through a pergola made of filmy floating hangings in black. There were black supports and a balustrade of heavy, twisted white glass which gave a mysterious effect and kept up the illusion of spirits and sprites.

Romaine said that her only purpose in decorating her interiors was to bring them in harmony with her mood and provide potential backgrounds for her paintings. She was attempting an eclectic mix of styles; for massed shadow effects on light, misty backgrounds. "Each ensemble had its white accent which sent the half-toned figure back to a second plane. Colors I used only to show up these half tones, which alone interested me . . ."

She had no intention of making a career out of interior decoration, but soon found herself being asked to give lengthy advice on the choice of lamp shades and cushions. She tried to comply, even though she was more interested in general principals than specifics. What she considered a fever for arranging things was to embroil her in perhaps her most painful encounter with Parisian society; and the person in question was Henri Bernstein.

Henri Bernstein, "Monsieur H." in her memoirs, was the son of a rich Jewish businessman of Polish stock, and his mother was the daughter of a New York banker. Manet painted him when he was six and when he went to Cambridge University he was already known as a celebrated dandy who owned 147 pairs of trousers and spent his money on gambling.

By the time Romaine knew him, Bernstein, two years her junior, was famous in Paris as the playwright of highly melodramatic works in the boulevard tradition of the "eternal triangle." What his plays might lack in psychological plausibility, they compensated for in a sure dramatic sense. Bernstein was so prolific that for ten years (from 1904 to 1914), there was not an evening when a play of his was not being performed somewhere in Paris.

Bernstein wrote two plays in the aftermath of the Dreyfus affair, in 1894, which exposed the extent of anti-Semitism in France. One of them, Israel (1908), was the story of an anti-Semitic young aristocrat who, after publicly insulting a Jewish banker, discovered that the banker was his father.

Romaine took a lively interest in the theater, but her tastes ran to Russian dramatists, the works of the Italian poet Gabriele D'Annunzio, and "those great artists who are held, not by reality alone, but rather by its significance." She considered the work of the popular Bernstein to be totally insignificant; full of dramatized platitudes. She disliked his manner, his ceaseless self-promotion, and his smug conviction that he was sexually irresistible. She thought he was grotesque: "big features jutting forward from rounded shoulders, . . . green complexion, long arms and trembling hands . . ."

As chance would have it, Bernstein passionately admired Romaine, and particularly her decorating style. Since he was a friend of a friend, Romaine was persuaded to give him advice.

She went to his apartment reluctantly. Her theory was that an interior should reflect the psychology of its owner. Bernstein's flat, which was full of pretentious Empire furniture, suited him perfectly. Everything was in atrocious taste, but particularly the bedroom, with its great canopied bed with the columns on a dais, and then the tiny bathroom with a white porcelain bidet (conspicuous, since Bernstein was a bachelor and had installed it, presumably, for the benefit of guests), in the shape of a swan. Romaine's instinctive revulsion was followed by irritation and exasperation. Really, she told the persistent Bernstein, the only thing to do is throw the whole lot out and start again from scratch. Obviously, nobody is going to follow such drastic advice, she told herself, and she left, glad to be rid of the disagreeable business.

She had reckoned without the determination of Henri Bernstein. He did just as she directed. He gave all his furniture to the concierge, but now he did not know how to proceed, she was told. Romaine was obligated to help him refurnish.

"Knowing how futile it would be to touch on such subtleties as intervening tones, I set Monsieur H. in the dangerous direction of blacks and whites. Besides, was it appropriate that he should nestle in the mystery of grays?"

Bernstein carried out her scheme meticulously, and then invited her for lunch to see the final effect. She approved. It was all done to shock, in spectacularly bad taste. Even the menu was written on a black slate and, at the climactic moment, a dog was let into the room: a black-and-white Dane.

Romaine heartily hoped she had seen the last of Henri Bernstein, but this was not to be the case. She went every week to a celebrated literary salon conducted by Madame Muhlfeld, widow of a well-known journalist and one of three sisters, who had each married well.

They were Jewish, although Romaine did not know it. Madame Muhlfeld was ambivalent about it, according to André Germain, who knew her well and wrote about her in *La Bourgeoisie Qui Brûle*. She said that she was only one-fourth Jewish and "between her lips, the epithet of 'Jew' took on a pejorative sense."

Madame Muhlfeld had the most important literary salon in Paris before World War I, frequented by the poets Paul Valéry and Anna de Noailles, Cocteau, Jacques-Émile Blanche, the painter and writer; Marie Laurencin, Paul Claudel, André Gide, and François Mauriac, who called her salon, "our café."

According to Romaine, Madame Muhlfeld was tiny of stature, lame, and generally misshapen, but balanced upon her stunted figure was a huge head with classical features. She was, in fact, partially paralyzed, and because of that earned the nickname of *"La Belle Otarie"* (the beautiful sea lion), a play on words since there was a famous dancer of the time called *"La Belle Otéro."* Germain took a more benevolent view of her. "As fragile and minute as she was, her astonishing and magnificent face elevated her above all other women. Her beautifully formed features, her large Oriental eyes dreaming with the heavy memory of buried civilizations, her marvellous shower of hair, gave her a look both ancient and fabulous, as if she were a sacred courtesan. . . ."

Both agree, however, that Madame Muhlfeld gave compliments indiscriminately; in fact, buried her guests in a shower of them. While Romaine sat in tongue-tied silence, the hostess would shoot such compliments in her direction as, *"la magnifique et superbe artiste."*

Bernstein was eligible; Romaine was beautiful. It was obvious that he was attracted, but what to do about Romaine? Madame Muhlfeld decided to take the initiative. Why not marry Bernstein, she suggested to Romaine one evening at dinner. Romaine was affronted. In her memoirs, she said that she worded her refusal none too gently. She told her friends that what she said in the shock of the moment was, "I don't want to marry that dirty Jew."‡ It just came out before she knew what she was saying, she told people later.

It was a public insult, bound to become general knowledge since Madame Muhlfeld was Jewish herself. Nothing could have been more brutal, more calculated to add salt to wounds still raw from the Dreyfus affair. Nothing could have identified Romaine more damningly with the bigots (those who throw the stones), or placed her at a vaster distance from enlightened opinion.

Yet Romaine was unable to see it in this perspective; even to admit that she had been at fault. She uses the incident in her memoirs as proof of the vindictiveness and backbiting of French society. She is on the defensive and indignant. When she went to the next Muhlfeld party, she said, the hostess was no longer smiling. Everybody else in the circle looked equally rigid. They were whispering false stories about her behind her back.

"So they have found me out at last, I thought; they know how much I dislike being here. It serves me right for trying to look as if I enjoyed these dismal *corvées*. I was very angry with myself and on returning home, gave vent to my feelings by jerking down the curtains of my bedroom window, rings and all."

She was angry with herself, she believed, for pretending to like something she didn't. By transferring her anger to this issue, she could excuse herself and accuse the rest.

What Romaine could not bear to face were strong guilt feelings for having, in the folly of the moment, made such a cruel remark. She tried to justify herself to herself for the rest of her life. In old age, when she was living in Nice, she refused to return to Paris because, her friend the painter Édouard MacAvoy said, she thought she had enemies everywhere as a result of the Henri Bernstein incident. "I told her, 'But Romaine, he has been dead for years.' It didn't make any difference. She was convinced that 250 people were waiting for her with knives and revolvers."

The incident also demonstrates her inability to accept the idea that she had any part to play. The ideal image that she had substituted demanded that she be saintlike in her perfection. Saints do not get angry, they do not lash out at others in a rage; and so such acts

‡ *"Je ne veux pas épouser ce sale Juif."*

simply did not happen. Since she could take no genuine pride in the worthless person she felt herself to be, she had to invest in what the psychoanalyst Dr. Karen Horney calls a neurotic (or spurious) pride, in the image of herself as a noble being fated to be misunderstood and victimized: "I *had* to be the martyr," she said once. What was tragically imposed from without developed, by degrees, into the only way she could see herself.

The Henri Bernstein incident was one reason why Romaine decided that Parisian society, with its rigid formalities, its ritualized teas, dinners, and receptions (which she called grown-up games), was to be avoided at all costs. Since the conversation was so boring that she had memorized every ornamental flourish on Madame Muhlfeld's Japanese teapot, why go there? Or anywhere else?

To make a cutting retort was not characteristic of her. Her pattern was to withdraw from those who had offended her and into herself; to barricade herself against the world. "I would draw the curtains at the close of day and retire into my library. There for hours at a time I read and studied and tried to be as happy as I had once been in Capri . . . Indeed it was with the very stones that were finally flung at me, that I built up the strong walls of this inner sanctuary . . ."

But Romaine was not above making barbed forays into the enemy's territory. She shared her mother's quick sense of the ridiculous, but her humor centered itself around the poignant disappointments of life, those private personal tragedies that were the raw material for amusing stories told on oneself, with only an occasional flare of irritation which revealed how angry one was at having dared to hope for anything. Directed at others, her sense of humor had its subterranean purpose: the settling of old scores. People became grotesques, like Henri Bernstein with his green complexion and trembling arms, and there are two or three portraits in which her dislike for the sitters results in unmistakable caricature. The ridicule is usually so deft that the sitter is unlikely to see what is obvious to everyone else.

People said that Romaine disliked Madame Errazuriz on principal, simply because she was a socialite. Perhaps there was some rivalry between the two women, since Madame Errazuriz had been heard to declare that she was using black, white, and gray as a decorative scheme ten years before Romaine thought of it. Or perhaps it was simply the natural antagonism of strong personalities.

Madame Errazuriz was, her friends said, a very frightening woman whom everybody adored; a Chilean who had married into an enormously wealthy family and then bought houses in London and Paris which she ran, as she did her husband and daughter, with a whim of iron. At the turn of the century everyone was painting her portrait: Helleu, Sargent, and Boldini. Her taste in art was discriminating (she was an early and generous patron of Picasso) and she arranged a nearly priceless collection of paintings in rooms furnished starkly, but with great discrimination.

"A bunch of tightly packed peonies, in a glass goblet on a brass table, should have been painted by Manet. The curtains are made of sprigged white muslin. Every object on the tea table seemed likewise beautiful and simple—the great glass jar of marmalade, the champagne beakers and the brass-ended wooden trays," Cecil Beaton wrote in *The Wandering Years*, after visiting her house in Paris in 1935.

Beaton admired her taste and Bettina Bergery, who also met her in her final years, admired her courage: "She left Paris in her nineties to live in Chile, saying, 'I want you to remember me as I am, not when I am old,'" and her sense of the fitness of things: "She had a way of making just the exactly right comment about a subject. For her, everything in life was a question of proportion. Even behavior was 'disproportionate.'"

But to Romaine, Madame Errazuriz was a smug, vain, slightly ridiculous figure, who liked to dress up in absurdly overornamented clothes; small and squat, smothered under feathers, veiling and tassels, her tight mouth pursed into a smirk of self-satisfaction. It is doubtful whether Madame Errazuriz ever realized that she had been so mercilessly ridiculed.

There was another reason for Romaine's withdrawal from the world of tennis and titles, of kid gloves and calling cards. Her move to Paris in 1905, her purchase of an imposing house, and her assiduous attention to social obligations meticulously observed, had been in the service of a goal: to win a new love. She had lost her.

The affair, which seems to have had particular significance in Romaine's life, was the latest in a long line of love relationships with women, which began at St. Mary's Hall in New Jersey. Such affairs probably went no further than the silent agonies or rapturous moments alone that Romaine records, but a sexual initiation could have come soon afterward, in 1895. Having escaped from her mother and celebrated her freedom by defiantly taking biking lessons, the latest craze, Romaine had made one of her first solo trips in the Bois de Boulogne. In the middle of the park, something went wrong with the bike and Romaine was forced to make a stop at what was then known as the Pavillon Chinois. She gave her bike to a *chasseur* (servant) to have it repaired, sat down and started drinking a lemonade.

The room began to fill up and a particularly boisterous group of people came in. Romaine, who detested being on such close terms with noisy humanity, was about to leave when a beautiful woman, fashionably overweight, and covered with jewelry, came up to her table. She had the most alluring eyes Romaine had ever seen; "they actually dazzled one."

The woman, never named, fixed Romaine with a compelling look. Then she sat down at Romaine's table without a word. She ordered an *apéritif*, "and kept looking at me as she drank it . . ."

Romaine did not send the beautiful stranger away in indignation. She did not make her escape in embarrassed astonishment. She knew perfectly well what was involved when the stranger, with a ravishing smile, courteously suggested that they go for a drive in her carriage, and she could not have been too surprised to discover herself lunching with her new companion.

This might have been the moment when she discovered the sexual implications of love between women. Women of Romaine's generation would have had the greatest difficulty being initiated into physical love. Love between women would have been an even more shameful and impenetrable secret, and in such cases, the only hope for the young was to be taken in hand by older teachers, much as teenage boys used to be encouraged to look among their mothers' friends for their first mistresses.

Being a woman of her generation, Romaine would never have committed such a subject to paper. One can only assume that she indulged in physical love with other women, although, given her eventual partner, that is a safe assumption. The manner in which she made love to women is her secret.

In the record of this encounter with the seductive stranger, Romaine is having lunch. Then, with no warning, she seems to be on an upper floor, apparently a bedroom since something has gone wrong and the stranger is giving vent to her rage by throwing a set of toilet articles into the quiet street below. Servants appeared and recovered the ivory-backed brushes, combs, and looking glasses with such matter-of-factness that Romaine suspected it must happen often.

Romaine gives no reason for this display of temper. Did Romaine repulse her advances? Was Romaine, as unskilled and unversed as she must have been, a disappointing lover? Insufficiently jealous? As elsewhere in the memoirs, Romaine prefers to draw a veil over delicate matters by ignoring an incident's implications.

She is almost as uncommunicative about a second incident, which took place later that day when they were back at the Pavillon Chinois having dinner. In the middle of the meal, a tall dark woman who had been watching them ominously rushed up and threw a bottle of water at Romaine, hitting her nose. There was blood and Romaine was taken off to the ladies' room to be sponged with cold water.

It was a lover's quarrel, the beautiful stranger said. The tall, dark woman was insanely jealous, that was all. Why, she wanted to know, hadn't Romaine hit her back? To the seductress, the incident must have presented the delightful prospect of two women battling it out for her favors. But to Romaine, it would have been unpleasantly reminiscent of Ella's scenes. All Romaine wrote was, "It was hard to make her understand that I had never hit anyone in my life; also that I was ashamed of a row in such a crowded place."

The origins of homosexuality in women have been studied far less than in men, and competing arguments are presented: that it results from a disturbance of the endocrine glands, or is a case of early conditioning. Without entering the debate over whether lesbianism is always caused by unconscious neurotic factors, or is the result of free choice, a field in which I am not qualified to argue, I believe that Romaine's particular case fits the hypothesis put forward by Dr.

213

Charlotte Wolff, who studied over a hundred case histories and wrote about them in *Love Between Women*.

The dominant pattern, Dr. Wolff found, was a girl whose relationship with her mother was poor to start with, so that she does not develop a vital sense of inner security. Her father plays an insignificant role since he is either weak, immature, or actually absent, as Major Goddard was. The third factor in her development is that her mother prefers a son.

Like the women Dr. Wolff studied, Romaine was placed in the impossible position of depending for her approval on a mother who would always compare her unfavorably with a boy. Instead of taking the path some girls adopt, that of becoming outwardly "feminine" and competing with her mother for male approval, Romaine developed a hatred of men, born out of original envy for St. Mar. She despised her own sex, which Ella did not value, rejected its trappings and identified with the powerful sex. She became a tomboy for Ella, who would have preferred a boy.

What Romaine wanted was what she had never had: Ella's all-accepting love. "The homosexual woman is generally looking for a mother . . . and, in many instances, the mutual dependence of the couple . . . is more important than the sexual satisfaction which each may obtain from the other," Anthony Storr wrote in *Sexual Deviation*. "Emotional incest with the mother is indeed the very essence of Lesbianism," according to Dr. Wolff. Only this can account for Romaine's profound sense of having been cheated by life and her adamant refusal to forgive Ella. This must be at the core of her search for another woman; an ideal relationship to substitute for the one she never had.

At any rate, for her the hunt was on, and as so often happens, she was recognized by the women she was looking for. She might be picked up casually in a restaurant in the Bois de Boulogne or she might, in the case of the love affair which brought her to Paris, have met her adored one in the very best circles.

The lady was a musician, very knowledgeable about art, an American ten years Romaine's senior, who had married into the French nobility. Romaine does not say, but she was the former Winnaretta Singer, daughter of the inventor of the sewing machine, now the formidable and rich Princesse Edmond de Polignac. According to Francis Steegmuller in *Cocteau: A Biography*, she had a Dantesque profile and "beneath her hatchet-like exterior and nasal voice, she had a considerable musical culture; her drawing room was the scene of frequent concerts both classical and avant-garde."

Romaine painted her. She found her profile both enchanting and disquieting. "The head is bent forward with profile emerging from out a profusion of dark hair," she wrote, describing a photograph of her idol. "The lowered eye escapes detection. The nose is arched and noble, but the mouth with its protruding lower lip shows strong atavistic ruthlessness ever active in self-defence . . ."

The lady had a forcible character and a dry wit and Romaine could not understand why she would choose to squeeze herself into the narrow box that marriage into French nobility implied. But, like Ella, the princess found impeccable bloodlines the *ne plus ultra* of her ambition: she "valued this borrowed remnant of other days above all else . . . and willingly cramped herself to fit its form."

Since social position impressed this princess, Romaine would acquire it. She cultivated people assiduously and her salon was soon filled with marquises—genuine or otherwise—princesses, dukes, and duchesses; suffering their intolerable garrulity in the pursuit of a larger goal.

Then Romaine was offered an unparalleled opportunity to impress: She was presented to King Edward VII.

It happened in 1908, when Romaine was staying at Carlsbad. She was invited to a tea party somewhere near Marienbad. The king would be there. One must dress accordingly. Romaine, who liked having photographs taken of herself at critical moments in her life, recorded the clothes she bought for the occasion: a long white dress enriched with embroidery and an ornately flowered hat perched on a mass of curls. One end of a long black veil swept over the hat and fell below the waist, and the other end was looped gracefully over an arm. She fingered a delicate parasol, and her face, as fashion dictated, was perfectly vacuous.

The king arrived and Romaine curtseyed deeply, then observed him with her intent and secretive gaze. He was, she said, thickset, ruddy and middle-aged and immensely dignified; he had that "limited perfection" many Englishmen learn to acquire. He had a very paintable face, with watery blue eyes, and she briefly considered painting him, then decided against it (as she did a number of others, including Montesquiou, Somerset Maugham, Georges Clemenceau, twice premier of France; Gertrude Stein, and Ezra Pound.)

The king was just as observant, and Romaine felt herself being summed up with "the most royal inaccuracy possible."

At tea, she sat next to Lord Admiral Fisher who confided, by way of introduction, that the queen always called him "Jacky Fish." The conversation ambled along until the moment when a small vase of field flowers suddenly fell over. The admiral tried ineffectually to right it. Romaine sprang to his aid and forced the vase upright with a vigorous gesture. The king was admiring. "We always need the aid of the ladies, don't we?" he asked the admiral.

After tea, the king came over to talk to Romaine. What did she think of the Royal Watercolour Society? Romaine, who had never heard of it, managed to consider that it ranked very highly indeed. The king asked what she was working on and she told him about the portrait of Madame Cloton Legrand (which she later exhibited at the Galeries Durand-Ruel).

"He knew her and evidently some thought amused him, for after repeating her name, he laughed heartily. Without knowing precisely why, I laughed too."

The king laughed because Madame Legrand was an "awful old cat," one of Romaine's friends wrote after hearing about the incident. Romaine must have shared this opinion of the lady, who was however a close friend of Robert de Montesquiou, the eccentric poet, art critic, and homosexual who is considered to have been the model for Proust's character, Baron de Charlus. Montesquiou so admired Romaine's portrait of Madame Legrand that he hung it in his famous Paris house, the Pavillon des Muses. After his death, Romaine bought it back.

But Montesquiou detested the Princesse de Polignac and, after Romaine had exhibited the portrait (present whereabouts unknown), he wrote in *Le Figaro* that the princess looked rather like Nero, only much more cruel; "one who dreamed of seeing his victims stitched up by sewing machines."

Romaine also believed that the princess was ruthless. Perhaps the impossibility of ever meeting the princess' exacting standards presented the ultimate challenge. There seems to have been very little contact between them. Like royalty, the lady exacted homage and Romaine genuflected. Afraid of ridicule, Romaine never told the lady of her secret fear, that Ella was still directing her life, or what she felt in moments of particular unhappiness: that Ella's inimical power had somehow become embodied in that friend. "At times," Romaine said revealingly, "I even thought she resembled my mother."

The end of the affair is not recorded, but the fact that it appears to have been so obviously motivated by Romaine's search for a second Ella must have doomed it from the start. Romaine only states that she set to work with increasing frenzy, filling her canvases with sad and dejected figures, while she struggled to regain her equilibrium. The loss of the princess caused a further contraction into herself and a rejection of those whose company would only serve as a painful reminder of what might have been.

One of the few people Romaine went on seeing afterward was Aunt Minnie (Lady Anglesey), whom she had met several years earlier at Versailles, a delicate, old porcelainlike figure, seated amid clusters of the pale and delicate white porcelain flowers she loved to collect.

She, too, was an American, with a finely chiseled and aristocratic face which Romaine contemplated painting. Conversation with her was as amusing as it was exasperating; "with each slight puff of her breath, feathery thoughts were wafted from place to place . . . A vocabulary was not necessary; mere chirping and twittering answered just as well."

Lady Anglesey was perfectly willing to pose, but she wanted to be painted as Boldini had pictured her when she was thirty. Romaine wanted to record the beauty that age had given her; and so nothing was done. But Romaine went on visiting her at Versailles for several years, not completely able to abandon the idea.

Romaine did not say exactly when she met Natalie Barney and Natalie didn't remember, but it is likely that they met just before the start of World War I because the two women whose portraits were cut out of the Cocteau portrait, which Romaine was painting in

1914, could have been the Barney sisters. The resemblance is slight, but the circumstantial evidence is strong: the seated figure wears a beautiful pendant which exactly matches the one Romaine gave to Laura Dreyfus Barney, younger sister of Natalie, and which that lady gave to the National Collection of Fine Arts in 1972. It comprises two stones of black onyx surrounded by diamonds, hanging by a black velvet ribbon, and was designed by Romaine and made by Mauboussin, 29, Place Vendôme, Paris. The standing figure that could be Natalie wears a plumed hat and what looks like a tie. She leans against the railing, looking introspective but certainly independent.

They called Natalie "the wild girl from Cincinnati." She was known all over Paris for her wealth, social connections, poetry, aphoristic writings, and scandalously unorthodox life. Romaine even knew what Natalie Barney looked like, since she had often seen her out walking in the Bois de Boulogne followed by an insignificant little woman dressed in Oriental clothes who, Romaine discovered later, Natalie fancied embodied all the splendors of the East when she danced, though Romaine privately considered her performance inferior.

Romaine was predisposed to like her long before they met, if only because society made it so plain that it did not. At one of Aunt Minnie's receptions, which, according to Romaine, were usually patronized by American society women of the pouter-pigeon variety (her cartoonist's eye summing up the full-bosomed, sway-backed silhouette of the Edwardian female), Romaine overheard one stiff comment that Natalie would be received again in society when she returned to her mother's friends.

"Looking around at these smug and puffed-out members of society, I decided that Natalie Barney had doubtless made more inspiring friends elsewhere."

One afternoon, Natalie Barney herself was in the group Aunt Minnie had invited to take tea, eat cakes, and play cards. They went home in the same car; and that was the beginning.

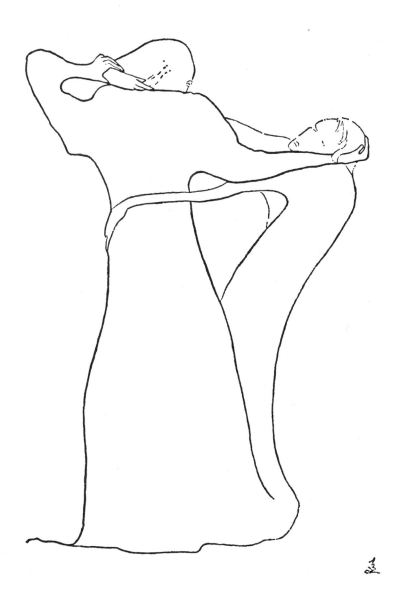

The Dead Friend

14

He changed the world about me and lifted me from a state of deep despondency. (*Memoirs*)

. . . I haven't the strength to come back to a place which saw the birth and death of so many illusions and so many good intentions. Everything has become only a very distant dream . . .*

It is much easier to imagine that Gardone Riviera is a vast stage set from a nineteenth-century comic opera—spread out on a hill beside a lake—than to believe that it is real. Yet it does exist, and so one was right after all to innocently believe in that papier-mâché world, where grape vines climb over wrought-iron balconies, the sun sinks in an orgy of violet, and tenors with voices like purple plums hurl banalities at black-eyed gypsies. Common sense reels, and artistic judgment is powerless before the improbability of Gardone.

I drove there one evening in late fall through a blizzard. The countryside out of Milan is a flat, monotonous plain with only an occasional crumbling farm building or church tower to break its horizontal uniformity. The cold had stripped the earth bare and clouds rolled down and smothered it; snow fogged the landscape like white smoke

---

* " . . . je n'ai pas la force de revoir ni de me réinstaller dans un endroit qui a vu naître et mourir tant d'illusions et tant de belles intentions. Tout n'est devenu qu'un rêve très lointain . . ." Letter from Romaine Brooks to Gabriele d'Annunzio, September 1910.

and one advanced into a void, in which clouds had become the swirling land.

I awoke the next morning in Gardone to a clear blue sky. I looked out of my hotel window onto trees, flowers, olive trees in fruit, palms, the orange-tiled roofs of buildings and walls bleeding orange and brown; a lake glittered in the still air. The foothills of the Alps are in the background, covered with snow; but through some fluke of nature the area surrounding the lake has a subtropical climate and leaves stay on the trees all year round. The perimeter of the lake has been developed with expensive hotels but a kilometer up the hillside there is the old village of Gardone, with its narrow winding streets, its wrought-iron balconies, its ruined walls gently crumbling under the weight of a lushly flowering rose, its creaking lanterns and rotund peasants in soiled overalls and caps jammed on their heads, sitting at tables outside a trattoria. Across from this village, rising against a tapestry of Lombardy poplars and blue-green hills, is the monument to the memory of Gabriele d'Annunzio.

It is called Il Vittoriale Degli Italiani, which translates roughly as The Victory Monument of the Italians, and, like the village in which it is so aptly situated, it presents the same challenge to one's sense of the probable. It is a fantastic memorial to one man's megalomania, a preposterous ship of death. It is the tomb in which Gabriele d'Annunzio sealed every random act of his life, barricading himself against the horror of oblivion. It is the completely characteristic response of a man whose extraordinary gifts as poet, dramatist, novelist, essayist, orator, philosopher, and man of action were poured out over his life, as if to blot out persistent inner voices. His shortcomings were on the same heroic scale. He was capable of the tenderest love and the most cynical treachery; of sublime exaltation and maniacal despair; of the most delicate insights into human nature and a willful ignorance of his own motives that was almost suicidal. He saw himself as a martyred genius, comparing himself with Napoleon and Dante.

Yet one cannot jump to the conclusion, as some did, that he was a fraud. His poetry in particular has established a permanent place for him in Italian literature, and *Alcyone* is considered the best book of Italian poems since Leopardi's *Canti*. D'Annunzio's paradoxical aspects reflected much of the brilliance and the most glaring shortcom-

Ida Rubinstein, 1917. (Charles Phillips; National Collection of Fine Arts)

*Renata Borgatti au Piano, circa
1920.* (National Collection of
Fine Arts)

*Miss Natalie Barney,
L'Amazone, 1920.*
(Musée du Petit Palais, Paris,
France)

Una, Lady Troubridge, 1924. (National Collection of Fine Arts)

Marchese Uberto Strozzi, 1961. (National Collection of Fine Arts)

ings of the Italian national character. For many Italians, he came to symbolize the mystique of patriotism. He was the hero who would transform their reality into a vision of true grandeur by his act of self-immolation. Grandeur and heroism are not words in much currency today, which is perhaps one reason why, outside Italy, Gabriele d'Annunzio's memory has disappeared, despite all his efforts, eclipsed by the cataclysm of World War II, which his extreme right-wing political views and support of Mussolini indirectly helped to further. He died in 1938 just before it began.

D'Annunzio moved to Gardone Riviera after World War I and spent the remaining seventeen years of his life constructing his own memorial in what he was pleased to call "living stones." He used an old country house as the kernel for a small universe of arches, columns, walls, allegorical statuary, pillars, tombs, fountains, steps, bells, tiled courtyards and paths, a museum, a library, an amphitheater where his plays could be produced, and a still-unfinished mausoleum, looking like a half-submerged submarine, for the mortal remains of his body and those of ten other men who fought with him in World War I. A pillar commemorates the rear-guard battle he fought at Piave; another symbolizes calm before danger. The plane in which he flew over Vienna on the first propaganda raid (he dropped leaflets instead of bombs) hangs in the auditorium. The Fiat in which he guided his followers to battle is mounted in the courtyard. The boat that figured in the assault on Fiume in 1920 was ingeniously taken apart and reassembled plank by plank on the side of a hill overlooking the lake. No object that might serve to make the passage of his life, however trifling, and no foot of space was overlooked, that might be consecrated to the greater glory of Gabriele d'Annunzio.

D'Annunzio's private rooms preserve the moment of his death thirty-six years ago. There sit the spectacles on the writing desk, the quill pen, the pencils, the toothbrushes, the soap. The Chinese silk robes he liked to wear, carefully pressed and moth-balled, hang in the wardrobe. Each object on his bedside table is placed exactly as he left it. The last written papers and the last works in preparation, are laid out carefully on the table of his studio. There is an old retainer, a man with cheeks like wrinkled crab apples and a smile of fanatical devotion, who cares for the 30,000 books of the library, who dusts each of the thousands of objects, the hundreds of pictures, and plumps up the dozens of pillows. Then he goes out of the old house, carefully closing the brown wooden shutters and locking all the doors behind him.

So he lies embalmed, this latter-day Pharaoh—whose servant has willingly walled himself up in the same tomb—a man who paradoxically thought of himself as an outcast. The theme of martyrdom occupied one of his major works, and D'Annunzio devoted a room of his house to lepers (in the Middle Ages a leper was considered a sacred being whom God had touched, and he used the word in this sense). A marble statue of St. Sebastian stands beside a bed on a dais, surrounded by chamois leather curtains. The bed was in the shape of a coffin and the room was the one to which he often went to be alone.

D'Annunzio was correct in supposing that visitors would be affected by the weight of such accumulated detail. After walking through these rooms, heavily draped and curtained and carpeted, which suffocate the senses with their single insistent, overpowering theme, one does indeed begin to believe that Il Vittoriale is a city peopled with dead souls (*La città morta* is one of D'Annunzio's works, and it was Romaine's favorite). But the effect is the reverse of that intended. D'Annunzio could not postulate a universe where immortality might be synonymous with change. With indefatigable zeal, he hurled himself at his unattainable goal. So one admires the *trompe-l'oeil* cleverness of his creation, the ingenious perfection of the discarded carapace, but with detachment. One wonders about a man who could inscribe, "I have what I have given away" (*Io ho quel che ho donato*) over the main gateway of Il Vittoriale; and asks oneself how much he really understood.

Gabriele d'Annunzio was born in Pescara in the Abruzzi in 1863, and was writing poetry before he was out of school. He published his first book of verses at the age of 16, following this early success by an outpouring of poems, lyrics, short stories and novels. He established his literary reputation with *Il trionfo della morte* (*The Triumph of Death*) at the age of twenty-nine. By then he was in Rome and making his name as a brilliant journalist.

One of the turning points in his life came in 1896 when, already married, he met Eleonora Duse and embarked on a famous affair. She was the inspiration for a series of plays and performed the leading roles with great success in Italy and France. D'Annunzio became a deputy in the Italian parliament, where he was establishing himself as a compelling orator. He was already becoming a legendary figure, not only for his accomplishments but the heroic scale of his debts and love affairs. When Romaine Brooks met him in 1909, D'Annunzio had just moved to voluntary exile in France, leaving Eleonora behind, and was having an affair with a wealthy Russian woman, Nathalie de Goloubeff.

He was, a French actress said who met him, short and somewhat plump, with small shoulders and rounded hips. He had tiny feet and there was an impression of well-padded arms and legs that added to the disconcertingly feminine aspect of his appearance. In addition, he was extraordinarily vain, and his wardrobe would have been elaborate, even for a courtesan: an endless series of meticulously matched outfits for every hour of the day and every imaginable occasion.

His head had the fine modeling that would have inspired an ancient sculptor, but there was something morbidly sallow about his pock-marked skin; something repellent about the pale, bluish-green eyes, with their almost invisible lashes and eyebrows. To be blunt, he was short, fat, and ugly. Yet, in attempting to explain why so many women found D'Annunzio irresistible, the actress, who seemed just as susceptible to his charm, cited an "extraordinary verbal power" and the "musical timbre of his voice."

Romaine met him one day at a lunch given by the Italian artist Capiello, whose highly colored posters were having a fashionable vogue. She had read D'Annunzio's books although (she wrote) it took a considerable stretch of the imagination for her to understand the masochistic agonies of his doomed lovers. But whether she entirely liked D'Annunzio's work was secondary. He was the center of malicious gossip in Paris, which naturally disposed Romaine to defend him. She too considered herself an exile, even if living in a palace; an "exile from nowhere."

During the meal they were seated on the same side of the table and whenever she could, Romaine would lean back in her chair to examine him at length.

She does not seem to have been put off by his ugliness, his small-ness, or his peacocklike manner of dressing so foreign to her own tastes. She does not seem to have found his conversation particularly mesmerizing either; what struck her about him at once was the almost superhuman energy that manifested itself in the slightest gesture. When D'Annunzio picked up a knife and fork, they became weapons with which he ravaged his food, and when he declined a dish, the force of his "No!" shook his body. He seemed to Romaine like an elemental force of nature; someone from another epoch.

She also noticed that when D'Annunzio spoke to a woman, the most beguiling smile would transform his face. But when he with-drew into himself, as he did from time to time, his mouth would pull downward into what she described as the bitter pleat (*le pli amer*). She had never seen such an acerbic, crucified look.

Romaine was simply curious about him, that was all, and he was making no attempt to charm her. He saw her, she said, as just an-other society woman, and not even the voluptuous type he fancied. They might never have become friends but for a casual remark which D'Annunzio made after lunch. Capiello was showing his brilliantly colored canvases when D'Annunzio suddenly leaned over and whispered, "And to think how much can be expressed without any color at all!"

The comment summed up Romaine's artistic philosophy with such accuracy that she found herself inviting him to come and see her work. D'Annunzio was obviously surprised and amused at the idea that she was a painter. But he expressed a polite interest and they set a date.

Having invited him, Romaine had her usual attack of stage fright. The characters of his novels lived and died on a heroic scale. If it were not for D'Annunzio's unerring sense of humor, Romaine wrote, the emotional intensity of his works would have verged on the ridicu-lous. But there they were, larger-than-life figures whose passions spilled blood all over the page. Romaine mentally compared them with her own pale, melancholic, life-denying creatures and decided that it would be ludicrous to hope that D'Annunzio would look at her work twice. By the time he arrived, she was prepared for the poet to be polite but evasive.

D'Annunzio could not have been more flatteringly impressed. As soon as he entered the room, he went up to the portraits and began to compose a poem to each in turn, by way of a dedication. It was the beginning of a friendship which lasted for thirty years.

That year in Paris was, D'Annunzio said later, "the period of my great debauch." He had always been a Don Juan, according to his lifelong companion and secretary Thommaso Antongini (*Quaranta Anni con D'Annunzio*), but now his urge for new conquests had become compulsive. He would promise a woman anything in order to succeed: that he would divorce his wife; that he would make her the heroine of a new novel. He would make up a flowery new name for her, like Nontivoglio or Meliadusa. There were at least six Donatellas and unnumbered Amarantas. He sent flowers and, if the woman were particularly impressive, a pet as a gift, usually a dog. He bombarded her with telegrams. Most of all, he wooed her with words. He was, Antongini said, so extraordinarily persuasive and seemed so sincere, that each new woman believed him—against the evidence.

Yet, behind the flattery and the seeming sincerity, was a sinister undertone which Antongini reports on with apparent approval. It seems that D'Annunzio never, or almost never, meant a word he said. When Antongini once gave D'Annunzio an onyx cameo representing Venus and Mars "in that special posture which, Roderigo Borgia, the cardinal, described as 'a dreadful sin, but a most ingenious and intelligent combination of two people,'" D'Annunzio accepted it with the comment that he always used such "scabrous objects" in seduction. "These are my working tools." (Quoted in *The Poet as Superman* by Anthony Rhodes.)

At that stage of their friendship, Romaine took the rumors of D'Annunzio's predatory amours calmly, listening with amused disapproval when he talked about them. She thought his boasting showed bad taste, and she could not understand why a man who was so discriminating in other ways showed such a lack of it in his choice of mistresses. But if he hoped to make her jealous, he was unsuccessful. She simply dismissed his philandering as another of his rococo characteristics.

The year they met, Romaine was moving into a peak period in her life. Her work was beginning to yield the fruit of dedicated effort, to gain her influential admirers and a reputation as a highly original talent. She was going to build a new studio in her house on the avenue du Trocadéro. She was going to buy a new house by the sea. Perhaps make a trip to America. Her letters are postmarked from Florence, Spain, Versailles, Monte Carlo, and London (where she had an exhibition in the summer of 1911). She was thinking of establishing a home for abandoned children in London not, as she explained to D'Annunzio, because she liked children that much, but because she had some theories about raising them that she would like to try out. Didn't he think "Drucilla" was a pretty name for a girl? She was giving parties and at work on some of her best canvases.

D'Annunzio's enthusiasm for her work might well have given her the courage to agree to the exhibition at the Galeries Durand-Ruel; it certainly added to her zest. Like Virginia Woolf before the publication of a new novel, Romaine's panic before the ultimate test that an exhibition, or even the visit of a famous man to her studio, represented, teetered on the edge of madness. When D'Annunzio praised her canvases in words that seemed to demonstrate an almost uncanny understanding of her spirit, it was the vindication she had dreamed of for years. She had always believed that only the most delicate sensibilities could appreciate her work and here was the proof. A wave of grateful relief was followed by the intoxicating thought that she must indeed be a very great painter if such a great man thought so. No wonder she liked him.

From the start, they enjoyed each other's company enormously. She would invite him to her parties and then monopolize him for hours discussing the English poets, teasing him, joking with him, and telling him her most irresistible anecdotes. "Like you, I don't laugh any more," she wrote a year later. "Do you remember how we used to spend hours laughing with each other? How delightful you were! I remember each change of mood on your face, so full of charm and infinite expression . . ."

She would sing him Debussy's songs, or they would go riding or take long drives through the Bois de Boulogne. They went to a fair at Versailles one afternoon and Romaine shot down one of the egg-shells bobbing over the jets of water of a fountain. Her prize was a glass bowl containing a tiny red fish, which she gave to D'Annunzio.

He named it St. Sebastian on the spot and carried it back with elaborate care.

He gave her books, a dog they named Puppy, a photograph of himself as a teen-ager, inscribed "The child at the guitar, the little poet-musician who turned out so badly"; and two photographs of himself in his early twenties; a slight figure in stark white, glimmering against a romantically black forest, surrounded by the delicate and ascetic silhouettes of white Russian wolfhounds.

She used to send him great baskets of fruit. ("I shall haunt you," she wrote, "with a great plate of fruits which every evening, whether you are alone or not, will be tipped over your naked body, battering you about, and not one will enter your mouth. That will be my revenge!")

D'Annunzio did for Romaine what John Fothergill had accomplished in Rome: He showed her the alternative to melancholic resignation. "Indifference is my normal state," she wrote to him. "I can shut myself up for months and not see a soul," but this proud resignation hid a longing for what she felt had been denied her: an existence in which she might be happy at last. One of her favorite quotations came from Keats's *Ode to a Nightingale*: "Charm'd magic casements, opening on the foam/Of perilous seas, in faery lands forlorn." Since she was convinced that life's riches would always be denied her, it would take an act of magical power to wrench away the veils separating her from the bliss one might glimpse in a dream, or in the vision of a poet.

D'Annunzio managed to make that world real for her. "He changed the world about me . . ." The force of his energy tore away the barriers between her and life, at least temporarily; and she could experience what she had not been able to feel on Capri, had in fact taken as a personal affront: the beauty of life. His poet's intuitive sense became the lodestone by which she could breathe, taste, bathe herself in a sea of colors; take a child's artless pleasure in being. It was not to last, but that it could happen at all, seemed like a miracle.

Her memoirs speak of his character in the most generous terms. He was, she said, completely incapable of petty prejudice and unable to speak unkindly of anyone. He detested what he called the Gallic wit and would take her to task whenever she indulged in such mocking humor.

". . . I remember our discussing the *Titanic* disaster. I mentioned a woman who, it was said, had managed to escape in an all but empty boat, after having persuaded the boatman to row quickly away from the sinking ship. 'What a coward!' I exclaimed, echoing the general verdict. '*Ma che!*' retorted D'Annunzio. 'How can she be courageous if she is born timid? How can you judge her if you don't know her?'"

His servants were devoted to him. Whenever he rang his bell, they would fall all over each other in their zeal to be the first to answer it. He, in turn, went to great lengths to avoid hurting their feelings. He kept a row of small bird cages on the windowsill of his sitting room, and when Romaine asked why he didn't put all the birds into one large cage, D'Annunzio replied that he could not possibly do that. Each specimen belonged to a different servant and, "They want me to show interest in each of their birds separately."

Romaine found his amorality harmless, his extravagance innocent and childlike, and his sense of the ridiculous, irresistible. Bit by bit, she began to assume the role of chief confidante and to supplant the *"maîtresse en titre"* who had figured most prominently in D'Annunzio's life for the previous two years: Nathalie de Goloubeff.

D'Annunzio had met her in the international social circles he cultivated. She was twenty-five, blond, and had a statuesque way of holding her chin that Rodin captured in a bust he made of her. She had the almost Grecian beauty (the broad brow, the short, straight nose, the grave and almost sexless stare, the prettily modeled chin) which his epoch fervently admired. Nathalie de Goloubeff sang divinely, and her extremely rich husband had the further virtue of being incapable of jealousy. Romaine dismissed her as "a beautiful statue," but for a time D'Annunzio endowed her with every virtue the way, Romaine said, he was inclined to do. He would rename some mistress, "La Bella Cigna Nera" (The Beautiful Black Swan), and then Romaine would discover that the lady had nothing more distinctive than a long neck.

D'Annunzio renamed Madame de Goloubeff "Donatella," wrote rapturous letters in praise of her charm, her voice, her immortal soul and her physical divinity, and convinced her that she could not live without him.

When D'Annunzio moved to Paris in voluntary exile, it was, he insisted, to be near his Donatella. Perhaps he meant it. What Donatella realized, after he had been there for several months, was that he was not her possession, a captive celebrity to be reserved for a few choice friends and worn, so to speak, like a badge, but a thoroughly independent figure who was cutting a swathe in Parisian social circles.

Their idyl of bliss had been flawed from the start. The first months of ecstasy were followed by increasingly bitter quarrels during which, Donatella discovered, D'Annunzio could become vicious and unscrupulous. Then, he would disappear. "Please be indulgent," he wrote once. "A moment comes in love when one has either to die or commit murder. I understand that very well. The middle road is to flee."

The theme of killing or being killed in love was almost a leitmotiv for D'Annunzio. His inscription on one of Bakst's sketches for D'Annunzio's play, *The Martyrdom of Saint Sebastian,* reads: "Each must kill his love in order that it may be reborn seven times more ardent." (*Il faut que chacun tue son amour pour qu'il revive sept fois plus ardent.*)

Nevertheless, the period of D'Annunzio's "great debauch" was exquisite agony for this pathetically insecure woman. As Donatella sensed him slipping from her grasp, her determination to hold on to him became fanatical, deathlike in its grip.

Donatella was ignored because she had worn out everyone's sympathies. In a society where the one inadmissible act was an undisciplined display of emotion, Donatella's excesses had made her an object of ridicule. It was said that she made scenes everywhere D'Annunzio went, that she carried a gun so as to kill any woman she found him in bed with, and that, one morning, after being out all night, D'Annunzio had found her curled up on his doorstep.

D'Annunzio appeared to feel the same contempt. He complained to everyone who would listen that it was insupportable; Donatella had become a tyrant. How, he asked his friends, could he be rid of her?

In the summer of 1910 Romaine took a house, the Villa St. Dominique, outside the village of Moulleau, five kilometers from the summer resort of Arcachon on the Bay of Biscay. It was not a particularly beautiful coastline. Barren sand dunes gave way to a thick, impenetrable, and desolate forest. But it was isolated. It was a harmonious solitude for Romaine, who felt herself at peace in the garden, where the only sounds to be heard were the grate of cicadas and the rush of the sea. Because it had three ancient pines in the garden, she had renamed it "The Three Writhing Pines" (Les trois pins tordus) and moved in with her furniture, her paint brushes, her cook, and her British chauffeur, Bird.

One night early in July 1910, D'Annunzio made a cloak-and-dagger departure from Paris. He registered in one hotel, then slipped out of the back door to another and took the same rapid route through a third. At the last moment he made a dash for the railway station and caught the Sud Express, traveling under the pseudonym of M. Guy d'Arbes. He arrived at the Villa St. Dominique the following morning.

The degrees by which the friendship between Romaine Brooks and Gabriele d'Annunzio progressed, can be seen in dim outline against what evidence remains of those weeks at the Villa St. Dominique in the summer of 1910. There is, to begin with, an account in the memoirs, in which ironic amusement has long since triumphed over feeling. In sharp, clear pencil strokes, Romaine simplifies, minimizes, and caricatures to present an acceptable outline to the outside world.

In contrast to this are the 123 letters and 148 telegrams† from Romaine to Gabriele in the archives at Il Vittoriale (many undated) that give a confused, tortuous, and infinitely more complex picture of what must have happened.

The outlines of Romaine's relationship with D'Annunzio were further obscured by her belief that she and this poet in exile were comrades in adversity, artists against the world; and nothing more. She believed it so firmly that so did everyone else. Even as acute and suspicious an observer as Antongini concluded that Romaine Brooks was

† In French. Although D'Annunzio and Romaine Brooks were both trilingual, they appear to have used this language as an accidental result of having met in Paris. She signed herself "Cinerina," the name he gave her, which approximately translates as "Little Gray One."

one of the two or three women in D'Annunzio's life with whom he had a platonic friendship and nothing more. He was wrong.

D'Annunzio was, Romaine says in her memoirs, very relieved to be invited and to escape the complications of his life in Paris. She was making preliminary sketches for a portrait of him and all seemed to be going well, but . . . "I suspected that he was not so free as he had liked me to believe, and my suspicions proved to be well founded."

One day several trunks of clothes, which D'Annunzio had been waiting for impatiently, arrived from Italy: shoes, shirts, waistcoats, and a particular pink hunting coat in which he wanted his portrait painted.

He had just gone upstairs to put it on, when Bird burst into the room. It seems that there was a certain lady outside who demanded to be let in; it could only be Donatella. How was Bird to deal with her? Do anything you like, but don't let her in, Romaine said, remembering the gun. So Romaine paints the principal characters in her reconstructed drama: a frantic blond woman, poised at the front door, ready for murder, a terrified chauffeur, and herself as an innocent bystander, vacillating between panic and helpless laughter.

Enter the principal actor in his favorite pink hunting coat, breeches, and boots. There is a madwoman outside, he is told. D'Annunzio simply refuses to listen: "He had come down on purpose to be admired; nothing else mattered." He begins to pirouette around the room and Romaine notices idly, the way her eye would fix on some totally incongruous detail at a moment of crisis, that the stiff pleats of his pink coat stuck out in a funny way at the back.

Agitated voices were heard coming from the garden. Exhausted by his efforts and looking even paler than usual, D'Annunzio flung himself on a couch and sat there in deep gloom, refusing to say a word.

Bird returned to announce that the lady had gone away but not, he explained in cockney accents, without protest. "He had been obliged to detach her hands from the bars when she tried to climb over the gate."

The brief account ends with the information that Donatella moved into a house in the dunes close by and then became dramatically ill. The whole incident had disturbed D'Annunzio: "For a long while D'Annunzio remained silent on the couch." Romaine decided that he somehow needed to be the storm center for such a whirlwind of passionate feeling. She felt small and out of place. Romaine's decision to leave was the result of a "mysterious weight"; though whether she means a sudden insight or an overwhelming depression Romaine does not say. She invents an urgent call to Paris. En route, her hand is caught in a door. She is too sick to return. The next time she saw Montesquiou, he was very concerned about her injured hand. "When I told him that my hand had never been crushed at all, he refused to believe me."

The reason why I left, she says in one of her first letters to D'Annunzio after the incident, "was because of my enormous pity for the poor woman who was agonizing in the dunes. Your description of her trip was heartrending. I felt myself infinitely to blame in the whole affair. When she was far away, I must confess that I hardly thought about her, but once she had moved close to us I was haunted and to tell you the truth, that was the reason for my departure."

They sent each other letters and telegrams almost every day, D'Annunzio urging her to return and Romaine inventing excuses. She had "enormous clots of blood under the skin," she wrote with relish, or she was in bed with terrible bronchitis, or she was miserably undecided and he must help her decide what to do for the best.

Bit by bit, Romaine began to abandon the façade of the impersonally generous friend who was urging him to "go to her, you were meant for each other"; who could pretend in her memoirs that she remained immune ("His fire could warm but it could not burn"). Bit by bit she began to reveal the truth.

It seems that they had quarreled. She had found a strange pair of women's black riding gloves among her things. D'Annunzio accused her of having planted them in a fit of jealousy, to stir up trouble. Romaine, protesting her innocence, asked why he was always so ready to think the worst, to find the most devious motives in frank and open actions, and why life around him had to be a perpetual whirlwind of insults and hysterical bitterness. Why, she wrote, do you only listen to my enemies and reject one of your truest friends?

They tried so hard to understand each other, she said in a letter, and made "the most pathetic and amusing mistakes. For you, I became the eternally changing Sphinx" (she added an exclamation mark

234

here), "and for me, you were the stranger before whom I could only murmur, 'How curious!' It's strange," she wrote, "how different we are. Your genius needs wings to take flight, but you yourself will always be firmly rooted to the earth, safe and sound. Whereas, while my words are always sensible and sane, my actions can be dangerously impulsive and very far from being understood by mediocre people. Happily, such moments are rare and even my idols can't remove my wings." (An apparent reference to him.) "No doubt, once the first disillusion is past, I should thank them heartily for opening my eyes."

Then came the letter which expressed her truest feelings. "You were disappointed that I was not your charming ideal," she wrote from 20, avenue du Trocadéro, in a letter whose first page is missing, "and I am angry that you never understood my real love for you, how I adored you, how much tenderness I had for you, how much I wanted to protect you. I wanted to serve you with all my strength, to guard you and save you from petty annoyances. I thought you were ill-starred, like all great genius. You came to me with your troubles and I wanted to run to you with open arms, to shield you with my love, far from dangers and problems. I gave you my first spontaneous and simple response. My only thought was what should I do to make him happy? You spoke to me constantly of your disgust for 'the Fraulein,' and of your desire to escape. That's how I conceived the idea of a refuge, thinking that I would save you and prove my love for you; I never doubted your sincerity . . . You spoke of your love for me and I tell you simply that I believed you (don't smile). When I received your telegram calling me 'unique friend,' I wept with tenderness, joy and hope. I told myself, he has only me, he wants only me, I will be everything to him and I will do everything for him; he will never regret having given me the title of 'unique friend.' Alas! Alas! Alas! Alas!

". . . In four days, this world of dreams was destroyed, nothing, nothing was left; no more of the sad and abandoned poet, no longer a vulgar woman to flee from, no longer the gentle and protective and consoling role, nothing; I had become the enemy, the cruel one, the lying woman; all my acts of love put under the worst light by cunning, suspicious and distrustful eyes . . . Dear friend, believe me

235

that true love does not simply consist of the brutal and banal act. There are so many other things whose very existence you ignore . . ."

This tone of mournful, almost despairing reproach had changed in a later letter, which also demonstrates her split-image view of herself. "I am painting a sad and comical little being and while working I talk to myself in this fashion: 'Romaine, you are a great artist. All your powers and all your thoughts are in your art. How is it that you are now attempting another role whose outcome will mean slavery and imbecility? By taking refuge in your art, you can get the better of nature's traps. Now you are descending from your throne to mingle in the intrigues of the crowd. Romaine you are an elect of the gods, yet you become an ordinary female and concern yourself with the things the least tart in the street knows and always will know better than you. I talk this way, dear friend, probably with a lot of vanity but also with a little sadness, because I would have liked to sit down on a stool beside a throne higher than my own. Alas! The king is almost never there . . . it seems he descends every night to give dreams to a woman beside the dunes and when he comes back, he sleeps all the time with his feet on the footstool . . . It's sad."

She would never come back to him, she said, because "Your destructive power is stronger than you and everything that comes near you is annihilated. I had hoped that because I had so much respect for your art, you would have had a little for mine . . . But it was not so; I was for you only another female to destroy."

In the dozens of letters Romaine wrote, a picture emerges of the kind of ideal love she had imagined for them. It was, above all, noble: "Ask me, dear friend, to run with you my hand in yours against the most frightful giants, against all the dangers of this world and the next and, if the goal is the summit, I will do it fearlessly." She would be his guardian angel, would nourish and protect him. In her generous immediacy of response, there was a great deal of the caring concern she felt for St. Mar.

Since her love was so selfless and undemanding, she saw her need to be incorporated into his life, to sit on the footstool beside his throne, to supplant the other women in his life, as perfectly reasonable. But she had reckoned without the "Maître d'Amour's" belief in

236

the safety of numbers, and she was jealous at last. "You seem to be surrounded by so many inextinguishable fires of love that I must confess I don't pity you enormously," she wrote sarcastically from Paris. "I am sure, caro, that you won't die of the cold."

Perhaps Romaine gave herself physically in those first days and perhaps this was why D'Annunzio's enthusiasm for her seemed to vanish and "all my acts of love [were] put under the worst light by . . . distrustful eyes . . ."

There is still the larger question of why Romaine who, at thirty-six, was a lesbian, should have fallen deeply in love with a man. Romaine gives no clues, but the bisexuality of human beings is well-established, and while most people center their desires around the opposite sex, an element of sexuality is commonly present in relationships between the same sex. Similarly, while others may concentrate on their own sex, they have the capacity for heterosexual relationships with a physical element.

What is harder to understand is why Romaine should have chosen the one man she might have had most cause to avoid. She could have been motivated by self-destructive feelings, or, like Renée Vivien, she might have needed to have her pride knocked out from under her before she were freed to love; it could have been one or both of these reasons. The question is most easily understood in terms of Ella's damaging influence and Romaine's subsequent distrust of all close relationships. Since to become too close to someone was a threat to one's very self, she would choose a man like D'Annunzio who was ultimately unattainable, with whom one could never be close, and who was therefore no threat.

Romaine wanted most of all to be loved. Yet D'Annunzio could not have given it and she could not have accepted it; and that is their tragedy.

What D'Annunzio might have felt for Romaine can only be guessed at from a few clues, the poems† to her work and one short story which was published in the *Corriere della Sera* two years later, in 1912. The former show that he knew what demons pursued her; he knew that she felt embattled and alone against the world, and what he admired was her indomitable, diamond-hard endurance. He

† See Appendix, p. 410.

237

correctly saw the link between this quality and the black and white of her art. But he also knew that her attempt to integrate herself around her art could only be a partial solution. On Easter Sunday 1914, he wrote a poem to her in English‡ which, whatever it lacks in poetic grace, is clearly a heartfelt wish that she will find the inner peace that eludes her.

Although he admired, even loved her, he was ultimately afraid of her, as his transparently symbolic short story of 1912 demonstrates. The story is about a woman painter whose magical singing voice (he called Romaine "a nightingale") has a transfiguring effect upon him.

D'Annunzio is so enchanted by her that when she asks him to part with his most precious possession, a beautiful dog who loved him like a woman, he consents. The story describes the tender and agonizing moment of giving the dog to the woman, who takes it away.

One evening at twilight the dog escapes and runs back to its master. D'Annunzio rushes to the artist's house. She has been attacked in the face by the dog and killed. He is forced to destroy the dog.

In this short story, D'Annunzio demonstrates that he did not see Romaine's love as selfless and altruistic, but extremely demanding. He believed that she wanted his most precious possession; and reacted like a man who feels himself attacked by some wild animal. Her need for love had come into conflict with his own deepest fear: that of being annihilated in love. No wonder he saw passion as a battleground where one either must kill or be destroyed. He was bound to withdraw and she to be frustrated, and in this love relationship, which has many parallels with the affair he had with Donatella, D'Annunzio played out the impasse that would continue to confront him for the rest of his life.

After this rejection from D'Annunzio, Romaine withdrew into aloofness. "Once more I return to my sad and sublime indifference," she wrote to D'Annunzio in late September 1910, "and in my solitude I shall try to describe my contempt and disgust for everything; I shall withdraw once again into the shadows and become a vague image, enveloped in the color of distances, gray . . ." People who did not know her well, thought that she had escaped unscathed. André Germain wrote in *La Bourgeoisie Qui Brûle* that Romaine

‡ See Appendix, p. 409.

never fell into the trap of being a victim since "she knew how to claw just as well as he did." But the indifference hid something else: It hid her disgust and contempt; it hid her desire for revenge.

She must have given their friends colorful and highly amusing versions of the events of the summer. "I have just seen La Brooks again," Henri Regnier wrote in his journal for October 26, 1910 (quoted in *D'Annunzio* by Philippe Jullian). "She spent the summer at Arcachon with D'Annunzio, whose portrait she was making, and Madame De Goloubeff arrived to reclaim him. There was a grand scene, during which D'Annunzio explained to La Brooks that Madame De Goloubeff gave him 30,000 francs a year, which he needed, but if La Brooks was willing to furnish the sum, she would have the preference. La Brooks a practical American, declined the offer."

Perhaps D'Annunzio really did want Romaine to provide a yearly allowance. But the figure of 30,000 is strangely similar to the £300 a year paid to John Brooks; the 300 francs a month from Ella. It adds an additional flourish to the rumors in Paris that D'Annunzio made his women friends pay the bills, and is an echo of Ella's contemptuous attitude toward the men one has to support.

There was a further way Romaine could be revenged upon the man who had so pointedly rejected her. "After everything, you can still write me a letter like the last one," she wrote from Paris. "You are astonished that I can still be distrustful and that your second call makes me run from, rather than toward, you. Who can put his confidence in a heart that has destroyed it? A great magician like you ought to know that.

"Well, I am sad about this banal ending, but the voice that brought me back to myself, is calling me. I have to obey it. The other person sees even more clearly than I, because she knows you better. 'The other person' is someone who came to see me once at Arcachon . . . You used to know her . . . Truth sometimes surpasses fiction. . . . ."

Romaine had good reason to be triumphant, since she had succeeded in something few women would attempt. She had snatched away from her lover someone else he wanted; a glorious figure who appealed to his imagination, if not his heart; a fantastical being whose human dimensions are lost now beneath a chorus of awed reminiscence. Proust was immediately intrigued, Jean Cocteau thought she was penetratingly beautiful; to her Parisian audiences she was the personification of Art and almost as divine as Sarah.

Ida Rubinstein was, in 1910, at the height of her fame as one of the stars of the Ballet Russe in company with Nijinksy, Karsavina, Pavlova, and Fokine. The first performance of Diaghilev's troupe in Paris the previous year had made an extraordinary impact; their second appearance a year later would influence the whole development of ballet in the twentieth century.

Ida Rubinstein was not an outstanding ballerina. What she had was an uncanny ability to mime a scene and the kind of instinctive dramatic presence that is always recognized although almost impossible to describe.

She was young, elegantly tall, and faultlessly slender, with a delicately modeled head set upon a swanlike neck. She had been born in Saint Petersburg (now Leningrad) of a wealthy Jewish family and by the age of twenty, was impeccably schooled and traveled and studying to become a ballerina. She was too tall, Diaghilev decided, but her innate sense of movement and gesture astounded him. He immediately cast her in leading roles that did not require virtuoso dancing, and it was as the Sultan's favorite wife in *Scheherazade*, or as Cleopatra, carried on stage swathed in jeweled veils, that she entranced her audiences.

Montesquiou, now fifty, saw in her the embodiment of a youthful androgynous ideal and became her devoted admirer, appearing at every performance with his gold-headed cane. There were many others, including a Mr. Mavrocordato, an elderly lover who was replaced by an even wealthier one, a member of the Guinness brewing family (later, Lord Moyne). Ida Rubinstein had a sumptuous town house on the Place des États-Unis, emblazoned with mirrors, where it was said she lived on champagne and biscuits, ordering fabulous dresses which (it was said) she wore only once. Her lovers showered her with jewels, and Montesquiou paid to have her portrait painted, looking like the Queen of Sheba dressed by Worth and crowned with white feathers. Whether she invented herself or others did it for her, matters less than the fact that her very appearance at a luncheon would cause people to stare in open admiration. Words were inadequate for Montesquiou when he tried to impress upon Romaine the particular effect his first meeting with Ida Rubinstein had upon him.

He described her entrance, her gestures, her manner, leading up to that moment of indescribable beauty when she had turned to him and said, "Monsieur, sit down."

"To him this was no anti-climax," Romaine wrote. "He was experiencing over again in imagination, just that other quality which gave distinction to everything she said or did."

She might have been a heroine out of a drama by D'Annunzio. Montesquiou took the poet to see one of her first performances (probably in 1909) and D'Annunzio demanded to be introduced. "His eyes, in which the regard seemed to lose itself before blazing forth, rested with pleasure on the bejewelled veils in which that magician Bakst took delight in swathing me, and the cadence of those mimed poems had gained his approval because I learned then from Montesquiou that the poet of 'Fuoco' had asked him what could possibly be done with me," Ida wrote years later (in the *Nova Antologia*, April 16, 1927). "'Write a tragedy for her!' Montesquiou replied." Two years later, D'Annunzio cast her in the leading role in *The Martyrdom of Saint Sebastian*.

When Romaine met Ida Rubinstein, probably in June 1910, she was as captivated by her beauty as everyone else had been. Ida looked like a heraldic bird, delicately knit together by the finest bone structure. Romaine remembers one white, snowy morning when they walked together around the Longchamps race course. Ida was wearing a long ermine coat which was open to reveal the bare, fragile chest, and the slender neck rising out of a feathery white garment. Her precisely modeled face with its delicate, birdlike nose, its languorous Oriental eyes and cadaverous skin, her black hair, partly veiled: Ida presented a study in black and white whose overtones of the outspread wing took immediate hold of Romaine's imagination. She was even more beautiful off stage. She was an apparition.

To Romaine, Ida's elusive personality, commanding presence, and outrageous style were less seductive than what she personified. She had a kind of ethereal sexuality, as it were, purified of the instinctual, animal, and female. She was more and less than a woman, as Montesquiou believed, and as D'Annunzio recognized when he cast her in the role of a boy saint. She was the third sex, a creature who has fused the attributes of both sexes into a superbly androgynous whole, and it was as the androgyn that Romaine painted Ida. Ida became Romaine's ideal nude.

Romaine first used her as the model for "Le Trajet," 1911, a symbolic work whose other titles make the thought explicit: "The Crossing," "The Passing," "Death," and "Femme Morte." A woman is lying full length, a stylized sweep of black hair hanging down over a couch that seems to have taken on the outlines of an enormous white wing. The painting is a powerful visual representation of Romaine's state of mind after her mother died, when she felt suspended between life and death in an agonizing limbo from which she finally wrenched herself free.

Romaine had painted another, less intensely personal nude study the year before: "Azalées Blanches." She only painted nudes during the period of her friendship with Ida, abandoning the form once that was ended. Looking at Ida's elongated curves in "Le Trajet" and a later study of her, "The Weeping Venus" (1915), one concludes that the artist, out of some inner necessity, must have exaggerated their length.

But a sequence of photographs in Romaine's effects, probably taken during World War I, demonstrates that Ida Rubinstein in the nude was exactly as Romaine Brooks portrayed her. She lies in various graceful poses on a divan covered with a silk throw and bolstered by huge, tasselled pillows, naked except for an oriental-looking headdress and a pair of white leather boots with black-leather toes. Her long-boned and delicate frame is not even slightly emaciated, but simply extraordinarily elegant. She would be *Vogue*'s contemporary ideal.

Although Romaine heartily admired Ida, she was never deeply in love with her. To begin with, Ida was too much a pawn in the game Romaine was still playing with D'Annunzio. Apart from that, Romaine was capable of appreciating Ida's creative accomplishment in establishing a larger-than-life role for herself, without ever being deceived. Romaine knew that behind this *trompe-l'oeil* accomplishment was someone with a "rather uncomfortable" inner life; a woman who was a great deal less than she seemed.

Ida was extremely well read and knew pages of Goethe and Nietzsche by heart and, Romaine said, liked to assert that Dostoevsky was a greater genius than Shakespeare. She had a superb gift as a mime, yet what she really wanted to be was a ballerina. Romaine, full of misgivings, would watch with a frown as this divine creature, inches taller than any other girl in the class, would jump and pirouette while the dancing teacher, not impressed, would talk about the *plus petite* pupil who was so much more talented.

Ida also wanted to become a great dramatic actress like Sarah Bernhardt. She would make Romaine listen for hours while she read, with a strong Russian accent, speeches as Sarah might have read them and then make Romaine choose the pitch of her voice that sounded better. Romaine, exasperated, chose the lower pitch, but Ida informed her that Sarah had preferred the higher.

The moment Romaine suspected that someone lacked good sense, she had a way of dismissing that person without a backward look. But something else happened that she had not bargained for. Ida fell madly in love with her. Her stage triumphs, her house, her loves, her life: she was willing to give up everything for Romaine. She wanted to buy a farm where they could live in pastoral solitude. She wanted to consecrate her life to Romaine. "I can't be loved like that!" Romaine said.

At the moment when Romaine was psychically withdrawing from Ida, D'Annunzio had fixed upon her his momentary, but mesmeric, attention. He had begun work on *The Martyrdom of Saint Sebastian*, a forerunner of current attempts, particularly in opera, to forge poetry, music, art, and the dance into an ideal form of total theater. *The Martyrdom of Saint Sebastian*, which had its first performance in Paris in May 1911, is remembered now chiefly for the score Debussy wrote for it. At the time, it was a *succes de scandale* (Ida appears in one scene almost nude) and a further triumph for its star. Costumed by Bakst, Ida played the boy saint with such a poetic sense of the part's pathos that her admirers were prepared to deify her on the spot. She seemed to have stepped down from a stained-glass window, Cocteau wrote, and when, at the climactic moment, she was shot to death by arrows, she hung against the tree "like the wreck of some gallant ship entangled in its rigging." (Quoted in *The Decorative Art of Léon Bakst*.) The part of St. Sebastian had great symbolic significance for D'Annunzio, and for a year their triangular relationship could be oversimplified as one in which D'Annunzio was temporarily obsessed with Ida, who wanted Romaine. But Romaine was still in love with D'Annunzio.

"I think of you all the time, as often as I breathe," Romaine wrote from Italy, "because I tell myself, *he* has breathed this air and I embrace him in taking it. I love to envelop myself completely in this atmosphere . . ." They saw each other in Paris: "I await you with impatience," she wrote early in the morning from the avenue du Trocadéro. "The sun is rising just for us. I have dreamed about you all night . . ." They took several automobile expeditions together, what she called "our little trips." One letter records their moment of parting. He has left on one train and she is waiting for hers.

"I am writing to you with the vase of faded roses in front of me. You are no doubt halfway there, since it is already eight o'clock, and no doubt our little trip has become the past, without interest. I have shut the door to your room, so as not to see its emptiness, and the waiter is bringing my solitary dinner. It's not very gay! Perhaps as sad as my memories of The Three Writhing Pines. Dear Gabri, my sadness is endless. You are wrong about me. You give birth to joy but also a continual sadness, since one can never be sure of you and doubt makes one hesitate . . ."

But whenever she was going to see him again, joy outweighed pain. "I shall see you again in seven days! We'll be together in the car again, holding each other's hands, while I look at the trees and you sleep. I see again your dear face surrounded by a leather helmet and almost lost inside an enormous fur collar. Do you remember your great sadness when you heard the evening bells and your tender awakening at the hotel? I haven't forgotten anything, even the rain of yellow roses and after that the horrible parting . . ."

Then the letter was sent that proved how much Romaine loved D'Annunzio, despite the "insults, injuries" and repeated misunderstanding. It is dated August 16, 1911, written at about 9 o'clock one evening at a restaurant table in Monte Carlo.

"Gabrielino, I must be in love with you to write to you without any reason—I am doing it for the pleasure of giving you the palpable proof of my constant thought. I have lost I have lost a pile of money and I am frantic—7 million francs is a lot of money . . . at the moment. But what does it matter. If I could have you at this moment just to myself, for one night—You say the word—I am mad about you—about your adorable body. I see you I see you in raw detail—completely naked on a bed in the painter's studio. Do you realize how much I was in ecstasy before your nudity. I am exalted by you, I am insane about you tonight. Never has a woman appreciated you as much as I. I run from you because I am sincere—because I could not live another minute . . ."

The page ends here. Cross written on both sides of the paper are, "I don't make comedy or drama, but I am dying for you," and, "If I could have you to myself alone for several days," and, "I'll succeed in getting you or I'll die." The letter is unsigned.

The overlapping scribbled words, the disjointed sentences, the absence of paragraphs, the use of dashes (which Ella often employed, Romaine never) the sentences written at right angles across the narrative (another mannerism of Ella's which Romaine avoided), the repetitions ("I see you I see you"): the disarray is complete for one whose handwriting is usually firm, clear, and orderly. That she was in love with a man, that she, for whom the physical act of love between the sexes was so distasteful,† should find his body desirable; most of all that she, who was too proud to run after him like his spineless women friends, should have written such a letter, must have been such an affront to Romaine's self-esteem, that such an admission could only be made if she were momentarily on the edge of insanity. She may have been.

One would expect this confession to be counteracted by letters that would, in a hundred subtle ways, restore the right distance. This does not seem to have happened. Instead, the myriad unseen threads that bound her to him were untied over a long period, as if Romaine could not bear to let go, even after she had given up hope. "I love you just the same and despite everything," she wrote in a

† She wrote in one of her notebooks, "The sexual act is a commotion, rather than an emotion."

telegram, "profoundly, sadly and without hope. I know the whole truth and I pardon you because you hadn't understood me and also since I had played at being indifferent . . ."

The same tone of melancholic regret runs through dozens of letters. "If I don't see you before I leave, believe me dear Gabri that I shall carry away a souvenir of certain moments of our 'friendship'!! [what other word to define a rather ambiguous relationship?] which will always be sacred to me, and precious; sparkling red jewels which I will wrap up in a tiny gray veil like a souvenir that is tinged by the sad perspective of the past . . . Adieu, adieu . . . Was it a vision or a waking dream?/Fled is that music:-/Do I wake or sleep?" Finally she sent back all his gifts, keeping only photographs and copies of his personally inscribed works.

"Yes, everything you tell me is very strange!" she wrote. "The very day I sent back the rest of your things, the little fish must have died." How could he, she said, respond so callously? "To celebrate the return of your souvenirs, the death of the fish and the definite end of something that hadn't even started—and you drink champagne!" She, at least, would go to visit the grave of "the little fish which died so tragically with the last good things of the past." But the little red fish's soul does not sleep in peace, she said in a telegram of October 3, 1911. "It will return to haunt you."

While Romaine was writing despairing letters to D'Annunzio, she was seeing Ida constantly and had begun work on a portrait of her, now in the National Collection of Fine Arts, as she looked one day walking through the Bois de Boulogne, in a flowing black cloak "with sharp lights on its white satin revers."

Ida was a difficult model because her moods were unpredictable. Romaine never knew whether she would be "in a state of exaltation" or depressed enough to be talking about suicide. Ida might never have posed at all, Romaine thought, if it had not been for a long, glass-covered terrace on the avenue du Trocadéro which Romaine had turned into a studio and decorated with masses of white flowers and black and crystal accents. Ida decided to submit because "there could be no more beautiful spot in the world from which to commit suicide."

Romaine's portrait of Ida in black, white, and gray, is lit with a flat light, as Whistler's portraits were, with only the suggestion of color in the clouds and the slightest highlight on the delicate nose and cheekbone. Her elaborate headdress is blown back slightly by the wind and her mouth is half open, looking as Jean Cocteau saw her, "like the pungent perfume of some exotic essence," ethereal, other worldly; divinely unattainable.

But, comparing this portrait with a sequence of photographs of Ida Rubinstein (probably taken during World War I, when Romaine was finishing another nude of her and Ida had refused to pose any more) one sees how far short Romaine's version falls of Ida's reality. The commanding quality of the mime's presence comes through clearly in the photographs. She sits on a couch, wearing an enormous loose coat of spotted fur, in a headdress that looks magnificently right on her but would look ridiculous on any other woman, resting against the cushions in a pose that is at once utterly relaxed and compellingly beautiful.

One can see from these photographs, not from the portrait, what intuitive grace gave such authority to her slightest gesture and why all of Paris was in awe of her. What Romaine has failed to capture is the reality of this command; the sinuous, almost tigerish, sense of movement. The woman Romaine painted is the partial vision the artist wanted to see: Ida as the symbol of her own inner, Other world.

A few months after Ida's great triumph as St. Sebastian in the summer of 1911, and at the moment when Romaine's affair with D'Annunzio was turning increasingly sour, Romaine began to paint another portrait of Ida with the play as the theme (called "The Masked Archer" and also, "The Persecuted Woman").

D'Annunzio had, after all, been martyred by fate. He was a "poor dear exile," even if the ills he suffered were those all great men have to undergo. He was her "dear St. Sebastian," and in linking him with the title role in her letters, Romaine shows that she knew how much D'Annunzio craved the ultimate immortality of sainthood. That seemed perfectly reasonable to Romaine, since she had felt herself a member of the select band of *lapidés* for years.

But she did not paint D'Annunzio as St. Sebastian. Instead, Ida Rubinstein, this time with blond hair, is the one tied naked to the post, about to receive the first arrow from a tiny dwarf in an outlandish, rococo costume, who stands on a table. His face is turned toward the viewer but its expression can only be guessed at, since he is masked.

The canvas is a revealing example of the path Romaine's emotions took as her affair with D'Annunzio came to an end. Her characteristic response that he, like the rest of the world, was perversely tormenting and abusing her, turned to anger and a ferocious desire to get even. So D'Annunzio is the one being pilloried here, his short stature further reduced to dwarflike dimensions, his vain love of costume ridiculed, and his own most fervent desire for glory mocked; as he is shown as the one who shoots the first arrow.

Romaine kept that half of the painting and destroyed the nude representation of herself. Perhaps D'Annunzio took the fatalistic view that he was condemned by fate for the role of tormentor, since a telegram from Romaine refers to the sadness of the archer. Perhaps Romaine was momentarily contrite. But then, she thought of the raucous voices of his other women and hardened her heart.

The poet finally sat (or rather, stood) for his first portrait at St. Jean de Luz in 1912. Romaine was always going to find houses that, like the château at Mentone, had a commanding view of the sea. She chose one with an uninterrupted view of Atlantic coastline, intersected by the long dark line of a breakwater, and painted D'Annunzio against this background. "Huge waves dashed against this barrier and leaped high into foaming pinnacles in the air. What better symbol could there be for the portrait?"

Even though D'Annunzio hated to pose, he would arrive punctually each morning and stand with a look of grim determination on his face, "like a soldier at his post." Fortunately, Romaine added, the expression was momentary.

By the time the portrait was painted, their love affair had ended, and a friendship had developed that would last until D'Annunzio died. Once reconciled to the role of friend, Romaine could see D'Annunzio again as the martyred victim of fate and painted him this way. No trace of the malicious tormentor remains in these agonized eyes raised toward heaven, and in this distorted mouth; only a man battling against inhuman odds.

Although D'Annunzio might rebel outwardly at this view of himself: "I can accept the mouth but not the eyes!" he declared, it was the one he wanted to see. And so Romaine became what she had been at first: a perceptive, supportive, diverting companion, who one could think of as a brother (her letters are signed "Fratellino" and "Vostro Fratello"), not to be confused with one's other amours (although D'Annunzio covered his walls with women's photographs, Romaine was not among them because, he told her emphatically, "You're not a woman!"), and who would enjoy the joke as much as he did when he read his love letters aloud.

The portrait was a great success. When Romaine put it on view at the avenue du Trocadéro, *tout Paris* came to see it. Romaine expected adverse criticism and it came. "Does D'Annunzio know you have painted him?" one viewer whispered, apparently convinced that the portrait had to be some "awful form of vengeance." Somebody else said, "His mouth is like the crater of a volcano. D'Annunzio arrived at the end to hear the reactions and laughed so much that "I wondered if his mouth would ever return to the famous '*pli amer*' of his portrait."

This work of D'Annunzio had a further importance for Romaine, since it was the first of her paintings to be accepted by a state museum. (Others were a self-portrait of the same year against an identical background and the portrait of Cocteau.) Léonce Bénédite, then conservator of the Musée du Luxembourg (later, the Musée d'Art Moderne) had decided to add the work to his collection and even wanted Romaine to paint his portrait. (She decided against it since, she said, he looked too much like an Old Master.) This painting was probably the main reason why Romaine was awarded the Légion d'Honneur some years later.

Finally, the portrait led to an essay on her art which D'Annunzio wrote for the Italian magazine *Illustrazione* (April 1913). At one point, when she was angry with him, Romaine had sternly told D'Annunzio never to write about her: "Insult and wound in me the friend, mistress and woman—I can take it—but I beg you, don't insult my art!" But the mood passed.

Ever since he saw her exhibition at the Galeries Durand-Ruel in 1910, D'Annunzio wrote, he had been impressed by her ability to portray character.

In fact, she carried the cult of truth "to the point of cruelty, immune to any shadow of adulation and even of piety . . .

"The choice of subject, the decorative positioning of the figures, the apparently bizarre search of the details, the implacable acumen of the design, the repugnance toward any and all showy effect, the analytical study of the character reconciled with the synthetic expression of line, a certain ironic melancholy, a certain sad cruelty, a certain discreet play of mysterious allusion; everything reveals a special nature, a lucid and free spirit, a closed and guarded sensitivity that does not wish to enrich itself unless it be cultivating and exploring itself, hostile toward assimilations and deforming contacts."

D'Annunzio concluded that Romaine Brooks was the most profound and wise orchestrator of grays of modern painting. "These pages from your pen will be a real treasure," she cabled him from Paris the month the article appeared. The article represented more than that to her; it was proof of her worth. She kept the original, in D'Annunzio's own hand, locked up in a beautiful carved wooden box with a secret key that folded up into a small gold bar so that it would never fall into the wrong hands.

"No doubt a benevolent fate has foreseen that you are divesting yourself of past happiness in order to be reborn in an even more glorious future," Romaine wrote to "her poor exile" a few years before World War I. Neither could have known how prescient her words were. The great holocaust was, indeed, the period of D'Annunzio's ordeal by fire, and he survived it brilliantly, covering himself with titles and medals and earning a permanent place in the affections of his countrymen.

To be tilting against impossible odds brought out the best in Gabriele d'Annunzio. Given leisure, tranquility, and freedom to work, he would fritter away his time while complaining that his friends never let him alone. He did not, Romaine said accusingly, seem to know what he wanted; he would spend months in brooding indecision and letters from the "dear comedian" were never entirely free of a "recurrent sadness and apathy."

But, presented with his native land in peril, all of D'Annunzio's resourcefulness rose to meet the challenge. He returned to Italy from his self-imposed exile and made a speech in Genoa that roused his countrymen to a fervor and is cited as the single reason why Italy entered the war against the Austrian Empire. D'Annunzio aroused to action was irresistible to Romaine, for whom his vitality seemed almost supernatural and infinitely seductive. As before, he was transforming her world by injecting into it "the aspiring note" she had lost, and the war years were the warmest and truest period of their friendship.

At the outbreak of World War I, D'Annunzio was renting an elegant Louis XIII town house in the Marais quarter of Paris, and for months a stream of distinguished politicians from France and Britain came and went. He was preparing his speech for Genoa and read it aloud to Romaine. He was also writing another long poem‡ to accompany one of her new paintings, "La France Croisée," that of a Red Cross nurse, symbolizing France at war. The painting bears a kind of resemblance to Ida Rubinstein, and she may have posed for it. It is one of Romaine's favorite attitudes: that of a woman in three-quarter face, turned to face whatever horror lies ahead with implacable calm.

The poem links the theme of Christ's suffering on the cross with that of a nation at war. "Oh face of ardor, oh pity without sleep/ Courage which will never refuse the communion cup/Strength which makes a sacrifice of Your flesh/And a libation with Your ruby blood!"

Through Christ and this challenge to its survival, France, the poem says, will be reborn. Instead of fearing danger, one should go to meet it rapturously; one should throw oneself in ecstasy on the funeral pyre: ". . . exult/In your blood and be glad in the depths of your anguish/Even though the only flower you might cut/Is that of the hero born from the mysterious unknown." Be prepared, D'Annunzio told a condemned generation, to die in your millions.

The poem was printed in full on the front page of *Le Figaro* and rapturously received. D'Annunzio had caught the mood of the moment, or rather, it coincided perfectly with his own. He seized upon World War I as his personal crusade. It presented an opportunity to transcend self-doubt, to purify his soul, and to ensure his own immortality in the ultimate sacrifice of the battlefield.

Romaine was traveling with Ida in Switzerland when war broke

‡ See Appendix, p. 410.

out. Going back in the train, Ida spent the night on her knees praying to God to avert the calamity. Romaine was merely exasperated. These mass suicides were inevitable, she thought, since mankind simply would not practice birth control. The war was simply an infernal nuisance, one that interfered with her work, and Romaine tried to ignore it for a while. But seeing that one couldn't avoid dealing with the war, Romaine responded with her usual vigor. She put her paintings into storage in Bordeaux where it was safer. She refurbished her cellar as an air raid shelter and armed Bird with a pickax. She set up a fund for French artists who were wounded at the front. She wanted to join a unit and attempted unsuccessfully to harden herself by driving in an open car during very cold weather; she had to go to bed with back pains. She remembers sitting on her black-and-crystal terrace and watching the Zeppelins drop bombs around the Eiffel Tower.

D'Annunzio had joined a unit in Venice and served with it briefly before transferring to the Italian air force. When Romaine read that Venice, too, was being bombed, she decided to join him there before it was too late.

Venice in early spring was damp and cold, but it seemed lovelier than ever. Black lines of people streamed over the bridges and through the narrow streets. Romaine would go out with the intention of feeding bread to the pigeons and then, seeing beggars eyeing the crumbs voraciously, would end up distributing coins. In her spare time, she would lie in bed under a red eiderdown to keep warm, reading books on the *Risorgimento* and thinking, with fond pride, how like those patriots D'Annunzio was.

D'Annunzio was stationed not far from Venice and was directing aerial combat and bombing raids, types of warfare then in their infancy and in which the Italians took an early lead. He was living in the smallest palace on the Grand Canal, which Romaine described as an eighteenth-century chocolate box full of bibelots. There was a collection of clocks, every one of which D'Annunzio had set going, and the tiny drawing room would jangle with the discordant collision of a dozen delicate pendulums.

Since he insisted upon it, the palace was stiflingly hot. Every window was bolted shut, but even so one could smell the fumes of the gas with which the palace was heated, a block away. The rooms were so hot that "the wax candles drooped in their bibelot candlesticks, while others melted and ran up against the ornate mirrors."

D'Annunzio was seldom there. Even though Romaine realized that he could only pose at rare intervals, she took a villa on the Zattere and began to paint a second portrait of the new Commandante, wearing a heavy, pleated blue-gray military cloak over a black dolman edged with astrakhan, and standing in front of a seaplane which is taking off behind him on the blue Adriatic waters.

The view of himself as a leader, defiant, cutting through all the obstacles on his path toward a glorious horizon, was even more compelling than the first for D'Annunzio. Romaine would often find him alone in her studio, examining the new portrait intently. In a gesture rare for her, she gave it to him and he wrote that it would have a place of honor in the hall he was building at Il Vittoriale. His wishes were not carried out and the portrait is buried in an obscure corner of the museum annex in semi-darkness, its somber colors further muddied behind a pane of all-reflecting glass.

D'Annunzio had a particular reason to remember those sittings, and described it in *Nocturne*, a reminiscence he published after the war.

"I can't seem to shake off my black mood. Cinerina is there, she is all eyes and chin; it's no longer a woman but an artistic will, with her white linen smock and her sober paintbrushes in her hand. I take up the pose and begin to dream. I don't hear the things she is saying in an attempt to make pleasant conversation. The time passes. . . ."

Then D'Annunzio received the news that one of his closest friends, Giuseppe Miraglia, had just been killed. His plane had fallen into the Venetian lagoon. "This tragedy hit D'Annunzio very hard and I doubt if he ever got over it," Romaine said.

A vein of increasing disillusion runs through D'Annunzio's letters from the front, which are written on expensive paper and emblazoned with crests: *Per Non Dormire, Io ho quelque ho donato,* and finally in 1918 on paper with an orange crest, *Semper Adamas, Prima Squadriglia Navale, Il Commandante.* The man who thought he could fight and win against great odds was discovering just what odds the advent of modern warfare presented. His friends hurled themselves against the machine and it mowed them down, one after the other.

Then D'Annunzio, who could sigh with envy over another man's noble death, long for a *"bonne blessure"* (beautiful wound), and say that he was thirsting for "bitter water," was given his wish. His plane was forced to make a crash landing, his head was wounded, and the sight of his left eye impaired. He kept seeing flashes of colored lights. An occulist diagnosed it as a detached retina and prescribed rest in a darkened room.

Romaine was extremely concerned since she knew how critically D'Annunzio's writing career was threatened. She arranged to have a famous Parisian oculist make the trip to Venice for a consultation. The doctor, who thought at first that the eye might have to be removed, reported that this was not necessary for, he wrote, "D'Annunzio's health is excellent; his vitality that of a young man."

While other specialists gave conflicting opinions, the eye grew steadily worse. D'Annunzio was in constant pain. Reading tired him, he said, but he found that he could write well enough if he only looked at the page occasionally. He had already learned the trick by writing in semi-darkness. He would love to recuperate at Arcachon, as Romaine was urging, but did not dare to travel that far. "I would like to be free to live in a lonely villa surrounded by a shadowy forest, where I could gather back all my forces in the open air."

D'Annunzio was placing his pain "into your beloved hands." Romaine responded with the concern with which she would always sustain and console those she loved. She thought constantly of him "who fights in vain, with his solitary and desperate courage"; as D'Annunzio wrote despairingly. She praised his "winged heroism," anguished over his losses, fussed about his health, and reassured him that he was a genius and a hero. "Take very good care of yourself and plenty of gondola rides in the open air," she wrote. "I kiss both eyes and wish that your health will be completely restored. I think of you constantly . . ." And, "I have feared for you so much these days dear friend and I received your letter today, with joy. But I am heartbroken that yet another friend is dead. What sadness here," she cabled in June 1917. Then, "It takes great souls to appreciate the grand gesture."

Romaine's concern had another, and practical, aspect. While he was at the front, she took charge of St. Dominique, the villa at Arcachon that D'Annunzio had rented after she left it, and where all his furniture, paintings, bibelots, and, most important, his hundreds of valuable books, remained during the war years.

D'Annunzio had always lived as if money were beneath consideration. Periods of spending with seignorial splendor were followed by the inevitable ignominious retreat before a pack of creditors. That he could continue to live so ostentatiously beyond his income, was surprising in light of the gossip that followed in his wake. But there was always someone new who did not know his reputation, as in the case of the couple who rented him the Louis XIII house, the Hotel de Chalon Luxembourg, at the outbreak of World War I. Flattered by his impulsive manner (D'Annunzio came upon the house by chance as he was out walking and insisted upon subletting it) and somewhat overwhelmed by his munificence (after inviting them to a handsome lunch, D'Annunzio presented them with two pedigreed dogs as a parting present), the couple in question had no reason to be suspicious; until the rumors about D'Annunzio's profligacy caught up with them. After a few months of paying the rent, D'Annunzio seems to have forgotten about it. Someone finally paid the bill, and it was being rumored that the person was Romaine.

D'Annunzio's spendthrift ways had seemed like one more oddly endearing quirk of character. But, when Romaine thought that he (or anyone else) was making calculated use of her friendship, she was outraged. During the war years, when the importance of protecting D'Annunzio was uppermost, Romaine's attitude changed again. One ought to help one's friends in need; be the quintessence of generosity, if necessary. And D'Annunzio was in need. The rent at St. Dominique had not been paid, there were other outstanding bills, and by the end of World War I all of D'Annunzio's possessions were to be auctioned off to pay his debts.

Romaine, who had been doling out a thousand francs here or there for years to pay D'Annunzio's two remaining servants, rose to the occasion. She offered to buy the house but it had already been sold to a wealthy merchant from Bordeaux. She and Natalie Barney pleaded with the new owner without success. The only concession he would make was to allow more time for D'Annunzio's effects to be removed from the house.

Someone had to dismiss the servants, pack up the clothes, and close the house. Someone had to save D'Annunzio's library, for sale at a cost of several million francs, and as dear to him as life itself.

When D'Annunzio found out who had bought his treasured books, he made Romaine take him to her lawyer, where he signed a document to the effect that a certain percentage of the income derived from his works, should be paid to her until the borrowed sum was fully reimbursed.

Having agreed that her generous gift should be considered a loan, Romaine did not forget. That D'Annunzio appears to have defaulted on their agreement is made clear by a letter from her lawyer in 1929 in which the lawyer, S. K. Archibald, reports that he has received some 50,000 francs in settlement of a claim against D'Annunzio. It was, presumably, her share of the income from his works that had been promised ten years before.

D'Annunzio needed Romaine to take care of his affairs because, despite his wounded eye, he had flung himself back into the conflict, and in an early propaganda raid had dropped leaflets over Vienna urging the Austrians to surrender. He fought off the Austrians at Piave and took part in the successful counterattack. He served with such distinction that he had attained the rank of lieutenant colonel by the end of the war, was in charge of a naval squadron, had written several books on the technique of aerial warfare, had been awarded the gold medal for valor, four silver and two bronze medals, and had been created an officer of the Military Order of Savoy.

All that remained was the final flamboyant and heroic gesture which would elevate D'Annunzio to the role of supreme patriot. The armistice agreement provided that opportunity. A secret promise that Italy would be awarded Fiume and Dalmatia as one of the rewards for entering the war had not been honored, D'Annunzio claimed. So he assembled a force of men—variously estimated from 300 to 12,000 —and marched on Fiume. He took it on September 12, 1919, and held it for fifteen months. The gesture proved futile (at least until

1924, when Italy annexed Fiume), and D'Annunzio was forced to withdraw. But his grand gesture had fired the Italian imagination and "D'Annunzianesimo," as a political philosophy, passed into the language. He could have become a dictator, if he had wanted the role. He did not.

D'Annunzio retired to Il Vittoriale and spent the remaining years of his life, until he died at the age of seventy-four in 1938, writing letters, revising his enormous volume of writings, contemplating his own death, and planning his meticulous monument.

(Mussolini capitalized on D'Annunzio's fame. He made several ostentatious visits to Il Vittoriale, made him the Prince of Monte Nevoso and the president of the Royal Italian Academy, and borrowed many of D'Annunzio's ideas in the pursuit of his own glory. It is believed that the title of "duce" was originally given to D'Annunzio and that Mussolini took the idea for his band of black-shirted followers from D'Annunzio's similarly clad marchers on Fiume.)

D'Annunzio as the spurned and lonely man of genius, or the doomed warrior, was one thing; D'Annunzio as the focus for national adoration was something else. Romaine lost interest, partly because D'Annunzio no longer needed her and partly because her relationship with Natalie Barney had become the absorbing focus of her life. Her letters to him became rare and in 1926 he wrote to ask why she did not reply to his telegrams; why she went to Venice without coming to visit him, and accused her of having "cruelly forgotten" him. He closed with the sentence, "I kiss you with a very reproving mouth."

But Romaine was still a fond friend (she signed her letters "Always the same Romaine,") and a fervent defender, and she visited D'Annunzio at Il Vittoriale several times with Natalie Barney. That lady was not at all impressed. He was "the magnificent stranger" to whom one could never be close; she said. He had become "a precious little object in old ivory" and if in old age D'Annunzio seemed to be reclusive and embittered, as if he thought life had cheated him, then "the third act is always difficult to bring to a satisfactory conclusion." So Natalie summarized, with the insight detachment imparts, a man whom Romaine would always see as an elementary force of nature, like Ella; for whom there was no explanation except that of paradox.

Romaine went back for a last visit to Il Vittoriale one cloudless and still afternoon, when she was in her sixties. She had grown heavy with the years and her jaw, which had always been pronounced, had begun to dominate her face; but there was the same look of vital alertness in her eyes; that of a woman who is amused and undeceived. She liked to pull a felt hat down decisively over her forehead and knot a satin jabot around her neck and wear decorous skirts, well below the knee but short enough to show off the still-slim curve of her calf and the elegant shape of feet shod in the very best leather.

So perhaps she walked, an unremarkable figure in an expensive fur coat, whose beautiful new shoes would have clipped an instant echo from the intricately paved walks. Perhaps every monument, every stone, every carved surface brought forth a rush of mingled responses: glimpses of trees flicking by overhead as one drove in an open car, of faded yellow flowers in a vase, a pirouetting figure in a pink hunting coat, a restaurant table in Monte Carlo.

Or perhaps Romaine, walking through those reverberating courtyards, could summon up only the memory of Natalie's deep, appreciative chuckle as she read D'Annunzio's love letters; only the sense of futility that had overwhelmed her as their affair came to an end. "Sometimes the past appeared to me vaguely like a dream," she wrote to him, "but I am too lazy to see it as anything more than so many stupid, foolish and wasted efforts . . . a childish effort to try and join water with fire. . . ."

In her memoirs, Romaine says that she turned for a last look at the lake, that lake which forms such a faultless backdrop for the open-air theater where D'Annunzio planned to have his work performed. She was thinking of his motto, *Per Non Dormire* and was suddenly aware of a light shadow, "moving swiftly over its smooth surface." So Romaine hopefully concluded, and embellished, the pages.

On Wings of Love

15

Ceux qui ne mettent pas leur âme dans leur chair sont indignes de la vie.
(Those who do not put their soul in their flesh are unworthy of life.)

Et comment ne pas aimer l'amour qui, chaque jour, nous laisse insatisfaits?
(And why not love love which, every day, leaves us unsatisfied?)

Amour: église pour deux—où nous restons seuls.
(Love: a church for two—where we remain alone.)

From *Pensées d'une Amazone,* by Natalie Clifford
Barney, Émile-Paul, Paris, 1920

By the time Romaine met Natalie Clifford Barney on a certain afternoon early in World War I at Lady Anglesey's tea party, both had become figures on the Parisian scene. Natalie was the focus for a Bohemian circle of poets, musicians, and writers, and Romaine, having established herself as an artist of rare gifts, was painting regularly, if not constantly, and choosing among the parade of faces those that interested her.

The interlude with D'Annunzio, so profoundly disturbing and disillusioning, had settled something in Romaine's mind. From that time, her relationships with men could be amicable, tender, even intense; but they were never romantic. For romance, one chose women; there was one woman.

The woman who was to play a central role in Romaine's life for the next fifty years was called the Amazon, for her habit of riding in the Bois de Boulogne every morning, carrying a cane, dressed in a bowler hat and a black bow tie. Anatole France had said, "I kiss your hand with a sacred terror."

Natalie Clifford Barney was writing poems and essays and bringing together, in her salon on the rue Jacob, the most renowned writers of the early twentieth century, the aristocratic élite, and the homosexuals of a particular world. She mastered the elegant and difficult art of the aphorism yet, because she wrote in French and very little of her work has ever been translated, she remained virtually unknown in her native land.

This extraordinary figure was born in Dayton, Ohio, on October 31, 1877, the daughter of Alice Pike Barney, an artist, dramatist, and all-around esthete, and, Albert Clifford Barney, son of the founder of the Barney-Smith Railroad Car Foundry of Dayton, Ohio, and a prudent financier in his own right. Natalie described him as a bit too short for his good looks and something of a womanizer, who liked to repeat the compliments he was paid as proof of his powers of seduction. There were many such compliments. When one of his partners stumbled and fell with him at a dance, she commented adroitly, "Few women's falls have been as pleasant as mine."

From the first, Natalie and her younger sister, Laura, led an unusually free and privileged life. Their early years were spent living in a mansion just outside Cincinnati, surrounded by immaculately kept lawns, with their own playgrounds stocked with goats, baby alligators, parrots, and pony carts. They traveled between Ohio, Washington, and Bar Harbor, Maine, and, as soon as they were old enough, to London and Paris as well. They were given, Laura said, extraordinary freedom for their day.

Horses were the first love of Natalie's life, and France and the French came a close second. She had a French governess who would read stories from Jules Verne aloud and refuse to translate. "I wanted to understand them so much that I learned French fast." She also had Louisa Miller Este, her grandmother's oldest sister, who spoke French all her life, read yellow-backed French novels, gave elegant dinners in Baltimore complete with *pâtisseries* and a barrage of fine wines, and was enchanted to discover that the young Natalie could speak French without an accent. "You are someone after my own heart," she told her.

Natalie adored her mother although, like most children of her class, it is likely that she saw very little of her. "I sustained such a love for my mother," she related in *Souvenirs Indiscrets*, "that I have a vivid memory of her sitting by my bed, looking more beautiful than any of my dreams, before she went off to some party."

Natalie would wait long hours for her mother to return, listening for the rustle of her dress as she passed her room and for the proof that nothing dreadful had happened. Then she would creep out on bare feet toward the ray of light filtering out from under her mother's door. "I was trembling with emotion and cold," she continued, "but I couldn't persuade myself to leave until she had turned her light out." (Translation from the French is the author's.)

In those days, such an overwhelming desire to have one's mother back, safe and sound, would be taken as proof of a child's extreme affection. Now, it might well be seen as the anxiety of a child who fears abandonment. ·

From early childhood, there was a certain quality about Natalie's face, a sense of independent self-assertion, that fascinated artists. Her mother studied with several famous teachers, including Whistler and Carolus Duran. The latter painted a handsome portrait of Natalie aged eleven, dressed as a page, and her mother, who began to specialize in portraits of the famous, including Whistler, George Bernard Shaw, and Wanda Landowska, painted Natalie again and again. There was "Natalie in Fur Cape," at the height of her disturbing good looks at the age of twenty-eight, a plumed and cocked hat on top of her billowing hair, and there was "Natalie with Flowing Hair," her lustrous eyes almost lost beneath masses of blond locks. Underneath this pastel portrait, her mother had commented in French, "Sombre without being bored and sad without distress," revealing that she was as puzzled as her contemporaries by Natalie's enigmatic personality.

Then Natalie and Laura were sent to Les Rûches, a fashionable girls' boarding school in Fontainebleau just outside Paris, which completed Natalie's assimilation into the French culture. It was run by Marie Souvestre, an extraordinary figure whose influence on the young Lytton Strachey, according to his biographer, Michael Holroyd, was profound. She was as formidable a skeptic as she was intellectually brilliant. Every idea had to be brought under "a sort of hammering logic," Beatrice Webb wrote in her diary, "and broken into pieces unless it be of very sound metal."

Natalie Barney came under the influence of this hammering logic and made it her own. She asserted her right to live her own life, and there was nothing anyone could do about it, even though her mother, outwardly a Bohemian but basically a snob, would have liked Natalie to move in correct circles.

But Natalie had no intention of allowing herself to be so circumscribed. Unlike Romaine, she did not accept the path of conforming while chafing under others' restraints; she simply rose above them.

Natalie's achievement was remarkable, given the social climate of her day; even in Paris, which has a long history of tolerating eccentric behavior, and even with the special advantages that economic independence gives a woman. She managed to carve out a life for herself in the most rarified and exacting of worlds and be accepted on her own terms. She made others bend to her will, by the certainty of her convictions. She never evaded, explained, or apologized. She was what she was.

It is agreed that Natalie was not conventionally pretty, but what she had was even more seductive to those men and women who fell in love with her. She had, one said, a voice with a timbre like a violoncello. Another spoke of her profusion of hair, massed in great careless clumps around her head. A third was mesmerized by her eyes, as blue as gas jets, and her kind or savage stare, depending on which writer you read.

Early photographs of Natalie show her sitting beneath a pine tree, wearing a starched white shirt, a bowler hat, a bow tie, and a black riding coat, a slim cane poised between her hands, or looking back over her shoulder, or with her sister Laura, one hand on her hip and an expression of insouciant amusement flickering in her eyes, that showed her command of herself and her world.

There is another photograph that her epoch would have considered daring in the extreme. She is a wood nymph, lying back over a rock on a fern-covered floor that might be the forest of Fontainebleau or perhaps the woods around her house in Bar Harbor, her hair hanging down loosely; quite naked.

Too many clues are lacking for the emotional factors predisposing Natalie to lesbianism to be clear. There are hints that her mother seems to have been indulgent and even fond but emotionally distant and lacking the slightest insight into her own emotions or those of her children; that Natalie feared abandonment from an early age; and that she considered herself a feminist from the moment when she had seen a woman and a dog pulling a milk cart between them in Europe, while the husband walked blandly alongside. The theme of feminism runs through many of her aphorisms. "In England, nothing is for women—not even the men!" and, "Marriage? Maternity? The child also limits the woman and then abandons her."

Natalie might have been a rival with her father for her mother's affections; learning to compete with him for women as he competed with other men. He was a Don Juan; she became one. Before she was twenty, Natalie had begun to pursue women with the combination of imagination, courage, and boldness that many of them found irresistible; even if they were highly paid courtesans.

She writes with some pride of the manner in which she seduced Liane de Pougy, one of the last in a line of famous cocottes whose behavior, at the turn of the century, both stimulated and scandalized the public imagination. Such a woman, as Colette painted her in *Gigi,* could not only satisfy the most eccentric of male appetites, but would be socially correct, well-schooled, able to play, recite, sing, dance, and decorate with charming accomplishment. Such a woman was capable of an intelligent conversation and, finally, would know how to spend money. The more famous she was, the more psuedo-respectable her status. Such a woman would have presented a formidable challenge. Natalie fell in love with her first glimpse of Liane one day in the Bois de Boulogne.

She began, Natalie says in *Souvenirs Indiscrets,* with the usual flowers and letters. Liane finally agreed to a rendezvous. Natalie must have pretended to be a man, because she had rented a page's costume from Landolf for the occasion. The moment came when Natalie was ushered into Liane's boudoir, in semi-darkness. Natalie made out the dim outlines of a form, stretched out on a chaise longue and went down on one knee in front of it. She offered a bouquet, and launched into the poetic speech she had composed for the occasion. Then she heard an unmistakable feminine giggle coming from behind a screen. Standing hastily, Natalie discovered that the lady on the couch was not her goddess at all but an imposter.

Then Liane appeared, her ravishing head covered with short curls like one of Fra Angelico's angels, and her supple body swathed in a diaphanous white fabric. She looked so ethereal that Natalie was surprised to discover that she was, indeed, flesh and blood. Her hand came down on Natalie's shoulder as heavy as marble and her handshake was extraordinarily vigorous.

As they went for a ride in the Bois, Liane inspected Natalie with a gentle and ambiguous look. "I already like your hair and the shape of your spirit," she finally remarked. Liane was moved enough by the resulting affair to write a thinly disguised account in a novel titled, appropriately, *Lesbian Idyll,* and to make Natalie the heroine, Miss Flossie. The relationship ended abruptly when Natalie's father discovered her reading a long love letter from Liane and sent his daughter home to the States for two years.

By the turn of the century Natalie was renting her own house in Neuilly surrounded by trees and fountains just in front of the Île de Puteaux. It was a charming small lodge (*pavillon*), which had the advantage of an apartment on the second floor with a separate entrance for guests. Natalie considered separate quarters essential since she had, she remarked, learned very quickly that living on close terms with someone was the quickest way to destroy affection. "To live alone, my own master, was essential, not for egotistical reasons or any lack of love, but in order to give more freely of myself." (*Souvenirs Indiscrets.*)

From the start, Natalie had the gift of turning a reception into an event. There was the afternoon in May when Colette, who was then bent on a music hall career, gave a performance in the garden of Pierre Louÿs' *Dialogue au Soleil Couchant,* while the author, and Natalie, looked on.

"It's possible," Colette said in *Mes Apprentissages,* "that he didn't listen, because we were better to look at than to hear. But we thought

266

that, under its umbrellas and its fashionably large hats, all of Paris could think of nothing but us. . . ."

That was the same afternoon that a naked woman dancer, who was already notorious, appeared on a white horse harnassed with emeralds. When Colette was invited back to see the same dancer give a demonstration of Javanese dances in the nude, her husband wouldn't let her go. Her name was Mata Hari.

Everyone came to Natalie's parties, from the start. People were intrigued by her impudent and mocking sense of the scandalous perhaps, or her dramatic flair; like the evening when she gave a Persian dinner and a small boy, concealed above a skylight, showered the guests with rose petals; or the costume ball which included a performance of the eighteenth-century play, the Duc de Lauzun's *Le Ton de Paris*. Or it was her talent for persuading the already famous to attend, like the time when Wanda Landowska played the harpsichord and Colette acted in *La Vagabonde*, with Paul Poiret as her partner.

In those days, Colette of the slanting eyes was being locked up in her room by Willy to write books about Claudine. She described, in *Claudine S'en Va*, a certain Miss Flossie, Liane de Pougy's heroine, an American more supple than a scarf. "She smiles frankly at me, her eyes fixed on my own, until a quiver in her peculiar left eyebrow, as annoying as an appeal, makes me drop my gaze. . . ." This appeal, so disturbingly insistent, had its effect. When Colette and Willy separated, Colette moved into the apartment above the *pavillon* in Neuilly and was Natalie's co-hostess for a time. She left to attempt domesticity again with Henry de Jouvenal, but they remained on excellent terms. Colette wrote, "No serenity as cruel as yours, Amazon," but some years after that she had tempered her judgment of Natalie and could write affectionately, "Your calm face! Have I ever loved it more?" They remained friends until Colette's death.

All of this took place years before Romaine met Natalie, and it is doubtful whether she would have approved. Natalie was, to be sure, a Bohemian like herself, but the band of musicians and performers, friends of Sacha Guitry, which Natalie was gathering around her, would not have appealed to Romaine. Their earnest attempts to revive the Golden Age of Greece, all those harps and Greek dresses, would have had too strong an appeal for Romaine's sense of the ridiculous. Colette, who hated classical verse, might be persuaded to join the audience the day that Natalie produced the two acts in verse that she had just written, based on some fragments of verse by Sappho, and the Greek wife of Raymond Duncan played a musical accompaniment. Romaine would certainly have been forced to leave, stifling some undiplomatic laughter.

The circle of women poets that also surrounded Natalie would have been more to Romaine's taste. It was fashionable, in turn-of-the-century Paris, for women of the leisure class to write poetry and hold recitations in elegant drawing rooms, to the accompaniment of *pâtisseries* and harps. Such dilettantes were given the ridicule they deserved in the literary magazines. But Natalie's friends were more in earnest, more authentic. There was the Countess Anna de Noailles, whom everyone wrote about constantly, particularly Cocteau; and Lucie Delarue-Mardrus, who had married Dr. Jesus Christ Mardrus, the translator of a famous version of the *Arabian Nights,* generally considered the greatest woman poet of her epoch. Then there was Renée Vivien.

Natalie met her some ten years before Romaine did, in 1897. This exotic figure, whose work is enjoying a certain cult revival, was considered a poet of extraordinarily promising gifts cut short by her death. Renée Vivien was, like Natalie and Romaine, the product of two cultures. Her mother had been Hawaiian and her father was Scottish. (Her real name was Pauline Mary Tarn.) But she shared Natalie's love of all things French, and shortly after being presented at the Court of St. James's, Renée fled to Paris to become a poet.

When Natalie met her, Renée Vivien had long, straight blond hair falling to her shoulders and a heart-shaped, flowerlike face. Romaine kept a photograph of her in knee breeches, showing a straight and delicate leg, wearing a velvet jacket and striped waistcoat. A lace kerchief is tied in a high, old-fashioned way under her chin and her hands are barely visible beneath long lace cuffs.

There were so many puzzling contrasts about Renée Vivien. A lingering air of innocence, of childhood barely relinquished, seemed to be in grotesque contrast with the dissipated life she led. Her insistence on making light of everything: "Oh my dear little Colette," she would exclaim in a childish lisp, "how disgusting this life is!" before bursting into fits of laughter, was in ironic juxtaposition with the intense, romantic verses she wrote after the style of Baudelaire.

Renée Vivien was, in fact, in love with death, as Natalie discovered. At the age of twenty, when they met, Natalie was studying the difficult art of classical French verse, and she was told that Renée also wrote poetry. Natalie was not much interested. Renée seemed charming, but superficial. Then Natalie heard the first of Renée's many poems in French on what was to become an obsessive theme: the peace which death would bring her. Natalie's protective instincts were aroused, what her friends used to call her Girl Scout's impulse to help, along with the curiosity that is the prelude to infatuation. How could one give Renée a renewed interest in life? How could Natalie interest her in her own, Natalie's, life?

Renée was living in an apartment remarkable enough to be described in several memoirs. Romaine talked about a tunnel-shaped Japanese bed, lit from within, and carved doors with Oriental lattice windows. Colette remembered air which, "like stagnant water, slowed down my steps, the odour of incense, of flowers, of overripe apples . . . One day, when the spring wind was stripping the leaves from the Judas trees in the avenue, I . . . tried to open the window: it was nailed shut. What a contribution such a detail is, what a flourish it adds to a theme already rich! What a quantity of lurid gleams and glints of gold in the semi-darkness, of whispering voices behind the doors, of Chinese masks, of ancient instruments hanging on the walls, mute, only vaguely whimpering, at the banging of a door beneath my heavy hand." (*The Pure and the Impure.*)

Renée would invite her friends to lunch in this setting. It was served Oriental fashion on the floor, on cracked Damascus ware. They were given strips of raw fish rolled on glass wands, shrimps, *foie gras,* and salads seasoned with pepper and sugar. There would be cocktails beforehand: Russian, Chinese, and Greek alcohols, and a very good Piper Heidsieck brut with the meal. Renée, in fact, subsisted on fruit, a few spoonsful of rice, and alcohol, to which she was already addicted. She later added drugs to her terrifying list of weapons of destruction and died of anorexia, at the age of thirty, weighing sixty-six pounds.

Renée both lived for love and feared it. Natalie, she said, was the quintessence of her wildest longings, "less beautiful and more strange than I ever dreamed," and the agent of her destruction. The first time Renée caught sight of "those sharp eyes as blue as a wave," she had a presentiment that this was the feared face of her Future.

Renée might have been like Philip, meeting Mildred in Maugham's *Of Human Bondage*, attracted to qualities she felt lacking in herself; looking for a stronger, superior being; someone perhaps even openly arrogant and proud. Philip, the dependent one, responded with anger when he first met Mildred but, almost at the same moment, fell desperately in love and ruined, or almost ruined, himself.

The reasons, the psychiatrist Karen Horney said, lie in the fascination the arrogance of others exerts on the dependent person, and his own need for surrender. "He craves to surrender himself body and soul, but can do so only if his pride is bent or broken." Renée also feared the destruction of self which such a love sacrifice would bring with it; but her need for love was stronger.

Natalie was not a sadist; she loved Renée with a passion, but she could not abandon herself to feeling, the way Renée wanted her to do. She did not want to fuse into a common self. A part of her had to remain inviolate, virginal, as Renée said; to stay in its own house. Renée's rapturous desire for oblivion carried implicit demands: to be with Natalie every hour, to be constantly praised, courted, fondled, desired. After each night spent together ("The night is for us what the day is for others," Renée said), Natalie would receive flowers and poems of almost embarrassing fervor: "How many kisses can describe the languor of your body/How many rhythms of love, how many fervent poems/Honor sufficiently the one whose beauty carries/Desire on her forehead like a diadem?"

Natalie reflected, with her usual detachment, that she had become the pretext for a new obsession, replacing Renée's former themes of death and solitude. "It was love—but a facet of love which had scarcely found a poet since Sappho." But more than that, she needed the magical quality which Renée's delicate imaginative gifts brought to their encounters; to the first night in a white room filled with lilies and a white bed, to the white frost of snow that iced the streets as Natalie left in the morning; to the duels with crystal swords by moonlight and gallops with white horses across moonlit sands. Natalie loved, she said, her poet's melancholy soul, and searched for it in Renée.

But, as soon as Renée began to move closer, Natalie withdrew. She had not asked Renée to love her to madness. She refused to take responsibility for Renée's sufferings. The more Natalie withdrew, the more clinging Renée became. She would never have Natalie, she said frantically; Natalie was incapable of being faithful to anyone.

With a great effort, Renée would wrench herself free. Then Natalie would find herself nostalgic. Where was Renée? What was she doing now? Who was she in love with? The moment she would return from a trip to Bar Harbor, Natalie would hurry to Renée's apartment on the avenue du Bois. "Mademoiselle has just this moment left the house." Natalie would spend hours of anxious waiting until Renée returned. The car would appear; a brief glimpse of a white face; then it would swing past Natalie without stopping.

Then Natalie was the one writing love poems to Renée in the Sapphic idiom: "I wait, I keep a vigil . . ./I hope on, vainly, I count the moments/And don't know what to do. Ah, my double thoughts!/ For what other love are these inconstant looks,/These plaited tresses?"

Natalie would find a dozen audacious ways to deliver such poems, so that they would not fall into the wrong hands. She would ask the help of Emma Calvé, who had just sung the title role of *Carmen* in the United States. They would dress up as street singers and steal to the avenue du Bois at night, and when they came to Renée's shuttered windows, Emma would begin singing, *"J'ai perdu mon Eurydice, rien n'égale ma douleur"* (I have lost my Eurydice, nothing equals my sorrow) and Natalie would pretend to be picking up coins until the moment when Renée opened her shutters. Then Natalie would seize a bouquet, with her poems attached, and hurl it through the window.

Natalie in love was, in fact, a formidable adversary. When Renée once refused to see her, Natalie had herself dressed up in white and carried to Renée's house inside a white satin coffin, carrying a lily. The gesture appeared to have had its desired effect on Renée although, had it been directed at Romaine, it might have boomer-anged.

Then Natalie discovered that she had a rival. Renée was being kept by an enormously wealthy Jewish woman, a Dutch baroness who had been nicknamed "La Brioche," who had a face as hard as a Valkyrie, but who had gained some strange hold over Renée and was showering her with gifts.

This must have been the woman who, Colette said in *The Pure and the Impure*, Renée referred to as The Master. The woman never materialized, but would send exotic gifts by messenger. It might be a collection of ancient Persian gold coins, or glass cabinets of exotic butterflies, or a miniature garden of bushes with leaves of crystal and fruit of precious stones.

This was the woman who intervened with finality when Natalie and Renée went to Mytilene, intending to found a new colony of lesbian poets in honor of Sappho. They had scarcely established themselves in two small villas, joined by a common orchard, when letters and telegrams began to arrive. Renée could not give her up, but she could not renounce Natalie either. Her state of mind was expressed in a short poem, *Cri*, in which her ambivalent feelings for Natalie are powerfully expressed: "As the moment arrives when the fireflies begin their wild dance/The hour when the desire of the moment begins to burn in our eyes/You will tell me again those flattering words in vain/I hate you and I love you abominably."

Whether Renée Vivien committed suicide as a result of her affair with Natalie Barney is a persistent rumor that cannot be verified. Natalie certainly felt a kind of responsibility for her death since she wrote, "Separated, then once more irresistibly drawn to each other to fall in love all over again, our persistent love affair went through all the stages of a deadly attachment which, perhaps, only death could end."

Or perhaps the other woman, "La Brioche," whom Renée said would kill her with her insatiable desires, was the reason for Renée's deliberate self-destructiveness. Her death is mysterious and sad, a testimony to a profound lack of self-worth. It is also tragic, since she had a poetic gift which might have deepened as it matured. No one who saw her in her final months in 1909, pale, her hands trembling, was in any doubt about her fate. "Above all, please let me not love again, oh God!" she wrote.

Renée Vivien is buried in the cemetery at Passy and the epitaph she wrote for herself is inscribed on her tomb:

> Voici la porte d'où je sors . . .
> O mes roses et mes épines!
> Qu'importe l'autrefois? Je dors
> En songeant aux choses divines. . . .
>
> Voici donc mon âme ravie,
> Car elle s'apaise et s'endort,
> Ayant, pour l'amour de la Mort,
> Pardonné ce crime: la Vie.*

The deadly attachment Natalie wrote about was in its final stages when Romaine met Renée Vivien. Although they were guests in the same house, she and Natalie were not to meet for another six years. Colette saw Renée as a figure of fantasy, ambivalent and remote; Natalie saw Renée as a doomed poet. But Romaine, who disliked ornamented surroundings as much as she avoided artificial personalities, looked beneath the surface and seems to have seen a waif from her own childhood. She remembers a thin face bowed beneath the weight of some early sorrow like St. Mar and what she appears to have felt for Renée was the sympathy of the jointly afflicted. There was a momentary void in Renée's life; she seemed desperate for companionship and Romaine soon found herself drifting along with her.

The friendship did not last. Renée in love played a calculating game and must have told Romaine about "La Brioche" and Natalie.

* The poem was translated by Natalie Barney:
> Here the door through which I passed
> —Oh roses mine and thorns, both mine!—
> What matters now to me the Past?
> Who sleep and dream of things divine?
>
> My ravished soul, from mortal breath
> Appeased, forgets all former strife,
> Having, from its great love of Death,
> Pardoned the crime of crimes—called Life.

An old friend was very jealous of Romaine, Renée hinted. Fine, Romaine decided. She disliked having her emotions manipulated, and in this case, her attachment to Renée had more to do with pity than love. Romaine used it as a reason to end the friendship.

Renée was very upset and sent a friend to intercede. She was all alone and wouldn't Romaine reconsider? Romaine would not and learned a few months later that Renée was dead. Romaine tried to absolve herself from the guilt she felt by telling herself that Renée had not been signaling for help; she had simply been looking for someone to drag down with her into the abyss. But Romaine continued to feel an obscure responsibility for Renée's death; one of the first links she had with Natalie.

Natalie, who had just moved from her house in Neuilly into a seventeenth-century mansion on the rue Jacob to be nearer Renée, was in despair. She wrote poems in which she described the effect Renée's death had on her: "My heart, which I believed to be hard and impenetrable/My heart has just reopened under an old wound." The following year she published *Je Me Souviens*, a long reminiscence about the emotional stages of their relationship, in which she had transmuted their tormented love affair into something starrily remote: "I remember her on the balcony with all the stars of the night and the darkness of the sky in her hair. I remember how the earth, covered with a blanket of snow, reminded me of our virginal bed of love and how everything seemed made for the memory of our love." Gradually the image faded, became more shining, more inaccessible, bearable. Then Natalie sent her poetry to the most powerful man she could think of.

He was the star of a literary world into which Romaine had not yet ventured, and almost a legend by the time Natalie met him: Rémy de Gourmont. This poet, novelist and spokesman for the Symbolist movement, had a formative influence on T. S. Eliot and Ezra Pound and was the publisher of the influential *Mercure de France*. Very few people had seen him for years. In 1910 he was fifty-two and suffering from lupus, a rare tubercular disease of the Middle Ages, which he was said to have contracted from poring over old manuscripts in the Bibliothèque Nationale. The disease had led to disfiguring facial scars, and De Gourmont had hidden himself in a cell of books on the rue des Saints-Pères and would only see close friends; among them Guillaume Apollinaire and André Rouveyre.

His influence continued undiminished and his approval was to be courted diligently. Natalie's daring was rewarded. They exchanged letters and then the momentous day arrived that De Gourmont agreed to be taken for a ride in her carriage.

Their conversation was so stilted that Natalie was surprised to receive a charming letter proposing that they meet from time to time. So their relationship began.

People who knew him were astounded that Rémy de Gourmont would allow Natalie Barney to ask things from him that he would not do for anyone else: go for a drive, for a boat ride, or appear, masked, at one of her costume balls. They were even more intrigued when he began to write essays in the *Mercure de France* that were open letters to a mysterious Amazon who was, it turned out, Natalie Barney. These elegant essays on the sexes, on chastity, will, sympathy, pleasure, love, and sensation, are the conclusions of a man whose gentleness, sensibility, and humanity glitter like the rarities they are, on every page. He asked little and gave abundantly. Natalie knew how much she was being honored. He was, she said, "the most balanced, the most erudite and the most sincere" of persons.

The letters demonstrate a mutuality of understanding that was, Richard Aldington wrote in the preface to the English edition of *Letters to the Amazon*, "neither a flirtation nor a passion. It is a kind of liaison of minds. . . ."

Perhaps. Or perhaps Rémy de Gourmont, who knew he was dying, chose to lavish his affections on someone he could never have physically, considering that she gave him everything he needed and as much as he could accept. He wrote, shortly before he died in 1915, "You came and raised me from the dead. I saw, I loved you, I love you. I owe you that, I owe you everything, gentle friend." (*Souvenirs Indiscrets.*)

What De Gourmont gave Natalie in turn was literary prominence. If she were being ostracized by her mother's friends because of her scandalous attachments with women (Her response to that was, "I considered it [a scandal] the best way of getting rid of nuisances"), Natalie was gaining something which, to her, was much more valuable: the acceptance on equal terms of an artistic and intellectual élite. An extraordinary assemblage of famous men and women came to the house on the rue Jacob for the next fifty years to meet Rémy de Gourmont's Amazon who was, Sir Harold Acton said (in *Memoirs of an Aesthete*) as much the muse of the *Mercure de France* as Gertrude Stein had represented *Transition*. Natalie's book, *Pensées d'une Amazone*, was written on the strength of Rémy de Gourmont's admiration. She was still being called the Amazon years after she gave up riding horses.

Natalie's Amazon-like prowess in an artistic milieu which, if Bohemian, was nevertheless exclusive, her independence, her wit, and her erudition, would have been immensely seductive for Romaine. Since they met in maturity (Romaine was forty-one and Natalie thirty-eight), their relationship lacked the sharp immediacy of those first virginal encounters between Natalie and Renée, or the passionate involvement of Romaine's early months with D'Annunzio.

They went away on trips together to Annecy and Aix-les-Bains, they wrote each other letters, gave each other books and music boxes. Romaine had necklaces of sapphires made for Natalie to her own design, and Natalie wrote poems to Romaine which speak of her qualities of mind rather than her physical charms. The relationship might have had a certain nostalgic appeal for Natalie, rediscovering in Romaine another lost poet haunted by thoughts of death. For Romaine, bored with Ida and at a safe distance from D'Annunzio, it promised even more: the union with another that she had sought from childhood; the all-accepting and loving closeness she had never received from her mother.

They had so much in common, not just because both had been born to the same generation of American families made wealthy by industry; or because they had similar French upbringings and had been accustomed all their lives to social privileges and obligations; or because they shared that curious sense of otherness that an expatriate, no matter how comfortably established, will feel about his surroundings; or because they had similar artistic tastes (Romaine politely deferring to Natalie on matters of literature, and Natalie to Romaine on matters of art).

The strength of their uncommonly enduring love affair was contained in the delicate balance of their opposing temperaments. Natalie said many times that she considered her life to be her work of art, and her poems, essays, and aphorisms only the by-products. Romaine lived for her art, driving toward her goal with a single-mindedness that Natalie admired without reservation. Romaine detested large gatherings of people and would go to great lengths to avoid them, while Natalie hated to be alone and surrounded herself with crowds of friends all her life. Romaine was mistrustful of others and painfully self-conscious. She never learned to deal with the devastating wit of the Paris intelligentsia. Stung, she would blurt out words she later regretted. Natalie, however, had Cocteau's confident gift of the retort. She could make the one remark that would deflect the barbs of others without permanently alienating them; a gift that Romaine rightly considered rare.

Natalie found something admirable about the least-promising newcomer, managed to transform ex-lovers into friends and would overlook glaring faults. Like John Brooks, Natalie asked very little from her friends, except to be intermittently amused and occasionally delighted. Romaine, however, would drop people like Cocteau, who genuinely wanted her friendship, because of some slight, imagined or real. She expected her close friends to be all things to her and would feel cheated when they inevitably disappointed her in some way. Natalie almost never fell out with anyone, whereas, if one were a friend of Romaine, one could expect to be a combatant on a perennial battleground. When there were overtures of reconciliation to be made, Natalie made them.

The Romantic Romaine (as Somerset Maugham called her) could, for all her common sense, think in terms of malevolent influences from other spheres. Natalie's analytical, detached, and philosophical temperament made such speculations impossible for her. Romaine poured out her feelings in an incoherent flood of drawings, memoirs, and long conversations. Natalie would be silent, until she had condensed her thought to its most succinct and polished expression. Romaine was capable of a poetic insight into her emotional problems. Natalie tended to dissect passion until it was drained of an emotional basis. What remained were shrewd rationalizations.

Like Renée, Romaine wanted to be all things to her lover; to possess and be possessed. She thought of passion as pure and spiritual, on a "higher" plane. To Natalie, it was a much more practical matter of how much sensuality could be gained for how little expenditure of feeling. She was, outwardly at least, self-sufficient, which was what Colette meant when she spoke of her cruel serenity. To make Natalie admit that she had any emotional needs was difficult as Romaine, who was fundamentally faithful in love, discovered.

Through the vicissitudes of their long affair, there was an implicit tolerance and tenderness, attested for by the six hundred letters they wrote to each other between 1920 and 1968 (the earlier correspondence is lost) while Romaine was in Capri, London, New York, Fiesole, Santa Margherita Ligure, Venice, or Nice, and Natalie stayed in Paris at the rue Jacob. They had the same circle of friends and adored long, giggly conversations over lunch and dinner, went dancing, swimming, and for long walks. Romaine fussed over Natalie's health and household and lack of exercise, and Natalie took on Romaine's career as a cause to espouse, as enthusiastically and maternally as she had promoted Renée.

Natalie in love was anxious, tender, placating. She gave Romaine repeated assurances of her uncritical admiration. There was no greater painter. There was no more beautiful or desirable woman. Even Romaine's voice suited her physique to perfection, unlike those of some lesser women, and Natalie adored listening to it. She idealized every aspect of Romaine, as if Romaine were a goddess to be worshiped, or a god whose displeasure meant the end of her existence. Although the facts of their frequent separations indicated otherwise, Natalie believed that what she wanted was union: "Alas to be one," she wrote to her "Angel darling" in Venice; "we who are so agreeably, so irreplaceably two together—a stronghold above the bleak and bland and banal world."

Although Romaine might have realized that her physical distance acted as an aphrodisiac for Natalie, Natalie remained innocently unaware of that possibility. "I try to follow your flight," she wrote one night when Romaine left Paris for Capri, "imagine where you are resting tonight . . . worrying for fear you may have added to your cold . . . but soon I hope for a reassuring wire from you, treasure of mine, who are my genius and all my worth and care."

For herself, Natalie detested travel and only did it in order to meet Romaine in Venice, Beauvallon, or Aix-les-Bains. "I am a little tired and bewildered," she wrote in mid-journey. "Towns and trips seem so strange to your wanderer. My dreams walk with silent feet over the balcony into the room, and most gently touch your sleeping eyelids goodnight—"

Natalie's nice poetic fancy was brought into play whenever she sensed that she might be losing Romaine. After a long stay in Washington, Natalie's plans to return were tinged with fears that she might have lost Romaine. "Lovers are quick to fear and words are the stars by which they must read the signs—I hope I've read them wrongly and that the over-sensitive chords that vibrate from me to you are not being tampered with."

Romaine, Natalie decided, must have found someone else: "I know that you have not bathed without everyone on that hot island [Capri] desiring you—that they could follow the glimmer of your perfect form to the ends of the earth." Yet, Natalie continued, perhaps none of them understood the inner Romaine the way she herself did. Surely Romaine would not lightly abandon such a valuable friendship, so mellow and sweetly perfected?

"I fear, I suppose, that relentless quality I've seen at times in you, that getting rid of everything quality . . . If I meet with that I must change into some dumb devoted pitiable animal—that you may stretch out your hard and just and gentle hands to me!" Natalie concluded, "I carry a warmth that is my love for you—Will you accept it amongst the fallen leaves of this Indian summer of ours?"

Believing herself to be loved brought out the very best in Romaine. She wrote clear, bold, and lengthy letters to her Nat-Nat, her darling, kind friend, exhorting her to "play your little music box darling and keep cheerful"; telling Natalie at Honfleur visiting the Duchesse de Clermont-Tonnerre that she was "glad Nat-Nat is cooking in the sun and hope she will come back sound and well"; writing, "Always remember, Nat-Nat, I prefer Nat-Nat to being alone, but alone to being with anyone else." She signed herself Angel Birdie and, "All love from poor little Angel, who wishes she had wings."

Romaine's letters to Natalie are less lyrical than the latter's, and express her feelings less candidly than her letters to D'Annunzio. It was as if her feelings for Natalie ran so deep that even Natalie must never know of them. Only in her notebooks, which no one else would ever see, could Romaine dare to wrestle with the profound emotions that Natalie aroused in her, attempting, less successfully than her friend, to pin them down in aphorisms: "From magic interchange of smile and look, there may spring an intimacy which can have the intensity of an abstraction. This sudden intrusion may die at birth, or it may become part of our life, making unreality of all that it excludes."

Romaine was accurate in sensing that her love for Natalie had become the central focus of her life, and that reality itself was receding into the distance. She would have happily considered the world well lost if she could have lived forever surrounded by the safe walls of this newest dream of love.

Life*

16

It now astonishes me that I was not more wary of people. I had no need of them and besides so much real trouble had come my way that though petty scandals and malicious intrigues could not harm me, they did make me extremely angry at times.

Indeed it was with the very stones that were finally flung at me that I built up the strong walls of this inner sanctuary.

At the end of World War I, Romaine returned to Capri for the summer. She had not been back for several years, but Brooks, still her husband in name at least, was there and so were some of her old friends. She might have been moved by an obscure urge to rediscover the island where she had been so happy twenty years before. Then, she had been a poor student. Now, she was a painter of consequence, who had two paintings hanging in the Luxembourg, and a subject for articles in British and French art magazines, which attempt to dissect the clinical aristocracy of her painting. She moved in elegant circles and had powerful friends.

She had changed in other ways. If being alone had sustained her youth, now it had become a necessity, almost an obsession. "In my youth I asked for the gift of solitude and now I must accept the strength and weakness that come with this gift." One had to be alone, since one was never going to be understood by others. Romaine did not understand that since she saw herself as someone who was open,

* Also called, "La Durée."

283

frank, and loyal; whose nature abhorred petty acts and required situations that were "clean, sure and straight"; who would have the courage to clear the air when the occasion demanded it by saying the hard truths.

Solitude was essential during the depressions that sometimes overwhelmed her, when she could feel her total apathy in the inert weight of her hands. At such moments, people and the world receded into a mist. "I shut myself up for months without seeing a soul," she wrote to D'Annunzio, "and give shape in my painting to my visions of sad and gray shadows." At such moments, all she asked was that the wind not blow too hard, that the sun not shine too fiercely and that she could somehow be warmed. A fierce internal struggle was raging beneath this apparent indifference to life since, "I want to have enthusiasm and when it dies I feel as if a part of myself had died . . ." She wrote in a notebook, "I fear those shadows most that start from my own feet."

Romaine liked to design her own writing paper in soft beiges, blues and pale grays, with a silver border, using an ornate silver monogram. Her writing paper of this period contains a new symbol: a tiny drawing of a stick figure in a boat, heading into the wind, enveloped by what seems to be an enormous wing. Romaine explained that it was herself in a ship without a tugboat that no one could restrain. An expression of flight, or of a long journey toward some distant goal, or of the conviction that she was doomed to meet her fate alone.

Capri was about to change markedly. The end of the war would bring with it a new prosperity. Handsome German boats disgorged wave upon wave of tourists, more than the island had ever seen before; tourists with cameras, who wanted first-class hotels and liveried porters and elegant menus, who paid well for newspapers, dances, theatricals, and games of tennis. They thought Capri was such a quaint old place that they would tear most of it down to make room for their private villas. Morgano's Café, where one could laze away an evening on the dim terrace or join a friend for a game of dominoes, would be taken over by a smart young set insisting upon floodlights so that they could dance on the terrace. The old crowd would see the changes and regret them, but they had not been driven out yet; neither had Brooks.

He had been living out the war in one of the handsomest villas on the island, which he had rented with E. F. Benson and Somerset Maugham: the Villa Cercola. It was a glorious old house which one reached by a twisting alley of steps leading up from the town toward Tiberius' palace. One passed through a gateway in a whitewashed wall into a spacious interior: six bedrooms, two dining rooms, two bathrooms, and a long studio at the back looking over a terrace and, beyond that, the bay of Naples. There was a short, vine-covered pergola and a garden full of grapevines and olive trees and, E. F. Benson said, a great stone pine "which whispered to the slightest breeze and rooned when sirocco blew." (*Final Edition.*)

Romaine, who bought it a couple of years later when their lease ran out, adored it. She set about replanting the garden, where nothing had been tended for years and overrun by a strange blue flower which seemed to need no water and thrived in the driest and sunniest weather.

On hearing that Romaine was due to arrive in August, John Brooks hastily moved out to the smaller Villa Salvia. "The arrival of this striking personality was a sensation," Faith Compton Mackenzie related in *More Than I Should.* "A heat wave, hot even for Capri in August, sent temperatures up. Feverish bouquets of exhausted blooms lay about the big studio, letters and invites strewed her desk, ignored for the most part, while she, wrapped in her cloak, would wander down to the town as the evening cooled and sit in the darkest corner of Morgano's Café terrace, maddeningly remote and provocative."

Romaine's arrival on Capri in the summer of 1918 had been remarked upon by two people who took the most animated interest in the effect it produced. They were Sir Compton Mackenzie (Monty) and his wife, Faith. They met Romaine through Brooks, and Faith in particular was to become a close friend and wrote about Romaine in her memoirs. Sir Compton, a novelist, playwright, and biographer who wrote more than a hundred books, many of them best sellers, also described Romaine in his autobiography and made her a central figure in his novel, *Extraordinary Women.*

Compton Mackenzie was thirty-five that summer. He had served with the British Army in Gallipoli and Greece and had been invalided out with dysentery and leg ailments. He and his wife had taken the Casa Solitaria, another striking villa on Capri. The house perched on the side of a cliff with a matchless view of the sea. It was paved with tiles of baroque design and contained a curious collection of furniture, including Maxim Gorky's writing table.

Romaine was still exploring "the color of distances, gray." She had come to paint, but everyone was tanned "the color of old chestnut," which was most irritating. The only person who had retained a painterly pallor was Monty Mackenzie, since illness and work had kept him indoors. She offered to paint him.

The portrait was never made, but that Romaine would have suggested it is not surprising. Compton Mackenzie was an uncommonly handsome man, his features only saved from actual beauty by a look of somber determination. The effect was to suggest an intense and secretive inner life which, from Romaine's point of view, would have been much more interesting. He was, at that moment, energetically set upon a writing career. He had already published several works, including *Sinister Street*, a novel based on his youth, which Henry James had admired. His memory for names and events was prodigious, and he was making use of every conversation, every scrap of gossip, every incident, and every interesting new personality that might come his way.

Extraordinary Women, one of his less important novels, presents a portrait of the lesbian group that had temporarily taken over the island until the men came back from the war. The plot, which the author described as a "theme and variations," requiring feats of imaginative dexterity that left him exhausted, centers around their romantic intrigues. The book attracted considerable attention when it was published in 1928 (it was called "a farcical tour de force"), and it was one of the first to deal with the subject of lesbianism. It was allowed to be published by the same Home Secretary who banned Radclyffe Hall's *The Well of Loneliness* since it was not, like the latter, an impassioned plea for the acceptance of lesbianism, but a comic-opera view of the subject; an approach the British Establishment heartily approved of. (Its author was rather disappointed.)

Compton Mackenzie seemed to give very little thought, then or later, to the underlying causes of lesbianism. It was a "predisposition," like homosexuality and, like homosexual circles, full of petty back-biting and endless, frivolous love affairs. There were women who

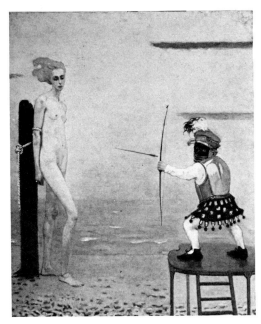

The Masked Archer, *painting by Romaine Brooks, 1910–11.*
(Maître Léon· Marie Emmanuel)

Portrait of Fothergill by Romaine Brooks. (Meryle Secrest)

Natalie and Romaine in Geneva, probably not long after they met, circa 1915. (Natalie Clifford Barney)

Romaine and Gabriele d'Annunzio, circa 1915. (Maître Léon-Marie Emmanuel)

Renée Vivien, Paris, circa 1900. (Maître
Léon-Marie Emmanuel)

Lady Anglesey, 1902: inscribed to Romaine.
(Maître Léon-Marie Emmanuel)

Self-portrait, 1900, age twenty-six. (Maître Léon-Marie Emmanuel)

Drawing of Romaine by Edouard MacAvoy. (Meryle Secrest)

Romaine, circa 1925. (Maître Léon-Marie Emmanuel)

Natalie Barney, nude study. (Natalie Clifford Barney)

Natalie Barney in Florence during World War II at the Villa Sant'Agnese. (Maître Léon-Marie Emmanuel)

Natalie in riding costume. (Natalie Clifford Barney)

Natalie and Laura Barney. (Natalie Clifford Barney)

Natalie in front of the Temple of Friendship during the '20s. (Natalie Clifford Barney)

Villa Cercola, Capri, circa 1920. (Maître Léon-Marie Emmanuel)

Château Grimaldi at turn of the century. (Maître Léon-Marie Emmanuel)

Romaine and Natalie, circa 1935, in Pari(s)
(Natalie Clifford Barney)

Romaine and Natalie at Beauvallon, France,
1936. (Alice DeLamar)

made fools of themselves and there were the few genuine inverts; those one respected. Romaine was one of the latter.

She was small and dark, Compton Mackenzie says of Olimpia Leigh, and at the height of her beauty. Romaine was forty-four and her hair had been cropped short so that a lock or two would fall over her smooth, high forehead. She appears in a photograph, taken on the terrace of the Villa Cercola, as she must have looked to Compton Mackenzie: "'Like a nightingale with shapeless wings wrapped around a little body.' That was exactly the effect of Olimpia in her draperies. But her body though little was not shapeless and her throat though tawny as the nightingale's was beautifully modelled, and her eyes as dark and bright . . ." She had a "low, thrilling voice," "burning eyes"; she had "the air of a crouching nightingale."

Olimpia Leigh was a composer and Greek scholar, famous for having set almost all of Sappho's poetry to music, perhaps the greatest female creative mind since Sappho, and "to be loved by Olimpia Leigh even for five minutes gave any young woman who cared about it a cachet not obtainable since the days when young women could boast of being loved by the mighty Sappho herself." ("The portrait of her is an exact one in psychological terms," Compton Mackenzie said. "I found as a writer that, if you want to avoid libel actions, you change the background but do nothing to change the character.")

What made Romaine so alluring to her author was her air of self-sufficiency: her complete indifference to what anyone else thought or did. His wife, Faith, echoed the verdict. Romaine was "a figure of intriguing importance, because for the first time I met a woman complete in herself, isolated mentally and physically from the rest of her kind, independent in her judgments, accepting or rejecting as she pleased. . . ."

Such Olympian detachment was bound to be irresistible to one foolhardy enough to attempt the heights. Rosalba Donsante, the flirt of the island, elected herself as Olimpia Leigh's next conquest. Rosalba was modeled on Mimi Franchetti, daughter of a Baron who had composed several operas, whose mother had been a beauty of such rarity and renown that when she appeared in her box at the opera the rest of the audience would turn in their chairs to stare at her.

Rosalba was just as beautiful. "Every feature was in proportion and every feature was clear cut. Her mouth curved up at the corners like the mouths Leonardo da Vinci loved to paint; and like Leonardo's saints and sinners her face was heart-shaped, so that her mouth broke into flower above a slim and pointed chin."

She liked to wear short accordion-pleated skirts and bow ties, go without a hat (to show off her glinting bronze hair), carry a cane, and smoke cigarettes stuck in long holders of white jade. All this striking of poses was bad enough but what was worse, her author said, was that Rosalba was an unregenerate troublemaker who tested her skill at breaking hearts out of sheer perversity. The most he could say in her defense was that she had charm, and she "cheered things up."

His wife, Faith, was more generous. Just to look at Mimi Franchetti would almost compensate for everything else. "Who that saw her will ever forget the black silk Pierrot of carnival night, whose great white ruff framed a small Greek head?"

Hearing that Olimpia needed a piano to practice on, Rosalba sent one and was quickly rebuffed. Rosalba realized that all her self-confidence would not be enough unless she could convince "her adversary" that she could be equally aloof.

" 'I am so sorry that I have bored you with my piano,' she [Rosalba] said haughtily.

" 'Yes,' Olimpia agreed, 'it was an infernal nuisance.' And in the same breath she added, 'I rather like your hands.'

"Rosalba cheered up, and laying her hands on the table regarded them, and the three signet rings on her boyish fingers.

" 'They are not so nice as other parts of me,' she said at last.

" 'I didn't say they were nice hands,' Olimpia responded. 'I said, "I rather liked them." '

" 'For me that makes them nice,' Rosalba declared with a smile.

"(Olimpia got up, wrapped her cloak around her head, and walked away without a word.)

" '*Tu sais Olga,*' cried Cléo with one of her huge laughs as she banged her fist down on the table, '*elle est vraiment impayable. Eh, eh, tu auras à faire, ma poupée d'amour.*' " (pp 246–47.)

Such courtships the author explained, were complicated by the fact that both were women. Although one might assume the masculine role, the pose seldom survived "such a searching test as court-

288

ship" and eventually both took turns at playing "the maiden loth. And they are both at any crisis of emotion apt to become as passive as ordinary women. Which is, if you come to think of it, a little humiliating."

The affairs were brief because passion, between women, had nowhere to go, Compton Mackenzie wrote. "Normal love" might eventually develop into friendship, even though "what a woman really means by friendship with a man is being able to depend on him to look out trains for her in Bradshaw," while what a man means by the term "is complete relief from all responsibility either for her emotions or her trains." It was even more difficult for two women to pass from passion to "a humdrum talking-about-clothes friendship, because though a woman may forgive a man for a failure of emotion at last, since that is what she has been perpetually expecting, she is not going to forgive another woman. Her physical responsibility is so slight compared with a man's that there is simply no room for excuses."

Olimpia hesitated briefly before deciding that she wanted nothing from the tiresome Rosalba, who was not even the type she fancied. To live with Rosalba would be "exactly like having a nephew about the place"; she preferred girlish girls. So Olimpia summoned Zoe, a beautiful American girl, from Paris. To learn that she had a rival only made Rosalba more determined; and she gave lavish dinners every night. (Her author makes amusing use of the knowledge that a sunburn was anathema to Romaine that summer, by having Olimpia profess the same dislike. Knowing this, Rosalba schemes to get Zoe sunburnt and succeeds.)

"We know what an atmosphere can be created at a dinner-party by one jealous woman," the author commented. "At Rosalba's parties there were often eight women, the palpitations of whose hidden jealousies . . . was in its influence . . . as potent as the dreadful muttering of subterranean fires before an eruption."

Olimpia might accept and then not show up, leaving everyone to "agonize" over her empty chair. Or she might refuse and then appear halfway through dinner, in a cloak of fine white wool, her brown legs bare except for white sandals. She would not sit at table but would draw up a chair beside everyone, "and what the company suffered under her burning gaze might be hard to make credible."

She would leave with Zoe. Rosalba would counter by hiring four local barbers to serenade her house. One by one the lights in Olimpia's windows would go out.

There are others on the fringe of this charade. One is Rory Freemantle, supposedly modeled on Radclyffe Hall, who is supporting Rosalba. She wears a monocle, affects men's clothes with such success that it is hard to believe she isn't one, writes bad poems which she publishes herself under a pseudonym, likes to breed bulldogs, and appears to play the role of the unappreciated in love: "'I,' thought Rory, 'I am just one of those great clumsy marbles fit to be leant against eternally.'"

What everyone found so absurd about Radclyffe Hall was that she should seriously propose a marriage with Una, Lady Troubridge. What is so ridiculous about Rory Freemantle is her hopeless infatuation for Rosalba, which has everything in common with that of a "foolish middle-aged man." In a long, stern speech, Olimpia tells Rory how stupid she is, for thinking that she, Olimpia, could be even slightly interested in Rosalba; for trying to write poetry, since "'I think all women are stupid who imagine themselves artists when they are . . . nothing more than sexually starved'"; and for dressing so ridiculously when, Olimpia concludes, delivering the *coup de grâce*, "'I look in vain for any single masculine quality in your mind.'"

Marguerite Radclyffe Hall, who became "John" to her friends, was born in about 1886, daughter of an English father and an American mother and spent her young womanhood hunting, writing poetry, and traveling. When she was in her late twenties she fell in love with an older woman, "Ladye," who encouraged her to publish her poems and write short stories and novels.

In 1915 she met Una Vincenzo, the daughter of Captain Henry Ashworth Taylor, who had become the second wife of Admiral Sir Ernest Troubridge. Una seemed an unlikely subject for a grand passion. In later years, Sir Harold Acton described her (in *Memoirs of an Aesthete*), as "a short-haired elderly dame in masculine attire . . . Though she discoursed about dogs and looked as if she breezed in from some English vicarage, she did not help put Evelyn [Waugh] at his ease."

Una was somewhat taken aback by John's militant lesbianism.

Nevertheless she fell in love and left her husband to move in with John. Sir Ernest countered with a famous suit for the return of his conjugal rights, citing Radclyffe Hall as co-respondent.

This was enough, but then Radclyffe Hall published *The Well of Loneliness,* a plodding but painfully honest novel, which sets out in detail the kind of life she and women like her are forced to lead; their sense of guilt, their despair, and their need to be taken seriously by society.

The book caused an uproar. Newspapers called it "perverted decadence" and it had to be withdrawn in Britain, where it could not be sold until after World War II. It did rather better in the United States, where it was judged not to be obscene, and elsewhere. It was translated into eleven languages and had sold a million copies by the time its author died in 1943.

Romaine never thought John could write, and in a letter to Natalie Barney she dismissed *The Well of Loneliness* as "a ridiculous book, trite, superficial, as was to be expected. A digger-up of worms with the pretention of a distinguished archaeologist." Radclyffe Hall had based one of her characters on Romaine, although exactly which one is unclear, and Romaine considered it no likeness: "She has watched me with the eye of a sparrow who sees no further than the window-pane. I find myself (?) chirping, pecking, hopping, just as she would do herself."

If Romaine invited them to Capri, it was because of her fondness for Una and, in 1924, Romaine took a studio in London at 15 Cromwell Road, to paint Una's portrait. Una had begun to wear mannish clothes: stiff shirts, high collars, and tailored jackets, along with the monocle and earrings that became her trademark.

The sittings caused a strain on the friendship perhaps, Romaine decided, because she had made her dislike for John's literary pretensions too obvious. There was the further question of whether Una really liked the portrait. She told Romaine that she was well pleased, but to friends she said, "Am I really like that?"

It was obvious to those who saw the work the following year (in four cities: New York at the Wildenstein Galleries, Chicago at the Art Institute, London at the Alpine Club, and Paris at the Galerie Charpentier) that Romaine had meant the portrait to be a caricature.

She wrote to Natalie, "Una is funny to paint. Her get-up is remarkable. She will live perhaps and cause future generations to smile," and in old age, whenever the subject of the portrait was brought up, Romaine would roar with laughter. Whether you were a lesbian or not, if you made yourself look ridiculous, Romaine considered you fair game.

Una, Lady Troubridge, Radclyffe Hall, and Mimi Franchetti might strike Romaine as bizarrely amusing, nothing more; but Renata Borgatti was a different matter. Mrs. Hamish Hamilton, wife of the London publisher, knew her through her first husband (and Mimi's cousin) Luigi Franchetti, who had shared a flat with Renata in Rome.

"She was an extraordinary woman, a pure freak of nature," Mrs. Hamilton said. "She shouldn't have been made like a woman because to all intents and purposes she was a man, and she treated women exactly as if she were one. She looked rather like the young Liszt and I haven't met a woman yet who was not ready to fall into her arms, if Renata wanted her . . . She and my husband parted when they ended up by quarreling. Over ladies, of course."

Compton Mackenzie also considered her some kind of biological aberration, a man whom some unkind fate had given a woman's body; doomed to suffer from unrequited love since, "the masculine side of her nature was so dominant that she sought women as she found them, without waiting for those who were temperamentally akin to herself . . . Her gray eyes were half the time clouded with the preoccupation of why she had been made as she was."

This "freak of nature," who has the coltish charm of Romaine's portrait of Peter, the young English girl, was the daughter of Giuseppe Borgatti, a famous Italian Wagnerian tenor, and had begun her musical career by accompanying her father on concert tours. In later years she was performing on the concert stage with major European orchestras and was particularly known for her recitals of Debussy, a composer Romaine also loved.

Renata Borgatti appears in *Extraordinary Women* as Cléo Gazay. She has "a straight nose and the jutting brows that hold music within them, with a finely carved chin out-thrust less as a sign of obstinacy than for some austere determination of mind. Her feet are large like a man's and her clothes are flung around her without any regard to the fashion of the moment. They are not so much clothes as curtains hung up to exclude the night or let in the day as desired."

At the end of World War I, Renata was poor, studying music, and giving free concerts for friends in her studio on the Punta Tragara, or performing for groups of the Mackenzies' friends at the Casa Solitaria. Faith's memories of Renata are nostalgic with remembered pleasures of those performances:

"I long to cry: Ah, but you should have heard her at the Punta Tragara, playing music because she loved it, with divine irresponsibility and some wrong notes, because she never practised enough. You should have seen that silhouette swaying to the music in the candlelight which flickered because outside the wind was booming from the south-west. You can't tell unless you hear her like that, what an artist Borgatti is!"

But Renata, who played like "a man of undisciplined genius," and was always judged that way, according to Monty, retained a few "feminine" weaknesses. One evening, after the group had gone to hear someone at a concert, Mimi Franchetti presented Faith with a bottle of absinthe as a gift. When the Mackenzies returned to the Casa Solitaria that night, they found that the kitchen door had been kicked in, Faith's room was in an uproar, jewelry was stolen along with a cheese and a bottle of absinthe, and Faith's portrait had been turned upside down on her dressing table. Although the matter was dropped, at Monty's urging, the local police decided that Signorina Borgatti was the guilty party.

Monty told Faith to shrug off the whole business. "So long as these ridiculous women are indulging in these ridiculous love affairs, we shall have these exhibitions of tormented and disordered nerves. If Borgatti did it, that bottle of absinthe Franchetti gave you after Bim's very successful concert may have filled her with green-eyed jealousy . . ."

The fact that his wife, Faith, was involved, however innocently, in "ridiculous" lesbian love affairs, may account for the occasionally testy tone of *Extraordinary Women*. It is the tone of a man who finds himself facing the uncomfortable possibility that he is a rival with another woman for his wife's affections. In this case, aping the male role had gone much too far.

This, perhaps, was the reason why the episode impressed itself on the author's mind. In any event, the same incident returns, its details intact, even embellished, in his novel; but with a different cast. This time, Olimpia is the one whose house is broken into, the back door kicked in, and jewelry stolen. It is her photograph that was turned upside down on the dressing table; to it the thief has added a large moustache and beard. The incident and opera buffo scene which follows with the local carabinieri, provides the climax to those variations on a single theme which the author has been inventing for eighteen previous chapters.

For Renata it was Mimi Franchetti that year; but the following year it became Romaine. Photographs of Renata in Romaine's effects show her in a one-piece belted swimming outfit, her shapely legs propped carelessly against a boulder and an unflattering swimming cap jammed over her head; or in profile, her hair slicked back, gazing at Romaine with undisguised passion. There is another photograph of them with a group of friends, in which Renata's arm is linked lightly and possessively through Romaine's.

In casting Romaine in the role of a detached observer, Compton Mackenzie could not have known that she rather enjoyed the Byzantine implications of the passions flickering through a group of women and giving rich overtones to superficial conversations. Romaine was enough of a flirt to enjoy the idea that she might be the focus of a jealous intrigue. Natalie, who played the game consummately well and savored its particular delights with exquisite amusement, always understood. Besides, there would have been something engaging about Renata's frank acceptance of her lesbian role, a subject about which Romaine was always equivocal; and something unique about Renata's extraordinary ability to look like a frankly handsome youth at one moment and then, with an unexpected wealth of hair flowing around her shoulders, to reveal a disarming femininity. Such ambivalence was not enough to engage Romaine's interest permanently and, a year later (1920), Romaine was writing to Natalie from Capri that she was trying to avert another visit from Renata and declining to help her out financially, "as in the past."

Romaine's portrait of Renata Borgatti is the enduring souvenir of that transient relationship. It is one of her most powerful works; a spare, tightly controlled, dramatic portrait of a pianist at a moment of complete concentration. But there is more to it than that. The painting conveys a sense of silent space, even mysticism, which has a great deal in common with the Symbolist movement. The way Romaine has used balance and interval, even the small but telling details, such as the particular browns and duns chosen, and Renata's extreme, almost deathlike pallor, are directly related to the portraits of Lévy-Dhurmer. Romaine may even have known that painter, ten years her senior, since he was a passionate admirer of Renée Vivien and designed the covers for her volumes of poetry.

Although Romaine disdained movements and disliked the suggestion that she had been influenced by anyone, she would have been temperamentally in tune with the Symbolists; with their fascination for interior landscapes, for the occult, for eccentric and bizarre ways of life, and dissonant moods. Romaine would always believe that a strange atmosphere surrounded her, that "things happened which I have nothing to do with and which even frighten me sometimes." It was a dread of the irrational, which Ella would have perfectly understood. The portrait of Renata contains this mystical dread, coupled with an emotional atmosphere that is both intense and icily cold; qualities that distinguish all of Romaine's best works.

And so the convoluted plots which the extraordinary women wrote for themselves spun themselves out as intricately as a tango; so intricately, in fact, that even the principal dancers could not see the pattern their feet were making and considered themselves only spectators. Romaine was avoiding everyone, she wrote to Natalie; "I prefer having no obligations and making no efforts."

Just the same, she showed up on Morgano's terrace, that summer and the summers which followed, flopping a pair of wet and sand-encrusted espadrilles down on the chair beside her, while she wiggled her toes under the table; and perhaps she nodded perfunctorily to Respighi and his wife or F. Scott Fitzgerald and Zelda or stole occasional glances at D. H. Lawrence, who Brooks said was such a brilliant writer, who might be "nervously (fingering) his beard while being unnaturally polite to a hostess who bored him." (*Town and*

Country, April 15, 1926.) Such international celebrities were taking over Capri, while those who had discovered the island cherished it and added their own rich, rococo and somehow sublimely appropriate qualities to its ambience; struggled against the onslaught or tried to ignore it.

Uncle Charley was still there and Romaine must have seen him often. He was older but still handsome and was looked after by three or four pretty girls in the Villa Narcissus while he painted his interminable pictures of Vesuvius in sun and shade, by night and morning, in mist and rain; paintings that E. F. Benson thought looked curiously like bad copies of first-rate works. Uncle Charley's beard might be whiter and his halo of hair thinner, but he was still disarmingly hospitable, raising his glass to toast his guests and telling them to "Drink hearty."

Baron d'Adelsward-Fersen, whom Compton Mackenzie made the central character of *Vestal Fire*, a novel about Capri's homosexual circle and companion volume to *Extraordinary Women*, was still living in his remote villa near the ruins of Tiberius' palace, and was still inviting friends in to while away tedium in his opium den furnished with so many ingratiating couches. (He died a few years later of an overdose of cocaine.) Romaine, like Faith, would have gone there for tea instead since she sternly disapproved of such excesses; perhaps to take another look at a portrait of herself that was hanging on his wall. (The artist is not known, nor are the present whereabouts of the painting.) It showed, Faith wrote, a young woman seated on a chair, her elegant legs displayed to good advantage in black knee breeches, and one white-cuffed hand dangling; and full, challenging eyes. John Brooks always wanted it.

Romaine was giving parties, to which she would invite the Mackenzies. They were all mad about dancing and since Romaine had one of two wooden floors on the island (the other was in the Quisisana Hotel) she often gave the dances. Or she would take her Decca portable over to the Mackenzies, along with her Chinese manservant to play it; ever so subtly, Paul Whiteman's "I'm Going South" and Vincent Lopez' "Adoring You" would be replaced by "Ah Fim Loo" and "Shanghai Lullaby."

Romaine would be summoned occasionally to Anacapri for dinner with Dr. Munthe, who had become a legendary figure on the island for what were believed to be his miraculous healing qualities. He was almost blind and never went out in the daytime but would walk out at dusk . . . "and the peasant folk looked on him with awe and affection as he passed, stilling a crying child, or laying a hand on an aching head." (E. F. Benson.) It was there, one weekend, that she met the Marchesa Luisa Casati.

Everyone had painted La Casati: Augustus John, Giovanni Boldini, Kees Van Dongen. She was legendary and self-invented, like a D'Annunzio heroine miraculously come to life who lives out all of that poet's most extravagant and lurid fantasies with the clockwork precision of the beautiful doll in *The Tales of Hoffmann*. What mattered was her improbability, and like film fans a decade later, the public would have been annoyed, even offended, if she had ceased to live up to their illusions. So she gave lavish costume balls on the canals of Venice, contemptuously accepting and discarding lovers; living with leopards, monkeys, and snakes; inspiring fads for gold evening capes and wide-brimmed hats with cascading feathers, and giving rise to dozens of silent screen beauties with cadaverous skins and eyes like searing coals. That there was something sinister about this outrageous, wealthy, spoiled woman, only added to her allure. Her audience was scandalized and thrilled when she appeared one night in her box at the Paris Opera with one arm dripping blood; the neck of a chicken had been slit over it.

As with Ida Rubinstein, Romaine was admiring but not overawed. "She is a bit too sloe-button-eyed for my taste," she wrote to Natalie, adding a descriptive little sketch; "and the white of the eye is red." But La Casati had taken a fancy to her, and so "she must be bounced up again" for dinner. La Casati wanted a new portrait of herself, and only Romaine could do it.

Romaine was flattered and amused and indecisive. "I should like," she wrote, "to paint a *chef d'oeuvre* but also hesitate before the ordeal." She said she had no equipment; Uncle Charley supplied the canvas. She said she would not go up to Anacapri; La Casati announced that she would pose in the Villa Cercola three times a week. Then Romaine, desperate for a way out, decided that she must paint La Casati nude, knowing that she didn't want that. "Very well, I'll be nude," La Casati said; and that was that.

One of La Casati's male admirers was willing to pay any sum for the result. Romaine refused to sell the painting because she detested it: "It wasn't me." Romaine's assessment is correct. What she had seen in Rubinstein was an exquisitely refined, even etherealized, sexuality which seemed to embody an ideal. Faced with La Casati's bitch-goddess, Romaine was baffled and took the fantasy for fact. As Kees Van Dongen painted her, this beautiful eccentric retains an essential femininity, however haughty and calculating; in Romaine's portrait she is desexed and has become a raging figure bent on vengeance, with ropes of hair writhing like snakes and feet like claws. Romaine kept the canvas rolled up under her bed for years.

Though not as constantly in each other's company as they had been twenty years before, Romaine was still seeing John Brooks. They liked and depended upon each other to some extent, and even if each condemned the other heartily to others, the complaints, after so many years, had taken on the ritualized aspect of old and barely remembered feuds. Romaine fell back into the habit of asking Brooks for advice (she was rather flabby, she wrote to Natalie, but Brooks assured her that since everybody climbed on Capri, her muscle tone would soon be restored), and she was pleased when he pronounced Natalie's poems in English as "extraordinarily good. I am glad of his appreciation as he certainly knows his English language," Romaine wrote.

Brooks was comfortably installed in the Villa Salvia, which was small but quite charming, with a kitchen, a tiny dining room, bedroom and living room; looked after by a woman who cleaned in the morning, cooked lunch, and left a cold dinner for him. His sitting room was lined with books and he was still playing on the same piano, now hopelessly out of tune; still studying the same tattered copy of Beethoven's sonatas.

He hardly looked older, although he was almost sixty. As the years came and went, his face took on a more ascetic and ecclesiastical aspect; "He might have been the model for some mitred adoring bishop in a 'Nativity' by Bellini," Benson wrote. He was still reading Meredith and Walter Pater, studying Leopardi by night and D'Annunzio's verses upon awakening. He had sent his translation of the Hérédia sonnets to a publisher, but nothing came of it. Now he had embarked on a translation of Greek epigrams, with his characteristic "indolent industry," as Benson put it. Benson's judgment of Brooks' translations, while severe ("a careful translation devoid of any rendered magic") is accurate, if a sampling of Brooks' poetry* is any judge; it is ploddingly conventional and so awkwardly phrased that it seems to have been written by a man deaf to the music of language.

Brooks never left Capri and some said, although Pino Orioli didn't believe it, that Brooks had never seen an electric tramway. As before, he seemed to be living on air although, as before, his secret sustenance was the money his long-suffering friends provided and which Brooks, out of an excess of delicacy (they assumed), never mentioned. Or perhaps it was Brooks' blithe, incorrigible assumption that to be supported by his friends was no more than his due. Benson relates that Brooks had discovered an excellent piece of land for sale and was proposing that he, Benson, buy it and build a villa, so that Brooks could live there; a proposal that Benson found intensely irritating. Nevertheless, his friends were obliged to rescue Brooks again and again, as he teetered serenely, from the verge of financial ruin. He often did not have enough money to buy another day's supply of coke for his stove.

Brooks' perpetual tranquility was, for the Mackenzies, one of his most endearing characteristics. They invited him to dinner constantly even if he did tend to fall asleep afterward and was getting rather deaf. Monty had discovered, quite by accident, that he could concentrate superbly well if someone were playing the piano, and when Faith could not, Brooks was called upon for the necessary background noise.

The years passed and the Mackenzies left Capri. Monty moved to Herm, one of the smallest of the Channel Islands, and Faith spent much of her time in Paris, where she visited Romaine in her new studio on the Quai de Conti, or had lunch with her and Natalie Barney and then went on to the Folies-Bergère to see Josephine Baker being lowered from the ceiling in a basket of roses. Faith met Mimi Franchetti at one of Romaine's parties; no longer as slim as a

† See Appendix, p. 414.

wraith and attempting to write poetry, but as charming as ever. She also met Ford Madox Ford, Mary Butts, the actress-wife of Maeterlinck and an "exceedingly interesting" person, a Dr. Marx whom Faith advised to see a psychoanalyst for his yawning fits, before she discovered that he was himself a prominent psychoanalyst.

Romaine's visits to Capri slowed and finally stopped ("Olimpia Leigh and Bébé Buonagrazia left Sirene by the early morning boat at half-past four"), and Brooks saw less and less of people. The Misses Perry had died and so had Baron Fersen and Mr. Jerome, the historian of Tiberius; Norman Douglas had moved away and the island was full of a fashionable crowd whom Brooks did not take the trouble to know. He didn't seem to mind. His memory often returned to those days when he had written a *Masque of Mithras* and performed it one night in the Mithraic cave; he played Apollo, barelegged and holding a lyre.

"Well, well, he had had a good time, there were still his translations to polish, and he was really feeling too tired for social life if there had been any." (*Always Afternoon.*) He could not walk as much any more. He was having difficulty eating. His financial situation worsened at the same inexorable pace, and Brooks, now very ill, was faced with the prospect of eviction. Friends came to the rescue again with a "loan," and Brooks decided to take his doctor's advice and go to the mainland for a checkup.

The trip exhausted him and he took to his bed. As Faith sat beside him, a package came in the mail. It was his translation of the Greek epigrams, which yet one more publisher had rejected:

"That was too bad—too bad—a life's work, you might call it. He wouldn't, no, he wouldn't bother to send it off again . . . Really there was little more to be said, or done. That pain was suddenly much worse. He hardly spoke again." Brooks died on May 31, 1929, of cancer of the liver.

"The mountains and the sea, the temples of Paestum, the snowy cloud above Vesuvius . . . the shimmer of famous towns all round that coast, the white villas of today, the brown ruins of yesterday, the old plainsong of the husbandman chanting at his toil upon the stony hillside, the tinkle of goat-bells . . . all were fused up here in an eternal now: time and space, the works of man, the might of nature.

Pompeii was not more dead, Naples not more alive." (*Extraordinary Women.*)

In the winter of 1971, Sir Compton and Lady Mackenzie were living in a corner house on one of Edinburgh's most imposing Georgian squares. Coming up from London in the train the countryside was all black and brown; clods of earth turned over for the winter, blackened stems, black woods and gray branches, and flocks of gulls settling in the fields among shaggy sheep with black faces. A city of black houses climbing the hills, surrounded by blackened tree trunks; and silhouetted against a grass of a swelling, intense green. Gusts of wind swirled the leaves up into the air and deposited them in a slippery, decaying mass, in the gutters.

Inside a subdued light; a reproduction of Botticelli's "Birth of Venus" over the fireplace, fitfully lit by the flames and, in the far corners of the room, the looming mass of books, the vast library which goes to the University of Texas after his death. Cups of milky tea and a sponge cake that melts in the mouth like clotted cream.

For Compton Mackenzie, as for Romaine, there had been something basically inimical about Capri; or perhaps it was the too-insistent, too-alluring, eternal present from which he had fled, to other islands tinged in more muted hues. On Herm in the Channel Islands and later in the Outer Hebrides, Sir Compton wrote like a man possessed, from 3 P.M. to 7 A.M., with a half an hour each for tea and dinner; living on "Phospherine, Alexine, Ovaltine, Sanatogen, cheese and Victoria plums"; writing one book after another including *Whiskey Galore*, which became the film *Tight Little Island*, endless newspaper and magazine articles, founding a magazine (*The Gramophone*), writing the first million-word novel, *The Four Winds of Change*, and, at last, his autobiography, *My Life and Times*, in ten volumes.

After Faith had died, he had married his devoted secretary, Chrissie, who had presided over the birth of so many novels. They were married for a year; she was operated on for cancer and died. Then he married her sister, Lillian, the present Lady Mackenzie.

Sir Compton was eighty-eight‡ and still almost as vigorous in body

‡ He died a year later, December 13, 1972.

as in mind; an astonishingly attractive, strong, sculpted face, with high cheekbones rising cleanly above a beard. He was wearing a tartan jacket and a red shirt and green velvet corduroy pants and brown leather sandals. He sat in a chair as if ready to leap up at the least sound, and one could see his irritation at the enforced idleness in the way he would fold his fingers on top of each other, where they would tap about restlessly. Even his toes twitched.

He was quite blind. "I can't," he said simply, "see my hand in front of my face." He could no longer write novels although he was mastering the trick of dictating articles, and he could pin point the direction of voices so accurately that it was impossible to know that he was not actually looking at the speaker. He could grope his way unaided from the library to the sitting room for tea and put a plate back on the table beside him. He smoked a pipe, and when he could not immediately light the match, would delicately finger its ends to be sure he'd used the right one.

He talked about the valuable relationship between writing and the unconscious, using one of his experiences as an example: In 1910 when he was writing *Carnival*, he had been searching for a simile for the effect of the headlights of a hansom cab in the blinding rain. He didn't get it, but fourteen years later he dreamed he was standing at the corner of Charing Cross Road, watching Napoleon and the French Army entering London with their fixed bayonets flashing under the arc-lights. When he awoke, he realized he'd found the simile and immediately wrote the scene into *Rogues and Vagabonds*. He was dreaming a great deal now, he said, and in his dreams, he was reading articles he was in the middle of revising.

Despite his disclaimer that his phenomenal memory was failing him, Sir Compton seemed to be slipping easily in and out of the decades and talking with a passion; a torrent of names, dates, facts, incidents; constantly leaving the main thread to pursue some fascinating new byway or other. When forced to listen, he would indicate boredom by beginning to twirl a red handkerchief with increasing violence. It brought the speaker to a speedy halt.

He had cloistered himself away from the main literary movements deliberately, he said, since he detested "fads" in literature or anything else; and was glad because he didn't think his work had dated as much as, say, Aldous Huxley's; whoever read *Chrome Yellow* any more? Yes, he thought his work had held up very well, even *Extraordinary Women*.

He could no longer remember Romaine's features, but he remembered her impact on Capri that summer; and of course Brooks, who had been a homosexual and never pretended not to be, "but there was nothing feminine about him"; and since Brooks couldn't have invented it, it must be true that Romaine liked him when she was a poor student on Capri but threw him over the moment she'd inherited some money. He talked about that idiotic literary faddist, Gertrude Stein, and about the ridiculous Radclyffe Hall and Lady Troubridge: "I can see them now going into the theater wearing dinner jackets and starched white fronts with their skirts. Of course people were going to stare at them, and they'd decide they were being persecuted and walk out." He reminisced about Romaine's long friendship with Natalie and about the way the subject of lesbianism was once as taboo as, say, homosexuality had been at the time of Wilde. The attitude then had been, "These things don't happen in England." "The change over my lifetime," he said, "has been incredible." He paused. "Of course they're all dead," he said, as if that thought had just occurred to him.

He had known them all and made use of their lives, insofar as it interested him, to illustrate opinions formed in advance. In the case of *Extraordinary Women* ("extraordinary" used in the occasional British sense of "curiously odd"), his attitude differed very little from that of the late Victorians. Lesbianism was not something he found shocking, as they had, since he observed everything with the impersonal curiosity of a microbiologist; but he saw no reason to regard it as other than a kind of bizarre emotional set that such women chose out of perversity. In his attitudes toward what were the prerogatives of the "masculine" mind and what the deficiencies of the "feminine," he demonstrates an unmistakable tone of male superiority and the prejudices of his generation.*

So Romaine appears in *Extraordinary Women* to illustrate, by her own behavior, the inanities of others. Although she is the author's

* Raymond Mortimer called the book "an expression of male pique and wounded vanity."

mouthpiece, her point of view was very close to his own. Qualities of mind could be given sexual labels; there was behavior appropriate to each sex, however much one might rebel against such social mores. There was only one escape hatch in the possibility that there could be a few "genuine" inverts, who could avert universal censure by not transgressing society's rules; by not dressing up in men's clothes and making themselves look ridiculous; by not thumbing their noses at convention; by outwardly impeccable behavior. Only then did they have the slightest hope of leading independent lives.

Romaine is not a very attractive figure in *Extraordinary Women*. She is too remote, too self-righteous, too maddeningly superior in her cool objectivity. Sir Compton Mackenzie saw her independence of mind ("One should be a slave," she often said, "to nothing except one's tooth brush"), but not the underlying sadness, the fatalism ("Life is a procession of funerals"), or even her sense of humor. However one-dimensional, the view of her is valuable in demonstrating the impression she made on others. She might think of herself as doomed to be undervalued and rejected by the herd, but others immediately recognized in her a forceful, even overwhelming personality. What Romaine thought of this view of her is not known; but, since she does not bother to mention Olimpia Leigh in her memoirs, she was probably not convinced.

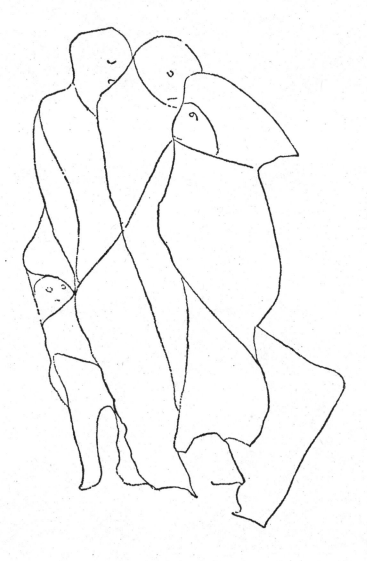

The Inevitable Line*

17

We are what we can be, not what we ought to be.

From Romaine Brooks' notebooks

The apartment in Passy, where Romaine concentrated upon what many believe to be her best work, was built in 1925 and designed to her specifications. It was on a corner of the rue Raynouard, ten top-floor rooms on a story and a half, to accommodate her request for a high-ceilinged studio. It had a tower-shaped roof, and its balconies looked then over flower gardens running down to the Seine; nothing stood between her and an uninterrupted view all over Paris. Its height meant air, light, and a sensation of being buoyed-up in space; all the qualities Romaine was looking for every time she moved.

People who visited her there had similar reactions to this and an earlier basement apartment on the Quai de Conti where Romaine moved in search of a less formal environment after she gave up her mansion on the renamed avenue du Président Wilson. When Madame Berthe, Natalie's housekeeper, paid her first visit to the Quai de Conti, she was convinced that she had wandered by mistake into a funeral parlor, and Bettina Bergery, who lunched at the rue Raynouard frequently in the '30s, thought the apartment "rather mournful"; though she noted that it was decorated with lacquered Chinese pieces in black and gold, that there were large expanses of fastidiously

---

* Also called, "La Ligne Inévitáble."

polished parquet floors, and that there was an emphasis upon light, shade, and balance that would be considered contemporary. Romaine's homes were always meticulous, unlike Natalie's house on the rue Jacob where the dust would fly out of the sofa as you sat down because Natalie never noticed her surroundings; "she liked literary ladies and rose tapestries."

Or perhaps what disconcerted Romaine's visitors were arrangements of furniture that conveyed their inhospitality: rows of hard wooden chairs without a hint of upholstery that one was, a friend complained, obliged to pull out from the wall and make a grouping of oneself, if one intended to have a conversation.

Romaine was well pleased with 74, rue Raynouard and continued to sublet the apartment for years after she had left Paris and bought and sold houses in Santa Margherita Ligure, Beauvallon, studios in the Latin Quarter and Carnegie Hall, New York (there were fifteen moves in ten years). It was not designed for entertaining but to please her eye, which required a free, uncluttered space broken at calculated intervals by some beautiful object; perhaps a Vuillard, or the handsome outlines of a Greek charioteer with one arm extended, or a fifteenth-century painted wooden dog from Venice, or the painting of her first nude, posed behind a fat black pot containing two burgeoning white azaleas, and, forming a frieze in the background, two sailboats, motifs of the painted Japanese mirror she loved so much. A minimum of curtains, perhaps semi-transparent or pulled back, to give her eye full rein to wander over the uninterrupted expanse of sky and clouds which her high, safe perch provided.

She had been drawing for years, and her letters to D'Annunzio and Natalie are often embroidered with fanciful doodles: an hourglass with Time running out, a Mona Lisa in full grin, a sketch of a woman in a fancy hat, or a resplendent wing arching out under her signature of Cinerina, that is unaccountably attached to the forehead of a beautiful young man with closed eyes. Since she had always drawn so easily, she attached very little importance to it. It was something she had to do because she was an artist; an outlet for self-expression that might seem more necessary in times of stress or boredom, that was all. Then one day Romaine sprained her leg and thought at first that it would have to be operated upon. She was forced to spend some weeks in bed at rue Raynouard, and perhaps it was then, as her eye surveyed a changeless, eternally changing expanse of open sky, as it meditated on the shifting outlines of clouds curling their dissolving shapes into a translucent shimmer, as one day melted into another and the faint, persistent sadness, seemed to empty itself into those limitless vistas; that she might have picked up a pencil and paper and followed the line wherever it went.

There was a line that traced out at first what looked like the delicate inner markings of a shell, and became by degrees a long cord that had caught tight and was attempting to mummify a silent figure, stiff and conquered, except for its rebellious eyes. There was a curve taking on the form of writhing hair and spiked ears and arms circling fast a frantic figure trying to free itself. There was a bold sweep that caught up and defined the tight, desolate shape of a departing woman, and there was a muffled, cloaked figure hiding its face and walking away, ignored, except by a dog.

There were tiny little skeletons, looking obscurely like baby monkeys, tucked into tombstone beds and bewailing their fate; there was an orchestra of such half-formed and misshapen spirits tugging at the skirts of an implacable Death. There were those who were bound, those who had died, and those who were cast aside.

Wings appeared, not disembodied, as they were in letters, but attached to a most beautiful horse looking back in mild surprise as he is held from flight by two determined-looking demons. Wings grew out of the shoulders of a man and a woman, falling like cloaks to the ground where they became a rasping, sharp-beaked bird. They flowed like banners or sails into the air, where a very small person was attempting an impossible upward climb.

Things sometimes struck one as funny, in which case one might discover a solemn little innocent trundling along with an organ, ignored by everyone ("L'Orgue de Barbarie"); or one might see an ironic parallel between a gabbling, gobbling fowl and a society woman with a fan; or one might be as much appalled as amused by the loathsome and fleshy outlines of the grossly fat figure trying to capture another ("Enemy Fat"). One meditated upon the occult and discovered the bodies of two figures confronting floating and enigmatic heads; one wanted to gaze upon a blank surface ("Terrestrial Reflections") in order to see whatever unknown depths existed, even if the sight were terrifying. One discovered, in this chorus of demons and saints, half-human beasts and beastlike humans, a final haven beyond good and evil where, as snakes writhed outside, a child slept in the safe center of its mother's curled body.

Everything surprised her. Romaine never knew where the line would go and followed with mingled pride and astonishment the way it would become a form; the way its sure sweep would give shape to the most inchoate emotions, feelings that could not be grasped at any other way, because they were formless. The drawings were, she decided, "indelible thoughts." They became a way of summing up, in which she could pour out all her sense of loss, her aloneness, and all her anguish, in its terror and simplicity. Romaine drew steadily for a year and frequently in the years that followed.

Romaine Brooks' drawings were certainly influenced by the artistic climate in Paris at the turn of the century. One sees, in the beautifully articulated curve, the influence of Art Nouveau and, in the choice of subject matter: fantasy, psychic manifestations of Death, bizarre beings and other worlds, the Symbolists' interest in interior landscapes. Her eerie, intensified and highly wrought forms have something in common with Aubrey Beardsley and recall, in their progression toward ever more simple statements, the perfection of a Japanese print. But whatever the similarities, Romaine succeeded in the alchemy by which an artist transcends such influences and makes his own statement.

Since Romaine hid nothing from her, Natalie was the first to discover them and to insist that they be exhibited. Romaine was reluctant. In the first place they were just drawings; she shared a "serious" painter's prejudices about what was important work and what wasn't; and in the second place, no one was going to understand them. She was so sure they would be misunderstood that she attempted to explain them. "These drawings should be read," she wrote in the exhibition catalogue for a showing at the Arts Club of Chicago in 1935. "They evolve from the subconscious. Without premeditation they aspire to a maximum of expression with a minimum of means. Whether inspired by laughter, philosophy, sadness or death these introspective patterns are each imprisoned within the inevitable encircling line. . . ."

Romaine was obliged to explain to her age what ours has recognized as an uncanny awareness of unconscious forces, expressed with subtlety and power. Her drawings are like a kind of automatic writing, like the most boldly simple dream where the symbols are unmistakable, because the dreamer has a direct link to his unconscious. Had she known what they meant, Romaine might have tried to disguise or distort, but because she remained naïvely innocent about the possible meaning of her drawings, their message is clearly, beautifully, and simply expressed.

A few critics recognized the insight her drawings showed, coinciding as it did with a growing interest in psychology. They are "rare, strange, with unexpected and troubling arabesques," Louis Vauxcelles wrote in the *Excelsior* when 101 drawings were exhibited at the Galerie Th. Briant in Paris in May 1931. "They are willingly esoteric, hermetic, always with a severe graphic quality and stripped almost to the abstract. One must think them dictated to the author by who knows what demon, or else that she was plunged into the most profound reverie, or was hypnotized . . ."

Vauxcelles was in a minority, and Romaine was not too surprised. "They thought I should be doing something else, perhaps," she said. "But that's the way I am, it's me, so I'm going to continue, because I needed to express myself." So she would draw a few more from time to time and put them in a trunk or under her bed, along with the Marchesa Casati.

The drawings stayed in trunks for years, long after Romaine had stopped thinking of herself as an artist ("I am dead," she said) and had been forgotten. By the late '30s, a defensive note is creeping into appreciations of her work by writers who find it increasingly necessary to explain how it could have remained unaffected by the major revolution in art taking place in Paris at the start of the twentieth century. At least Mary Cassatt had been strongly influenced by Degas and the Impressionists; Romaine Brooks acted as if the Fauvists, the Cubists, and the Abstract Expressionists did not exist.

To art critics, she began to seem like an anachronism; a figure unaccountably left over from the *fin de siècle*, obstinately set upon chronicling an increasingly irrelevant world and one that would vanish completely after World War II. The situation was further complicated by the fact that her work never had a market value. Her economic independence allowed her to paint freely, but because she never needed to sell, she never let them be bought, never had a dealer, and was not obliged to undergo the rough but useful competition by which an artist can assess his monetary worth. Because she could paint at whim, she did so erratically; clinging to an artistic vocabulary that was becoming increasingly out of style. She was never forced by economic circumstance to work steadily and become a painter to be reckoned with, instead of an ignored one.

By the time Édouard MacAvoy, the French portraitist and landscapist, professor at the Académie Julian and president of the Salon d'Automne in Paris, met Romaine in the 1960s, she was almost completely forgotten, and those who did remember her name would have added, "But she must be dead by now?" It was MacAvoy, who had admired the severity and simplicity of her work in the '30s when he was an art student, who went through the old notebooks, who re-examined the drawings and brought them to public attention in the March 1968 issue of *Bizarre*, which was devoted to her work. In it, he sought to establish that, in the earliest drawings of her teens, Romaine was already moving into an abstraction that predated Picasso. "In her drawing of 1891 titled 'Woman with a Fan,' Romaine Brooks risked certain formal solutions 52 years before Picasso dared to attempt them (around 1943)." MacAvoy called them images that came from the depths of her nights and predicted that the drawings would take their place in the history of art.

While others might make less bold assertions, we are far enough away from her epoch to see it in perspective, and the final verdict on her work may well be weighted in favor of her drawings. Those who saw the exhibitions at the National Collection of Fine Arts in Washington, D.C., and the Whitney Museum in New York in 1971, agreed that here was a little-known, highly original artist whose drawings, as well as portraits, merited a fresh evaluation.

At a moment when interest in her work was receding, Romaine was taking another direction: she was writing her memoirs and illustrating them with drawings. The first section deals with her childhood and young womanhood, ending with a series of chapters on D'Annunzio. The second deals with the war years she and Natalie Barney spent in a handsome old house, the Villa Sant'Agnese, a ten-minute walk from the Ponte Vecchio on the outskirts of Florence. They lived there through food shortages, bombings, and the Allied invasion, while Natalie continued her social round and Romaine mostly wrote. The section is in the form of a diary and mingles querulous complaints about Natalie, who, Romaine said, constantly nagged the servants, and grotesque descriptions of an odd assortment of friends (there is a woman who keeps sucking on a bruise). The tone is one of suppressed rage at the war and life in general.

She was writing or, it would be correct to say, rewriting her memoirs; for she polished and repolished rigorously for thirty years ("I've written my memoirs in English, French and Italian," she told Madame Berthe.) She seems to have decided to become a writer and so each sentence would be given every possible phrasing and every phrase examined in a dozen different ways before it was allowed to stand. Even the typewritten version, in which she had help from the American writer Allan Ross MacDougall who had ghost-written other famous peoples' memoirs ("He was good," someone said, "with difficult people"), underwent many revisions. Though parts of the memoirs had been completed by 1938, when the sections dealing with St. Mar were published in the British magazine, *Life and Letters To-day*, Romaine added a later section dealing with the war years spent in Florence with Natalie and did not try to find a publisher until the '50s.

Her obsession to refine until the work has reached perfection says a great deal about her character, and it is sad that the memoirs are not better than they are. They have been written with care, but if her approach to her drawings was often symbolistic and literary, her point of departure for her writing was visual. She saw events in loose successions of images, and so the narrative will pick up a thought, drop it for fifteen pages, and then circle back suddenly; dissipating the force of the point the author is trying to make and accounting for the memoirs' disjointed quality.

The main problem with the memoirs, however, is one that threatens all autobiography: a lack of perspective. Incidents that the reader finds trivial anecdotes at best are treated at great length, while others that require analysis, such as what life must have been like for a lesbian in a socially correct and intolerant world, or her marriage and hasty flight from John Brooks, and her fifty-year friendship with Natalie Barney, are either given the most cursory treatment or not discussed at all. Romaine was, in fact, ambivalent. While she wanted to make the clearest possible statement about her life, she was afraid it would be too well understood, and she was irrationally afraid of giving offense. She could not have her work translated into French, she told Natalie in 1952, because "that might bring all sorts of trouble as people of that epoch may still be alive. I thought to have seen in Paris the dressmaker who destined me for the cocotte world. I am sure it was she and that she recognized me . . ."

Having satisfied herself that she had a final version, Romaine began the disheartening round of publishers in London and New York, making use of every possible influential friend: Natalie Barney, Somerset Maugham, Alice B. Toklas, Bryher, and Sir Harold Acton; without success. Romaine was neither deterred nor persuaded that a single word needed to be changed. She was still hoping to have the memoirs published (by the Smithsonian Institution Press, as a counterpart to the 1971 exhibition) a few months before she died.

Natalie was the central figure in Romaine's life in those days; weaving her way, every Friday afternoon, in and out of the crowds of people who came to her weekly receptions; a mixture of literary and other lions, philosophers, professors, members of the Académie Française, those who were or would become famous, and all the rest, decreed by money or social position to mingle in that select group, who went in the hope that a little of the brilliance would rub off on them. Before World War I Natalie had been something of a social outcast, considered a Bohemian, and her circle of friends was composed of lesbian poets, homosexuals, or those famous people, like Wanda Landowska, whom she knew through her mother. She was giving costume balls in those days, but then she was told that the house was too old for dancing and that the floors might collapse. So she became "more literary." As Rémy de Gourmont's Amazon, Natalie Barney was a power to be reckoned with after World War I and the pivot of a brilliant salon.

Natalie Barney was in her forties. She had gained weight, the bridge of her nose had thickened perceptibly, her eyebrows had become distinctly bushy, and the knifelike outline of her nose, which had always prevented her from being a beauty, seemed even more pronounced. It was that nose, Sir Harold Acton said, that made her clear-cut intelligent features increasingly academic, like a medallion of Alfred de Vigny. None of it made any difference. Natalie had discovered her own style, wearing soft white flowing gowns by Lanvin or Schiaparelli with a large white fox skin, or wonderful lustrous black satin gowns with a stole of the same fabric twined around her neck, and her hair was in the same luxurious mass around her head, precariously held in place by hairpins and liable to slide back down into wild disorder. She was an abstract goddess like Minerva, they said; she was the Ice Queen.

So many people idealized Natalie Barney. Perhaps it was her humane, humorous tolerance of others' foibles, since Natalie was virtually unshockable, or what seemed like an enviable inner serenity, or a genuine and kind interest in everyone she called her friend. (She wrote once, "Where friends are concerned I am extremely lazy; when I give my friendship I don't take it back.") Or perhaps it was her wit, so droll and succinct and telling, or her quick intelligence, or the impudent sense of fun that drew them all to the rue Jacob, since one never knew quite what to expect. They came for fifty years.

Natalie Barney had been living since 1909 on the rue Jacob, once called the Chemin du Pré aux Clercs and later, the rue du Colombier, which dates from the Middle Ages. Her house, which was at least three hundred years old, was hidden in a courtyard and popularly (but erroneously) believed to have been the home of the actress Adrienne Lecouvreur (1692–1730), a great interpreter of Racine.

What made No. 20 a kind of miracle on the Left Bank was its garden, a small oasis in a jungle of tightly packed streets, and a remnant of the great seventeenth- and eighteenth-century gardens which once stretched from the rue Jacob down to the Seine. It contained a tiny Doric "Temple d'Amitié," now decreed a national monument and probably built during the First Empire or the Restoration, and a disused well which Natalie Barney never bothered to explore. The Germans cleared it out during World War II and found that it led to an underground cave and a passage going underneath the Seine to the Louvre.

"You can't believe the charm of the house," Bettina Bergery said. "First of all there was a curtain of ivy over the walls and a huge tree in the courtyard, now chopped down, which hung over the house. There was this lovely rambling garden with its eighteenth-century temple and it dominated the house. Inside, one found a green aquarian light. Everything was subdued and warm. Plus a big greedy table of food where we all used to eat like mad."

"Why do I remember Fridays as gray-green, and dim as if there had always been a light rain?" wrote Eyre de Lanux, the artist and writer, in an unpublished manuscript. "Was it always that half-season? I cannot remember sun or any bright light, nor can I remember any loud or discordant sounds. Muted."

It seemed to be transfixed, this house on the rue Jacob, at the moment when the visitor stepped through the door in the wall which barricaded it from the street, crossed the cobbled courtyard and had been greeted by Madame Berthe, always smiling, who remembered everyone's name; had wandered into the salon, vaguely red and packed tight with sofa beds covered in brown velvet, with lavish fur throws, with tapestries, portraits, photographs, vast mirrors, the grand piano on which Landowska and Darius Milhaud played, a bust of Natalie's close friend the poet Milosz, a portrait of Natalie as a page at the age of eleven, painted by Carolus Duran, her mother's art teacher; objects which loomed out of a perpetual semi-darkness since, Natalie said, "I have lived in the twilight and when I am not there, my things are sleeping." Everything would be overcast with the faintest air of disarray or neglect. A lingering trace of someone's Oriental scent would mingle with the decaying smell of roses wilting in a vase. There would be a box of half-eaten chocolates on a table beside a lute whose strings were broken; and a stack of new copies of Natalie's essays, their pages uncut, would be covered with dust.

One walked through the house into the dining room, dominated by a large hexagonal table with a lace cloth, spread with a sumptuous feast prepared by Madame Berthe, who was more than a housekeeper, who had become a confidante, Natalie Barney's amanuensis. She was the kind of old-fashioned cook who might go to the Gare St.

Lazare just for cheese and to the rue du Cherche-Midi for bread. "There would be a list of guests and food as long as the kitchen wall," she said. "We would have 20-60-100 people. Somehow we could seat everybody. We served sandwiches, cakes, fruit, crystallized strawberries, tea, port, gin, whiskey, everything. The whiskey always disappeared fast when we had American guests."

There were Madame Berthe's famous chocolate cake and harlequin-colored little cakes and triangular sandwiches, "folded up like damp handkerchiefs," Bettina Bergery said, and pitchers of fruit cup, and the Duchesse de Clermont-Tonnerre presiding at one end, pouring regal cups of tea, and the green half light from the garden filtering into the room, "reflecting from the glasses and silver tea urn as from under water." (Eyre de Lanux.)

One might wander out into the garden, more like a miniature forest with its rambling paths and iron chairs balanced at forlorn angles on the uneven ground; paths which might be packed with leaves. One attempted the hammock, which every year lost one or two more strings and finally became so hazardous that friends removed it. One inspected the marble fountain, long since choked with weeds, which stood in the middle of what had once been a lawn. One regarded one's image in the mirror ingeniously covering a side of the house, or walked up and down the steps of the Temple d'Amitié. Or one watched the rain drifting through the leaves like smoke in that garden where the sun never penetrated, where, Colette wrote in *Trois, Six, Neuf,* aqueous plants grew which "wreathe the interiors of wells." One waited for the unmistakable impression one always had at Natalie's, that she was allowing the past to coexist harmoniously with herself in that house; of the past and future blurring into an eternal present.

One came to see Ezra Pound, looking like an erratic mixture of American flamboyance and European correctness in, Jean Cassou said, "a cowboy hat, a little moustache, a pointed beard, lorgnons and an umbrella," perhaps leaning forward intently as he waited for the moment to crash the cymbals, playing some very percussive and experimental music in the School of Varèse with some experimental young American composer; or to see Colette, looking exactly like one of those Persian cats with bows, Aileen Hennessy said, or to meet the writer André Germain, who drew portraits of them in *La Bourgeoisie Qui Brûle,* who was tiny, ("a wicked little vest-pocket Voltaire," Dolly Wilde called him) and whose statue, designed for his grave, was in the Temple d'Amitié. Natalie used to point it out, adding, "Inside is André Germain, smaller than nature."

One watched the extraordinary Dolly Wilde, seated next to the old historian Professor Seignobos and drawing him out on the subject of *Lady Chatterley's Lover,* the only novel he had ever read, and which Dolly had given to him; or one eavesdropped while Colette, now elderly and arthritic, wearing sandals, "with toes like bunches of carrots," Bettina Bergery said, talked interminably about Sido, her mother. "She was always rolling her 'rrrrs' and talking with her mouth full and she smelled of raw onions to show you how sensitive and *près de la terre* she was. She had the most revolting table manners I have ever seen."

One went to meet the literary lion of the afternoon, who might be a pretentious and forgotten poet like Anna Wickham, a burly lady fortified in advance with wine and garlic and sedulously courted by a group of other ladies, while real celebrities like Sherwood Anderson might languish unnoticed, according to Acton. One went to talk to Natalie, like the young American poet Alan Seeger, who adored the work of Renée Vivien and might have made an important name for himself if he had not been killed in the World War I trenches. Or one went to play one's own work, like George Antheil, who thoroughly enjoyed the incongruity between the antiquated audience of French millionaires and bearers of ancient titles, in an antiquated drawing room with priceless antique furniture, and his own experimental First String Quartet (1926). "What they may have made of it I often wonder," he wrote in *The bad boy of music!* "for this particular little quartet was by no means a mild number."

One went, like the British writer Richard Aldington, out of homage to Rémy de Gourmont, whose *Lettres à l'Amazone* he had translated as an "act of literary piety"; and saw Natalie as the aristocratic product of an old school, with impeccable, even courtly manners. When he took a London publisher friend to visit the Villa Trait d'Union at Beauvallon, the summer home Natalie and Romaine built in the '30s, and the publisher, finding himself disastrously underdressed, had borrowed Aldington's jacket, several sizes too large, Natalie tactfully "saw nothing untoward and soon discovered that they had common friends among the English peerage. He still speaks of her with infinite respect." (*Adam International Review.*)

One went to concoct a new literary magazine with Natalie, as Sinclair Lewis did (unfortunately their collaboration never went further than an inspired title: "How to Live by Those Who Have") or to write poetry with her, as Ezra Pound did:

> Thoughts of pleasant tints are leading my dream-mind
> Back to the dynasties of the delicate,
> Who value a poem and a friend,
> As the deep possession of their lives.
> (*Transatlantic Review*, October 1924)

Their collaboration was tempered by Pound's opinion that Natalie's writings were the product of mental laziness and that her book, *Pensées d'une Amazone,* was full of unfinished sentences and broken paragraphs, although lit by occasionally sublime comments such as (Pound quoted in *The Dial*, October 1921), " 'having got out of life perhaps more than it contains.' " Natalie still found that comment irritating forty years later. "I was thinking of how wrong Pound is," she told the writer Mary Blume (*Réalités*, February 1966). "How lazy it is to write a lot. If you can put a whole novel into a few sentences, why not?" Such occasional disagreements did not affect their friendship, and the once-ebullient Pound returned to the rue Jacob after his experiences in World War II had made him silent and sad. He would sit in the garden without saying a word, "walled-in like his own statue," Bettina Bergery said.

Or one no longer came, like Paul Valéry whose reputation Natalie had made, according to the publisher Samuel Putnam (*Paris Was Our Mistress*). The time-honored function of the French salon as a gathering place for literary speculation had not altogether disappeared, "and what you heard in the drawing room one day you would not be surprised to read a day or two later in *Le Figaro, Le Temps* or *Les Nouvelles Littéraires.*" There were those who said that Valéry, now a member of the Académie Française, had become sententious and ungrateful; but Natalie was much too adroit to be pitied. "After a number of typically Gallic two-edged remarks had been tossed about, including a few in damning defence of the absent one, Miss Barney spoke up. 'Le pauvre!' she exclaimed, and quickly added: 'By the way, have you read So-and-So's latest?'"

One of the few exceptions to the pattern of those who were very good friends or had once been good friends, and the list was a very long one, including Ford Madox Ford, Marie Laurencin, Djuna Barnes, Anna de Noailles, Germaine Beaumont, the Princess Marthe Bibescu, Rainer Maria Rilke, William Carlos Williams, James Joyce, Paul Morand, Sherwood Anderson, Virgil Thomson, and Isadora Duncan, was Marcel Proust. He succumbed to his curiosity, like the others, after a year's exchange of letters. Perhaps it was his friend the Duchesse de Clermont-Tonnerre who persuaded him to visit, or Salomon Reinach, who kept talking about the wild girl from Cincinnati, or Gide, who had been known to comment that Miss Barney was one of the few people one ought to see, if one had time. Whatever it was, the great moment came when Paul Morand waltzed past Natalie Barney one night at the Bal des Petits Lits Blancs and said, "Proust is longing to meet you." The meeting took place in November 1921.

Since Proust only came awake when everyone else had gone to sleep, Natalie had agreed to stay up well past her bedtime; and since he could not bear the cold, she had taxed the house on the rue Jacob's antiquated heating system to the limit. He arrived close to midnight in a starched white shirt and black tails; his dark eyes "ringed with black by the vampires of solitude," looking more like an embalmed corpse than a man. While she sat, draped in the white ermine chasuble she used as a bedspread, Proust talked and talked of high society and how Madame Greffulhe's laugh sounded like a Belgian carillon.

Natalie Barney was extremely uncomfortable. In the first place, she had the impression that she was being steadily observed, though she could never catch him looking at her. In the second place, she had wanted to discuss literature, but all Proust wanted to talk was gossip and there was no stopping him; "It would be easier," she decided, "to stop a Sorbonne professor in full lecture." (*Aventures de l'Esprit.*)

Perhaps Proust was merely being polite with a woman whom he expected to be only worldly. Perhaps such acute observers were each waiting for a sign from the other; each hesitant before the ordeal of friendship. At any rate, neither would take the first step, and although Proust did come back (since Madame Berthe remembers him visiting for lunch afterward, looking very much the old novelist, cold and difficult to approach), they never surmounted the barriers.

So many others came that it hardly mattered; men who, like Rémy de Gourmont or Lord Alfred Douglas, to whom Natalie was briefly engaged, found the taste of friendship heady and enjoyed hovering on the edge of a delicate uncertainty while they tried to decide whether they, or she, wanted more. One of them was Bernard Berenson.

"At Salomon's [Salomon Reinach's] that red-letter day when I met you I very deliberately fell back in the hope you would catch up," Berenson wrote shortly after they met in 1917. "I did not send my book to you for fear it contained nothing to interest you. Yet now that you want to become better acquainted with me I can understand your wishing to see it . . . I now love my friends nearly as much for what I don't as for what I do approve and admire . . . And I would not for the world have friendship consist of identities. I want it to be an embrace of divergences."

In the same letter, he wrote, "Your notes—they are too exquisite to be called letters—are so life-enhancing that I sincerely wish I could receive them every day. At all events I am enchanted with your verses about my visit to you in the snow. I like your comparison of the falling snow to the scattering petals of the rose, and I love the line 'Fleurs du froid effeuillées par l'hiver.'"

Letters from the art scholar, collector, and connoisseur veer between what seems to have been a genuine delight in her originality of mind, a kind of old-fashioned courtliness, and a veiled appeal. Natalie parried that appeal with masterly tact, managing to seem a passionate admirer whose admiration was untinged by the slightest ambiguity. "What you say about the 'quality of time' is so true that I can live on it," she wrote to him, "and when the memory of having seen and heard you is no longer real and present enough—I shall travel towards you, to find out that you are the friend I want?" A little later, she wrote, "You and I, B.B.—friends, as only those who have not been lovers can remain," evading the implications of his words to her; i.e., "Yours as much as you will" and, "I kiss your feet."

"Berenson always said he was in love with Natalie and even said he went to bed with her," Sir Harold Acton remarked. "He said she woke up next morning and exclaimed, 'I thought you were a woman.' But I don't believe it. That was old man's boasting."

Later, when Natalie and Romaine were living in Florence through the war years, they saw a good deal of him at I Tatti on the hill near the village of Settignano. Berenson would come to greet them, a slight but immaculate figure, always wearing a fresh *boutonnière*, touching them with his delicate and graceful fingers, "with a rare sensibility," Natalie wrote in *Traits et Portraits*. "His glance has the purity of a star, but be careful, because he can become provocative or malicious . . ."

They would have tea and Romaine, at full volume, would read another chapter from the memoirs. Then a young Berenson relative, looking exactly like Nijinski, according to Natalie, would dance in a dress the color of a dead leaf and make them forget momentarily the encroaching straitjacket of old age.

Berenson's visits to them were an equal success, with the exception of one afternoon when, the Marchese Strozzi recalled, "He sat between them on a sofa. Berenson took the hand of each and commanded, 'Now make me laugh.' Neither could think of a single thing to say. Berenson got glummer and glummer and went off in a huff."

He was still coming to Natalie's Fridays after the war when, Bettina Bergery said, "He was a tiny little ectoplastic kitten with blue eyes, trying to shock people. He came back from a visit to the Louvre one day saying that the 'Raft of the Medusa' was the only good picture in it. Everyone thought he had to be joking . . ."

Romaine stayed aloof, perhaps because, according to Acton, he genuinely liked her, but didn't take her at her own evaluation as a great artist. As she began to doubt that her work had lasting value, it became unusually important that others think so. That to one side, she did not enjoy Natalie's parties, even if she was often there, wearing high collars and a cravat with a lock of hair dangling and looking the picture of elegance, Eyre de Lanux said. "She would look perfect today. She would wear a three-quarter length coat of wonderful black broadcloth and a little white collar. Her demeanor was one of elegance and retirement."

There were a few people willing to pierce the barrier of that forbidding silence. One of them was Bettina Bergery; like Romaine a transplanted American. She married Gaston Bergery, who had fought in World War I as a young man and was wounded in the stomach, then rose fast in the French diplomatic service, went into politics, and had formed his own party, the Common Front, before World War II. "It was rather uncomfortable, like Servan Schreiber," his wife said, "but more serious, because he was against both sides, the Communists and the Right. He had an originality of thought which separated him from the others. He was the only one who voted against World War II. He said, 'It's stupid, we are unarmed, they can go around the Maginot Line,' which of course they did, but that kind of talk made him very unpopular for a time."

Bettina Bergery worked for the couturier Schiaparelli in a public relations capacity. She led a social life that brought her into contact with every leading figure in the haut monde of the '30s. "All the young men I got to take me to parties while Gaston was working, ended up working for him instead. Dali and Jose-Maria Sert were among them.

"Then there was Gide. They used to be all sitting about in our living room signing things and licking envelopes. Gide would come in, to see the young men, I used to think unkindly, and he wanted the paper and a cup of tea and to be made a fuss of, and he used to be pushed off on me, because everybody else was busy, you know. Gide was very ponderous, he weighed a ton and I suppose I was rather unkind to him. Cocteau told me off. He said, 'He's a very important writer and a very unhappy man. You can't go on needling someone who is bleeding already.'"

Romaine and Natalie were one more set of characters in the bizarre society in which Mme. Bergery found herself. She regarded them with the curiosity of a born diarist. She has, said Janet Flanner, a "rare humorous sensibility for life and has a sense of reception for eccentrics . . . that is quite exceptional; she is a great gossip in the highest sense of the word . . . she is an animated journal." She saw them with a loving, undeceived eye. "In the last years of her life, Romaine and Natalie looked like Tweedledum and Tweedledee with their caps," she said. "But in her middle years, Romaine was very smart, the way people are now, with trousers and a cravat.

"Romaine had charm, you see. A physical charm like that and a sweet smile. She had a slight American accent, sort of Henry James, the white fence and the willow tree. One day I heard her say, 'Laura birdie, it's in the pocket of your *wrapper.*' There was a moment in her life when she looked like Picasso, the same nose and chin and the same 'pistol eyes.' He was an abominable man and there were lots of ways in which she was like him, the reflexes and defences were so like him.

"Then he had lovely little seed pearl teeth and his eyes could be so soft and then they could look like pistol shots. Like an animal that can't resist making cat scratches. Romaine was the same way."

Natalie had eyes like the blue in gas jets and an extraordinary way of laughing, like a schoolgirl's, and she was intellectually brilliant and rather frivolous. Romaine's glance was harder, round and hard like Picasso with little bulging eyes; and while she lacked Natalie's brilliance, there was "a tremendous sense of worth, riches, talent, much more than Natalie. A gold nugget; something there true and solid." Natalie would talk about everything under the sun, but, Mrs. Bergery said, Romaine was more likely to limit herself to saying something definitive about art. Natalie never talked about herself, but if you asked Romaine a question, "you had a good 15-minute reply, because she was rather interested in herself."

Both of them had "beautiful old-fashioned manners," paying attention to the smallest needs of their guests and making each visit to the rue Jacob a delight because of their thoughtfulness. Romaine played the role of a second hostess out of a heroic sense of obligation and duty, hating every minute of it, and sometimes she would have to leave in the middle of a reception. "Natalie has hundreds of friends," she once said, adding, "but I couldn't bear it." Where people were concerned, Romaine had always been difficult to please and would take irrational dislikes. When Mary Blume went to interview her one day on the rue Jacob, Romaine took one look at her and rushed in to

Madame Berthe to say, "How can I talk to her? She has such *ugly* arms." Romaine complained in her memoirs that she was meeting at Natalie's the "very hornets," those idle and malicious society women, that she had hoped to escape for ever. She felt herself imprisoned by her friendship with Natalie, but it was useless to complain because Natalie never understood; Natalie, who could always parry the most devastating shaft with a wit that was used "neither as a weapon of defence nor of attack, but rather as a game," soared above such "petty vindictiveness."

Romaine was certainly abnormally ready to take offense, but that she was in an unfriendly atmosphere, cannot be doubted. They were, Paul Valéry said, "hazardous Fridays."

"There was no camaraderie anywhere. Nothing you would understand as real friendliness," Eyre de Lanux said. All sorts of famous men and women would be lined up along the wall and one might be introduced for the fifth time to Gertrude Stein, in a thick tweed suit and heavy boots and her knees wide apart, without a flicker of acknowledgment from her. Those who were famous no longer needed to be indulgent to the young and struggling, they were too exalted for that; or perhaps too ferocious. "It was all tooth and nail, a rather vicious atmosphere and Romaine stayed aloof from this kind of intrigue."

Romaine, who was so silent in large groups, who had said, "I am on top of the table or underneath it, saying nothing," liked small groups, the smaller the better. In a friendly atmosphere, she became talkative, even exuberant. "When she told a story, it was like setting out a painting," Madame Berthe said. "She had a way of lifting her arm and saying, ah! . . with such élan. They were in fits of laughter."

Those who were handpicked for lunch at the rue Raynouard said the same thing. "She wouldn't have put up with a lot of Miss Barney's friends," said Aileen Hennessy, the artist. "I think people did bore her . . . She was still painting and I had been told before I met her in the '30s, 'Oh she's a real bitch.' I asked why and the reply was, 'Have you seen the portrait of Lady Mendl?' [A reference to Romaine's portrait of the decorator Elsie de Wolfe, later Lady Mendl, in damning mockery of that lady's simpering expression.] "I was told that she could be devastating [and Madame Berthe confirms that many people found Romaine formidable], but she never was with me. When I saw her I would always think, oh good, because she was such good fun."

Romaine might have a lunch for four or five and include Ida Rubinstein. "She wore," Bettina Bergery said, "a lot of tarnished gold lamé and fishnet, with a terribly thin, pointed face. I remember her wearing a black-and-white coat and white stockings, all very untidy and spilled on.

"Natalie said at that lunch, 'We all got what we wanted. I got my salon, Romaine became a painter and Ida became a famous ballerina.' As I recall, Ida said very little. All of that was before the war, a very long time ago, and I never heard Natalie talk about her."

A terribly thin and pointed face above a dress of tarnished lamé were what remained of the divine creature who, Gérard Bauer of the Académie Goncourt wrote, D'Annunzio had invented out of his exuberant concept of luxury, his ornate art. "She was not exempt from a garish taste and romantic excesses under which is buried today, one hopes temporarily, the work of the author of *The Martyrdom of Saint Sebastian*." (*Le Figaro*, October 17, 1960.)

The degrees by which Ida Rubinstein ceased to be "long, thin, hieratic, with almond eyes, a mixture of Queen Nefertiti and the mosaic of Torcello," and became a pathetic, forgotten figure, can be charted in the cycle of changing tastes, which decrees that one generation will find ludicrous posturing the art which its parents have idolized; and also what Romaine had long suspected to be Ida's stubborn lack of good sense. Ida persisted in trying to become a ballerina, dancing in the works she had commissioned from Ravel, *Boléro* and *La Valse*, in tutus made by Lanvin, and towering above every partner, long after her unsuitability for the role became painfully evident to her audiences. In *Bolero* she danced on the table and people said, "Madame falls off every evening, into the drum."

Ida persisted in thinking that she could become a great dramatic actress, affecting the Bernhardt manner for decades after it had become *de trop*. She mounted her own productions of the works of Paul Valéry and Arthur Honegger and Shakespeare's *Anthony and Cleopatra*, as translated by André Gide, and playing the title role in *La Dame aux Camélias* with a pronounced Russian accent. As her style became increasingly irrelevant, she faded into obscurity and died in Vence at the age of seventy-five in 1960. Romaine no longer wanted to see her, although Ida had sent her a loving invitation and friends were willing to drive her there. "She's no longer like an orchid," Romaine said.

Romaine liked the people she liked, and they were not Natalie's society friends but artists like herself. "If you were an artist," the novelist Bryher said, "it was quite simple; you could do anything you liked with Romaine. But you had to have tact. You could say, 'How is the work going?' but not, 'What are you working on?' That was quite unsafe." Romaine was not a part of Gertrude Stein's circle either, although she was, like Natalie, on excellent terms with that lady and her companion, Alice B. Toklas. They moved in different spheres. "Natalie," said Bryher, who married Robert McAlmon and talks about Hemingway, Gide, and Pound in her memoirs, *The Heart to Artemis,* "was inclined to know the conventional French and was already considered a bit too Right Bank and smart, outside our group. She never would have turned up in a café at six in the evening. Whereas we had one coffee at the Dôme or the Rotonde and it had to last an hour or two. There was a great gap."

Gertrude seems to have been rather more a fixture of Natalie's receptions than vice versa. While she and Natalie discussed literature, perhaps the former's latest work, in which Natalie might find "a rare and primeval innocence," Romaine and Alice might be off in a corner somewhere, to be joined by Madame Berthe, discussing recipes. (One of Madame Berthe's best dishes, a Romanian sauté of mixed vegetables and veal, appears in the *Alice B. Toklas Cookbook.*) Or Romaine and Natalie might run into Gertrude on the Left Bank walking her poodle Basket.

Or they might meet at Shakespeare and Company, Sylvia Beach's famous bookshop on the rue de l'Odéon, and commiserate silently, as they did the night that Edith Sitwell set out to immortalize Gertrude Stein in a lecture and never mentioned her name once. It was admiration tinged with a certain amusement, since neither Romaine nor Natalie could resist poking occasional fun at that increasingly odd-looking couple. "Alice T. is withering away under the stress of moving into a new flat," Natalie wrote to Romaine in New York in 1938.

"Yet she sweetly made me some sweets [candies] which when presented on Friday, repelled all but Dr. Mardrus, who recognized in them the Oriental touch? I am afraid 'the bigger one,' who gets fatter and fatter, will sooner or later devour her. She looks so thin. . . ."

Or Romaine and Natalie might visit Gertrude and Alice at the latter's summer home in Belignin, sitting on gaily striped canvas chairs, Gertrude in the favorite position in which Picasso painted her, her moccasined feet spread wide apart. She looked just like the old gypsy lady Natalie used to visit when she was growing up in Bar Harbor, Maine. It was one of those afternoons that Romaine was seized with a sudden desire to paint the group. "We are due at another party," Natalie said, regretting it later. Romaine contemplated painting Gertrude Stein for a long time. In the twenties, she was inviting Gertrude to her apartment at 13, Quai de Conti to read her work, saying that she would ask a few of those whom she had found sympathetic and asking if she would sit for a portrait. In 1930 Romaine was still asking, commenting that "no one has occupied so important a place in my mind as yourself." But the portrait was never made because, Romaine said, Gertrude decided that her hair was too long and cut it so short that the artist drew back in horror. (It might have been the response the sitter intended.)

Romaine was happiest when she could have Natalie all to herself; lunches for two in the dining room of the rue Jacob which might take hours, since Romaine ate slowly, and in which Madame Berthe would join, since she loved a good laugh; tickets for two at the cinema, followed by tea and cakes at Potel et Chabot on the avenue Victor Hugo. They both loved such lavish confections, and as Natalie grew ever more majestically plump, her jawline disappearing into a high collar and gored grosgrain skirts falling over chubbie knees, Romaine was also gaining weight. Since she had always been lean, with undeveloped breasts, flat hips, and slender legs, the onset of extra poundage would be enough in itself to make her depressed; as her friends saw, it offended her esthetic sense, but it also put her in peril of becoming ugly. Romaine anticipated the critical eyes of others and shrank from them.

Romaine had painted Natalie in 1920 wearing furs, her hair bound loosely around her head, beside a tiny jade horse that Romaine owned, to symbolize the Amazon. There is a dim snowy scene in the background. One makes out the hazy outlines of the house on the rue Jacob through a white fog and the vague aqueous shapes of trees, with boughs spreading out like water lilies. There is the most enigmatic of expressions on Natalie's face. She does not seem lost in profound thought; she seems to have transcended it, as if she were in some other framework of existence.

It is not a characteristic look. Natalie, in the company of those who interested her, was the most animated of listeners, and her gaze was mesmeric. The painting was exhibited in London, New York, and Paris through the twenties, hung in the dining room at 20, rue Jacob until Natalie Barney moved out and is now in the collection of the Musée du Petit Palais. It is puzzling and unsatisfying to the outsider's eye; a most private work.

Perhaps Romaine was trying to express a fundamental aspect of their psyches. They shared the view that life had frustrated them, and looked elsewhere: to art, to poetry, to philosophy, and theories of other existences, to experience tinged with nostalgia, to myth, to symbol, to images as haunting and repetitive as dreams, to the other sex inside themselves, for fulfillment. Romaine tried to express this inner state with her haunting line drawings. Natalie tried to do it with a book, *The One Who is Legion,* her only major work in English. It was privately printed in London in 1930, the same year that Romaine executed so many drawings and two years after the appearance of *The Well of Loneliness;* was limited to 560 copies. Romaine Brooks provided two illustrations, her only venture into this field.

They had collaborated once before on a painting and poem, *The Weeping Venus* (see Appendix, p. 413) on the feministic theme that Nature makes martyrs out of women by condemning them to reproduce, a fate from which only death can release them. Ida was again the model for this nude study, started just as World War I began, but refused to continue the arduous sittings. Romaine tried to find someone else to pose, but never could find a woman with such extraordinarily delicate legs, and try as she might, Ida's features were not to be altered or erased. So the painting was never finished.

The One Who is Legion is written on the theme of the androgyn, a concept which also interested them, in Romaine's case through Ida

329

as D'Annunzio's boy saint and, in Natalie's case, through Renée and Sappho. It was an idea in the literary atmosphere in those days. Virginia Woolf had just published *Orlando*, and T. S. Eliot was to refer to Tiresias, "in which the two sexes meet," in *The Waste Land*. Since his poem appeared after excerpts from *The One Who is Legion* had been published in *The Dial*, the speculation is inevitable that Eliot was influenced by Natalie's philosophies.

It is the story of a spirit, a One in "Beyond Time" who takes over the life of someone who has committed suicide and completes it.† One has the most extraordinary sensation reading through the book. The narrative does advance, yet it is written in such a disjointed and aphoristic style that the reader finds himself asking, "Who?" "What?" and going back again and again in an attempt to pick up the thread. The writing befuddles the mind like a drug.

Yet the book contains some beautiful passages. There are descriptions of a graveyard, which might be the forest of the rue Jacob, secret, rustling with lamentations: "A triumphant vegetation of undergrowth, overgrowing everything, bends down under its supple labyrinth trees caught with their branches in the tresses of bindweed." It might be the labyrinth of Highgate Cemetery, where Una laid John (Radclyffe Hall) to rest. It is like the forest Romaine describes in her short story, *Riviera Jungles,* a flytrap, a snare. It is the landscape of fantasy which Le Grand Meaulnes sets out to discover in Alain Fournier's novel of the same name.

The book contains precise sensual images, "Our hands, little bodies of nakedness, left free as children at play and unashamed, given into one another," and, "A luxurious and luxuriant womanhood, sleek-helmeted, rounded as shining sea-lions washed up by the last wave." Other passages are so elliptical as to be impenetrable, like, "Here we seem to be in a place of half-measures in which to confuse our divine entity, become nebulous as a satellite, a spiritual parvenu, subject to lost currents." They skid off the mind like chalk across a blackboard.

---

† This was a favorite theme of Natalie's. Years later, in 1951, she wrote of her late friend, Dolly Wilde:

> As long as I have memory
> Of her, our ill-starred friend,
> By thought and word and prayer, I'll try
> —Like threads of some torn tapestry—
> Her broken life to mend.

Behind such ambiguities, there are clues to Natalie Barney's inner state. "We've met with too many persons and allowed them all to cross and join in us," she wrote. "We shall never get ourselves clear now." The only way to become enough to oneself, to become whole, was to embrace this inner fragmentation. Her main theme:

> A double being needs no other mate—
> So seraphita-seraphitus lives;
> Self-wedded angel, armed in self-delight,
> Hermaphrodite of heaven, looking down
> On the defeat of our divided love.

Natalie's response to the possibility that she had been short-changed by life was ironic and detached. What she seemed to feel was the suffused and impenetrable regret that Romaine has painted. In Romaine's case, the incomplete being damned by fate was so linked in her mind with St. Mar, and through him everything that was mystical, incomprehensible and divine, that her work contains much more anguish, much more awareness of the lonely passion of the martyr. While Natalie's novel is directed toward the resolution of a dilemma, the completion of an unfinished state, Romaine's drawings, the first the naked and deliberately sexless body of a starry, god-like spirit hurtling through space and the second, the dangling limbs of a martyr in limbo, present the inner impasse, the double self that *she* felt herself to be. The two drawings are not her best work; but they are her clearest statement.

As well as collaborating on matters of art, Romaine and Natalie joined together at a more mundane, but equally symbolic, level. They had a joint Swiss bank account, made plans to be interred in the same tomb, and in the early '30s they designed the "Villa Trait d'Union" ("The Hyphenated Villa"). It was a handsome house built to their specifications, so as to have a common meeting room and loggia spanning separate quarters and individual front doors. It was set in pine woods outside Beauvallon, and they enjoyed many harmonious summers there, spending their days apart and coming together for meals. Natalie must have got the idea from the two little houses joined by a garden which she and Renée shared on the island of Mytilene, and her *pavillon* at Neuilly had a self-contained apartment where Colette lived for a time. Her philosophy was that the only way to sustain a living-together relationship was by maintaining a physical distance—and separate entrances.

"For me, to live alone as my own master is essential," she wrote in *Souvenirs Indiscrets*, "not for egotistical reasons or any lack of love, but in order to better give myself. To bathe in passionate intimacy on a daily basis, while living together in the same house and often in the same bedroom with the loved one, has always seemed to me the most certain way to lose somebody."

The arrangement appeared to work well for both. Each continued her style of living, Romaine perhaps drawing, swimming, or working on her memoirs and Natalie giving slightly less elaborate versions of the receptions at the rue Jacob, and inviting Dolly Wilde, the Duchesse de Clermont-Tonnerre, John and Una, Gertrude and Alice, Sir Francis Rose, Alice DeLamar and Aileen Hennessy. Natalie was inclined to wear a suit and blouse with a high, tied collar, and Romaine, looking tanned and increasingly handsome, like an elderly statesman, might wear a loose weskit, a string tie, sleeves rolled up above the elbow, culottes, and Roman sandals; or a sweater with a pretty chiffon handkerchief sticking out of its breast pocket.

The "Villa Trait d'Union" had one continuous annoyance. The famous architect who designed it, had given it a flat roof and made no provision for rain. "Every time it rained, it rained indoors as well," Maître Emmanuel said with a chuckle. This practical reason re-established the contact between Romaine and her sister Maya's family.

After St. Mar and Ella died, Romaine saw increasingly less of Maya. Maya, she believed, had walled herself up in a stultifying bourgeois marriage. It was because Maya was made so extremely uncomfortable by her sister's defiant refusal to conform, that Romaine was obliged to be circumspect in her writings and use pseudonyms. To her family, Romaine was the aunt one didn't talk about, and she had turned her back on them. When Maya's daughters, Beatrice and Liliane, were little, Romaine had sent Beatrice in particular many presents and letters. (Beatrice also had artistic talent.) Romaine was horrified when she learned that Beatrice was to marry a French lawyer, a certain Léon-Marie Emmanuel, in 1921. How, she demanded to know from Maya, could you let your daughter be sold into a life of slavery? That effectively ended all communication until 1930, when Beatrice and Léon-Marie (Boni) Emmanuel happened to be staying at a hotel in Beauvallon. They sent Tante Romaine a very cool note. About forty-eight hours later, as they were sitting on the beach in swimsuits and robes, Tante Romaine appeared with Natalie, wearing a high, stiff white collar and a foulard. She informed her nephew that she had come for legal help. It was a matter of a leaking roof. Boni helped, and went on helping with other legal problems, building a tenuous link between Romaine and her relatives in Nice.

The "Villa Trait d'Union" was the physical proof of a relationship both Natalie and Romaine believed would last until the end of their lives. (Unfortunately, it burned down during World War II.) They felt so sure of each other that Romaine could tolerate Natalie's infidelities, and even tell her about her own occasional adventures. If the affair became onerous, she would contact Natalie with good-natured exasperation and say, "Do send me a telegram saying that somebody is dying."

And Natalie's flirtations were interminable. What gave spice to her receptions and added to their allure was the possibility that, in that endless sea of new faces, there would be a particularly interesting face. Her urge to conquer continued to be as impetuous and vernal as in those early days with Renée. She would meet someone and disappear for days. "Once she simply left. She had gone to sleep with a married woman," Madame Berthe said. "Finally she called me up four days later, with no explanations. She said, 'Berthe, there will be ten people for dinner tonight.'" Madame Berthe continued, "There were some women who weren't worth it, but how can you explain love?"

Natalie was not always the pursuer. She had been watched, Madame Berthe said, by a neighbor who had remarked upon a charming procession of ladies to and from 20 rue Jacob. When her passionate letters went unanswered, that neighbor gained entry to the house on some pretext or other while Natalie was out (it was before Mad-

333

ame Berthe's vigilant reign) and installed herself on Natalie's bed, naked. How Natalie responded is not recorded.

The goings-on at the rue Jacob became a subject for gossip almost at once and Natalie, a notorious woman to be avoided at all costs by respectable ladies. ". . . for already, when Evangeline appeared at tea with the Duchess Clitoressa of Natescourt, women in their way (the Bourgeoisie be it noted, on an errand to some nice church of the Catholic Order, with their Babes at Breast and Husbands at Arm) would snatch their Skirts from Contamination . . ." (*The Ladies Almanack.*)

Mothers of adolescent daughters went to elaborate lengths to avoid having them cross the threshold of 20 rue Jacob. Monique Grossin, Maître Emmanuel's daughter, recalled that when she was in her teens, and Natalie was "an old lady" as far as she was concerned, Natalie fired her with enthusiasm to go to college in Paris. She was mystified when her parents told her that it was out of the question, refusing to elaborate.

Even Romaine considered that Natalie had lived "years in dank unhealthy houses among many dank unhealthy people," and, into the twenties there was the same aura of scandal about her. "A lady who came to my bookshop with a letter from Miss Barney seemed to have got very little benefit from her visits to the rue Jacob," Sylvia Beach wrote in *Shakespeare & Co.* "She looked overwrought and hissed in my ear, 'Have you anything more about *those unfortunate creatures?*'"

The Ladies Almanack: Showing their Signs and their tides; their Moons and their Changes; the Seasons as well as a full Record of diurnal and nocturnal Distempers was privately printed in Paris in 1928 and written under the pseudonym of "A Lady of Fashion." When it was reprinted in 1972, its author was acknowledged: Djuna Barnes, once considered the most important woman writer in Paris for her novel, *Nightwood,* and her short stories, notably *A Night Among the Horses.* She knew Natalie and her circle well; had, in fact, employed Madame Berthe and recommended that she see Miss Barney when Madame Berthe decided that she wanted to find a family which would be traveling. When the book was republished Miss Barnes, who called it "a slight satiric wigging," did not further explain that it was a burlesque of a particular lesbian circle, namely Natalie's. Radclyffe Hall appears as Lady Buck-and-Balk, Una is "Tilly-Tweed-in-Blood, [who] sported a Stetson and believed in Marriage," the Duchess Clitoressa of Natescourt is the Duchesse de Clermont-Tonnerre, and Natalie is Evangeline Musset.‡

When Evangeline's father discovers that his daughter's tastes are unusual, and takes her to task about it, she replies, " 'Thou, good Governor, wast expecting a Son when you lay atop of your Choosing. Why then be so mortal wounded when you perceive that you have your Wish? Am I not took after your very Desire, and is it not the more commendable, seeing that I do it without the Tools for the Trade, and yet nothing complain?' "

This scandalous figure was by now "a witty and learned Fifty." She was far from pretty, but "so much in Demand, and so wide famed for her Genius at bringing up by Hand, and so noted and esteemed for her Slips of the Tongue that it finally brought her in the Hall of Fame . . ."

It is difficult to see what made Natalie appear quite so corrupt or made her so vulnerable to this kind of sexual mockery, thinly disguised as fiction. Perhaps what was so shocking was that her tastes were different, which meant disgusting, decadent and even threatening, to her contemporaries. In addition, she made no bones about it. Far from acting like the social outcasts they were, she and her friends were openly seducing all comers and were most skillful at satisfying their lovers; a quality that would seem to recommend them to our sexually more tolerant age.

They seem harmless, even disarming, this band of ladies, who loved fine food and good conversation, who wrote poetry and gave receptions at which they were most meticulous hosts, who had indefatigable flirtations and sexually satisfying affairs. There is no evidence that their encounters contained any hint of the morbid or sadistic. While sexologists were defining the supposed difference between vaginal, as opposed to clitoral, orgasm, and writing that a real woman can only get the former, or "mature" response, with a man, these women were finding out without fanfare what Masters and Johnson were to document later: that there isn't any difference.

‡ Identified from the Janet Flanner-Solita Solano papers at the Library of Congress.

"Men have skins," Natalie wrote, "but women have flesh—flesh that takes and gives light." And so the likelihood that vague, wicked, and delightful acts were being practiced behind a serene facade lent the final allure of the forbidden to an invitation to 20, rue Jacob. There must have been plenty of guests who found an excuse to go up the circular staircase followed around by a brown velvet rope; who paused, as if breaking into an Egyptian tomb after centuries of silence, before pushing open the double doors, expecting . . .

Perhaps a "love feast on the fallen bedclothes," where a bed stood in the far corner of that high, pale, still room. Perhaps she had stood on this bearskin rug, "her body's line uninterrupted by any bathing suit . . . Her breasts, uplifted centres, where heart and senses unite and exalt each other—no longer closed eyelids of flesh, but remoulded in the glow of the fallen daylight, again they looked at us." She was embellished by the gray-and-white starred bedspread which matched the curtains on the French windows; was resplendent under the pale oval of that dim ceiling; she was more compelling than the shimmer of green outside that both challenged and defined the room's stillness. All the objects in the room, the old tiara askew on top of a heavy brown wardrobe, a clutter of letters, an old cane, a china vase of a white swan's torso, sensuously curved, were reflected back by that mirror, which "recorded the gesture through arcades of watery distance and vistas of drowning lights." (Quotations from *The One Who is Legion*.)

"The warmth of her in our blood . . ." The room is as silent and impenetrable as Natalie in old age; as white as the vast landscape of her mind, those empty spaces that the wind sweeps across; as faded as the cheeks of her withered, peach-soft skin; as enigmatic as her utterances. There are only three photographs of a woman in a top hat, arranged in the shape of a fan, on a cluttered desk. I go back down the stairs.

Romaine liked, by teasing little remarks, to make it clear to Natalie how safe and unthreatened she was by these minor, but persistent, threats to their union. "Is Nat-Nat enjoying her new friend?" Romaine wrote from London in 1924 and, "I miss Nat-Nat a lot at times; but am glad she is getting over her honey-moon etc. while I'm away. Don't like it when she looks drunk & all to one side." She even tolerated Elisabeth (Lily), the Duchesse de Clermont-Tonnerre, whom Natalie had known for ever, a writer and *grande dame* of impeccable lineage: her father was the Duc de Gramont and her stepmother was born a Rothschild.

Elisabeth de Gramont had married Philibert, a wealthy man with a handsome black beard and equally imposing ancestral holdings. He turned out to have reactionary views: "He thought a woman's place was in the home, doing tapestries and receiving 300 cousins," Bettina Bergery said. The Duchess' attempts at rebellion were not always successful. "When people first had cars it was considered daring for women to drive, although they all drove for a bit. The Duchess stole the Duke's car and went out for a joy ride and he spanked her."

The Duke and Duchess had a beautiful old house at Nos. 67 and 69 rue Raynouard (now demolished; it was opposite the apartment where Romaine lived) with long gardens sloping gently down to the Seine. There were two summer houses, where the Duchess used to give candlelight dinners, serenading her guests with a string quartet playing the music of Rameau and Debussy. She entertained on a lavish scale, "in gold lamé rooms where you had lunch by candlelight. All those people had much more personality than we do today and they weren't afraid of grand gestures."

The Duchess and her husband knew Proust, who would often arrive at their eighteenth-century château at Gisolles, hours late, since he explained cheerfully that he had been obliged to drink seventeen cups of coffee along the way to calm his asthma. Proust thought Lily had the most fresh and ravishing voice he had ever heard, and said that her laugh was like the notes of a bullfinch. Natalie believed that she had developed a sixth sense, one of pleasure, based on the exquisite delight she took in touching; in this respect she was very like Berenson. "And when one admired the elegance of her bare feet on the beach, she contemplated them for a while, as if for the first time and, bringing them together, agreed: 'They are very sweet.'" (*Souvenirs Indiscrets.*)

Natalie made it clear to Romaine from the start that she did not intend to give Lily up. So the *ménage à trois* continued for many years, and while it made Romaine uncomfortable at times, she found it endurable. In the first place, Natalie's passion for the Duchess had

337

more to do with friendship than love, and in the second place, Lily's tact was exemplary and her behavior impeccable. Whenever Natalie was invited to the country, the invitation was extended to Romaine. Lily wrote several graceful essays in appreciation of Romaine's work (she called her "the greatest painter of our epoch") and Romaine responded with a sympathetic portrait in which Lily appears in front of the handsome outlines of her country house, like one of her own romantic ancestors, all heavy-lidded eyes and ruffled jabot.

Romaine had a more distant but equally cordial relationship with Eyre de Lanux, a writer and also an artist who was a protégée of Natalie's. She was a slim, beautiful American girl with black hair, great black eyes, and a ravishing smile, who had met Pierre de Lanux (a high-ranking French official who was lecturing in the United States to persuade America to enter World War I immediately) when she was a teen-ager. She married him at the Armistice and left at once for Paris, where they were lent a third-floor apartment overlooking the courtyard of 20 rue Jacob, and the house of Natalie Barney. Eyre would lean out of the window to watch the procession of men and women passing through every Friday afternoon. One day at "La Maison des Amis des Livres" run by Adrienne Monnier, she met Natalie Barney. "I believe we are neighbors?" Natalie inquired, and a seven-year friendship began.

Eyre remembers very little about those Friday afternoons. She was overawed and at a loss; too young to take advantage of the situation. She adored Natalie, but from a decided psychic distance and more or less obeyed like a good child when it was decreed that Romaine was to paint her portrait.

Romaine had perhaps been intrigued by Eyre's vivid good looks, or saw something that reminded her of Ida, since she posed Eyre the way she had posed Ida as a Red Cross nurse defending France ten years before. There is the same steadfast gaze, but the symbols (the woman as huntress in front of an icy mountain landscape and the figure of a goat) recall Romaine's letters to D'Annunzio in which she describes her vision of an ennobling love, which will take those involved to the peak of human aspiration; where the air is crystally cold and pure. Eyre remembers visits to an enormous studio in grays, whites, and black, with dozens of canvases standing around the wall, and posing in the center of the room. "I thought her work uninter-esting. I was very snobbish in my 21-year-old mind." They scarcely spoke yet, years later, when Eyre had a minor car accident and was left alone and penniless, she was astonished to receive a check from Romaine, without a word of explanation.

After years of friendship, Romaine and Natalie had worked out an understanding that was almost a marriage, and had arrived at that comfortable state where neither had any illusions left. They were as solicitous of each other as mothers. Natalie was constantly sending Romaine medicines, and Romaine, in turn, worried about Natalie's health. "You must be careful never to let your legs get cold. In Dieppe they were like *ice,*" Romaine wrote from London in 1924, and in New York ten years later, "I can see Nat-Nat propped up in bed, blue cushion, blue knitted pyjamas [*sic*] perhaps writing essays with beatic [*sic*] expression; but alas quite oblivious of insidious dampness creeping into her tiny bones. All the nice pink cushions of flesh won't keep the rheumatism away. Never let the *calorifère* [heater] die down even when hot outside; that is my advice."

They took responsibility for each other's cars, keys, and servants and grumbled at each other's self-indulgences with the resignation of old lovers: "Of course you find comfort in your new friends and manage to get a fair amount of amusement out of it all," Romaine wrote from London in 1924, where she was painting Una's portrait at a studio in Cromwell Road. "I must also seek in the future for friends but they must have some value other than the physical; & as we don't like each other's friends, it is best to keep them apart."

Romaine was extremely dependent on Natalie. She seldom dated her portraits and almost never signed them. The possibility of having her work rejected was so painful that she became compulsively self-abnegating, retreating behind a barrier of pride. She began to need Natalie to take over at a certain point, to have Natalie drop a deft word to this or that museum curator about Romaine's latest *oeuvre,* to arrange to have a booklet on Romaine's work printed, to plan a limited-edition volume of Romaine's drawings, 70 *Dessins,* to have certain works placed in the "right" museums. Natalie organized the practical aspects of Romaine's life indefatigably, though Romaine de-clined to return the favor and reacted with extreme irritation and

339

many heavy underlinings if Natalie so far forgot herself as to ask for similar favors in return.

Romaine was dependent and also demanding. If she had tolerated a certain person on Natalie's account, then it was up to Natalie to bail her out at the first hint of difficulty. While in London Romaine invited Toupie, a friend of Una and Johnnie's, to a party. Toupie declined and appears to have boasted to a mutual friend that Romaine was trying to seduce her.

"I only asked T. because you wanted me to do so," Romaine complained. "My first impulses are always correct. I knew that I should be exposing myself to some silly disagreeable misunderstanding by inviting T. Why give second-rate conceited people the occasion of showing their silly fangs . . . As I made this mistake through your advice, don't you think it is up to you not to write to T. again?"

Perhaps Natalie was conciliatory, because then Romaine decided that Una and Johnnie were somehow "deeply displeased" with her, and made a second demand. The couple had become very cool about the portrait, Romaine wrote. Although she had introduced them around to all her friends, Una and Johnnie did not seem at all disposed to return the compliment.

"I asked to know May Sinclair and her [Johnnie's] answer was when she came back [from her cure], that is to say next autumn! Now Lady T. intends seeing you in Paris, of course you must do as you want, but it would please me when she writes that you simply gave her the answer she gave me, 'with pleasure if you are here when I come back.'"

That she might have been subjecting Natalie to a kind of emotional blackmail in asking her to dislike the people she disliked, never occurred to Romaine. In that way, she was very like Ella. Those who loved you were under a certain obligation to you. If they did not live up to your expectations, you were justified in reproaching them, in being aloof, sarcastic, angry. Romaine invited Natalie to London. She was willing to drive to the coast to meet her. But then Natalie said she could only come for three days. Only three days! Romaine complained. One could hardly do anything in that time. Well, she supposed that Natalie was too tied to her life in Paris. Natalie needn't bother.

She ended her letter with the words, "There are a lot of amusing things to do but I've no one to do them with. As usual am isolated when I need bucking up & getting away from myself. After my month's hard work & solitude I certainly won't come back to all the worries of Paris until I've had some sort of a good time."

In her autocratic expectations, her attempts to make Natalie choose between her and other friends, her efforts to make Natalie feel guilty and in other ways, Romaine was often irrational. She would drop the remark in casual conversation that she didn't know how long she could stay where she was, "because there seemed to be evil emanations coming out from under the floor boards," said Alice DeLamar, who visited her at her Carnegie Hall studio and the villa Romaine bought in the '30s at Santa Margherita Ligure (and which she rented for a time to Pavel Tchelitchev). "We all looked embarrassed as this seemed a bit 'nuts,' but she was that way occasionally."

Romaine decided that the English literati were somehow angry with her. After lunching with Maugham in New York in 1935, she wrote to Natalie that the latter had just written his autobiography (*The Summing Up*) and mentioned Brooks in it. "It is my impression that the book will be used to humiliate me in some way," Romaine wrote, although how she could have thought so is difficult to imagine, since Maugham never mentions her name once. Her adolescent's supersensitivity to slights, real or imagined, was becoming a fixed conviction that people were out to get her.

That Natalie was at a loss to know how to deal with Romaine's irrational dislikes for people and her apparent conviction that enemies surrounded her, can be seen in the short essay she wrote on her in *Aventures de l'Esprit* in 1929. Her own gift of the retort was the perfect weapon in summing up certain people, with a Scorpio's devastating accuracy. Of a priest she disliked, she commented that he was a priest out of poverty, a philosopher by necessity, and a sensualist by preference. Having made such a statement, Natalie forgave and forgot.

She was baffled therefore by what seemed, in Romaine, to be a nursing of grudges, a resentment always seething under the surface, and a growing misanthropy. "She is totally lacking in spitefulness or venom," Natalie wrote defensively, "but when her hypersensitivity makes other people suffer, it is only her way of expressing her own suffering." One can see how desolate the artist really is by looking at her self-portraits, Natalie wrote; but she protests too much and one is aware of her discomfort. It was an aspect of Romaine's character that she could not explain.

However, Natalie had her own way of keeping Romaine at a certain psychic distance. "Nobody dominated anybody in that relationship," Bettina Bergery said. "Natalie politely concealed an absolutely iron will." Natalie's affairs, besides being a source of reassurance to the ego, could be depended upon to keep Romaine off balance and counter what seemed like a demand for total attention, total love. Perhaps Natalie's affair with Dolly Wilde had no more serious purpose than that to begin with. It became much more.

Dorothy Ierne Wilde was the daughter of Willy, who people said was even more brilliant than his more famous brother and who died of drink shortly after his daughter was born. Since Dolly Wilde looked a bit like her uncle Oscar, the comparison was inevitable. She had the same indolent charm, the same marvelously urbane and inventive wit and her own particular gift for the resplendent phrase. There was, when she first appeared in Paris society in about 1916, a particular, almost mythical freshness about her, Alice B. Toklas said; along with a joyous spontaneity that no one could quite convey. The psychiatrist Dr. Charlotte Wolff, who met Dolly in 1936 when the latter came as a patient suffering from depressions, commented, "She was very sick at the time, but she was so beautiful; she was radiant. I shall never forget how she stood in front of the fireplace. I've met hundreds of women in my life, but this woman I never forgot."

Dolly was well read. She loved the Brontës and Max Beerbohm, Tolstoi and Madame de Staël, and letters from Whistler were in her family papers. She was a born writer: "Not a visual person, she didn't see in images, she saw in phrases," Bettina Bergery wrote, but one was never able to persuade her to publish, although Natalie tried. Dolly lived in the impotent shadow of her brilliant uncle, unable to use her gifts or ignore them. When H. G. Wells declared on meeting her, "How exciting to meet at last a feminine Wilde!" she was delighted, just as her vanity was hurt if her relationship to Oscar were not acknowledged.

Nobody knew how she managed to exist. Perhaps she had a small private income, but Dolly was always financially embarrassed. She had an apartment in London for a while, and then she didn't have it and seemed to be living off friends in London, or Paris, or Venice, drifting between houses like an unwanted relative. What little money she had, she squandered. "When she sent flowers they were the most beautiful and apt to be the most expensive and her telegrams and long-distance telephone calls ran into a ruinous number of words and minutes," Natalie recalled in the privately printed volume she arranged to have published, *In Memory of Dorothy Ierne Wilde*. Once Dolly had tea at a café with a wealthy male friend. To punish him for having so much money, she removed the little round top-knot from two dozen brioches, declaring that this was the only part she liked to eat; and left him to pay the bill. When she died in 1941, she owed £500. In those days one could live for a couple of years on such a sum.

"It seems to me I must have first met Dorothy Wilde at Madame Bousquet's," Bettina Bergery wrote in *In Memory of Dorothy Ierne Wilde*. "In those days Marie-Louise Bousquet received in a suite of oblong rooms, where there was a great deal of red velvet. Dolly called them the *chemin de fer* because she thought they were like the first-class carriages of an old-fashioned railway train. I saw Dolly there, sitting between Gide and Jacques-Émile Blanche, who were both laughing at something she had said and how surprised I was to hear the grave Gide laughing so helplessly. . . ."

Dolly's wit was mythical and inclined to be barbed. Arriving at a party in the rue du Bac in the '20s, "Like the wind she came, blowing away the banalities of the talk. Boredom that a moment before had hung like a thickness over the room was chased away. She said, 'You all look as if you were waiting for the Coffin to be brought in.' A famous revue actress was there—severely dressed in a tailored suit, pretending to read a book of poems written by one of the ladies present. Dolly who had not met her before, on being introduced, raised her beautiful voice and said, 'It can't be you, I've always imagined you in tights and ostrich feathers.' And to our hostess, very slightly aside, 'What is she here for? Darling, it can't be for her mind.'" (From Allanah Harper.)

She was sarcastic and she was kind and she took such a delighted interest in other people's lives, and particularly their love affairs, that they found themselves confiding more and more secrets for the pleasure of her delicious responses.

"'It's not hopeless,' she says, 'nothing is hopeless, darling. Have you tried Lysistrata's system?—Oh, he's trying it! Really! Then what about Krafft-Ebing? Have you tried feather boas and perfumed them? and lace petticoats and wigs and whips and masks? . . . Have you tried spells? Remember how Dicky succeeded with her Duke, you should try that. It's better than Isolde's magic philtre, and you won't die of the after-effects, and I've found a recipe in a book of magic I bought on the quais and can loan you, but don't try it on Italians, they can't digest it. Lucretia Borgia used it and you know what happened at her parties . . .'"

There was an unfulfilled literary character about her, Janet Flanner wrote, not because Dolly was Oscar's niece or could or should have been a writer, but because she was like a character out of a book. "On the street, walking, or at a Paris restaurant table, talking, or seen in the dim, sunset light of her rue de Vaugirard flat, remote in its inner court, she seemed like someone one had become familiar with by reading . . . She was made for adjectives such as writers use, in long novels, where the description of the characterizations becomes intense, intelligent, elaborate, fanciful, and repeated with variations until it clothes and embodies the personages in words in which they take their form and reference and which have made them seem to come alive . . ."

Which have made them seem to come alive. To an acute and undeceived eye, there would be something fictionally contrived about the life Dolly Wilde led, floating from Marie-Louise Bousquet's Thursdays to Natalie's Fridays in a shabby, stained black suit enlivened by a Schiaparelli scarf that Bettina had given her, at first svelte and then drastically overweight but always, with "that particular floral quality in physical appearance which was the bloom of her charm," Miss Flanner said. It was a magnificent facade and behind it existed a most unhappy woman.

344

"I used to see her in Paris between the wars," Aileen Hennessy said. "There was a lot of opium smoking going on then and we were all quite used to it. I used to entertain on Sunday afternoons at 5 P.M. It was a very English institution, very stuffy. We read *The Tatler* and *Town and Country* and gambled on backgammon and had cold tongue, boiled eggs and ham salads. A real high tea. It was a mad success.

"Dolly got to hear of it and used to arrive. She would rush to the ladies' room and return with white powder coming out of her nose and blowing it ostentatiously; she had obviously been sniffing cocaine. My sister thought, what a waste."

Everyone said, "What a waste." Gertrude Stein remarked bluntly, "She certainly *hadn't* a run for her money." "Did she go home to those untidy bedrooms or borrowed flats so empty that all the bottles in the closet couldn't fill her inner void?" Bettina Bergery wrote. "Then did she think with fright of her future and of Oscar's past? . . ." Natalie believed that "Her love for life was too great and so she had to destroy it, 'For all men kill the things they love.'" Dolly, as relentlessly bent on self-destruction as Renée had been before, ruined her body with drugs and alcohol and was being treated for cancer when she died of an overdose in London.

Behind the facade of self-sufficiency Dolly was avid for love, capable of infatuations that combined a schoolgirl's vulnerability, even gaucheness, with an extravagant romanticism. She yearned most tenderly toward an ideal lover who would, indeed, bring her to life, whether it were a man or a woman. "I remember so vividly her bringing J.R. to dinner on the Quai de Conti soon after she had found her way into the false paradise of which he held the key," Victor Cunard wrote. "I had never seen her look so radiant and her eyes were of a dazzling blue."

Dolly Wilde met Natalie, one does not know how, in 1927, and wrote to her from London in July. "I am in a trance and reality is only you and love," she said. "What a world I am heir to now—what miraculous rights I possess, what secret bread is mine . . ."

She went on writing to Natalie, from Mayfair, Chelsea, Venice, Dinard, Rome, the Isle of Wight, until she died; long, darting phrases full of effusive descriptions: "I have been asleep all this golden afternoon and now it's tea-time and life is a dreamy, yawning affair full of stillness and quiet"; and, "I am just home from Lady C's ball. It was so glamorous and brilliant—with the lights shining down on exquisite women and the summer air coming through the long windows making the flowers tremble"; and, from the Isle of Wight, "Here I am embosomed in Beauty—wrapped up in the scented sachet of summer."

It was almost as if she were transfixed by Natalie, as a mouse is by an owl's glare. She had been turned to stone by moonlight; Natalie was "as far away as a remote star—but the longest spears of your light strike into me with deadly precision." Natalie had "set such a seal upon my lips that I still feel the line of suffering formed between them." Natalie had enslaved her. At the thought of seeing her, Dolly was ecstatic: "I cannot believe I am really going to see you. The idea is to be flirted with deliciously—but actually realized— impossible . . . I come to you thrilled and full of love—met you how you like! Oh! but love me, love me, darling." The threat of losing Natalie was unbearable. "Such coldness has stopped the warm current of my thoughts, and diverted them into horrid channels and treacherous eddies and whirlpools. I imagine you cross and ir- ritable and—far worse—indifferent . . . Don't, don't slip away from me —don't short-circuit your magic."

Infinitely vulnerable, her letters to the Amazon vacillate between delirious joy and despair. She took an overdose of sleeping pills, "unconsciously, in my sleep, I took the whole bottle . . ." Natalie mustn't worry for a moment as it would all be over in a week or two "and then I'll come to you (if you will have me darling) and we'll spend a happy spring together and forget all this sort of horror. . . . I *really* mean to take a new lease of life and I feel, somehow, that things are going to be different. . . ."

Then Natalie ran away with an actress. She was infatuated with the lady, giving her jewels and furniture, and after two months of that Dolly cut her wrists in a hotel. Natalie sent Madame Berthe, who sat by her bed for eight days. "She said, 'Don't leave me, don't abandon me,' and I wouldn't, the poor creature."

Dolly misjudged the situation between Natalie and Romaine. She must have thought, because Romaine remained aloof, that both had

346

left passion far behind. One must, of course, be deferential, and Dolly's letters to Romaine betray a childlike, almost abject eagerness to please and appease: "Often, I am afraid, I must *appear* impertinent as, alas! I have the defects of my qualities to turn the slogan round! I mean a certain quality I possess of enthousiasm [*sic*] & spontaneous truth in admiration, makes me over-eager to express myself without stopping to consider the effect on the other person, who may possibly misunderstand the spate of words! . . . If one *does* convey a wrong impression, I realize now, one must blame not the other person but a lack of sensitiveness or deference on one's own part. . . . An artist here complimented me the other day on my visual taste—and I realized how *enormously you* had influenced me that way and how *much* I had learnt from you. I remember one of the very first things you taught me, though its [*sic*] sounds trivial enough—the vulgarity of pink in clothes! I had just met you at Gardone and I had a silly pink dress. You intimated it very gently and politely, but the criticism widened in circles far beyond my silly little cotton frock, showed me in a flash the commonness of the whole school of 'blush-pink' and salmon-rose! . . . The cardinal virtue— the only necessary virtue—is 'quality'—you have it in everything you do and say . . ."

Romaine was not placated. She was bound to realize that the affair of Dolly was not like the others. It was lasting too long. Natalie, who detested having people live with her, was actually letting Dolly live in the spare bedroom.

Once before, when she had sensed that she was losing her, Romaine struck first: "Evidently we were not to see the New Year in together. But that portentious sign must be respected . . . You have been unconsciously voicing to me the death of the Old Year these last few days. But your trumpet blew loud and brassy sounds. Gentle-browed friendship & affection was stunned and deafened, she ran to be comforted elsewhere . . . Goodbye Natalie. Your fate is awaiting you and for your own good. Mine is over the uneven horizon's road, a goal never in sight. It is hard but why should you walk it with me, you whose goal is material and but the senses . . ." It is a ragged little letter, hastily composed and not to be compared in eloquence with the letters of renunciation Romaine sent to D'Annunzio. Its tone is half-hearted, and she probably regretted sending it almost at once. But it served its purpose, frightening Natalie into a realization of what she was losing. At this new moment of crisis, Romaine attacked again.

"Natalie, I received your very nice letters and 'am glad you are well' (with 'hell,' 'sorry' more appropriate).

"This letter is not in answer to your many friendly protestations, but a summing up of an intolerable situation, which in spite of many other disagreeable preoccupations still fills my mind.

"First of all there can be no possible misunderstanding about my friendship for you; that I have proved over and over again even to living in Paris for fourteen years more than was agreeable or desirable. My complete surrender to your generosity and sense of fair play has not been crowned with success. I find myself today faced with the fact that you are weak in all that concerns your personal vanity and that anyone so inclined can play on this, even to the point of changing your attitude to an old and trusty friend like myself. Your life at present, Natalie, is infested by rats and one of these rats is gnawing at the very foundation of our friendship.

"As long as you surrounded yourself by a not unfriendly tribe of second-rate young women, though unpleasant, I suffered it to pass; but when I am aware that you have chosen as confidant and friend one inimical to me . . . there is no course open to me but to ask you to shake the rat from out of your skirts or to accept my complete retirement . . .

". . . unless you as my personal friend can clean up your quarters . . . I shall not only keep away from your home as has been the case for some time but also break away from you altogether . . .

"So far I have never asked you to change anything in your way of living. I now ask you to change everything, otherwise there will be no longer
     Romaine."

Romaine's need for love was as insistent as Dolly's. But while Dolly crumpled when threatened with loss, Romaine had learned in childhood how to wrench herself free. Her solution was to cut the tie ruthlessly; to replace unrequited longings with anger. When she was rejected, Romaine became rejecting.

In their vacillations, they acted exactly as Natalie had with Renée and Romaine with D'Annunzio, with the difference that Romaine was never able to arrive at the same fond and tolerant distance. She was always vulnerable to Natalie, to the end of her life. Whereas Natalie, who had to "go away from the things I love," was always ready, at the moment when her lover was giving up in disgust, to say the words that would heal the wounds. But it was more than that. Natalie could only know how much someone else meant to her, if she were about to lose that person; about to be confronted with an unendurable sense of incompleteness: *"Richesse ou pauvreté/De n'être plus qu'à moi?"* (Is it riches or poverty/To be no more than myself?) she wrote in a poem (see Appendix, p. 415).

Whenever Romaine seriously threatened withdrawal, Natalie would be plunged headlong into despair and would set about repairing the damage, organizing trains and reunions in Annecy, where they parted, with all the skill she could muster. She juxtaposed these plans with passionate appeals: "Because the past is sacred ground to me, why must you take the promised land from my sight? . . ."

Natalie considered her numerous *affaires du coeur* as essentially frivolous; not to be compared with the great love she bore for Romaine. "The nearness of the flesh is an illusion," she wrote once before, "the nearness of the mind a sweet hourly delight . . . I am most tenderly thankful to you for all your beauty, and kiss your falling hands good-night—I'm not ungrateful, and sometime may know that this unstimulated easy everyday sort of an existence was a simple form of happiness—too good for me who am an 'erotic debauchée' undergoing a cure!"

So Romaine's letter had been a calculated gamble with the hoped-for results. Natalie wrote back to Romaine a couple of weeks later.

"My angel darling,

"Again between your little mushroom-lamp and music-box with your portrait of me looking on, and the vision of you seated sadly by my sick-bed I write to reassure you that not only in my house but in my life you will never again meet anyone you dislike.

"D. who rushed to London to seek comfort from her friend there writes: 'Alas, the full meaning of everything came over me with hideous force and I am ashamed to say I wept most of the way over—

349

But things cannot be like that—R. might as well insist on your killing me as not to see you.' I did not realize I had made the first blow so forcible, and I hope to be off before she returns, for I want to decide with you on the next step, so as to proceed according to your wishes and perhaps more cautiously so as not to change into a possible enemy one not unfriendly, and who has great appreciation of you . . . And since you affirm that it is 'gnawing at the very foundation of our friendship,' right or wrong, it must be sacrificed to our friendship—which is, as you should know—the most important thing in my life and my love for you is neither changing nor conditional and nothing, no matter what, would alter or corrode the pure metal of it—and I shall always serve under your near or distant banner for all the days or years of my life that remain, Romaine!"

Miraculously, Dolly survived the blow; they all survived. In time, Dolly was to know the feeling of the mistress who is supplanted by a rival, writing to Natalie, "I'd like to shout a friendly warning to your harem: 'Take care!'" . . . and even confiding in "dearest Romaine" that she was "very distressed" about "the Chinese situation." "As you know the whole affair in Paris made me *very* unhappy as I had begged N. not to start anything unless it was a real emotion. Two days after my arrival . . . well you can imagine what happened! It made my stay with N. very difficult and I only hoped it would soon be over—but I hear 'Wong Wong' [?] is to be secretary living at rue Jacob! *Please* don't tell Natalie any of this. . . ." Dolly thanked Romaine very warmly for the check she had sent. Having won, Romaine could afford to discover that the "rat" was more to be pitied than feared. Besides, she liked Dolly.

Romaine was a bit like Ella at that period in her life, "wandering where the wind listeth." She bought, then abandoned, a beautiful white mansion at Santa Margherita on the Italian Riviera, its elegant and simple lines jutting out like the brow of a ship over a steep garden filled with palms and fruit trees and its heavy wooden shutters open to the sun. Romaine went to New York for her first exhibition at the Wildenstein Galleries in 1925 (the New York *Times* verdict was that "genius rules a not yet perfectly competent talent"); she was in Paris painting portraits of aristocrats like the Duke of Alba, member of a noble Spanish family, the Baroness Émile d'Erlanger (beside a wild cat whose features, it was said, resembled those of the lady's husband), and an aristocrat of letters, the writer-diplomat Paul Morand, whose reminiscences fill out the human dimensions of the dramatis personae in Paris between the wars. He sits before a vision of his Château de l'Aile in Vevey, Switzerland, so submerged in his own thoughts that it's almost as if he were deaf.

Romaine returned to New York ten years later, timing her visit to coincide with an exhibition of fifty of her drawings at the Arts Club of Chicago (January 11–31, 1935). Her income still derived from the Waterman estate, now being managed by her cousin Wattie (Toby Dwight), the son of her mother's sister Clara, and Romaine's suspicions that the estate was being mishandled were confirmed in the crash of 1929 when one of its major holdings, the Kingston Coal Mine Corp., went bankrupt.

Although she had heard the rumors, Romaine still found her first meeting with Cousin Wattie something of a shock. "It became perfectly clear why the family estate was not prospering. Cousin Wattie was literally pickled in alcohol; this pickling process had been going on for years and acted as a preservative. Though I had always heard about his clubs, his . . . dinners, his ladies and his drinking habits, I was quite unprepared to meet him on his last legs as it were."

Romaine wanted most of all to see Chestnut Hill again (now demolished), but the sight of that was another shock. "There was no drive up to the house [any more], and the ugly Victorian structure, without trees to hide it, was visible from the road. On the other side of the house . . . still remained something of the old lawns, tall trees and flower gardens; but the splendid view was intersected by clusters of ugly buildings and the dark forests were no more . . ."

The plangent dream of childhood, the vision of an old country house, had sustained her for years. Romaine had built around it the persistent longing to find a real home that lay behind her aimless traveling, that made her dissatisfied with every house or apartment she tried to live in. She wanted to know from what she had been exiled. The hope was doomed because what she remembered had vanished. She realized that as soon as she walked into the old dining room, where she had spent so many hours listening to St. Mar's interminable prayers, that was once filled with the heavy mahogany chairs and black horsehair sofas of her childhood. They were gone and bad Italian Renaissance furniture was in their place.

Romaine returned to New York and took a studio at Carnegie Hall, alive with music, the home of dozens of painters, sculptors, violin makers, dancing and singing teachers. Her suite of rooms had the right light, high ceilings, large windows, and even a wood-burning fireplace. Romaine decorated it with her usual fastidious restraint, in black, white, and gray. She had a black sofa and chairs in the kind of angular and severely simple lines that are still in fashion, low tables of black Chinese lacquer, white wrought-iron accessories, and black-and-white striped rugs placed on a bare wooden floor. In this understated setting, a few handsome sculptures stood out in sharp relief.

Romaine had the inspired idea of blowing up a number of her drawings to the size of murals and papering them on screens or on the walls, over the fireplace, the doors, and down the sides of windows. The effect was striking enough to interest the American *Vogue* which at once saw the possibilities for its black and white fashion art. But Romaine turned them down.

She went to after-the-theater parties, which were extremely popular in the '20s and '30s, and it was at one of these that Alice De Lamar met her. Romaine was then sixty, but her hair was dark and there wasn't a line in her face. She wore very good-looking tailored suits and simple, dark afternoon dresses. She went to Esther and Chester Murphy's often ". . . and saw most extraordinary people, all rather drunk and Esther talking wildly about Jefferson and the Constitution and about you," she wrote to Natalie. "It was all rather mixed, but I gathered that she is still wildly in love with you. She begged me to ask you to write her a nice letter. Please do so, for she is really very gifted and she and Chester have been very nice to me. Chester says I am the most fascinating woman he has ever met. So you see what success I'm having . . ."

Romaine took Gertrude Stein and Alice B. Toklas to lunch at the Tavern on the Green. She went to see Mae West's latest film and Deitrich in *The Devil Is a Woman* and reported that Nöel Coward's film, *The Scoundrel,* received loud applause. She saw Central Park from the Plaza by night on a snowy evening and was enchanted with its Japanese effect, but horrified when she saw it from the ground by day. It looked like "nothing less than an abandoned farm-yard." She thought New Yorkers colorless, since they all dressed alike, and the food tasted like skyscrapers; but "Darky-Town" was wonderful.

"One melancholy and haunting tune was played, sung and danced most of the evening. 'Do You Remember.' It sounded like some other language and a very fat, dusky beauty in a short pink doll's dress with sash and white stockings rolled her eyes and as she sang made me feel the tragedy of her race."

It was her first exposure to a side of American life she knew very little about. Her artist's eye appreciated black beauty without pre-conceptions; her sense of social injustice saw blacks as outcasts like herself, and her appreciation of the literature, perhaps the work of Langston Hughes and James Weldon Johnson, could have formed her first link with Carl Van Vechten. Romaine had met this former music critic, six years her junior, through Gertrude Stein when Van Vechten was Paris correspondent for the New York *Times*. It seemed natural enough to look him up after he had returned to New York, where he had begun to write novels, was photographing hundreds of figures in the world of ballet and theater, and had become a champion of black culture.

Looking at the letters from Romaine to Carl Van Vechten now in the Beinecke Rare Book and Manuscript Library at Yale, one would almost believe that the telephone had not been invented. Dur-ing her year's stay in New York, Romaine wrote to him at least once a week, letters about books, his novel *Peter Whiffle* which she ad-mired, anecdotes about artists and D'Annunzio; letters offering proof that her memoirs were accurate, saying, "As you know I have been very fond of you & somehow I thought that perhaps you might be-come more fond of me if you knew what an awful life I had as a child . . ."

Because his personality intrigued her, she risked the danger of courting his approval, of giving him the authority to assess and eval-uate her. She admired him and asked for his advice and almost flirted: "Don't you ever answer a real letter?" she said. "I wrote you a four-pager the other day . . . but no reply. Yesterday put on my best red tie & sallied forth to Esther and Chester Murphy's anniversary party thinking of course to see you . . . no Carl—so drowned my disappointment in gallons of beer & danced till two in the morning at a low-class brewry."

Now that Brooks was dead, Romaine had applied for an American passport (she had become a British citizen through marriage) and considered changing her name back to Goddard. Van Vechten suggested that she change her first name to Roman. Although she reluctantly decided against it, she signed herself that way in letters to him. He called himself Carlo to her and sent her verbal bouquets of "Roses, Hyacinths, Carnations, White Lilies and pink Cyclamen."

In the flush of her enthusiasm, Romaine decided to paint his portrait, an impulse that came less and less often these days. They seem to have worked out an artist's agreement that she should paint his portrait and he should photograph her. She prepared for the task with her usual thoroughness: "I stand endlessly looking in at the shop windows displaying all kinds of artists' materials . . ." Then Carl began to pose, very "conscientiously." But Romaine was worried. "I've lost a little of my quickness and magic and my tones are rather different from former ones," she wrote to Natalie (January 29, 1936). "I find myself working nearly all the time and get up in the night to look at it."

She painted him on a wharf, his face composed and thoughtful, with faint Negro heads discernible in the black background. He was "the resplendent white king," she wrote to him and the heads were "an anthropological touch: good for those who search for a reason in everything." It is a grave, even imposing study, though Romaine took the sitter somewhat less seriously than he took himself. He gave Romaine two earlier self photographs and in both, wearing a watered silk robe or a top hat and white tie, with a gardenia in his lapel, there is the same fixed stare and self-conscious frown which must have been meant to dramatize, but somehow strikes the hollow note of posturing.

Van Vechten was delighted with his portrait and told Romaine that he would leave it to the Metropolitan Museum of Art in his will (it went to Yale). Romaine was also delighted with the portrait. She decided that she had painted a *chef d'oeuvre* and, she wrote to

Natalie, "The more I know Carl, the more I like him; he is in his way an aristocrat and I hope we shall always be friends."

But the fact that Romaine was so satisfied with the portrait made for strained relations between them. She never wanted her sitters to have their portraits, beginning with Fothergill. Her paintings were an extension of herself; and to give them up caused her real anguish. Since Van Vechten took a handsome photograph of her, in a pleated shirt, a dotted bow tie and a matching jacket, looking up with that shrewd glance of alert amusement which was typical of her, he must have felt that he had discharged his debt. She sent him the portrait with a grudging note, "I am giving you this portrait most reluctantly and only because I feel I have to."

Afterward, she couldn't let the subject drop. There are references to the way it was hung: "I think you ought to ask my opinion about the lighting. It was appalling in your last flat, but of course it went with all the rest"; and to his lack of finer feeling: "I know he [the portrait] would much rather have stayed with me—more congenial atmosphere. Less bric-a-brac about. Things have a soul when very much liked. I'm sure your portrait has lost its soul. But of course you won't notice the difference . . ."

When these hints were ignored, Romaine was forced to be more direct. "Let me say a few frank words. If there are not to be any amenities between us . . . don't you think you had better give me back the portrait. It was painted with my life's blood as you know and it is certainly a link between us. Give it back to me and this link is broken . . ." But she had succeeded too well in pleasing her sitter and the plea failed.

Romaine's portrait of Muriel Draper, painted during the same visit to New York, interested her less. She appears to have wanted to paint this lecturer, writer and celebrated hostess, whose Thursday afternoons attracted the *haut monde* of writers and musicians just as Natalie Barney's Fridays did in Paris, because her face presented a challenge. Delicate New England features with soft brown hair and blond eyes were married to a large, jutting, ugly mouth; the combination held the mingled revulsion-fascination of the grotesque for Romaine.

The result is an interesting work, in which the artist's fondness for strong, simple masses in dramatic contrast is receding. It is as if the painting is becoming looser, suffused with light like a water color, and line is taking over. These are the arabesques and liquid curves of the drawings and hint at the direction Romaine's work might have taken. Muriel Draper's body juts out like the prow of a ship, reminiscent of the stick figure in the winged boat which Romaine designed to represent herself. Like that motif, and twenty-seven other portraits, including that of Van Vechten, the sitter faces toward the left of canvas; an unexplained preference of the artist's. And, like almost all of Romaine's portraits, the sitter's eyes do not engage the viewer but seem fixed in furtive apprehension upon some distant scene.

Just before the outbreak of World War II Romaine returned to Europe for good. She was bitter at the relative lack of interest her work had aroused. She, who thought of herself as American first, had been cavalierly treated by her native land. Her drawings in particular, that most intimate aspect of her work, had been misunderstood or ignored. She had also come to the deflating realization that the home she imagined no longer existed; perhaps had never existed. She was as Natalie said, a stranger everywhere. So she should stay with those who at least valued her. They both knew that a war was coming and she would go back because, "I hope I shall be with Nat-Nat wherever and whenever that takes place."

As for the future, she was vague. At one moment she said that her friends would have to deal with the artist first, and not the *femme du monde*; at the next moment, that she was thinking of a series of portraits of all the women writers; then again, that she would not paint at all unless she really wanted to.

In fact, she thought of her artist's self as a separate and extremely fragile facet of her psyche; a person who came and went depending upon circumstance and whom the least noise, or interruption, or emotional disturbance, could frighten away. If the artist self vanished once more, it was because Parisian society was so disagreeable, and that was somehow Natalie's fault. But even Romaine recognized the illogic involved in that argument. Her artist's self was as unpredictable as a moth fluttering around a light and if it disappeared, one simply had to wait it out patiently, like one of Ella's moods; one had to coax it back again.

Then something else happened. Romaine was close to sixty-five and becoming a victim of the normal chills and aches of age; she thought she had rheumatism and she was complaining of frequent head colds in New York. She had always been something of a hypochondriac, despite generally excellent health. Now she thought of death as a malevolent force prepared to pounce at the first sign of weakness and carried a trunkful of medicines with her everywhere. She was vulnerable to any bizarre cure and, since she never thought much of doctors' advice, usually diagnosed and prescribed for herself. One day, she had some kind of fright. Perhaps it was a bad cold that made objects around her temporarily indistinct. Perhaps it was the normal deterioration of a once excellent vision. Whatever it was, Romaine became convinced that she was going blind.

It happened just after she returned to 74 rue Raynouard. Her apartment was on the floor above that of Laura Dreyfus Barney, Natalie's younger sister, who had always lived at a physical and psychic distance from the house on the rue Jacob. Laura had showed talent as a sculptor and even after she married Hippolyte Dreyfus y Cordozo, a wealthy lawyer and Orientalist whom she met in the lobby of a hotel in Egypt, and had become an officer of so many committees engaged in charitable causes, the sound financial advisor of the family, and finally a widow, she and Romaine had remained on good terms. What they had in common was the same distaste for people en masse, the same instinctive reticence, the same love of height and space and something else; a kind of like-minded philosophy. "We are not whiny and objecting, although we can get angry," Mrs. Dreyfus Barney said of them both. "We realize that life is a continuous onward march, so it's much better to do that, than sit down and wail about things."

It was because of Laura's delicacy of understanding, a sympathy all the more appreciated because it might be silent, that Romaine would have wanted to confide in her. They walked up and down the floor of Laura Dreyfus Barney's hallway, a vast and somber space furnished with heavy oaken pieces, in which the sheen of highly polished parquet provides the only gleam of light; the day Romaine

357

explained that her artist's career was over. One imagines the strong voice fading away, the half whisper, the silences charged with meaning; the hand falling back with finality. One senses the understanding coming from the other who, as an artist, would not need to be told what a poignant moment she was experiencing. Laura accepted the decision. She believed, with Romaine, that her sight was going. After all, she said, Romaine had been most imprudent. If she were interested in a book she would sit and read as long as her mind wanted to. Romaine was like that. And now, Romaine's body was exacting its retribution. . . . So, bit by bit, the regime began, of green eyeshades, of dozens of pairs of eyeglasses bought and discarded, of carrot juice faithfully consumed twice a day, of exercises for the eye that was farsighted and for the eye that was nearsighted; of weeks at a time spent in darkened rooms and, bit by bit, the retreat from the world of light.

Time Separates*

18

Au Passé À Peine Passé:
Passé, passé à peine et qui peut-être ment;
Présences d'ombre, avec quel coeur hanté les suivre
Ces souvenirs volés à l'angoisse de vivre?†

Natalie Barney

Those grave and stately rooms where objects had once been placed with precision, had vanished; and disorder was in their place. One could still see proportion in the height of the ceilings, and a pleasing quality in the expanse of glossy parquet flooring; but those objects that remained in the two rooms at 11 rue des Ponchettes in Nice where Romaine Brooks spent the final years of her life, were strewn about raggedly. It was the deliberate neglect of a way of seeing that had not so much lost its powers as become a negative force, impersonal and deadly.

One enters through heavy doors chained and double barred, into a dim hallway which contained a telephone, until the wire was cut, and beside that the numbers of the police and fire departments and a portrait of Natalie Barney by Bachrach.

Then through to the sitting room which, like the bedroom beside it, has french doors opening onto a dazzling terrace with the Baie des

---

* Also called, "Le Temps Sépare."
† "The past, the past scarcely past and which perhaps plays false,
　Presences of shadows, with what haunted heart should one follow them
　These souvenirs stolen from the anguish of living?"

Anges spread out below it, an apt setting for someone Natalie Barney always called her Angel. What furniture stands about is black, except for an easy chair indifferently slipcovered in white. There is a trolley containing rubber bands, pencils, notepads, a lamp hooded in black, and a variety of green eyeshades. The black bed faces a portrait of Romaine Brooks by Édouard MacAvoy, but that has been curtained over and hangs there on the wall, a hooded canvas, as puzzling and enigmatic as Magritte's painting of two lovers embracing with hooded faces. One beautiful object remains: a Japanese mirror with painted boats floating on its surface.

Drawing back the heavy black curtains which blot out the panoramic view, one discovers tatters of a once-white filmy fabric floating on the slight breeze like cobwebs. The air flows through the open doors and the rooms exhale a sweetish, cloying dampness, the smell of abandoned houses. Anna Cerutti, the housekeeper, sits at a card table, the sun falling against her strong blunt features and warming the stiffened legs and swollen knuckles. She smiles her hopeful, all-placating smile and is saying, "I don't know why; Madame was always like that. She did not want to see the day."

"How glad I am to think of you," the Marchese Uberto Strozzi wrote to Romaine Brooks, "on your terrace, where I imagine that you always are, looking on the sea and enjoying the pure briny breeze—How lovely and how soothing—And the flower market just behind you, and the magic rock above, and all the little streets at the back with their timeless memories of life. . . ."

He was "dearest Uberto," and they had known each other for years, although it was after Romaine moved to Fiesole, where for some years she had a little house perched on the side of a hill (the Villa Gaia—Mother Earth), that they became such close friends. This gentle and cultivated aristocrat who can trace his ancestry to the origins of the Florentine republic in 1292, owns a historic palace in Piazza Del Duomo at Florence; and has assumed, with devoted care, the burdens of traditional family obligation toward it. He observes Romaine with a subtle and tolerant eye, and perhaps what he admires is her rebellion, her determination to liberate herself and be enough to herself. Perhaps they see each other as joint victims of circumstance. At any rate, Romaine's letters to Uberto Strozzi have a spontaneity that she can never allow herself with Natalie, whose irony of thought carries an implicit demand. Perhaps these letters to "dearest Uberto" come closest to a true description of her state of mind.

He of course, in his desire to have her at peace, commiserates with her and placates her hopefully, almost as if exhorting her to be happy. She thinks he romanticizes her life. The truth, as she writes to tell him, is much more prosaic.

"After lunching as a rule with Natalie, I pass the long dark afternoons and evenings alone. N. has numerous friends that [*sic*] drop in at her hotel for tea (I dislike them all except the Lahovarys) and so just like at Fiesole, I sit by my window for hours (can't read by artificial light) and look at the lights across the bay. Sometimes a big star, meaning the ascent or descent of an aeroplane, sometimes, very rarely, a ship outlined by its golden lights passing along over the black waters, shows itself and then disappears into the distance. Then to bed after semolina pudding and milk. Such is Romaine's hectic life!"

Romaine had given up the Villa Sant'Agnese on the outskirts of Florence after World War II, and she never went back to the apartment on the rue Raynouard, although she rented it furnished for many years. She had taken the apartment in Nice, so as to spend the winters in its mild climate, perhaps because Nice was a city that automatically suggested itself, or because it carried so many echoes of Ella, appearing on the staircase, her moonlike face blank with despair. But Nice was too hot in the summer, and since Romaine could afford two houses, as well as two servants, she set about finding a summer home and discovered the Villa Gaia in Fiesole, climbing back in flights against a hill. It was cramped and inconvenient, but it had a secluded and rambling garden with an incomparable view over the surrounding hills.

"It is the high air that does me good and keeps me well and the expanse of sky and clouds over the hills exhilarates me," she wrote to Natalie in 1955, knowing that Natalie distrusted heights and liked to burrow in her nest; would, in fact, have liked to live in a cellar. It was a lovely view, Florence rosy in the distance and a misty expanse of hills, clouds, and sky. Even when one could no longer see the city, when it was blanketed in fog, up here one could see for miles: Each object stood out in triumphant relief; it was the penetrating clarity of reason, while down below lay stupidity befuddled by doubt. So Romaine decided on her mountaintop.

There was something equally self-isolating about the way she was cutting more and more people out of her life. To begin with, there were not many left. Dear old Aunt Minnie (Lady Anglesey) had died years ago and so had the enigmatic Princesse de Polignac and the terrible Henri Bernstein; John Fothergill had sunk into the obscurity of old age; and following his death, D'Annunzio's reputation went into a precipitous decline. Who talked nowadays about Dolly Wilde, Radclyffe Hall, Renée Vivien, E. F. Benson, Renata Borgatti, or even Norman Douglas? Romaine had survived them all and scarcely flicked a finger at their passing, except to send a clipping to Natalie, as on the death of Una, Lady Troubridge in Rome, or an unrelenting judgment as on the death of Cocteau; he was, she said, a minor poet and he didn't draw, he scribbled.

One still saw a few staunch friends, Willy (Maugham) and Uberto and Natalie and Yvon Bizardel, author and retired director of the City of Paris museums, and followed the lives of others like Bernard Berenson and was on cordially distant terms with Bryher, Sir Harold Acton, and his ailing mother (Romaine thought that the former's balding head looked like "an enormous Chinese egg"); and that was it. One cordially detested the rest and became very peevish if one was forced to give a luncheon at home for someone like Allanah Harper (because one didn't like to go to restaurants and have "ugly people" staring at one) and then be obliged to accompany the latter visiting another friend and the steps were so high and wide that one fell down. Her life was certainly becoming monotonous, Romaine wrote to Natalie, "and quite incomprehensible to most people. But as I was a child-martyr I can't be like others and now seek peace and quiet away from nasty people. Even friends," she added forebodingly, "are not always friends." And Natalie would insist upon sending her friends to seek Romaine out.

"Please," Romaine wrote to Natalie (November 24, 1952), "don't give anyone my address. A certain Mr. X appeared without warning one Sunday noon, rang forever and even shouted, trying to get in. I saw it was he in the peephole," Romaine said. "Sunday is my staying-in day and I was in nightgown and absolutely invisible. This morning he came again and I was in the W.C. [toilet] which as you know gives on the hall facing front door. Émile clumsily told him I was in bed. Even then he wanted to come in & shouted his name. Of course he will now be an enemy and all because you gave him my address."

There had been a time in Romaine's life when her retreat from the world was that of a hypersensitive spirit who shrinks in advance from certain rejection; who feels fated to be misunderstood. But now Romaine seemed to be taking a perverse pleasure in misunderstanding the intentions of others, even those who approached from the kindest of motives. When Natalie, knowing that Romaine wanted to learn more about the technicalities of engraving, asked some friends (a certain Madame Lahovary and her daughter, a specialist in this area) to drop in, Romaine took it as a personal affront; "certainly don't want," she told Natalie, "to fill up my life with unknown mothers and daughters." Natalie had to smooth things over with the right excuses.

While Romaine's boundaries shrank, Natalie clung like a limpet to the friends of a lifetime and they, in turn, clung to her. One went to the house on the rue Jacob in 1925 and Natalie, her hair massed low on her forehead like a halo, would be wearing a loose white chiffon overblouse belted with a thong at the waist, and the incomparable Madame Berthe would be nodding and smiling; one went in 1955 and Natalie was still there, looking like an abbess in something soft and white and with the same intent and inscrutable look which could break into a smile of childlike delight, and Madame Berthe was still chattering to the guests in a voice more bell-like than any cascade of laughter imagined by Proust.

But something had changed. The vital energies were draining from those faithful few who still came. Colette and Pound, Anna de Noailles, Otto of Hapsburg, and Bernard Berenson were slowing to a halt. First they moved like swimmers floating toward an underwater camera in grotesque slow motion and sliding away; and finally they were like chess players in some intricate maneuver whose next step everyone has forgotten; they were ranged like the stone statues of

Versailles in her *sous-bois* against petrified trees. Through them wandered a younger crowd, remarking on the lifelike quality of the waxworks, noticing that candle wax disfigured the brocade walls, and that there was, under a gaunt tree, the remains of a skeletal hammock.

Natalie herself, who began as a social outcast in 1910 and then became fashionably smart in 1925, had become an anachronism. If it is true, as Lord Kenneth Clark says, that one can only understand the experiments in art of one's own generation, Natalie had long since outlived her usefulness as a critic; this did not prevent her from continuing to survey the latest work in art and literature and to dispatch it with increasingly, and deftly, damning comment. After reading *The Grass Harp* in 1952, the latest work of her friend, Truman Capote, Natalie remarked that she feared "he was a one-book boy." Bernard Berenson lacked soul, it was true; there was nothing to be done about it. As for abstract art, Natalie had been to see Graham Sutherland's exhibition of two rooms full of "zig-zags and crazy-quilt designs. Well painted, but what for?" she wrote to Romaine. The fame of the people she had known always surprised her, like Colette, who hadn't deserved a state funeral. That demonstrated how much *la gloire* was something others conferred and how little reference it might have to the actual worth of one's work.

Natalie always invited Somerset Maugham to her parties, and Alan Searle would come if Maugham couldn't. Romaine was particularly fond of Willy. He was, after all, her oldest friend, as they liked to remind each other. Maugham wrote to his "romantic Romaine," his "dearest Romaine," she and Natalie were "dear glamorous girls"; he sent affectionate greetings from "your devoted old friend." He wrote to thank Romaine for a book of Natalie's, which he found full of sharp and clever observation, or to invite her to lunch (they were particularly fond of a restaurant on the quay at Nice called La Venise) or to grumble about the crowd at Vichy (September 6, 1950): "You can't think how many ugly people there are here and what mean faces they have. I haven't yet seen anyone, male or female, on whom one's eyes can rest with pleasure."

Natalie and Romaine agreed that it was dangerous for Willy to be taking Dr. Niehans' rejuvenation treatments in Switzerland, as well as futile to cling on at whatever cost to what was lost forever. What, Natalie wrote to Romaine in 1963, did she find on her visit to the Villa Mauresque? "A dead past?"

But Romaine continued to visit Maugham up to the very end, Searle said, when Maugham was crawling around on the floor and he dared not go out. In fact, Searle had only left the house twelve times in the final five years, and, perhaps this was why, after Maugham's death, he contracted Parkinson's Disease. Romaine and Maugham shared the same hostility to family obligation, and their bleak outlook on life developed at the same pace, so they continued to find themselves in agreement. Willy was always generously admiring of her portraits. He had even wanted to have his portrait painted by her, although his enthusiasm for her writings might be tempered with a certain reserve. So Romaine endured it, grumbling, when Willy persisted in admiring her Vuillard of a white rose on a plate; "Why at his age does he want things so intensely?" Romaine wrote to Natalie. And she would drive up to the Villa Mauresque for lunch with Gino at the wheel, completely hidden from view because she had installed gray curtains all around the car windows, and they would all laugh about things that had happened so many years before.

In old age, Natalie was surprised to find herself becoming famous. It was partly because the public had belatedly discovered the austere elegance of her writings (she published her last book, *Souvenirs Indiscrets* in 1960); also because the wave of nostalgia that embraced the twenties and decades even more remote than these from postwar Europe, brought with it an omniverous curiosity about the few who survived. Interviewers discovered her, critics wrote about her; documentary film crews set up cameras and lights at the rue Jacob. Natalie suffered their intrusions with the tolerant amusement of one who feels she has succeeded in leaving it all to the last possible moment. She was not even slightly affected by it. It was Romaine's immortality that she wanted, and she occupied her energies to that end; first, a booklet privately printed of Romaine's significant portraits and drawings; then, delicate maneuvers to have other works placed in national collections in France and the United States; further negotiations to have essays on Romaine's work appear in newspapers and, finally, exhaustive attempts to find a publisher for the memoirs. Natalie advised about pills, investments, servants, and wills. She supervised the renting of the rue Raynouard apartment and its eventual sale and kept track of the furniture and canvases deposited at various Parisian warehouses over the years. She was, in fact, Romaine's link with the outside world.

In a way that happened so gradually they hardly noticed it, Natalie had become the lover and Romaine the courted one. Perhaps it began after World War II when, after spending seven years in the same house, Natalie wanted them to live together and Romaine didn't. "I am wondering why you are taking it so much to heart," Romaine wrote from the Villa Sant'Agnese to Natalie in Paris in 1946. "Nothing has changed between us . . ." If Romaine now intended to return to art (a plan not acted upon), this automatically meant for her the return to a solitary life. Natalie was upset by the idea, Romaine said, only because she happened to be temporarily free "of the double distraction such as you've always had for someone or other since I've known you . . ." Romaine added that she loved Nat-Nat as much as ever and that they could visit each other often.

So the pattern of their lives took shape: letters, interspersed with frequent visits that Natalie almost always organized since, she said, "I am never quite happy away from you." Romaine was Natalie's bright Angel, the only one she loved for keeps. Natalie alone in Lausanne was sad, wandering around the shops they had visited together and melancholic as any lover avoiding, because the memory was too painful, the fountains outside the casino where they had lingered. But there was something equally maternal about Natalie's love. There were frequent exhortations to Romaine to eat more and better, to at least go out for lunch (since Natalie thought Romaine was becoming too solitary); constant reassurances of Romaine's greatness as a painter and much anxious concern. "I think of you every time I wake up in the night," Natalie wrote in an echo of the unease she felt at night as a child for her absent mother. Romaine meant more to her than anyone else, Natalie said. Life was not worth living without her. When Romaine visited Natalie in Paris, she usually took a room at the Hotel Continental, but finally she was staying at the rue Jacob in the bedroom, shrouded with tapestries and bed hangings, that had once been Dolly's. Natalie, spending a few days in bed, wrote, "I lie in your bed, the window open to the second day of summer: with the chirp of birds and the cuddling sound of doves and my thoughts of you!" Finally, Natalie was happily anticipating Romaine's next visit, to be spent "in *our* room here."

If Romaine needed someone to champion her, since she felt so defenseless against life, that person should be Natalie. Natalie would support her, save her even, as she had not been able to save Dolly Wilde and Renée Vivien. But Natalie had deep doubts about whether even she were equal to the task. She had a dream that she, Romaine, and Uberto were on their way up to Fiesole, "but neither of you seemed to know the way and I was hard put to it to discover the right road. . . ."

Romaine returned the loving concern, "You don't tell me about your personal news," she wrote in 1967 in an unsteady hand. "All your woes are mine. If I can't do anything at least you have all my sympathy which is what is most precious between friends. . . ." She quoted Matthew Arnold; to be true to one another was all that counted in an increasingly dreary and hostile world. As Natalie left after one of her frequent visits to the Villa Gaia, Romaine sat in the dark car at the station, "thinking about our long friendship which on my part is as great as ever; of our natures that differ fundamentally: you needing people as fuel for producing the sparks that animate your rare gift of rapid words and I needing solitude for creating . . . my world of art . . . But we meet in so many other ways and what a joy it is when we do meet!" The endings of her letters were always effusive: "All love darling. I think of Nat-Nat all the time."

Yet these reunions, so anxiously awaited, caused as much friction as joy. There were too many times when, after a month together, Romaine seemed to sink into apathy interspersed with sudden storms of rage. These outbursts worried Romaine, since she sensed their irrational quality. Natalie preferred to ascribe them to Romaine's excessive sensibility. Since this was an essential part of an artist's nature, Natalie was all for protecting it, even though she hinted delicately that it was the inevitable result of too much time alone. Work, Natalie decided, was the cure; work would fill in the time "far better than spent in anyone's company." Still Romaine did not paint, and there was another crisis a year later, in May 1957, during Natalie's visit to Nice. Natalie had not realized what a strain she was under, Romaine wrote; what an effort she was making "to keep in contact with your friends: to listen to endless tittle-tattle which your being the soul of indiscretion, reveled in, even when this tittle-tattle was about me; the desire to show off at my expense . . ." Romaine suddenly decided that one eye was bothering her and that she must spend ten days in a dark room. Uberto Strozzi was most concerned to hear about that. It was very dangerous to meddle with such delicate organs as eyes, he wrote, adding that he doubted whether there really was anything wrong with them. Natalie replied at once and there is a hint, in the draft of the letter she sent, that perhaps she had met someone new and that this was the cause of the trouble. If she had not realized Romaine's state of mind, it was because she was "a bit dazzled" (by the newcomer). Don't you remember, Natalie asked her, the way you felt after you first met Uberto, and how you blamed me if something went wrong between you? To herself, Natalie scribbled unfinished poems: "Our two opposed natures complete each other" and, "You have the power and the art/to hurt and harm my heavy heart." Her reply was sufficiently conciliatory for Romaine to continue her plans to come to Paris, and the always delicate balance of their friendship was restored.

Although Romaine had intended to resume her artist's career after World War II, and to take it up again in Fiesole and Nice, something had always intervened. There are several references to the intention in her letters, and none to the reasons that prevented it, whether it was really because of failing sight or might have more to do with a failure of confidence. What Romaine appeared to need was a new vision; someone who, like D'Annunzio, could make the world of art worth rediscovering and life worth living. That person presented itself in the guise of another portraitist: Édouard MacAvoy.

The French painter was more famous than Romaine Brooks, having painted the portraits of many of the brilliant men and women of the century, including Pope John 23rd, François Mauriac, André Gide, Pablo Picasso, Somerset Maugham, Louise de Vilmorin, and Général de Gaulle.

370

He was also younger (born in 1905), a short, slim man with hunched, square shoulders, and a sharply featured face which, like that of Cocteau, seemed designed to exist in profile in order to throw into uncompromising relief the high-bridged nose, the anguished mouth, and the shock of gray-white hair through which he ran his small, well-shaped hands. His energy was prodigious, along with the compelling quality of his artistic imagination. Meeting someone new, he would look fixedly for a moment or two, as if to make a trophy of the face, before his eyes sank back into themselves and, just as D'Annunzio before him, a look of profound inner exhaustion would cross his face.

MacAvoy had been asking Natalie Barney to arrange a meeting with Romaine Brooks for some time, since he considered himself almost her pupil. While studying art in the '30s, MacAvoy had seen Romaine's portraits in the Musée du Luxembourg and had been profoundly influenced by them. In imitating her austere approach, he was going against the trend of the period, which was to accommodate the style to the personage being painted, and toward what he called the *sens de Romaine;* that is, toward an uncompromising, sober, and subtle style, whose restraint would provide the optimum possible framework for a delineation of temperament. Like Romaine, it was not the outward form but the inner reality that interested him. But Romaine had been characteristically unwilling to meet MacAvoy. Natalie diplomatically showed Romaine some of his work. Romaine was admiring but still hesitant. Suddenly she gave in.

The friendship was a revelation for Romaine. Whatever his inner doubts and moments of despair, MacAvoy had a propulsive force that carried him forward, and his personality had a galvanizing effect on her. It was partly the compliment of knowing how much he had been influenced by her, partly his belief that she could and must paint again, and partly his D'Annunzian refusal to take no for an answer. His letters to his "*Sorella bellissima, carissima,*" have uncanny overtones of that poet. They are filled with large, confident phrases about her strength, her regenerative powers, her ability to find new depths in herself. She would triumph because she was indomitable, he told her; accurately sensing her most cherished notions about herself. She adored and, some believe, fell in love with Édouard. At eighty-five, she was childishly jealous of his attentions to other women, possessively anxious to have him visit her, and arranging to have him inherit her apartments in Nice. Her enthusiasm for him, he explained modestly, had most to do with her fear that she had not realized herself enough. At any rate, they made a pact: he would paint her and she would paint him.

He painted her in a jacket and pants, swiveling around in a chair to look behind her with a sharp eye, an empty artist's palette behind her and, in the background, her powerful portrait, "La Veuve." He wanted her to look, he said, like a kind of wild beast and searched for a pose both troubled and questioning to correspond with her profound internal dynamism. Since black and gray were her colors, those are the ones he used, and the widow's portrait, for him, was a symbol of Romaine's solitude.

The figure is still that of a woman, but barely. The cropped hair, powerful shoulders, and angular knees, even the rigidly placed, useless hands, convey an almost overwhelming male image. There is something about the distortion of one hostile eye, the flattened bridge of the nose and the set of the mouth, that speaks of a battered prize fighter; she looks like a self-opinionated, stubborn old woman.

Romaine's reactions to the portrait were helplessly mixed. She thought it was a work of art, yet she looked in vain for the remotest resemblance to herself: "Not one of my traits, even in caricature, although my face lends itself to caricature," she wrote to her niece, Béatrice Emmanuel. "I don't like the formidable stranger he painted."

With MacAvoy, Romaine temporized. He made her look too old, she complained, and after protesting ("What? Must I minimize those magnificent marks which your talent, your energy and your passion have engraved on your face, in order to please you?" he wrote in March 1960), he removed a double chin. None of us, he reflected, can face the fading physical truth. "You know Cocteau once said, 'Mirrors ought to reflect, that is, consider, before giving us back our likenesses.'"

Natalie didn't like the way MacAvoy had masculinized Romaine, "instead of portraying the 'double-being' with all its double charm which you preserve!" she wrote, after going one rainy and muddy afternoon in the fall of 1960 to see the work exhibited in the Salon d'Automne. She added that several viewers thought the work was a portrait of MacAvoy himself.

Romaine's objections had more to do with the inner image she carried of herself, which she had painted twice, and which the work in no way resembled. What lay behind her rocklike endurance was vulnerability, even terror. D'Annunzio's poetry had expressed it, but not this work, she felt. She was torn between an admiring love for the painter and disappointment with the work. So she bought the portrait, hung it facing her bed, and finally drew the curtains across it.

The portrait of Édouard MacAvoy by Romaine Brooks was never painted. There were physical problems; she wanted him to pose in the sixth-floor studio in Nice behind her suite of rooms; he wanted her to go to him in Paris. Both shrank from the undertaking, Romaine because it was a test to which she might prove unequal, and Mac-Avoy, because it would have placed great demands upon him (as Romaine's friendships had a way of doing). "She told me, 'I will never be able to do enough. I will have to see you from morning til night for six months.' But I hesitated, I couldn't interrupt my life for that long . . ."

Nevertheless, Édouard's faith in her had its result. She painted her last portrait the following year, 1961, of a man whose life was considerably less crowded, even placid by comparison, and who would be lovingly willing to undergo considerable discomfort if it would please her: the Marchese Strozzi.

Romaine had been talking about painting his portrait for a long time, and he was not surprised to find her looking at him with a contemplative eye. When at last she decided to do it, she set about turning one of her rooms in Fiesole into a studio. The room had, he said, exactly the wrong light, a south light, and so she uncovered the roof and replaced it with glass; then installed an intricate system of black curtains on pulleys to shut out certain areas; a telling demonstration of her perfectionism.

The sittings, he said, seemed eternal. He was not allowed to speak, the studio was excessively hot and, Marchese Strozzi says of the portrait, "If I look as if I am passing away, it's because there was no air. It was an ordeal."

Romaine stood throughout and, because she was becoming short-sighted at eighty-seven, was obliged to walk up to him, look at him intently, then walk back to the canvas and put it down. This went on for hours, and the painting was still not finished when Romaine stopped for fear of spoiling it.

The result has the immediacy of "La Veuve" rather than the more deliberate outlines of Romaine Brooks' other portraits. The marchese is in profile in a black velvet chair looking, as she wrote, ready to spring up and vanish at any second. "I must hurry to get you framed, if one can ever get anything done in a hurry here, and the frame may help to keep you in your chair." This view of him is consistent with the self-portrait he painted in a letter to her. He would, he said, eat a solitary supper in the tapestried dining room of the palace in Piazza del Duomo and then walk down to his room on the first floor. "I often wonder how many miles of rooms and halls and corridors I cover each day, a solitary and harassed ghost!"

Romaine had visited the Strozzi country house in Settignano outside Florence, and felt its ambiance: "Masses of black shadows against a lurid striped sky and great pine trees waving inky branches in the foreground," she wrote to Natalie; had seen Uberto's younger brother, Gerio, darting in and out of the trees like "an automatic spook" and, as she watched Uberto looking silently out of a window, had felt her imagination tugged with unease. In this delicate, elegiac work, Romaine was painting that part of herself which Uberto's secluded life represented to her. It speaks of inner phantoms, and perhaps for this reason the man in the chair is insubstantial, scarcely made of flesh and blood; and the mood is one of nostalgic regret rather than present pain. Most of all, it demonstrates how well she knew her sitter. As a final, telling detail, she has left the eyes unpainted. She was extraordinarily pleased with this achievement of old age, as she deserved to be. It is a great pity that she never painted again.

Painting Uberto Strozzi's portrait was probably the last happy act of Romaine's life. Left to herself, her preoccupations tended to revolve endlessly around her health. She took sunbaths and did daily exercises (to strengthen the back muscles, she said, after she found difficulty in hoisting herself up the last steep step of the continental trains); she marched up and down her garden in Fiesole and the Promenade des Anglais at Nice with soldierly stoicism; she consumed vast quantities of carrot juice daily for her eyes; she had massages, took vitamins, tried out various remedies for constipation and rheumatism and, when she discovered that she sometimes had difficulty swallowing, had all of her food puréed. She saw old age as a relentless enemy and eternal vigilance as her only defense. In fact, despite her continual aches and pains, her vague feelings of being "under par" that she blamed on "nerves" and, perhaps more to the point, despite the patent medicines and home brews which she swallowed with an abandon that terrified Natalie, she was in vigorous health.

Even her eyesight, which she was ready to imagine disintegrating at the slightest excuse, remained good. Her writing is as firm and confident as ever until mid-1967. By the end of that year, it has begun to falter and a year or two before she died in 1970, Romaine stopped trying to write letters herself and began dictating them to a secretary. But the specialist who told her that she would always see something was right. When Édouard MacAvoy accompanied her on her first plane trip to Paris at ninety-two or ninety-three, she looked out of the window and said, "Oh look at all those tiny villages down there!" And when Madame Berthe came to visit her the year she died, Romaine remarked, "I see you're still wearing that brooch I gave you."

Romaine's physical health gave less cause for concern than her mental state. Her seemingly sensible temperament had always had its irrational aspects, as she herself had acknowledged to D'Annunzio, and now what others would consider trifling annoyances were beginning to dominate her life. A little boy playing in the next garden, a neighbor in the apartment above in Nice who hung her laundry out over Romaine's balcony, the motorbikes whizzing up and down the narrow streets under her Fiesole garden, became acts deliberately designed to infuriate her. A day spent in a depressed and apathetic state might end with the "loud harangues" at Gino and Anna which worried Romaine because she could not seem to stop them. Natalie was even more disturbed to find that Romaine talked constantly in her sleep, and suggested tranquilizers.

Noise, in particular, drove Romaine wild. "An almost invisible window in my courtyard has suddenly burst with the loud popular life of Naples. A woman cook sings at the top of her voice, a baby screams and beats on some pan or other . . ." Every Quatorze Juillet in Nice, when there was a fireworks display over the Baie des Anges, Romaine would have to retreat to the studio at the back of the house, put pillows over her head and hold Anna's hand until it was over. She never made her peace with those loud, head-splitting sounds coming from St. Mar's piano.

At one time Romaine had a small but exquisite collection of paintings and sculpture. Besides the Vuillard, there were a Degas, a Renoir, a number of Picasso sketches, several of Conder's delicate paintings, a bronze statue by Chana Orloff, a fifteenth-century wooden dog from Venice, and a Greek statue of an archangel. Most of them were at Nice with her own paintings and, perhaps after the Villa Mauresque was rifled, Romaine became convinced that thieves would find her as well. To protect what could not be put in storage or sold, mostly her own works (which actually had no commercial value), she had her doors at 11 rue des Ponchettes loaded down with several more sets of bolts and bars and so convinced Anna of the danger that she was terrified to be left in the apartment alone.

One had to be on guard, Romaine felt, against "evil intentions." This was a further reason to be wary of newcomers, who might steal from you, or somehow swindle you out of your money. Even people one had known for years, like one's nephew the lawyer, might somehow enrich themselves at one's expense, although of course one had no proof. One might, because one could not find one's drawings, wrongly conclude (as she confided to Adelyn Breeskin), that someone in one's household was making a secret collection, implying Gino Scodellari. That devoted chauffeur, valet, and companion of her final years, was as incapable of a dishonest act as he was of being a connoisseur of undervalued art. This did not prevent Romaine from focusing her poisonous suspicions on him. She convinced herself that Gino might poison her for her money and had a clause inserted into one of her wills that, the longer she lived, the more Gino stood to inherit.

Equally virulent suspicions contributed to her final coldness toward Édouard. Romaine wanted him to inherit her property at 11 rue des Ponchettes because, she said, artists always needed money. She welcomed Janine Lahovary's suggestion that she make a nominal "sale" to him, along with the clause that he would take possession after her death. But when Romaine discovered that she had sold not one, as she had thought, but both apartments, she had a swift change of mood; and decided that it had been a plot to defraud her. It was Édouard's fault. It was also the fault of Madame Lahovary, for "sticking her Swiss nose into my affairs."

One needed to be on guard against the very earth itself. Those subterranean rumblings at Nice, forerunners of an earthquake, were portents one dared not ignore. Such seethings must be cooled by rain, Romaine thought. In another age she would surely have offered up a sacrifice to the Gods.

Above all, one must beware of trees. "We love nature but nature doesn't love us and everything around us uses us for the things they lack," she wrote to Natalie in 1965 in a letter mirroring the theme of her short story, *Riviera Jungles*. "Trees especially are our enemies and would suck us dry. Do you remember at Sant'Agnese how rheumatic I became sitting under the acacia tree? So darling be very careful about lying down on benches in your garden which certainly lacks no end of things and will pounce upon your life stream to feed them." Romaine's irrational conviction that the whole world was somehow out to persecute her, was distinctly paranoid.

So perhaps it is not altogether surprising that, in old age, Romaine should sever her friendship with the one person who had loved her steadfastly for fifty years, who had provided endless support, reassurance, admiration, and affection, and who had been willing to endure her increasingly irrational behavior for the sake of her strengths. The ostensible cause of her break with Natalie was the same battle they had fought for years. It provided the proof, to an increasingly embittered woman, that there was no one you could really trust.

Janine Lahovary, the friend of Natalie's whom Romaine had been so unwilling to meet in 1956, appeared in Natalie's life by chance. Natalie was in Nice one spring, and perhaps it was after lunching with Romaine that she had struck up a conversation on a park bench with this lady, the wife of a former Romanian ambassador living in

Switzerland. Madame Lahovary had married when she was a young art student and her husband a brilliant thirty-year-old diplomat at the League of Nations in Geneva. It was a union in which she had played, a little, the role of Galatea to his Pygmalion. As she matured she became very interested in psychoanalytic thinking, knew Jung, was reading the writings of the Catholic thinker Marie Nöel, and was working toward a synthesis of psychoanalytic insight and religious conviction. To her, life was a training ground for the soul, and she had gained much self-knowledge in coming to terms with a not very happy life.

She was younger than Natalie, still lovely and always impeccably dressed in coat-and-dress ensembles and expensive French shoes. A lock of hair invariably fell over her asymmetric features, giving the effect of disarming disarray in contrast to the correct elegance of her clothes. She had a way of leaning forward intently on the edge of a chair and, when walking of threading her arm loosely through that of her companion, which reinforced one's impression that here was someone in whom it was safe to confide, and who would always take the most generous view of things. Her tact with others was as much due to her sympathetic insights as the result of having spent years as a diplomat's wife; because of it, she would always avoid a confrontation.

Meeting Natalie, whom she immediately saw as a rare, even unique being was a revelation for Janine Lahovary; a kind of reward for painful self-insight. She deferred to her completely. It was Natalie's manner, which had its own grandeur, that dominated; and Janine who unobtrusively kept the wheels turning and who would deftly usher out those guests who might be beginning to tire "Naty." Janine admired Natalie's calm acceptance of others and herself; her quality of seeming to be grounded in herself. Janine saw Natalie as infinitely humane, though not divine; since Natalie was most clear about the importance of choosing those to whom one gave oneself. That, too, was something Janine felt the lack of in herself. It was an equally important friendship for Natalie, since it combined intelligent, loving companionship with the practical help on which a woman of her advanced years must depend. They saw a lot of each other until Nicolas Lahovary died in the summer of 1963; then Janine Lahovary moved to Paris to be with Natalie and was at her side when she died on February 2, 1972.‡ Janine Lahovary died a year later to the month.

Janine knew that Natalie was the only one Romaine had ever loved. She bent her considerable charm to gain Romaine's friendship, to be helpful in small ways, and to invite Romaine to stay at her Swiss country house whenever Natalie was there, since she knew that Natalie was never quite happy without Romaine. If she could not help taking sides (she thought the relationship endured because Natalie made all the concessions), she would never have presumed to come between old friends. Romaine responded to her overtures to a limited extent and even confided in her occasionally. But her distrust simmered below the surface and finally became open dislike and hostility. It was the old rivalry in which Romaine was competing with another for a faithless Natalie, just as she had competed for her mother. Unlike Lily de Clermont-Tonnerre, who had been the epitome of discretion, Janine Lahovary was insinuating herself between them, Romaine believed. It was jealousy that led to the final break; violent, irrational, inevitable.

When Romaine had rebelled before, Natalie had always given ground. But this was not a relationship that could be ended by ultimatums. Romaine refused to live with Natalie, but Natalie was psychically dependent upon others, she had to have someone and by now was physically dependent as well. Someone must watch over her

‡ "Natalie had a heart attack and then pneumonia an hour afterwards and died at night after a few hours of suffocation," Madame Bergery wrote to the author from Paris. "MacAvoy who came, and stayed all night with Natalie and Madame Lahovary, did one of his best drawings of Natalie on her death bed. Afterwards—during the night—she was taken to the crypt of the American Cathedral and then buried in the Cimitière de Passy at the Trocadéro.

"The funeral was on a Friday and her maid Berthe said, 'Mademoiselle's last Friday.' (You know she always received on Fridays.) About 50 people came. Madame Lahovary was very sad—and quite ill for the moment . . . A friend said at Miss Barney's funeral, 'Natalie wouldn't have come—she never went to a funeral in her life—She said they were barbaric' (and in fact Natalie answered when asked why she hadn't gone to her great friend Madame de Clermont-Tonnerre's, 'Why trail after an old dress that the owner threw away because it was worn out?') . . . Madame Lahovary answered, 'Natalie was so cerebral—That is the intellectual view—But the heart is less reasonable.'

"When you come back you must go and see her grave which was given her a few years ago by Paul Boncourt—for it's a cemetery that has been full, with no more places since 40 years or so—Typically 1900—all the old friends are there—including Renée Vivien. . . ."

diet, help her get dressed, help her walk, put her to bed, give her injections in the middle of the night, and that could no longer be Madame Berthe, who was also getting older and was ill.

Since Natalie had placated Romaine in 1957, over a new friendship which might have been Janine Lahovary's, Natalie tried again to convince Romaine that she loved her the most and that nothing could separate them. Romaine refused to listen. From her point of view, it was one more manifestation of Natalie's need to be liked, a need so compulsive that Natalie would cheerfully sacrifice her dearest friend to this end. Natalie was deliberately turning away from her; well, two could play at that game. But behind the stubborn facade she was deeply, fatally, wounded. The psychic hurt translated itself into the terrible fear that she was losing her eyesight. In June 1968 Romaine went back again to her dark room, to black curtains and bed. She refused to answer Natalie's letters and phone calls, would not go to Paris, and would not have Natalie come to her.

Natalie was very upset. She wrote to an old friend to intercede, since, "Anything seems preferable to me than to know her in a darkened flat and solitude." She began sending messages to Romaine in an unsteady hand, "Nat-Nat loves Angel." "From Nat-Nat's weak heart full of love for her Angel."

Natalie sent her own doctor from Paris so as to have news of Romaine and also to see whether ill health could be playing a role. The story is that Gino let him in. "Oh well," Romaine said, "since you are here, you may as well examine me, but don't think I am going to pay your bill." Then Anna Cerutti said, Romaine refused to take the medicine he prescribed.

There is a second version to the same story. Romaine told the Marchese Strozzi that the doctor was admitted on the pretext that he had news from Natalie, but that once inside he whipped out a hypodermic needle and put her to sleep, presumably in order to examine her. Romaine was furious. It became one more reason to get even with Natalie. She told Gino to "slam the door in Miss Barney's face" if she should appear.

When her letters and phone calls went unanswered, Natalie did appear. She wrote, from the Hôtel d'Angleterre in Nice, "My Angel, and cruel Love—After half a century of being our nearest and dearest, why do you treat me at present like an unwelcome stranger? That you 'wished to see no one' not even your doctor last night . . . Why can't I come now or tomorrow Monday just to be near you—and reassure us that all is as well as possible . . . Do please, I beg of you and our everlasting friendship, reassure me or let me go to you— Just for a moment—To put your head on my shoulder and carry out whatever wish you may express to your everloving and faithful friend Natalie."

Natalie must have returned to Paris without seeing Romaine. On July 9, 1969, she sent a last message. All it said was, "My Angel is, as ever, first in my thoughts and deepest in my heart." Romaine never answered it. She simply marked the envelope in heavy black ink and a large firm hand, "Miss Barney—Paris."

The break was tragic for Natalie, who was right in believing that her heart, which age had weakened, continued to beat chiefly out of love and concern for Romaine. She might write that life consists of subtractions, things one has to give up, but in truth she simply refused to accept that their friendship had ended and could write without irony, in an appreciation for the catalogue of Romaine's Washington exhibition, about Romaine's rare gift for the art of friendship. Nothing had changed, as far as Natalie was concerned. It was perhaps a saving solution; since Natalie had also said, "To live in hope is a great relief."

The break was much more destructive for Romaine, whose pride had been as final a barrier between her and Natalie as it had so many years before with Ella. She had had her revenge, but at a bitter price. There was no longer a lifeline to the outside world and no surcease from solitude. There was no longer night or day, since all one ever perceived was the dim glow from a black-hooded lamp, and so she was awake at night and ringing for Gino every two hours and wanting meals at strange hours, just as Ella had done.

Perhaps alone, between sleeping and waking, Romaine's thoughts spiraled back to the unresolved issues of her life in an attempt to come to a final confrontation, or a truce, if not a resolution. She was the hooded figure on a boat deck looking out, as the boat slips away, over the past (since the drawing was called "The Past" and also, "Departure"); she was perhaps the man in a stained brown suit huddled against a wall on the quayside at Nice whom she could have seen from her window if she had ever looked out. He has worked at the market by day, and now, after the market is closed, he sits facing the bay, and rotting cabbage heads roll in the gutter, alone, unnoticed; to wait all night for the market to open again perhaps; too remote even for pity. She was, they said, talking about Ella and St. Mar, those images of past pain which would always haunt her; and perhaps she was only dreaming that they were in the room. The unhappiness in the world is a constant, she had written; now she waited for death to release her from it. She begged Gino for pills; he refused in horror. She did not want to know when Madame Berthe came to talk about the coming exhibition of her work in the United States. "I don't care," she said, "I am dead."

She stopped writing to Édouard, and to the kindly Yvon Bizardel she explained that if he came to Nice, she would be delighted to put him up at a hotel but that she could not see him. Finally, she broke things off with Uberto. He had resisted the idea when she had decided to sell the Villa Gaia and live in Nice the year round: "I was anticipating with joy the approach of spring," he wrote in May of 1963, "as I thought it would bring you back, like the swallows, to your high-perched nest . . ." But despite his attempts to convince her that it could not have been the air at Fiesole ("so wholesome and dry") which disagreed with her, Romaine left, and Uberto consoled himself by sometimes daily phone calls during which they would chat for hours. When, finally, Romaine no longer came to the phone, Uberto sent messages. One day he asked Gino, "Do you give madame my messages?" Gino said that he had, but that Romaine's answer had been, "What's the use?" "It made me," the marchese said, "very sad."

Romaine's twilight life was interrupted only by the ministrations of Anna and Gino and occasional visits from Maître Emmanuel and his daughter, Monique Grossin. She shuffled what seemed to her servants to look like scraps of paper. It was a collection of notebooks, kept for years, in which she had written quotations, scraps of poetry, aphorisms, proverbs, and her own attempts at the succinct statement. They were found in the tangle of forgotten objects in forty trunks and twenty wooden boxes after she died, along with a hundred pounds of old medicines, the sixty silk scarves, the sixty-two identical berets, the twelve pairs of unworn shoes, the Moroccan and Chinese clothes, the lounging pajamas, the catalogues, letters, bills, bank statements, dried up tubes of oil paint, the drawings, a diary from 1903, a silver cigarette case from D'Annunzio, and 150 gold coins stuffed into medicine bottles.

In one of those notebooks, Romaine wrote, "My dead mother gets between me and life. I speak as she desires/I act as she commands/To me she is the root enemy of all things."

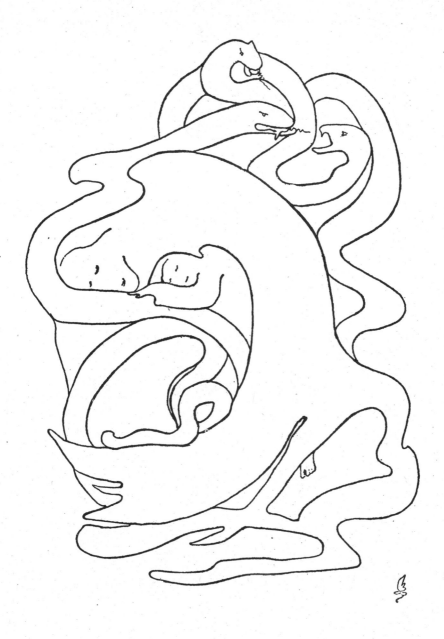

Epilogue: Unity of Good and Evil*

Then and there I resolved . . . to obey no other urge than that of my art, even though it might lead to the extremes of physical sufferings or to the depths of mental distress.

Why blame the cause of past tribulations if their effect in the present stands for strength and individuality? It pleases me rather to survey objectively the plant that survived the storms of that atmosphere of intense and adverse feeling.

Romaine Brooks was an artist of remarkable gifts who fought to express her talent in an age when women of her class were expected to be the amusing companions of prominent men, nothing more; and with the further badges of difference which sexually unorthodox tastes and an unhappy childhood have to confer.

As an artist, she succeeded on her own terms. To her credit, her contemporaries make no mention of the oddity of a woman painting, or label her art with the adjective "feminine" (or even, "feminist") which present-day critics sometimes use in order to subtly denigrate work by a woman. She was recognized as a serious painter on a par with her male colleagues and treated as such. She also succeeded in the perhaps more difficult task, even for the economically secure, of living an independent life with the lovers she chose, an achievement

* Also called, "Unite du Bien et du Mal."

which living in the tolerant '70s may make it impossible for us to fully appreciate.

Hers was a strongly destructive spirit and a fatalistic one. The pain inflicted on her in childhood led to the conviction that she was fated not to be happy; it was one that became tragically self-fulfilling. Yet one cannot confidently consider any woman completely self-destructive who survives to the age of ninety-six. In Romaine, powerful tides of despair and equally powerful tides of hope were evenly matched. Her character was forged out of these violently opposed emotions and, if its dominant coloration was the gray of melancholy, there was a counterbalancing theme of self-reliance, a courageous willingness to explore the dangerous waters of the psyche, and the ability to laugh at her fears, which continued into old age. She was, as a taped interview for *Bizarre* magazine shows, alert, amused and vital at ninety-three. Her voice is wonderfully expressive; full of wit and delicate shades of feeling. Phrases that look uncompromising on a page were modified, even robbed of their harshness, when she spoke them, since she shaded them with nuance. Talking of her mother, Romaine said matter-of-factly, "My mother scolded me. Grumbled at me. She didn't want me to be intelligent when my brother was not. Because my brother was—deficient. She wouldn't have it that it was me, the daughter, who had the brains." There was a pause, then an exclamation, "Aaaannngh!" full of meaningful overtones.

She sang scraps of songs, "A little bit of string, just a little thing." She was full of suppressed amusement as she told stories about Una, Lady Troubridge, and Gabriele d'Annunzio. She would begin to explain a certain drawing, then burst into astonished and derisive laughter at the part-men, part-animals, she had drawn and forgotten. "You know," she said, suddenly switching to English, "I have a sense of what's funny. Happily, because the things of life . . . One must laugh." Her voice trailed away to a whisper, "Because life isn't . . ."

She had, her nephew Maître Léon-Marie Emmanuel said, a luminous spirit.

As a strange and solitary being, Romaine remained at a certain distance from the world of artists and intellectuals which she frequented; someone fated like Frederick Rolfe, Baron Corvo, never to feel at ease anywhere. Like him, she saw herself as ill-starred and thwarted by those who should have known better. Corvo blamed

Catholicism for his disappointments; Romaine blamed her mother. One does not know whether Ella truly gave Romaine away to Mrs. Hickey, and it does not matter. What matters is that Romaine experienced the event as such, and this was the rock upon which she built her resentment. She directed her adult energies to righting the real and imagined wrongs of childhood, and her memoirs have to be seen in this light; to accuse Ella and vindicate herself. Similarly, if Romaine could not have normal friendships, it was "the herd" that was at fault, and Romaine parceled out the blame with a free hand. Yet she felt the lack of emotional satisfactions acutely. The need propelled her toward Natalie and provided a durable cement. The break that came was the result not of a lack of feeling but a failure of confidence.

Romaine had an ideal image of herself as a perfect being, a saint, Natalie's Angel, which coexisted with a second view of herself as powerless, unwanted, and unlovable. Such an inner fragmentation tends toward a very uncomfortable inner life. Because a perfect being is perfect, not even the slightest imperfection is tolerable. Such pitilessness helped her to attain a facade of integration, the "rocklike" quality her friends spoke about, but it prevented her from an acceptance of herself as a person with human failings, which is the road out of the psychic impasse. To have acknowledged these would have brought a murderous self-hate into play, and so in this sense, Romaine *had* to see herself as a martyr and others as accusers and accused.

Ella did indeed stand between Romaine and life, but not in the way Romaine believed. A person who sees only giants, Anaïs Nin remarked, is looking at the world through the eyes of a child. To pass into adulthood, each of us must forgive our parents their sin. This essential step frees us to break the umbilical cord of emotional dependence and become the sum of all our parts. It was a vital step which Romaine could not take, and so she was doomed to see Ella as an "elemental force of nature," not a human being; was doomed to remain emotionally bound to Ella in that circle of love-hate with which her repetitive, suffocating, encircling drawings are concerned.

Romaine's emotional problems gave her creativity a ready source of subject matter. The impulse to paint was further fueled by the need for an outlet for inner conflicts, and it is safe to say that if Romaine had not had this safety valve, she would have committed suicide. Her art is an attempt to apply balm to the wounds, alleviate the distress; come to terms with the pervasive despair.

But the creative urge was just that, an outlet for suffering and one that could offer only a partial solution. In such a case the emphasis is on expressing the problem and secondarily on realizing a work of art. The result is too often unsatisfying or, as in Romaine's case, focused obsessively on a single discordant theme. To have forgiven Ella would have released Romaine to see people as they were, not simply as characters in a private tragedy. To have been less obsessed by the need to be perfect would have freed her to experiment as an artist. To have discovered new aspects of herself would have led to deeper insights into others. To have let go of her rage would have removed the barriers between her and life.

I prefer to think of Romaine Brooks not as the stubborn, exasperating old woman she became, but the child she once was, with permanently startled eyes; the thin young art student huddled on the wooden bench of a rocking train; the successful portraitist in medieval velvet, on a terrace of black and crystal overlooking the Eiffel Tower; Compton Mackenzie's heroine with the low, thrilling voice and the impenetrable gaze, enfolded in a white woolen shawl. Romaine is alone in the studio in Tite Street or on the coast of Cornwall near St. Ives, concentrating, correcting, erasing, and beginning again; finding in her work the balm to old wounds and, occasionally, the solution and completion which she so profoundly desired.

She was, indeed, someone whom life did not defeat. She remained, as she wanted her epitaph to read, Romaine.

APPENDIX

Letters of Ella Waterman Goddard 1885–97.
1885

DeKeyser's Royal Hotel, London
To executors I. S. Waterman
Yours of March 29th with enclosed Duplicate Received.
In regard to my daughter Romaine's confirmation I think the child entirely too young to understand the nature of such a performance.
I attribute my son's sickness to the unnecessary religious pressure inflicted upon him by his grandmother. He was of a too nervous temperament to be bothered with such subjects. It undoubtedly retarded his recovery. So, naturally, I would have preferred Romaine to have waited until she had developed her mental powers.
However, I sincerely trust no harm will come from it.
Now that I am more comfortably situated & St. Mar has much improved, I have concluded to have her brought over here to Europe. As Romaine is so anxious to come I shall make arrangements for her to do so in June or July. The weather will then be most favorable.
I intend my daughters to continue their studies together as they are the natural companions for each other. . . .

> August 8, 1893 on paper of the Hôtel
> Athénée, 15, rue Scribe Paris

My dear Beatrice,
I have received your 2 letters—and also I found Mlle. Tavan's which I will answer in Paris—in a day or two. I know you wish to leave School this fall & have been thinking over 1 or 2 plans in which you might combine amusement & still continue your drawing & music some time.

I am glad you feel better—I think the pure mountain air is a tonic for a bilious spell—which is probably what you have—and a change of scene is better than medicine sometimes.

You have doubtless applied yourself to your studies somewhat closely —Mlle. Tavan thought you made very good progress.

I sometimes eat the "cheese" which however is not—I suppose—of your making at Gruyère.

Maya looked thin—a Southern *Spring* seems rather enervating to her —although she enjoyed Egypt in winter—So I thought the air of St. Moritz would set her up again—as the mountains generally do agree with her. And from what I hear it has been so far successful—although the weather was not favorable to outdoor excursions. She seems to require a high altitude once a year or so—

The mountains, however, do not agree with me so very well latterly —and I was advised not to take S.M.—last time he had rheumatic fever and as he is not prudent the changes of temperature are too much for him—in fact—for many people—I do not mind a little warm weather— unless it is enervating and dull—*Paris* is good enough for *me*—I had intended to run up to the sea-shore (Trouville or Dinard)—but it was so cool in July that a warm wrap was very necessary driving late in the afternoon—Recently the weather is warmer—but there are so many out-door resorts—although not many theatres are open just now—that one can keep quite comfortable and entertained—there always crowds—well-dressed—in the Bois de Boulogne—and the hotel is very comfortable and clean—My room's very airy and the Manager very attentive. I have been here 2 or 3 times before—. I was very sorry to learn of the deaths of my old friends Count and Countess de R—who generally resided in this Hotel.

I staid [sic] on his Mother's plantation in Cuba while visiting Cuba before St. Mar was born. He was of a very old French family and a *perfect* gentleman of the old regime of breeding—I had met him *before* I was married and I remember he was then *very* handsome—His wife was a Spanish Marchesa who had very large possessions in Cuba—and they lived regally—but before death they had some heavy losses—Slavery is no longer the paying institution of Cuba—and I think his wife gave too much to the "Priests"—and she also lent a good deal of money to the Spanish Royal Family when they were in difficulties—I doubt whether she got it all back.

His "brother's wife's mother" who was also wealthy was one of the kindest most devoted of friends to me in illness abroad—She died long ago—rest her soul!

The "old guard" is passing away—and their ranks are filling up—by EWG & Co—who will soon in her turn pass over to the great Majority —into the Silent Land—the land of the Departed.

Count de Buillet was a great gun among the French Spiritualists—I read that they are making a great Confederation—of different Nations— Headquarters in Paris—in order to facilitate "Spiritual apperations" [*sic*] who have perceived to try to make some especial [*sic*] universal "test"—or "manifestation" that will be generally convincing.

"Esperons!"—(?)

But when I casually recited that to a gentleman acquaintance "I hope not" he gasped and turned quite pale.

Of course there is a good deal of humbug—and some queer enough things which may be called "coincidence" by unbelievers—and yet are more or less convincing to the personal private experience of some others—

But this life and the next are slow & fast trotters which do not drive well in harness together—the condition must be so different that it would be a sufficient reason to be to us as "forbidden fruit" of knowledge—lest it should tamper with and clog the every day machinery of earthly life— In our hours of "waking dreams" we can luxuriate & live in the ideal— in our hope or belief of Spirit hereafter.—But "practicality" is the watch-word to guide our individualities here below—Into life's limit we are born and life must be our mould. "To be kind and considerate—to be charitable in theory as in act to those who differ in opinion as well as in matter"—are spiritual ethics for this world—and mighty hard ones to learn—I never will believe in Socialism. I believe it creates unhappiness & discontent—instead of curing it—People quarrel with their own be-cause they can't have or be somebody else's belongings or state.

Discontent *may* be immortality—may oil the rust of the wheels of progress—but it should be balanced by a centre of gravity—and keep with system—by a centrepetal [*sic*] power of "home, heart and thankful-ness."

I suppose you are not much edified at this long rambling letter—but as the "wind blows" so am I in a mood sometimes. I did not intend how-ever to be so serious—it is not very agreeable for your young nature— And not very "Parisian" certainly.

I like to go to the theatre and laugh—I went to the Cirque d'Été last night—and was quite entertained—there were wonderful, performing dogs—almost human!—graceful horses and an equestrian "Lois Fuller" who finally flew into the air and flapped her wings about the theatre under the changing rainbow tints of electric colored lights—It was quite an angelic performance—although a fallen one—as she finally lit upon earth—and ran back to her natural element—The Stables!

The fashions are 1835—pro. tem.—*before* I was born if you please!—leg-o-mutton sleeves, fan-tailed skirts—horned hats and tall combs—puffs at the side—

Quite a "Miss Fanny" style—Did you ever see the model for one in an old-fashioned "Girls' Book"? I will write soon again—Give my regards to Miss Tavan. I am very glad she found my letter agreeable—I am afraid I am not always so to everyone.

I nearly died laughing at your sketch of the mountain rambling.

You certainly have a good deal of talent for that—It is very entertaining—but be careful. And your libation to the Mountain Deities—is natural on the "Mer D'Eau"—but an especial act of devotion on your part to the Mer de Glace—

And you "Saw Stars" on the Donkey. I was quite sick on first arrival here—My friend also and a diarrohea which frightened me as we passed through Marseilles.—You know there has been and is Cholera in the South of France—Italy etc—but not *very* severe—in fact it is little nearly everywhere—and folks do not scare very much—It is usually the poor who live badly and imprudently. Suppose you are nearly asleep. So farewell for the present from your Affectionate Mother.

Excerpt from an undated letter, c. summer 1893 to Romaine Brooks

About your departure from school—I have had such a lot to attend to & write about—business & all sorts of things—and I have to look up Maya's movements pretty often of course.

I always feel that at least, you are safe,—and are well supplied with everything for a term—

But I do not forget you and I have thought, all considered, you had better travel in the direction of Paris—. I really want to see you—and I do hope you will act with good sense & consideration to your mother—and not let yourself be pulled about by the envious. You know that you have a little inclination to "Perversity." Haven't you? and you some times go a little two-sided—and some times a little wild-tempered, well—all have some faults—but it annoys me when I feel chilled by some of those actions—just when I want to do something for you—and feel a pride in you—In many things you are quite sympathetic—we have many similar tastes.—And it disappoints me when you are not always so—or not true to your *best* self.—and I become more exacting—or more indifferent apparently than I really wish to be. But I want you to act "straight" with me.

Anyhow I want to see how you are and what you need to fix you up a bit—and you can go to an art school probably here for a while—and sing also—and get a little fun—And then we can decide afterwards for the winter's location.

Terminus Hotel PLM. Marseille
1893

Dear Beatrice,

If you want more fine of course you can have it. But Mme. Givend told me you would not require much as she intended to have a large stove perhaps outside—so I considered the wood fine in a private family for your room. But coals cost more in Paris—although I . . . you only to charcoal—which rather astonishes me.

As I know you had an Astracan [sic] tippet and plenty of warm flannel—together with your new plush winter jacket—I know you should not be cold walking at this season—

I think I sent you a muff—before with your tippet—what did you do with it? I thought you would need one in Geneva in winter—If you've lost it—you should have bought a pair of flannel-lined gloves—when you got the others—until you could get another—as I was not there [in Paris] especially—

This was not to be thrown away at a caprice—I had a tippet & muff that I brought to Europe after I was married 3 years—and had bought 2 years before as a girl for me by my mother—In regards to money—when you have some, always spend for what is most necessary—and keep back a little until there is more pocket money—You had better let Mme. Givend get you a warm solid winter dress—perhaps a sufficiently cheerful color that you can walk out in or wear for usual little vacations of a few intimate friends. With the remainder of the money (I sent 600 frs) you can get a muff and buy a few yards of white silk to add to the length and drape the waist more if necessary of the silk I had made for you—with the neck and sleeves edged with a little lace it will make a very pretty muff & suitable dress for you on other occasions—You were very well pleased with the idea when you first came to me from Tavan's . . . And as for being left among strangers and not dressed up

397

I really think my dear Romaine you ought to be ashamed to bribe me just like that—You wished to leave school—you were willing to do anything agreeable you said—you wished to be in some such place as you are—to study—in addition you see something of Paris—You are not without cheerful society—You were content. I certainly did not intend to dress you like a caracature [*sic*] of fashion plates at your age—Nor trouble about your . . . concerning people whom your mother does not know the names.

Fragment of a letter, 1893, no address

My dear Beatrice,

I receive your letters which I find quite entertaining—and think you are having a good time—and great opportunities for French.

I do not mind, of course, if there is an occasional young gentlemen of their acquaintance *"en visite."*

I have not yet seen the Art School—but I will attend to it at my convenience.

Those accomplishments are extras which it will give me pleasure to afford you—as I can best do—but you must not get impatient or forget yourself or attempt to push me on or dictate such matters in a hurry. That I could not allow. You will always gain more with me by gentleness and consideration.

> Jan. 5, 1894   Poste Restante
> Algiers

My dear Beatrice,

I am glad you understand the motives of the persons you are with. I placed you there to *learn French*—which was all they undertook to teach. And I paid nearly double to have you very *comfortable*—and, of course they are to a certain degree responsible for your safety. But in regards to other lessons—or plans or arrangements of mine—it is none of their business whatever unless I choose to make it so—and any remarks thereon from them would be very bad form to say the least. When you left school Tavan thought a little change of *rest* from study would benefit you. Many people travel hundreds of miles in order to see the lively boulevards of Paris or to acquire an accent or fluency in a language. I gave you those & other advantages. It seems extraordinary after 3 years steady instruction in various branches of study—that you have not sufficient self resource for 2 months—I have taken pains to see you well dressed for a family life while away from me. If as you say—they tried to incite general discontent—or if they excited you about extra finery and things of no real importance—at a time especially when your brother was nearly at the point of death and your Mother so worried & tired,—why it was far worse than common.

The proof of good influence is in *right* direction of *right* feeling—not in utter selfishness & self seeking.

But why did you lend yourself to such things—That sort of people are pretty much alike—it is *their business* to "make" off of others & they keep a sharp look-out to general profit—but much also in their behavior depends upon the character of their charge—if it is well balanced & of good understanding there [*sic*] efforts will slide off like water from a duck's back—if they detect vanity & other traits which may be useful to them—they fan the flame—hoping to have a cat's paw. I dare say that couple are good to assist each other,—I and others, assist them both to their "extras." The old dame wrote to me a while ago that she could *not* keep you *unless I gave her entire authority over you* & a sum of money at her disposal. Fancy—that I would pay the piper to *their* tunes. It is very easy to use other peoples' money "*ad libitum*" in many ways. But I think while I get up the orchestra I will select the music. I could have boarded you for a while in a family who taught *singing* & *piano* and *French*—all first class—with your own room—for *less* than your pension where you are—and you would have been accompanied to [*sic*] for art Class—that I would designate if you liked to keep it up—They were nonpretentious—but seemed well-bred & very intelligent—but as I did not suppose you meditated becoming an Operatic Star—I chose your present as a more central locality, etc. The class I wished to investigate myself was one for 20 ladies only—under superintendance of an eminent American artist—but I lost the address—& it was evidently soon filled up . . .

It is so parvenue to value *everything* by a fancy price (except for the receiver!) But my dear Beatrice *you* are not Miss Vanderbilt—and it would be cruel to give *you* a false idea—Although I might not wish to advertize the actuality—But there is always plenty of *occupation* of *mind* for a *real* lady—indeed the daughters of the Princess of Wales make their own dresses for an occupation—as I have heard their mother—the daughter of a King—did for economy, once upon a time . . .

But you are not in Paris for that—However I saw there was a little play acting in all the posing—the varnish was a little thin—it might impose on those greenhorns who know nothing and are used to nothing and do not know what to do with their money—Of course certain little habits of refinement necessary to daily association for people of a certain education would probably not be wanting—but in regard to condition— they are teachers of their *own* language—thousands of English are employed in the same way with their own—And unfortunately the "teachermarm" is so apt to "shop" out of class. Self-assumption & assertion in social life is very *under*-bred—and when those useful folk take their hand off the plough of fallow ground & want to teach the waves how to roll & rule the stars in their courses—it is very comical. Declaration, & ranting, are quite interesting accomplishments sometimes however— although not very practical—it was said that the great Mrs. Siddons would ask for a "pot o' beer" so tragically that the waiter would fairly leap into the air. But I think you like a role occasionally—do you not my dear. I saw before leaving however you were beginning something "crooked" and I would have removed you had I the time. They were playing their little airs off on you—and you were inflating & giving one or two to me second-hand—like a dear, foolish little monkey, & soon were grinding me out like a coffee mill—Why—when I am interesting myself —in spite of St. Mar's sickness—why do you throw cold water on me— by impatience—and even by a spirit of dictation—which is absurd—but I suppose you do not realize it. You seemed inclined to turn your nose up at everything I began. Can you not see that there are times when, as you are doing nothing to help—the least is to try not to worry at me. Well —I won't scold—but it seems a pity that you are often so . . . and resentful of advice or restraint from your mother whom you could accept it from—in an attentive & pleasant spirit without humiliation—and by whose side you might have advantages—otherwise impossible to me— as you can comprehend. I do not suppose you are so stupid as not to understand her superiority—not only in the social advantages—but in so many more mental—to those employed—of course I do not occupy myself with the details of "tuning up" but on account of all this sickness I have been more reserved than necessary—but it is I am the only *"chef d'orchestre."*

I will let you know in my next what I can best do in the present for you. I am sending off G—s payment—You had better have your white silk arranged—unless you have already had it done with your money—I rather like Algiers—it is quieter than the Riviera or Cairo—but the Climate not quite so cold as the former. I have met some *very* pleasant people & some old friends . . . I send you a hundred pound note (fr 100) ack—St. Mar has his hours of pain—but we think he is in all easier

& better—New Years' eve he had a chill. I sat up all night—And had a bad rheumatic spell on New Years—but has improved since. With a kiss, Your Affectionate Mama.

Dieppe, Sept. 8, 1894

Dear Romaine,

I wrote a letter to you which I did not send as I expected to return to Paris—but I enclose it now. Since then I have received the miniature of Maya—and another letter of yours—speaking of it.

It is a good attempt for an amateur.—The upper part of the face quite like—The mouth a little crooked—but the *"tout ensemble"* Do one of yourself.

I took a fearful cold—and when I was better St. M. set in for another like it—He seemed pulling up again—but I never saw such weather —they say they have had no summer—it reminded me of England—rain-rain—then a little sun—then wind, wind—

But of course it is "tonic" if one can stand it—It was a rather severe change from Algiers—although it was bracing & refreshing.

We are obliged to light a little gas stove in the rooms—But St. M. has been able to walk out more freely than he would have done in crowded, dangerous Paris—and I also am able to run on the *"plage"* in the mornings—in careless attire—which is a great advantage—. I don't care a straw about "races" although I like to watch the little ducks and geese and ganders—take to the water—I expected to be in Paris long ago—Suppose I shall do so in a very few days.

I have not yet made up my mind where I shall take him this winter—

Algiers *agreed* with SM—and it is a very gay place—dinners, receptions, balls etc.

They elected me membre [*sic*] of the French "Circle" and of course I always invited whom I pleased members, also gave dinners etc. And also had standing invitations with English Club of course—There were 6 fancy balls—

As the Governor also gave good entertainments—there was always something going on—

The Governor's wife settled on me—And I found the really nice French people very pleasant. I also liked the English colony exceedingly—

But I *don't* like crossing over the water twice a year—it is inconvenient —the boats are crowded—and one is obliged to take places in advance.

401

And in winter the passage is *abominable*—although not *very* long—

I had such a lot of fine young beaux at my "once a weeks"—Princes and French & English officers—all really nice fellows—And of course the girls *ran after* me proportionately—They used to circle about me like a flock of doves—And did love me so! Well of course, this is human nature—And they were always begging to pour out tea.

But some of the girls were really quite nice—and appreciated anything I did.

A lady—my most *intimate* friend—gave a "strawberry *fête*" in the Moorish garden of her villa—which is beautiful—she being very rich—

It was really lovely under the orange trees—and the strawberries & cream perfect.

The drives were lovely—very green and fertile "*paysage*"—some of the old Arab houses are very interesting—and O—the English Colonists do give such *good* dinners.

I *may* return—but am not sure—I suppose if I do not—I should return some of the very kind hospitality I received—by little "*picque niques*" or dinners at G— of a few friends who will be "*en voyage*" for a while this winter.

However—"Kismet" I wander as the wind listeth.

Your affectionate Mama

Château Grimaldi
Mentone
May 21, 1895

My dear Beatrice,

I am astonished you do not write oftener to me & tell me what you do & who you see & what interests you most—My life is more or less monotonous under the circumstances but you must have plenty to speak about—and as I have already said to you—I have too many letters—business or friendly—to attend to already—and am not always able—But your correspondance is sufficiently limited and you can very well take a little trouble to write—even if it is not a pleasure to you—. I have been waiting to hear how you are getting on—and wished to send a little extra money for your "*habilement*". I enclose it here fr. 500—five hundred francs—and I would like you to send me the receipt & bills for what you spend it. [*sic*] I suppose you would like a dress & mantle—. . . but don't spend it in unnecessary rubbish—

I thought both you & M* would enjoy the change to a hotel—

* Maya

which is also quiet and *comme il faut*— . . . And kept on the old dame
to hover around when quite necessary for *"les apparences"*—

I was quite poorly for awhile and suffered a good deal—but have
managed to get underway again—St. Mar seems still to improve—He
takes lunch & tea in the garden with me lately—and if he doesn't once
climb—the fresh air should be a great tonic & medicine for him—

The garden is really lovely—I never saw so many roses Xccc—I am in
it nearly all day—. I have been quite besieged with callers—but have
not cared to receive any—

Of course while St. M was so ill I cared for nothing like pleasure—
and when he was better I felt ill myself—And some people insisted upon
my taking some distraction—but I was in too much pain to feel more
than a great fatigue often—

This month is certainly the most delightful here in regard to climate
—flowers ecc—and yet it is the time the strangers homeward fly—But
the Spring is pleasant everywhere—if not for its reality—for its promise—

I am not quite sure when I shall be on the move. I am having the
house put in order preparatory—so that I may be able to be on the wing
when the Spirit moves—I do not think it well for St. Mar to remain
through the approaching summer heat—I thought something of going
on to Venice for the Exhibition—but am not really decided—it will last
until late in the fall—

There are lots of birds in the garden now—and lots of frogs croaking
at nightfall—the Mosquito is just beginning to sound the tocsin—but
Nets are prepared to catch the lively angler—as well as the poor fish—

The view is always heavenly—and the house more comfortable—and
of course I feel in lighter spirits now when St. M.—is doing better and
profitting [*sic*] by this—Acknowledge receipt—and also mention the
Sum—it is businesslike—Hoping you are enjoying yourself & quite well.
I am your Affectionate Mother.

To Miss R. B. Goddard, Rue Scribe, Paris   Nice

Jan. 24, '97

I send you enclosed frs 700 for this and next month and 100 for the
Xmas present. E.W.G.

Don't forget to acknowledge receipt.

The Riviera Jungles

By Romaine Brooks

When on the Riviera I have always been fascinated by those dark unkept parks shut in by old walls and rusty gates, which one comes upon unexpectedly in the midst of a gay and sunny outer world. These enclosures seem to contain a force striving for isolation, and, in the effort they give out poisonous self-protecting scents. Here the magnolia trees hold flowers yellow and spotted black, their scent without sweetness would kill. The thorny and ragged eucalyptus mitigates, perhaps, with its medicinal fragrance the poisons of decay which enrich the black earth. Grey-bearded palm-trees resembling hugh primordial apes, others like Indian fakirs meditating with unbound turbans trailing around them, seem indifferent to their slim companions rising high in the air with plumage like leaves waving in some wind-blown exaltation.

Within these parks there is no human joy but triumphant unity of living and decaying nature with the black force of the earth.

The sun never penetrates these jungles nor does it touch the pale leprous house lost in their midst. What hybrid creatures live there? Their shell, another's cast off diseased shell, savage nature's whose lairs savage nature covers; leprous souls flaked by the scaling of leprous walls; perhaps dual natures seeking impersonal union with darker selves. Who knows?

If we breathe deeply the dark poisons creeping out from under these rusty gates we will find ourselves being drawn away from our sunny terraces by the magnetism of these Riviera Jungles.

From my pink villa a path led directly to one of these enclosures. My daily walk invariably brought me to the foot of an old wall where, seated on a projecting stone, I would pass the hours dreamingly looking up into the tangled mass of branches overhead.

One day I was started by a shower of leaves falling from a decayed and barely discernible summer-house which still clung to the walls. A figure was leaning over . . . Expecting the unusual I heard a voice in harmony with the sounds of nature inviting me to visit the park. My answer that no way seemed to lead there was followed by a gesture showing steps of moss-covered stones. Strangely enough, without hesitation, I climbed these and found myself facing the dweller of this particular jungle.

The erect figure seemed to tower over me like a tree, and the pale face with its wisps of black hair was round and expressionless like the moon. The voice drew me on and, as I followed my strange companion into the park, the meaning of its low whispering reached me: A philosophy of death and trees, of nature concentrating her poisons in these sunless jungles; of dark forces thrown back on still darker forces. Death the very essence; life but the overflow, the exaltations of death. Trees the highest, the most perfect of death's triumphant banners, attached to death by roots imbedded in the divine rottenness of all things. Humanity, crystalized disorders, accidentals on the earth, and like all moving things, food for the trees. Humanity will be destroyed by fire or washed away by water; whereas trees are hooked into the very bowels of the earth; they will exist as long as the earth exists.

The whispering ceased and I found myself being guided into an underground grotto held together by the intertwining of many roots.

My companion then turned to me and spoke: "You too have come to us. You belong to us. Here in this cave you will stay and meditate and then, from the call to earth, you will spring up into a tree. All the white roots you see here were formerly human bones of young creatures like yourself. I live on the sap of those who owe to me their new existence. When my time comes I shall be the tallest of them all, for my roots will spread round the earth many times." My companion then walked towards the cave's opening. I, sensing danger, dashed past the door which was about to close on me. I fled through labyrinths of trees, the roots holding me back, the dampness sucking me to earth. At last reaching the wall with one final effort I sprang over on to the other sunny side below. Gasping for breath. . . . I awoke. It was a dream. All was silent; the old wall and tangled mass of branches overhead were as before.

When walking home in half-dazed fashion, I resolved not to return again to the poisonous jungle of the old park. Perhaps I was haunted, for during the following nights I would dream of my dream and see through the window a great tree with the moon shining between wisps of dark branches.

One day a neighbor came to sit with me on my terrace. She was a gossip and I listened to her in half-awake fashion. When about to leave she said: "There has been unusual commotion in one of the parks near here; its owner has disappeared and the body can't be found." "The body can't be found!" I repeated now fully awake. "Oh, I see that you know nothing about the matter," said my guest, "it is the crazy proprietress of the old neglected park overthere. She refused to live in the house, preferring a sort of damp underground grotto where she would stay for days at a time. Now the grotto has caved in and though there has been much digging about the body can't be found . . ."

When alone, my dream drew me back to it. Did the mystery shroud a deeper mystery, I wondered. Then vividly came the words, "I will be the tallest of them all, for my roots will spread round the earth many times."

Untitled poem by Gabriele d'Annunzio to Romaine Brooks' color scheme.

> Je vois les blancs et noirs marbres au ciel d'automne
>   où la Nue a l'ardeur d'un Ange Combattant.
> Sur les fauves ravins du duf orviétan
>   se lever d'un seul jet, tel le choeur qu'on entonne
> Ainsi les noirs et blancs esprits de ton grand art,
>   O soeur, du crépuscule indicible, à l'écart
> Sur les sommets ardus, dressent de doubles charmes.
>   Et la nuit et le jour font un divin accord
> Dans ton aube ou se tient la tristesse sans larmes
>   Prête à venger ton âme et la vie et la mort.

À Romaine Brooks
     sur son
Portrait Peint Par Elle-Même

> C'est la mer d'Occident, que fatigua la rame
> de l'Ulysse dantesque arqué vers l'Inconnu,
> celle dont l'amertume ard ton visage nu
> frappé par ton démon au dur coin de ton âme.
>
> Nul sort ne domptera, ni par fer ni par flamme,
> le secret diamant de ton coeur ingénu.
> Debout entre le ciel morne et le flot chenu,
> tu ne crains pas le choc de la dixième lame.
>
> Voici dans tes grands yeux le feu qui fut l'espoir
> du souverain amour, avant que ton plus noir
> regard mirât l'intacte horreur de la Gorgogne.
>
> C'est la pourpre de Tyr qui double ton mantel
> de bure; et c'est le vent du courage immortel
> qui seul de tes cheveux rudement te couronne.

                          Gabriele d'Annunzio

To the georgian poetess
Romaine Brooks
peace

      Deep peace, red wind of the East from you;
      Deep peace, grey wind of the West to you;
      Deep peace, dark wind of the North from you;
      Deep peace, blue wind of the South to you;

      Deep peace, pure red of the flame to you;
      Deep peace, pure white of the moon to you;
      Deep peace, pure green of the grass to you;
      Deep peace, pure brown of the earth to you;

      Deep peace, pure grey of the dew to you;
      Deep peace, pure blue of the sky to you;
      Deep peace, pure soul of the poet to you!

·And by the Will of the King of the Clements
and by the grace of the black and white Love

   peace! peace!

   Gabri

Easter Sunday 1914

(written in English)

To Romaine Brooks' painting of France at war, "La France Croisée," also called, "The Cross of France."

Sur une image de la France Croisée
peinte par Romaine Brooks.

I

Ont-ils haussé l'éponge âcre au fer de la lance
contre sa belle bouche ivre du Corps très saint?
La Croix sans Christ, qui souffre au-dessus de son sein,
n'est que la double entaille acceptée en silence.

Mais son oeil est plus clair que la claire Provence,
mais son coeur est plus doux que le printemps messin.
Elle oint de sa douceur la force qui la ceint,
elle noue à ses pieds percés la patience.

Et le vent du combat et l'or du jeune jour
et les avrils non vus et l'amour de l'amour
et les chants non chantés vivent dans son haleine.

La bandelette pur à son front est un feu
blanc qui conduit les morts. Et l'on voit sur la plaine
tomber de son manteau la grande ombre d'un dieu.

II

Ô face de l'ardeur, ô pitié sans sommeil,
courage qui jamais n'écartes le calice,
force qui fais avec tes chairs ton sacrifice
et ta libation avec ton sang vermeil!

Sur quel bûcher, sous quel signe, pour quel réveil,
à quel avent ta foi chantait dans le supplice?
Plus haut que l'alouette à l'aube du solstice,
on vit soudain ton coeur bondir vers le soleil.

Car toute entière en toi lève la bonne race.
Là-bas, d'entre les neuf preux, sourit à ta grace
mâle, par les barreaux de l'armet, Duguesclin.

Tu as communié, dans ta sainte vêture,
sous l'espèce du sol. Mais, couronné de lin,
ton front semble souffrir d'une étoile future.

III

France, France la douce, entre les héroïnes
bénie, amour du monde, ardente sous la croix
comme aux murs d'Antioche, alors que Godefroi
sentait sous son camail la couronne d'épines,

debout avec ton Dieu comme au pont de Bouvines,
dans ta gloire à genoux comme au champ de Rocroi,
neuve immortellement comme l'herbe qui croît
aux bords de tes tombeaux, aux creux de tes ruines,

fraîche comme le jet de ton blanc peuplier,
que demain tu sauras en guirlandes plier
pour les chants non chantés de ta jeune pléiade,

411

Ressuscitée en Christ, qui fais de ton linceul
gonfanon de lumière et cotte de croisade,
"France, France, sans toi le monde serait seul."

IV

Et voici le printemps de notre amour. Exulte
dans ton sang et jubile au bout de ta douleur,
quand même tu n'aurais à cueillir d'autre fleur
que le héros jailli de la racine occulte.

"Sonnerai l'olifant," dit l'Ancêtre. Ô tumulte
des tes chênes! Ô vent de l'immense clameur!
Hauts sont tes puys, tes vaux profonds. On meurt, on meurt;
et chacun de tes morts dans ta beauté se sculpte.

Entendez le signal, combattants, combattants,
âmes prises aux corps comme aux ceps le printemps,
Comme aux poignées les fers, les bannières aux hampes.

Roland le comte sonne; et tout en est fumant,
et en saigne sa bouche, en élatent ses tempes.
"Frappez, Français, frappez! C'est mon commandment."

5 Mars 1915
Gabriele d'Annunzio

The Weeping Venus

Laid out as dead in moonlight shroud
Beneath a derelict of cloud:
A double wreckage safe from flight,
High-caged as grief, in prisoned night—
Unseeing eyes whose clustering tears
Tell the pure crystal of her years.—
No crown of thorns, no wounded side,
Yet as the God-man crucified,
Her body expiates the sin
That love and life with her begin!

From *Poems and Poèmes, au très alliances,* by Natalie Clifford Barney.
Paris: Émile-Paul, 1920.

Chapter V, Festival of San Costanzo—An Island Carnival†

Paganisme immortel, es tu mort? On le dit
Mais Pan, tout bas, s'en moque et la Sirène en rit.

What mean these flower-strewn lanes, these banners gay,
These blue-veiled maidens in this fair attire,
These gossips come to see and to admire,
These ruddy youths, who make such brave display,

A long procession files in slow array,
Aloft, a silver image gleams like fire,
Borne shoulder-high, amid a white-robed choir,
The patron saint moves on his festal way.

Great Pan is dead? Ah, no! He lives. 'Tis we
Blind with the scales of centuries on our eyes,
Have lost belief and thus the power to see.

These humble folk, in their simplicity,
Perceive the glory which around them lies
And commune with their Gods perpetually.

Ellingham Brooks

From *The Book of Capri* by Harold E. Trower—Ed. by Emil Prass, Naples, Piazza dei Martiri, 1906.

† The greater part of this chapter appeared in *The Gentlewoman* of October 24, 1903.

Untitled poem by Natalie Barney

Oh passé, cher passé
Pourquoi avoir lassé
l'amour dans ma pensée
Et la vie insensée
Que je vivais pour toi?

Retrouver l'équilibre
Triste à me sentir libre
Loin de ta cruauté—
Richesse ou pauvreté
De n'être plus qu'à moi?

BIBLIOGRAPHY

ACTON, SIR HAROLD. *Memoirs of an Aesthete*. New York: The Viking Press, 1971.

ALDINGTON, RICHARD. *A World Tribute to Natalie Clifford Barney*, in the *Adam International Review*. London, 1960.

ALEXANDRE, ARSÈNE. *Le Figaro*. May 20, 1910.

ANTHEIL, GEORGE. *The bad boy of music!* New York: Doubleday, Doran and Co., 1945.

ANTONGINI, THOMMASO. *Quaranti Anni Con D'Annunzio* in *The Poet as Superman*, by Anthony Rhodes. London: Weidenfeld and Nicolson, 1959.

APOLLINAIRE, GUILLAUME. *L'Intransigeant*. May 15, 1910.

BARNES, DJUNA (under the pseudonym of "A Lady of Fashion"). *The Ladies Almanack*. Privately printed at Dijon by the Derentière Press (recently reissued by Harper & Row).

BARNEY, NATALIE CLIFFORD. *Aventures de l'Esprit*. Paris: Émile-Paul, 1929.

—— "Poem to Dolly Wilde," from *In Memory of Dorothy Ierne Wilde, "Oscaria."* Privately printed in Paris. Articles from the same book, by Natalie Clifford Barney, Bettina Bergery, Janet Flanner, Victor Cunard, and Allanah Harper. Letters from Dolly Wilde, also from this book.

—— *Je Me Souviens*. Paris: Sansot, 1910.

—— *Souvenirs Indiscrets*. Paris: Flammarion, 1960.

—— *The One Who Is Legion*. Privately printed in London by Eric Partridge, Ltd., 1930.

—— *Traits et Portraits*. Paris: Mercure de France, 1960.

—— *Pensées d'Une Amazone*. Paris: Émile-Paul Frères, 1920.

BAUER, GÉRARD. *On the Death of Ida Rubinstein,* in *Le Figaro.* Paris, October 17, 1960.

BEACH, SYLVIA. *Shakespeare & Co.* New York: Harcourt Brace & Co., 1959.

BEATON, CECIL. *The Wandering Years.* London: Weidenfeld and Nicolson, 1961.

BENSON, E. F. *Final Edition.* New York: D. Appleton-Century Co. Inc., 1940.

BERENSON, BERNARD. Letters from Natalie Barney and vice versa, quoted in the *Adam International Review, A World Tribute to Natalie Clifford Barney.* London, 1960.

BLUME, MARY. Article on Natalie Barney in *Réalités,* February 1966.

——— Article on Romaine Brooks in *Réalités,* December 1967.

BREESKIN, ADELYN. Essay in *Romaine Brooks, "Thief of Souls."* Catalogue to National Collection of Fine Arts exhibition, March 1971.

BROOKS, ROMAINE. *No Pleasant Memories.* Unpublished autobiography.

COCTEAU, JEAN. Note from the performance by Ida Rubinstein, quoted in *The Decorative Art of Léon Bakst,* by Arsène Alexandre. London: The Fine Art Society, 1913.

——— *Paris Album, 1900–1914.* London: W. H. Allen, 1956.

COLETTE. *Claudine S'en Va.* Paris: Société d'Éditions Littéraires et Artistiques, P. Ollendorff, 1903.

——— *Mes Apprentissages; Ce que Claudine n'a pas dit.* Paris: Hachette, 1936.

——— *The Pure and the Impure.* London: Secker & Warburg, 1968.

——— *Trois, Six, Neuf.* Paris: Corréa, 1946.

D'ANNUNZIO, GABRIELE. Article on the painting of Romaine Brooks in *Illustrazione.* Italy, April 1913.

——— *Notturno.* Milano: Fratelli Treves, 1921.

DE GOURMONT, RÉMY. *Letters to the Amazon.* Preface to English Edition by Richard Aldington. London: Chatto & Windus, 1931.

DE LANUX, EYRE. Unpublished essay on Natalie Clifford Barney.

DOUGLAS, NORMAN. *South Wind.* London: Martin Secker & Warburg Ltd., 1917.

DRAPER, MURIEL. *Music at Midnight.* New York & London: Harper and Brothers, 1929.

FLAMENT, ALBERT. In *Le Trottoir Roulant.* 1910.

FOTHERGILL, JOHN ROWLAND. *Lest an Old Man Forget.* Unpublished autobiography.

GERMAIN, ANDRÉ. *La Bourgeoisie Qui Brûle.* Paris: Éditions Sun, 1948.

GLASSCO, JOHN. *Memoirs of Montparnasse.* Oxford University Press, 1970.

GODDARD, ELLA WATERMAN. *A Tale of Christmas Eve Masque.* Privately printed, 1902.

HALL, RADCLYFFE. *The Well of Loneliness.* London: Jonathan Cape, 1928.

HOLME, THEA. *Chelsea.* London: Taplinger, 1972.

HORNEY, KAREN. *Neurosis and Human Growth.* New York: W. W. Norton and Co., 1950.

JULLIAN, PHILIPPE. *Journal of Henri Regnier.* Quoted in *D'Annunzio.* Paris: Librairie Arthème Fayard, 1971.

—— *Prince of Aesthetes: Count Robert de Montesquiou, 1855–1921.* New York: Viking Press, 1968.

KNOWLES, SIR LEES. *The British in Capri.* London: The Bodley Head, 1918; New York: John Lane Company, 1918.

KRAMER, HILTON. *Romaine Brooks: Revelation in Art.* The New York *Times,* April 14, 1971.

—— *Revival of Romaine Brooks.* The New York *Times,* April 25, 1971.

MAAS, JEREMY. *Victorian Painters.* New York: G. P. Putnam's Sons, 1969.

MACAVOY ÉDOUARD. Writing in *Bizarre.* Paris, March 1968.

MACKENZIE, SIR COMPTON. *Extraordinary Women.* London: Martin Secker, 1929.

—— *My Life and Times, Octaves 4, 5, & 6.* Autobiography of Compton Mackenzie. London: Chatto & Windus, 1965.

MACKENZIE, FAITH COMPTON. *As Much As I Dare,* 1940, *More Than I Should,* 1938, and *Always Afternoon,* 1943. Three volumes of autobiography of Faith Compton Mackenzie. London: Collins.

MAUGHAM, SOMERSET. *The Summing Up.* London: William Heinemann, Ltd., 1938.

MUNTHE, AXEL. *The Story of San Michele.* New York: E. P. Dutton & Co., 1957.

Article in *Town and Country,* April 15, 1926, signed by R. N.

NOCHLIN, LINDA. *Why Have There Been No Great Women Artists?* Art News, January 1971.

ORIOLI, PINO. *The Adventures of a Bookseller.* New York: R. M. McBride & Co., 1938.

PATMORE, DEREK. *Passionate Friends*. London: *The Observer Magazine*, September 5, 1971.

POUND, EZRA, on the writing of Natalie Clifford Barney in *The Dial*, October 1924.

—— and Natalie Clifford Barney. *Transatlantic Review*, October 1924.

PUTNAM, SAMUEL. *Paris Was Our Mistress*. New York: Viking Press, 1947.

REGNIER, HENRI. "Journal of Henri Regnier." Quoted in *D'Annunzio* by Philippe Jullian. Paris: Librairie Arthème Fayard, 1971.

ROGER-MARX, CLAUDE. Introduction to exhibition at Galeries Durand-Ruel, May 2–18, 1910.

—— *Personnages d'Une Époque*. Figaro Littéraire, March 1953.

ROREM, NED. *The New York Diary*. New York: George Braziller, 1967.

RUBINSTEIN, IDA. "How I Came To Know D'Annunzio." Article in *Novo Antologia*. Italy, April 16, 1927.

RUDORFF, RAYMOND. *The Belle Époque*. New York: Saturday Review Press, 1973.

STEEGMULLER, FRANCIS. *Cocteau: A Biography*. New York: Atlantic, Little Brown & Co., 1970.

STORR, ANTHONY. *Sexual Deviation*. London: Penguin Books, 1964.

TAYLOR, DR. JOSHUA. Preface to *Romaine Brooks, "Thief of Souls."* Catalogue to National Collection of Fine Arts exhibition, March 1971.

The *Times of London*. Obituary for John Rowland Fothergill, August 29, 1957.

USHER, JOHN. *A True Painter of Personality*. New York: International Studio, February 1926.

VAUXCELLES, LOUIS. Writing in *Excelsior*. Paris, May 1931.

—— Writing in *Gil Blas*, May 14, 1910.

WOLFF, CHARLOTTE. *Love Between Women*. London: Gerald Duckworth & Co., Ltd., 1971.

YOUNG, MAHONRI SHARP, on Romaine Brooks in *Apollo* magazine. London: May 1971.

Index

Académie Colarossi, 136
Acton, Sir Harold, 117n, 314, 364;
  and Berenson, 322; and Fothergill
  portrait, 110–11; and Natalie
  Barney, 276, 315, 322; and
  Romaine's memoirs, 10–11; and
  Una, Lady Troubridge, 290
Adam International Review, 319
Addio al Protestantismo, 69
Adelsward-Fersen, Baron Jacquqes d',
  129, 296, 300
Adventures of a Bookseller, The,
  131–32
Alba, Duke of, 350
Alcyone, 222
Aldington, Richard, 275, 318–19
Alexandre, Arsène, 197
Algiers, 156
Alice B. Toklas Cookbook, 327
Alma-Tadema, Sir Lawrence, 75
Always Afternoon, 300
Anacapri, 124, 297
Anderson, Sherwood, 318, 320
Anglesey, Lady (Aunt Minnie), 217,
  218, 364
Anna. *See* Cerutti, Anna
Antheil, George, 318
Anthony and Cleopatra, 326
Anti-Semitism, 206–10

Antongini, Thommaso, 227, 232
Apollinaire, Guillaume, 198, 275
Apollo magazine, 198
Arabian Nights, 268
Arcachon, 255–56
Archibald, S. K., 256
Arts Club of Chicago, 310, 351
Assisi, 116
At the Back of the North Wind, 48
Aventures de l'Esprit, 320, 341
"Azalées Blanches," 197, 242

Bachrach, portrait of Barney by, 361
Bad boy of music!, The, 318
Baker, Josephine, 299
Bakst, Lev, 231, 241, 243
Ballet Russe, 240
Barnes, Djuna, 320, 334–35
Barney, Albert Clifford (father), 262,
  265, 266
Barney, Alice Pike (mother), 262ff.
Barney, Laura. *See* Dreyfus Barney,
  Laura
Barney, Natalie Clifford, 149n, 199,
  204, 217–18, 256ff., 261–80, 291,
  294, 295, 297, 299, 307, 308,
  314–32ff., 352, 361ff., 378ff.;
  death, 379; and Janine Lahovary,
  378–79; and Lord Alfred Douglas,
  185, 321; and Romaine's drawings,

310; untitled poem, 415; *Weeping Venus* reprinted, 413; World War II years, 312–13, 322

Barr (secretary), 43

Barra, R., 129, 134, 136

Baudelaire, Charles, 150

Bauer, Gérard, 326

Beach, Sylvia, 327, 334

Beardsley, Aubrey, 184, 310

Beaton, Cecil, 211

Beaumont, Germaine, 320

Beauvallon. *See* Villa Trait d'Union

Bénédite, Léonce, 249

Benson, E. F., 12, 123, 124, 126, 128, 131, 132, 285, 296ff.

Berenson, Bernard, 321–22, 364ff.

Bergery, Bettina, 307, 316ff., 323–24, 342, 379n; and Bernard Berenson, 322; and Colette, 318; and Dolly Wilde, 342ff.; and Duchesse de Clermont-Tonnerre, 337; and Ezra Pound, 319; and Ida Rubinstein, 326; and Madame Errazuriz, 211

Bergery, Gaston, 323

Bernhardt, Sarah, 342

Bernstein, Henri, 206–10, 364

Berthe, Mme. (housekeeper), 313, 316–17, 325–26ff., 333, 365, 380, 382; and Alice B. Toklas, 327; and Djuna Barnes, 334; and Natalie Barney's funeral, 379n; and Proust, 321; and Romaine Brooks' apartment, 307

Bibescu, Princess Marthe, 320

Bibliography, 419–22

Bird (chauffeur), 232, 233

Bizardel, Yvon, 364, 382

Bizarre, 312, 388

Blacks, 353

Blanche, Jacques-Émile, 208, 343

Blume, Mary, 319, 324–25

Boldini, Giovanni, 203, 211, 217, 297

Bolero, 326

Bonaparte, Jerome, 17

Boncourt, Paul, 379n

Bonheur, Rosa, 180

"Bonnet à Brides, Le," 188, 193

Book of Capri, The, 414

Book of Months, The, 126

Borgatti, Giuseppe, 292

Borgatti, Renata, 199, 292–95

Borgia, Roderigo, 227

Bourgeoisie Qui Brûle, La, 208, 238–39, 318

Bousquet, Marie-Louise, 343

Breeskin, Adelyn, 9–10, 376

"Brioche, La," 272

Brooks, John Ellingham, 12, 115, 123, 124, 126–28, 131–34, 138, 178–81ff., 298ff., 303, 314; after World War I, 283, 284–85; death, 300; and D. H. Lawrence, 295; in Maugham's autobiography, 341; poem reprinted, 414; and Romaine's self-portrait, 296

Brooks, (Beatrice) Romaine (*see also* specific friends, relatives, works): at boarding school, 75–79; at convent, 64–69; and deaths of brother, mother, 138–45, 167; drawings, 308–12; family background, childhood, 15–23, 27ff., 37–43, 47–55, 59–72, 75–84, 149–67 (*see also* specific family members); fear of blindness, 357–58, 370, 375, 380; goes to Paris to finish education, 79–82; left with family in New York, 37–43; marriage (*see* Brooks, John Ellingham); memoirs (*see No Pleasant Memories*); in music hall, 95–96; old age, last years, 5–10, 362–83, 388; and origins of her homosexuality, 213–14; residences (*see* specific homes, places); at St. Mary's Hall, 47–55; struggle to leave mother, 82–84, 86ff.

Bryher, 12, 314, 327, 364

Buillet, Count de, 395

Burlington, N.J., school. *See* St. Mary's Hall

Burne-Jones, Sir Edward, 107
Butt, Clara, 81–82, 114
Butts, Mary, 300

Caffè Greco (Rome), 106, 107, 114, 116
Calvé, Emma, 271
Capiello (artist), 225, 226
Capote, Truman, 366
Capri, 123–35, 138, 178ff., 283–301ff.
Carlsbad, 215
Carnegie Hall, 352
Carnival, 302
Casa Solitaria, 285–86
Casati, Marchesa Luisa, 9, 297–98
Cassatt, Mary, 196, 311
Cassau, Jean, 317
Cerutti, Anna, 5, 6, 112, 362, 376, 380, 382
Cézanne, Paul, 196
"Chapeau à Fleurs." *See* "Madame Legrand au Champ des Courses"
"Charwoman, The," 188, 193
Château Grimaldi, 33, 69–71, 140, 153–54, 161, 164, 173–74ff.
Chatto and Windus, Ltd., 112
Cheiro, 141, 143, 145, 166, 167
Chelsea (Holme), 184, 185
Chestnut Hill (Philadelphia), 16, 19, 40ff., 47, 351–52
Chicago, Arts Club of, 310, 351
Childe Harold's Pilgrimage, 117
Chrome Yellow, 303
Cimitière de Passy, 379
Cirque d'Été, 154, 395–96
Città morta, La, 224
City of the Soul, The, 185
Clark, Lord Kenneth, 366
Claudel, Paul, 208
Claudine S'en Va, 267
Clemenceau, Georges, 216
Clermont-Tonnerre, Elisabeth (Lily), Duchesse de, 317, 320, 332, 335, 337–38, 379n
Clermont-Tonnerre, Philibert, Duc de, 337

Cocteau, Jean, 8, 200–2, 249, 323, 372; and Anna de Noailles, 268; death, 364; and Ida Rubinstein, 240, 243–44, 247; Madame Muhlfeld and, 208
Coleman, C. C. (Uncle Charley), 129–30, 131, 178, 181, 296, 297
Colette, 266–67, 268–69, 272, 273, 317, 318, 332, 365; and Liane de Pougy, 265
Collier, John, 183
Conder, Charles, 184
Conder, Stella Maris Belford, 184
Confessions of an Innkeeper, 111
Corriere della Sera, 237
Corvo, Frederick Rolfe, Baron, 388–89
Corbet, Gustave, 137
Crampton, George S., 149n, 164–65
Crampton, Mrs. George S. *See* Goddard, Ella Mary Waterman
Cri (Vivien), 272
"Cross of France, The." *See* "France Croisée, La"
"Crossing, The," 242
Cunard, Victor, 345

Dali, Salvador, 323
Dame aux Camélias, La, 326
D'Annunzio, Gabriele, 8–9, 187, 193, 206, 221–58, 261, 284, 308, 312, 326, 338, 373; decline of reputation, 364; poetry reprinted, 407–12
D'Annunzio (Jullian), 239
Dead City, The (*La città morta*), 224
Dead Poet, The, 117
"Death," 242
Debussy, Claude, 243
Decorative Art of Léon Bakst, The, 244
DeLamar, Alice, 332, 341, 352
Delarue-Mardrus, Lucie, 268
Delville, Jean, 150, 165
"Demoiselles d'Avignon, Les," 196
Denis, Maurice, 189
"Departure," 381

De Wolfe, Elsie. *See* Mendl, Elsie de Wolfe, Lady
Diaghilev, Sergei, 200, 240
Dial, The, 319, 330
Dialogue au Soleil Couchant, 266
Douglas, Lord Alfred (Bosie), 110, 117, 184–86, 321
Douglas, Norman, 123, 128, 132, 300
Draper, Herbert James, 75
Draper, Muriel, 355–56
Dreyfus affair, 206
Dreyfus Barney, Laura, 218, 262ff., 357–58
Dreyfus y Cordozo, Hippolyte, 357
Duncan, Isadora, 320
Duncan, Mrs. Raymond, 268
Duran, Carolus, 263, 316
Durand-Ruel, Georges, 196–97
Duse, Eleonora, 225
Dwight, Clara Waterman, 16, 19, 175–76, 351
Dwight, Toby (Wattie), 351

Edinburgh, 301
Edward VII, 215–16
Eiffel Tower, 200, 201
Eliot, T. S., 274, 330
Emmanuel, Beatrice Phillips, 92, 162, 332–33, 370
Emmanuel, Léon-Marie (Boni), 6, 332, 333, 382, 388
Emmanuel, Philippe, 163
"Enemy Fat," 309
England. *See* specific places
Epstein, Jacob, 110
Erlanger, Baroness Émile d', 198, 350–51
Errazuriz, Madame, 199, 210–11
"Esquisse," 194–95
Este, Louisa Miller, 262–63
Excelsior, 311
Extraordinary Women, 285, 286–94, 303–4

Farraro, Don Alessandro, 134
Fauvists, 196

"Femme Morte," 242
Fiesole, 363–64, 382
Figaro, Le, 197, 216, 326
Final Edition, 285
Finch, Constance, 149n, 164
Fisher, John Arbuthnot Fisher, Baron, 216
Fitzgerald, F. Scott, 295
Fitzgerald, Zelda, 295
Fiume, 223, 256
Flament, Albert, 197–98
Flanner, Janet, 323–34, 335n, 344
Florence, 313, 322
Fokine, Michel, 240
Fontainebleau, 263
Ford, Ford Madox, 300, 320
Fothergill, Anthony, 112, 113
Fothergill, John (son), 112
Fothergill, John Rowland, 110–19, 364
Fournier, Alain, 330
Four Winds of Change, The, 301
France, Anatole, 262
France, 189. *See also* specific places
"France Croisée, La," 251, 410
Franchetti, Luigi, 292
Franchetti, Mimi, 287, 292, 299–300
Freer, Charles Lang, 128, 182

Galeries Durand-Ruel, 193–95, 196–97, 228
Garlerie Th. Briant, 311
Gardone Riviera, 221–24
Gaulle, Charles de, 370
Gauthier-Villars, Henri (Willy), 267
Geneva school. *See* Tavan, Mademoiselle, school of
Genoa, 250–51
Gentlewoman, The, 414n
Germain, André, 208, 238, 318
Gide, André, 208, 320, 323, 326, 343, 370
Gigi, 265
Gil Blas, 198
Gino. *See* Scodellari, Gino
Giotto, 116

Givend, M. and Mme., 79–82, 88, 157, 158, 397

Givend, Louise, 80–81, 82

Glackens, William, 38

Glassco, John, 185

Goddard, Mrs. (grandmother), 28–29

Goddard, Pastor, 16–17

Goddard, Beatrice Romaine. See Brooks, (Beatrice) Romaine

Goddard, Ella Mary Waterman (mother), 15–23, 27ff., 49, 60ff., 70ff., 82ff., 87ff., 107, 110, 123, 173ff., 202, 214, 217, 237, 245, 382, 383, 388ff.; cuts off Romaine's hair, 37–38; death, 143–45, 167, 173; family background, first marriage, 16–17; and involvement with Dr. Phillips, 91, 93; leaves Romaine with family in New York, 37; letters of, 393–403; mother-daughter relationship from former's point of view, 149–67; and poetry, 21; presentiment of sister's death, 175–76; relationship with son (see Goddard, Henry St. Mar); Romaine haunted by, 175; second marriage, 164–65; sends Romaine to learn singing career, 79; and son's death, 138–43; and spiritualism, 19–20, 21, 51; tries to groom Romaine for wealthy marriage, 76; visits Italian convent, 69

Goddard, Major Henry (father), 15, 16–17, 48–50, 152, 214

Goddard, Henry St. Mar (brother), 15, 18ff., 23, 27–34, 37, 60–61ff., 70–71, 83–84, 150ff., 174, 176, 214, 331, 382, 388; cause of death, 27–28; dies, mother's reaction, 138ff.; Dr. Phillips and, 90, 91; and George Crampton, 164–65; mentioned in mother's letters, 393, 400ff.; pseudonym in Romaine's memoirs, 11; Romaine buried beside, 6

Goddard, Katharine, 15, 27

Goddard, Maya. See Valbranca, Mary Aimée (Maya) Phillips

Godwin, Edward, 205

Goloubeff, Nathalie de (Donatella), 225, 230–33, 239

Goncourt, Edmond de, 197

Goupil Gallery, 197, 198

Gourmont, Rémy de, 274–76, 318, 321

Gramont, Elisabeth de, 199

Gramophone, The, 301

Grand Meaulnes, Le, 330

Grass Harp, The, 366

Grossin, Monique (Mme. Pierre), 6, 112, 113, 163, 334, 382

Grotta di Matromania, 131

Gruyère, 137–38

Guitry, Sacha, 267

Guy, Mme. (Paris widow), 87–88, 176, 177

Hall (Marguerite) Radclyffe (John), 199, 290ff., 303, 330, 332, 340; in Ladies' Almanack, 335; Well of Loneliness banned, 286

Hamilton, Mrs. Hamish, 292

Hamon, Count Louis, See Cheiro

Harper, Allanah, 344, 364

Heart to Artemis, The, 327

Helen (childhood nurse), 17

Hélène (school friend), 77

Helleu, Paul, 211

Hennessy, Aileen, 317, 325, 332, 345

Henning, Dr., 164, 165

Herm, 299, 301

Hickey, Mrs., 37–43, 47

Hickey, Mike, 40, 41

Holme, Thea, 184, 185

Holroyd, Michael, 264

Honegger, Arthur, 326

Horney, Karen, 210, 270

Hughes, Langston, 353

Huxley, Aldous, 303

Illustrazione, 249–50

Impressionists, 196

Inferno, 166

In Memory of Dorothy Ierne Wilde, 343
Innkeeper's Diary, An, 111
Interlude Hell, 101
Intransigeant, L', 198
Israel (Bernstein), 206
Italy, 250–58 (*see also* specific places); convent in, 64–69

James, Henry, 183, 287
"Jaquette Rouge, La," 193–94
Je Me Souviens, 274
Jerome, Thomas Spencer, 128–29, 130–31, 300
"Jeune Fille Anglaise, Yeux et Rubans Verts," 193
"Jeunes Filles," 200
Jews. *See* Anti-Semitism; specific persons
John, Augustus, 110, 112, 297
John XXIII, Pope, 370
Johnson, James Weldon, 353
Jouvenal, Henry de, 267
Joyce, James, 320
Jullian, Philippe, 239

Karsavina, Tamara, 240
Keats, John, 229
Kingston Coal Mine Corporation, 351
Kramer, Hilton, 195–96

Ladies Almanack, The, 334–35
Lahovary, Janine, 137, 138, 365, 377–79, 380
Lahovary, Nicolas, 378
Landowska, Wanda, 263, 267, 314, 316
Lanux, Eyre de, 316, 317, 323, 325, 338–39
Lanux, Pierre de, 338
Lanvin (costumer), 326
Laurencin, Marie, 208, 320
Lavallière, Mademoiselle, 95
Lawrence, D. H., 295
Lecouvreur, Adrienne, 315
Leicester, England, 113–14

Legrand, Mme. Cloton, 193, 197, 199, 216
Lesbian Idyll, 266
Letters to the Amazon (*Lettres à l'Amazone*), 275, 318
Lévy-Dhurmer (painter), 295
Lewis, Sinclair, 319
Life and Letters Today, 313
London, 60–61, 108, 115, 118, 161, 181–87, 189, 197, 205; Royal Academy, 108, 189
Louys, Pierre, 266
Love Between Women, 214
Lucifer, 63

Maas, Jeremy, 184
MacAvoy, Édouard, 209, 312, 362, 370–73, 375, 376–77, 382; and Natalie Barney's death, 379n
MacDougall, Allan Ross, 313
Mackenzie, Chrissie, 301
Mackenzie, Sir Compton (Monty), 128, 132, 285–94, 299, 301–4; *Vestal Fire* by, 296
Mackenzie, Faith Compton, 285, 287, 288, 293–94, 296, 299ff.
Mackenzie, Lillian, 301
"Madame Legrand au Champ des Courses" (portrait), 193, 197, 199, 216
"Maggie," 188, 193
Magritte (painter), 362
Mamie (cousin), 19–20, 21
Manet, Édouard, 196, 206, 211
Mardrus, Jesus Christ, 268, 328
Marienbad, 215
Marius the Epicurean, 117
Martyrdom of Saint Sebastian, The, 231, 241, 243–44
Marx, Dr., 300
"Masked Archer, The," 247
Mata Hari, 267
Maugham, Somerset (Willy), 123, 124, 128, 201, 216, 270, 277, 285, 341, 364, 366–67; and Brooks, 127, 131ff., 341; and Cocteau portrait, 200; MacAvoy portrait,

370; and publishing of Romaine's memoirs, 314; rejuvenation treatments, 366–67

Mauriac, François, 208, 370

Mavrocordato, Mr., 240

Memoirs of an Aesthete, 276, 290

Memoirs of Montparnasse, 185

Mendl, Elsie de Wolfe, Lady, 199, 325

Mentone. *See* Château Grimaldi

Mercure de France, 274ff.

Mes Apprentissages, 266–67

Meyer, Agnes E., 135

Milhaud, Darius, 316

Milosz (poet), 316

Miraglia, Giuseppe, 253

Monnier, Adrienne, 338

Monet, Claude, 196

Montesquiou, Robert de, 197, 199, 216, 234; and Cocteau, 201; and Ida Rubinstein, 240, 241–42

Morand, Paul, 9, 199, 320, 351

More House, 183

More Memoirs of an Aesthete, 110

More Than I Should, 285

Morgano's Café, 284, 285, 295

Mortimer, Raymond, 303n

Moulleau, 232ff.

Moyne, Lord, 240

Muhlfeld, Madame, 208ff.

Munthe, Axel, 128, 130, 135, 297

Murat, Princesse Lucien, portrait of, 193

Murphy, Chester, 352, 353–54

Murphy, Esther, 353–54

Musée d'Art Moderne, 200

Musée du Petit Palais, 199, 329

Mussolini, Benito, 223, 257

My Life and Times (Mackenzie), 301

My Three Inns, 111

Mytilene, 272

Napoleon Bonaparte, 17

National Collection of Fine Arts (Washington, D.C.), 8, 9, 12, 218, 312; Ida Rubinstein portrait at,

246; "The Charwoman" at, 188

New Jersey school. *See* St. Mary's Hall

New York, 37–43, 91, 350–51, 352–56, 357. *See also* Whitney Museum

New York Diary, The (Rorem), 203

New York *Times*, 195, 350

Nice, 5–8ff., 112, 209, 361–62, 372, 375ff.

Niehans, Dr., 366–67

Night Among the Horses, A, 334

Nightwood, 334

Nijinsky, Vaslav, 240

Nile, the, 155

Nin, Anaïs, 389

Noailles, Anna de, 199, 208, 320, 365

Nocturne, 253

No Pleasant Memories (memoirs), 5, 10–12, 17ff., 27ff., 82–83, 137, 312–14

Nova Antologia, 241

Ode to a Nightingale, 229

Of Human Bondage, 270

Omar Khayyam, 131

O'Neill, Mary, 17

One Who is Legion, The, 329–30, 336

"Orgue de Barbarie, L'," 309

Orioli, Pino, 131–32, 299

Orlando, 330

Otto of Hapsburg, 365

Pankhurst, Mrs. Emmeline, 184

Paris, 79–84, 85, 87–96, 136–37, 154ff., 189, 193–211, 225ff., 251, 307–50, 357–58, 368–69, 379ff. *See also* specific galleries, residents

Paris Was Our Mistress, 319

"Passing, The," 242

"Past, The," 381

Pater, Walter, 117, 175

Patterson, Elizabeth (Betsy), 17

Pavlova, Anna, 240

Pearson, Norman Holmes, 11, 12

Pensées d'une Amazone, 261, 276, 319
Perry, the Misses, 128, 129, 300
"Persecuted Woman, The," 247
Peter Whiffle, 353
Petit Duc, Le, 95
Phillips, Alexander Hamilton, 90–94, 153, 162, 164
Phillips, (Ella) Beatrice. *See* Emmanuel, Beatrice Phillips
Phillips, Liliane, 92, 162, 332
"Piano, Le," 194
Piave, 223, 256
Picasso, Pablo, 196, 312, 328; MacAvoy portrait, 370; Madame Errazuriz and, 211; Romaine's resemblance to, 324
Pissarro, Camille, 196
Poems and Poèmes, au très alliances, 413
Poet As Superman, The, 227
Poiret, Paul, 267
Polignac, Princesse Edmond de, 199, 215, 216–17, 364
Polignac, Comtesse Melchior de, 203
"Portrait de la Princesse Lucien Murat," 193
Pougy, Liane de, 265–66
Pound, Ezra, 216, 274, 317, 319, 365
Proust, Marcel, 203, 216, 240, 320–21, 337
Pure and the Impure, The, 269, 272
Putnam, Samuel, 319

Quaranta Anni con D'Annunzio, 227

Ravel, Maurice, 326
Raymond, Harold, 112
Réalités, 319
Redon, Odilon, 196
Regnier, Henri, 239
Reinach, Salomon, 320, 321
Renoir, Pierre Auguste, 196
Respighi, Ottorino, 295
Rhodes, Anthony, 227

Rilke, Rainer Maria, 320
Riviera Jungles, 177, 330, 377; reprinted, 404–6
Rodin, Auguste, 230
Roger-Marx, Claude, 197
Rogues and Vagabonds, 302
Romaine Brooks sur son Portrait Peint Par Elle-Même, A, 408
Rome, 105–10, 114ff.
Rorem, Ned, 203
Rose, Sir Francis, 332
Rouveyre, André, 275
Royal Academy (London), 108, 189
Royal Watercolour Society, 216
Rubaiyat of Omar Khayyam, 131
Rubinstein, Ida, 8, 240–44, 246–48, 251–52, 326–27, 329–30; Eyre de Lanux and, 338
Rûches, Les, 263–64
Ruskin, John, 188

St. Ives, 187–88, 193
St. Mary's Hall (Episcopal school, Burlington, N.J.), 47–55, 64ff., 149, 150, 202
Salon d'Automne, 196, 373
Santa Margherita, 350
Sappho, 272, 330
Sargent, John Singer, 183, 203, 211
Schiaparelli, Elsa, 323
Scodellari, Gino, 5, 6, 9, 10, 112, 367, 376, 380, 382
Scuola Nazionale, La (Rome), 106, 108–9, 110
Searle, Alan, 183, 201, 318, 366, 367
Seignobos, Professor, 318
Sert, Jose-Maria, 200, 323
Sert, Misia, 200
Sexual Deviation (Storr), 214
Shakespeare, William, 326
Shakespeare & Co. (Beach), 334
Shakespeare and Company, 327
Shaw, George Bernard, 263
Sinclair, May, 340
Singer, Winnaretta. *See* Polignac, Princesse Edmond de

Sinister Street, 286
Sitwell, Edith, 327
Smallwood, Norah, 112
Smithsonian Institution, 314
Snow, Mrs., 129, 134, 178
70 Dessins, 339
Solano, Solita, 335n
South Wind, 128, 134
Souvenirs Indiscrets, 263, 265, 266,
    275, 332, 337, 367
Souvestre, Marie, 263–64
Spreadeagle, The, 111
Stein, Gertrude, 216, 325, 327, 328,
    332; Compton Mackenzie on, 303;
    on Dolly Wilde, 345; introduces
    Van Vechten to Romaine, 353;
    Romaine takes to lunch in New
    York, 352
Storr, Anthony, 214
Story of San Michele, The, 128
Strachey, Lytton, 264
Strozzi, Gerio, 374
Strozzi, Marchese Uberto, 200, 322,
    362–63, 364, 370; portrait,
    373–74; Romaine breaks off with,
    382
Summing Up, The, 127, 132, 341
Sutherland, Graham, 366
Symonds, John Addington, 117

Tacitus, 129
Tale of Christmas Eve Masque, A,
    142–43
Tavan, Mademoiselle, school of,
    76–79, 156, 393, 396, 398
Taylor, Henry Ashworth, 290
Taylor, Joshua C., 196
Tchelitchev, Pavel, 341
"Terrestrial Reflections," 309
Terry, Ellen, 183
Thomson, Virgil, 320
Tiberius, Emperor, 129
Tight Little Island, 301
Toklas, Alice B., 314, 327–28, 332,
    342, 352
"Toupie," 340
Town and Country, 295–96

Traits et Portraits, 322
"Trajet, Le," 242
Transatlantic Review, 319
Trionfo della morte, Il, 224
Triumph of Death, The, 224
Trois, Six, Neuf, 317
Trottoir Roulant, Le, 197–98
Troubridge, Sir Ernest, 290, 291
Troubridge, Lady Una, 290–292,
    303, 330, 332, 340; death, 364;
    portrait, 199, 291–92, 339
Trower, Harold E., 414

Valbranca, Emilio, Comte de, 177–78
Valbranca, Mary Aimée (Maya)
    Phillips, 15, 23, 59, 61, 90ff.,
    141, 151–52, 156, 160, 173,
    332–33; marriage to Valbranca,
    177–78; mother's letters mention,
    394, 396, 401, 402
Valéry, Paul, 208, 319–20, 325, 326
Valse, La, 326
Van Dongen, Kees, 297, 298
Van Gogh, Vincent, 96
Van Vechten, Carl, 11, 353–55, 356
Vauxcelles, Louis, 198, 311
Vedder, Elihu, 128
Venice, 252–53
Vernet, Marcel, 95
Vestal Fire, 296
"Veste en Soie Verte, La," 194
"Veuve, La," 194–95
Victoria, Queen, 69, 138
Victorian Painters, 184
Vienna, 256
Villa Cercola, 285
Villa Gaia. See Fiesole
Villa Salvia, 285, 298
Villa Sant'Agnese, 313
Villa Trait d'Union, 331–32, 333
Vilmorin, Louise de, 370
Vittoriale Degli Italiani, Il, 222,
    223–24, 232, 253, 257, 258
Vivien, Renée, 237, 268–74, 330;
    Alan Seeger and, 318; gravesite,
    379n; Lévy-Dhurmer and, 295

Wandering Years, The, 211
Warren, E. P., 110, 115, 118
Washington, D.C. *See* National
  Collection of Fine Arts
Wasteland, The, 330
Waterman, Clara. *See* Dwight,
  Clara Waterman
Waterman, Ella. *See* Goddard, Ella
  Mary Waterman
Waterman, George, 16
Waterman, Isaac S., Jr. (grandfather),
  16, 42–43, 150, 202
Waugh, Evelyn, 290
Webb, Beatrice, 264
"Weeping Venus, The" (painting),
  242, 329
Weeping Venus, The (poem), 329,
  413
Well of Loneliness, The, 286, 291
Wells, H. G., 342
Whipple, James, 130, 131, 135, 138
Whiskey Galore, 301
Whistler, James McNeill, 135–36,
  182ff., 186, 188, 195, 205; and
  mother of Natalie Barney, 263; and
  redecoration of gallery for exhibit,
  196–97; and Royal Academy, 189

Whitney Museum, 12, 195, 312
Wickham, Anna, 318
Wilde, Constance, 183
Wilde, Dorothy Ierne (Dolly), 318,
  332, 342–48, 350; Natalie Barney
  poem on, 330n
Wilde, Oscar, 127, 183, 184–85;
  color scheme of dining room, 205;
  and Dolly, 342–43; and John
  Fothergill, 110, 117
Wilde, Willy, 342
Wildenstein Galleries, 350
Williams, William Carlos, 320
Willy (Henri Gauthier-Villars), 267
Wolfe, Elsie de. *See* Mendl, Elsie
  de Wolfe, Lady
Wolff, Charlotte, 214, 342
"Woman in Mourning," 194–95
"Woman with a Fan," 312
Woolf, Virginia, 330
World War I, 223, 251ff.
World War II, 313
Wunder, Richard P., 42

Yale University, 354; Beinecke Rare
  Book and Manuscript Library, 353
Young, Mahonri, Sharp, 198